WORKSHOPS IN COMPUTING
Series edited by C. J. van Rijsbergen

Also in this series

AI and Cognitive Science '89, Dublin City University, Eire,
14–15 September 1989
A. F. Smeaton and G. McDermott (Eds.)

Specification and Verification of Concurrent Systems, University of
Stirling, Scotland, 6–8 July 1988
C. Rattray (Ed.)

Semantics for Concurrency, Proceedings of the International
BCS-FACS Workshop, Sponsored by Logic for IT (S.E.R.C.), University
of Leicester, UK, 23–25 July 1990
M. Z. Kwiatkowska, M. W. Shields and R. M. Thomas (Eds.)

Functional Programming, Proceedings of the 1989 Glasgow
Workshop, Fraserburgh, Scotland, 21–23 August 1989
K. Davis and J. Hughes (Eds.)

Persistent Object Systems, Proceedings of the Third International
Workshop, Newcastle, Australia, 10–13 January 1989
J. Rosenberg and D. Koch (Eds.)

Z User Workshop, Proceedings of the Fourth Annual Z User Meeting,
Oxford, 15 December 1989
J. E. Nicholls (Ed.)

Formal Methods for Trustworthy Computer Systems (FM89), Halifax,
Canada, 23–27 July 1989
Dan Craigen (Editor) and Karen Summerskill (Assistant Editor)

Security and Persistence, Proceedings of the International Workshop
on Computer Architectures to Support Security and Persistence of
Information, Bremen, West Germany, 8–11 May 1990
John Rosenberg and J. Leslie Keedy (Eds.)

Women into Computing: Selected Papers 1988–1990
Gillian Lovegrove and Barbara Segal (Eds.)

3rd Refinement Workshop (organised by BCS-FACS, and sponsored
by IBM UK Laboratories, Hursley Park and the Programming Research
Group, University of Oxford) 9–11 January 1990, Hursley Park
Carroll Morgan and J. C. P. Woodcock (Eds.)

Designing Correct Circuits, Workshop jointly organised by the Universities of Oxford and Glasgow, 26–28 September 1990, Oxford
Geraint Jones and Mary Sheeran (Eds.)

Simon L. Peyton Jones, Graham Hutton and
Carsten Kehler Holst (Eds.)

Functional Programming, Glasgow 1990

Proceedings of the 1990 Glasgow
Workshop on Functional Programming

13–15 August 1990, Ullapool, Scotland

Springer-Verlag Berlin Heidelberg GmbH

ISBN 978-3-540-19667-9

British Library Cataloguing in Publication Data
Glasgow Workshop on Functional Programming (1990: Ullapool, Scotland)
Functional Programming, Glasgow 1990: Proceedings of the 1990 Glasgow
Workshop on Functional Programming, 13–15 August 1990, Ullapool,
Scotland. – (Workshops in computing).
1.Functional programming
I. Peyton Jones, Simon L. *1958–* II. Hutton, Graham *1968–* III. Holst,
Carsten Kehler *1962–* IV. British Computer Society V. Series
005.1
ISBN 978-3-540-19667-9
Library of Congress Cataloging-in-Publication Data
Glasgow Workshop on Functional Programming (1990: Ullapool, Scotland)
Functional Programming, Glasgow 1990: Proceedings of the 1990 Glasgow
Workshop on Functional Programming / Simon L. Peyton Jones,
Graham Hutton, and Carsten Kehler Holst, eds.
p. cm. Includes index.
ISBN 978-3-540-19667-9   ISBN 978-1-4471-3810-5 (eBook)
DOI 10.1007/978-1-4471-3810-5
1. Functional programming (Computer science) I. Peyton Jones, Simon L.,
1958– . II. Hutton, Graham, 1968– . III. Holst, Carsten Kehler,
1962– . IV. Title.
QA76.62.G58 1990   91–8692
oo5.1'1–dc20   CIP

© Springer-Verlag Berlin Heidelberg 1991
Originally published by Springer-Verlag Berlin Heidelberg New York in 1991

34/3830–543210 Printed on acid-free paper

Preface

The Third Glasgow Workshop on Functional Programming was held in Ullapool, Scotland, 13–15th August 1990. Members of the functional programming groups at Glasgow and Stirling University attended the workshop together with a small number of invited participants from other universities and industry.

The workshop was organised by Kei Davis, Jak Deschner, Kevin Hammond, Carsten Kehler Holst, John Hughes, Graham Hutton, and John Launchbury, all from Glasgow University.

We are very grateful for the support of our industrial sponsors: British Telecom, Hewlett Packard, ICL and Software AG. Their financial help made the workshop possible.

Thanks to Samson Abramsky, Tony Field, and Paul Kelly, all from Imperial College, for their help in refereeing many of the papers.

Glasgow University
December 1990

The Programme Committee:

Simon Peyton Jones (chairman)
Chris Hankin
Carsten Kehler Holst
John Hughes
Graham Hutton
Philip Wadler

Contents

Lifetime Analysis
Guy Argo 1

Compiling Laziness by Partial Evaluation
Anders Bondorf 9

Strictness Analysis in 4D
Kei Davis and Philip Wadler 23

An Algorithmic and Semantic Approach to Debugging
Cordelia Hall, Kevin Hammond and John O'Donnell 44

Abstract Interpretation of Term Graph Rewriting Systems
Chris Hankin 54

Compile-Time Garbage Collection by Necessity Analysis
Geoff W. Hamilton and Simon B. Jones 66

Improving Full Laziness
Carsten Kehler Holst 71

Towards Binding-Time Improvement for Free
Carsen Kehler Holst and John Hughes 83

Towards Relating Forwards and Backwards Analyses
John Hughes and John Launchbury 101

PERs Generalise Projections for Strictness Analysis
Sebastian Hunt 114

Functional Programming with Relations
Graham Hutton 126

Abstract Interpretation *vs.* Type Inference: A Topological
Perspective
Thomas Jensen 141

Analysing Heap Contents in a Graph Reduction Intermediate
Language
Thomas Johnsson 146

Is Compile Time Garbage Collection Worth the Effort?
Simon B. Jones and Michael White 172

Generating a Pattern Matching Compiler by Partial Evaluation
Jesper Jørgensen 177

An Experiment using Term Rewriting Techniques for
Concurrency
Carron Kirkwood 196

Type Refinement in Ruby
David Murphy 201

Normal-Order Reduction Using Scan Primitives
William D. Partain 218

Calculating Lenient Programs' Performance
Paul Roe 227

Problems and Proposals for Time and Space Profiling of
Functional Programs
Colin Runciman and David Wakeling 237

Solid Modelling in HASKELL
Duncan C. Sinclair 246

Differentiating Strictness
Satnam Singh 264

Generalising Diverging Sequences of Rewrite Rules by
Synthesising New Sorts
Muffy Thomas and Phil Watson 268

Concurrent Data Manipulation in a Pure Functional Language
Phil Trinder 274

Lifetime analysis

Guy Argo

Computing Science Department, The University, Glasgow G12 8QQ,
United Kingdom.

Abstract

A major obstacle in the efficient implementation of lazy functional languages is the high demands placed on heap-allocated storage. This stems from implementors' conservative assumption that all environments must be heap-allocated to avoid the block retention problem. The block retention problem is that variables which might be referenced outside the block in which they were created force their block to be stored on a garbage-collected heap to avoid dangling references. In this paper we examine an analysis technique called lifetime analysis which classifies variables into two classes: persistent, which may be referenced outside the block in which they were created; and transient, which are guaranteed never to be referenced outside the block in which they were created. Using this information allows the transient and persistent parts to be stored in separate blocks thus reducing the space consumed by the retained blocks. Unlike previous similar analyses, ours is for a lazy language but is wholly decoupled from the related problem of strictness analysis. This makes our analysis simpler and more modular. We then demonstrate how these techniques can be incorporated into an environment-based abstract machine like the TIM.

1. Introduction

Besides the overheads of implementing lazy evaluation, the major reason functional languages are slow is their high rate of heap-allocated storage consumption. So why is heap allocation necessary?

Stacks allocate space in a last-in-first-out (LIFO) manner. In order to use a LIFO allocation scheme we must be certain that no reference to an object persists after it has been popped off the stack. Thus to be able to use a stack for function environments, we must guarantee that no references to the environment persist beyond the context which created it. Languages like Pascal can guarantee this because they are strict and first-order, and thus the result of a function can never be a closure (representing either a lazy suspension or a function). As closures are the only run-time objects which reference environments, this is sufficient to guarantee that it is safe to use stack-allocated environments. Conversely, it is the inability to guarantee this condition that forces implementors of lazy higher-order languages to use the more conservative heap-allocated environments. However if an analysis were able to determine that a function would not export references to its environment then it's block could be safely allocated on the stack. Consequently we wish to classify variables into two categories: persistent, which may be referenced outside the block in which they were created; and transient, which are guaranteed never to be referenced outside the block in which they were created.

For the rest of the paper we will assume the following syntax for programs:

```
expr ::=    id                                          |
            constant                                    |
            let id = expr [; id = expr ]* in expr       |
            λ id+ . expr                                |
            ( expr+ )                                   |
            op expr expr                                |
            if expr then expr else expr                 |
            expr'id                                     |
            expr!
```

Let definitions may be recursive. The default evaluation order is call-by-name. To effect call-by-need we use the share annotation, e'v where e is a shared expression whose result will be saved in the variable v[1]. To effect call-by-value we use the force annotation, e! where if e is part of an application being evaluated to Weak Head Normal Form (WHNF) then e will also be evaluated to WHNF. Thus a conservative method to achieve lazy evaluation would be to coat every application with a share annotation. For instance:

```
let fact = λn.    if (= n 0)
                  then 1
                  else (* n (fact (- n 1)))
in fact 20
```

would be annotated thus:

```
let fact = λn.    if (= n! 0)
                  then 1
                  else  let $1 = (- n! 1)'$1 in
                        let $2 = (fact $1)'$2 in
                        (* n! $2!)
in fact 20
```

This is clearly inefficient. If strictness information is available then this can be rephrased as:

```
let fact = λn.    if (= n 0)
                  then 1
                  else (* n (fact (- n 1)!)!)
in fact 20
```

These annotations are provided by the strictness analyser in a previous pass of the compiler.

---

[1]It eases the task of implementation to make the variable updated after a shared expression explicit.

By performing the strictness analysis in an earlier pass, we decouple lifetime analysis from strictness analysis. This allows us to use better strictness analysers when they become available without affecting the lifetime analysis (except perhaps by improving the accuracy of its results). The accuracy of the lifetime analysis' results depends on the quality of strictness annotations. For instance, if a function is strict in an argument x then any variables referenced in the expression passed as x's actual parameter are guaranteed not to persist as the actual parameter is evaluated before the call. However if a function is non-strict in an argument x then the closure representing the expression passed as x's actual parameter may be returned as part of the function's result and thus we must be pessimistic and assume any variable referenced in the closure will persist.

2. The analysis

We will describe our analysis by explaining only a few important cases - once these are understood the rest can be worked out.

The analyser takes three arguments besides the expression it is analysing.

The first argument is the context which indicates whether the current expression is used in a strict or lazy fashion. Note that the outermost expression in a function body is evaluated in a strict context but for a nested expression to be evaluated in a strict context all the enclosing expressions must be annotated by an exclamation (!).

The second argument is an environment, $pset\_env_{eval}$, which maps variables to their $pset_{eval}$. The $pset_{eval}$ is the set of variables that may be referenced from the evaluated form of the given variable. Consider:

```
let from = λn.
        let from$1 = (+ n! 1)'from$1 in
        let from$2 = (from from$1)'from$2 in
        (Cons n from$2) in
(from 1)
```

Here the $pset_{eval}$ of from's body is {n, from$2, from$1} as n and from$2 are stored in the cons cell and from$1 must be retained to compute from$2.

Likewise, the third argument is another environment, $pset\_env_{uneval}$, which maps variables to their $pset_{uneval}$. The $pset_{uneval}$ is the set of variables that may be referenced from the unevaluated form of the given variable. For instance, in the code fragment:

```
let from$1 = (n! + 1)'from$1 in (from from$1)
```

$pset_{uneval}(from\$1) = \{from\$1\} \cup pset_{uneval}(n)$. That is, we must retain the variable $from\$1$ so that the share annotation's update can take place, and we must retain the variables $pset_{uneval}(n)$ so that n can be kept in unevaluated form since it will be needed if $from\$1$ is ever evaluated.

Note that if $from\$1$ and n were mutually recursive, our set equations would be mutually recursive necessitating that we compute the fix-point of the equations, i.e. their $pset\_env_{eval}$ and $pset\_env_{uneval}$ may depend on each other. For this reason, the result of the analysis is the $pset$ for the current expression and also augmented versions of $pset\_env_{eval}$ and $pset\_env_{uneval}$.

Note also that $pset\_env_{eval}$ is always a subset of $pset\_env_{uneval}$.

We will now examine the analysis of several constructs.

A constant in any context has no persistent component so the $pset$ returned is {} and $pset\_env_{eval}$ and $pset\_env_{uneval}$ are returned unaltered.

The persistent component of a variable, v, in a $strict$ context is $pset\_env_{eval}(v)$. The persistent component of a variable, v, in a $Lazy$ context is $pset\_env_{uneval}(v) \cup \{v\}$ as we must ensure that the variable itself persists.

In the case of an application, $(f\ a_1...a_n)$, we compose the analysis of the components of the application with respect to the $pset\_env_{eval}$ and $pset\_env_{uneval}$ i.e. the $pset\_env$s returned from the $pset$ computed for a_n are used in the analysis of a_{n-1}, the $pset\_env$s returned from the $pset$ computed for a_{n-1} are used in the analysis of a_{n-2} and so on until f has been analysed. The resulting $pset$ is the union of the application's components' psets.

The expression, $e!$, is analysed using the outer expression's strictness context. For instance, in the program:

```
let from = λn.
       let from$1 = (+ n! 1)'from$1 in
       let from$2 = (from from$1)'from$2 in
       (Cons n from$2) in
(from 1)
```

although the n which occurs in $from\$1$ is forced, it is part of a lazy expression, so it will be analysed in a $Lazy$ context.

Our last case is shared expressions. Recall that the expression, $exp'v$, means that after exp is computed, its result will be saved in the variable, v. This type of expression specifies an update - the possible run-time values of v are the union of all the shared expressions in which v is specified as the result variable. Thus the possible values of v's $pset_{eval}$ and $pset_{uneval}$ are the psets computed for all the shared expressions (in a strict context) in which v was the result variable. Fortunately, each variable can only be the result variable of one shared computation - sharing annotations are introduced by the compiler and it is guaranteed to introduce only one expression per shared variable. However as the analysis of a shared expression may change the values of $pset\_env_{eval}$ and $pset\_env_{uneval}$, we must still iterate the analysis until we reach a fixed point.

This completes the crucial fragments of our analysis.

So how good do we expect our analysis to be? If we implement a call-by-value language by annotating every parameter strict then our analysis will annotate all first-order functions to be stackable. (Higher-order functions may cause some environments to be heap allocated.)

2. Making use of lifetime analysis

In this section we describe two different implementation schemes that enable us to make use of the information derived from our lifetime analysis to improve the efficiency of our implementation. The first is a simple modification which allows frames to be allocated on the stack instead of the heap. The second is a more sophisticated technique which involves a two-level environment where the transient part is nested inside the persistent part - this allows the transient portion to be reclaimed before the persistent portion.

2.1 Using stack frames

A simple approach to making use of the results of our lifetime analysis is to implement stack frames, as they exist in strict languages such as Pascal. The idea is that if a function has no persistent variables then its whole frame can be put on the stack where it can be popped when the function exits, rather than on the heap where it must be reclaimed by a garbage collector.

We assume that the last action of a function is to save the function's result and resume the next continuation.[2] The stack frame is collected by ensuring a suitable reclamation continuation is waiting on the stack when the function exits. This continuation squeezes out the stack frame and resumes the function's original continuation. We assume that

---

[2]Note that this may cause a problem in abstract machines like the TIM which do not have an explicit representation for a higher-order value.

arguments are passed on the stack. Thus all that is required to create a stack frame on function entry is to set the environment pointer to point to these arguments on the stack and set up the reclamation continuation.

Unfortunately, in practice there are few functions whose entire environment can be allocated on the stack. Typically they are functions which are strict in every argument. Well-known benchmarks that fall into this category are nfib and tak. In our implementation, the use of stack frames actually degraded the performance of nfib by about 5% but sped up tak by about 15%. This is because when heap frames are used the arguments are pushed directly into the heap, thus stack frames incur the overhead of having to set up the reclamation continuation. We conclude that the optimisation is only worthwhile for functions of two arguments or more. Note also that we must be careful to optimise tail recursion to avoid poor space residency on the stack. This was not crucial before because environments were always heap allocated and so could be reclaimed by the garbage collector, but in our new scheme de-allocation must be performed explicitly to avoid poor behaviour.

It appears that we are not making the best use of our analysis as most functions have a mixture of persistent and transient arguments, a situation which can be detected by our analysis but not exploited by our implementation. In the next section, we demonstrate how to split monolithic frames into two-level frames whose transient portion can be reclaimed separately.

2.2 Partitioning the environment

Although stack frames improve matters somewhat they are still handicapped by being monolithic just like the original heap frames. The ideal would be a frame representation that allowed the transient part to be reclaimed separately from the persistent part whilst having the minimum of impact on the rest of the implementation.

Our proposed solution is to nest the transient part of the frame inside the persistent part. This is achieved by placing an extra pointer in the frame header which points to the transient part of the frame. The following diagram illustrates our proposal:

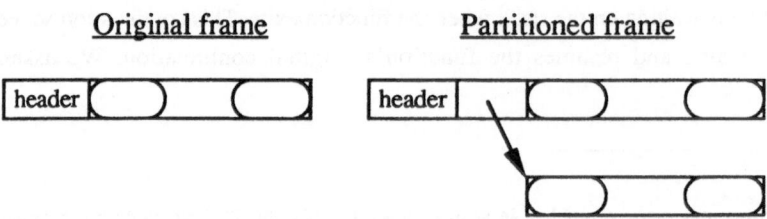

Original frame   Partitioned frame

For our new representation to work we must be careful that the garbage collector is modified so it knows about transient frames and does not try to reference a dangling pointer left by an expired transient frame. Note that we have placed no constraints on the representation of the transient frame so in principle it could be a stack frame.

The overheads of this system are: the complication of organising the construction of the two-level frame; using an extra level of indirection to refer to transient arguments. However in a lambda-lifted implementation where the frames are typically larger, this overhead may be worthwhile. We have not yet tested this idea in practice.

3. Related Work

Fairbairn and Wray [1987] pointed out that combinators which contain no nested applications and no share-annotated expressions are guaranteed not to export their environment. Unfortunately this condition is very weak. It can detect that $K \times y = x$ and functions of that ilk that do not export their environments but nothing much more complicated. The weakness of the technique is that it fails to take strictness information into account. Thus it assumes that the presence of nested applications automatically implies the presence of lazy suspensions but this is not necessarily true.

Hughes' suggested lifetime analysis [Hughes 1987], classifies arguments into two sets: persistent, which may be referenced after the function has returned; and transient, which will not be referenced after the function has returned. He did not suggest how the information derived from the analysis could be used. Hughes' original analysis was only applicable to strict languages, but he suggested solving this shortcoming by performing a combined strictness-and-lifetime analysis. Although we recommended this possibility in [Argo 1989], we subsequently rejected it because it committed us to a particular method of strictness analysis.

Jones and Le Metayer [1989] describe an analysis technique to reduce the cost in processing time of storage management operations implied by a program (possibly to zero). The goal of their compile-time optimisation is to replace as much as possible the allocation of new cells by the reuse of previously deallocated cells (in place updating). Their technique is based on the detection of sharing information. They illustrate their method by showing that all the cell allocations which occur in naive reverse can be implemented as in place updating.

Hudak [1987] analyses functional programs by abstract interpretation of reference counts. He is concerned with determining the loss of the last reference to aggregate data structures, such as arrays, in order to avoid performing a new allocation. It is shown how a functional encoding of Hoare's quicksort algorithm can be optimised to have space complexity equal to that of the imperative version. Hudak's analysis is much more powerful than ours, but also much more costly.

4. Conclusions

We have demonstrated a new analysis technique which determines whether a variable may outlive the context in which it was created. This analysis was decoupled from strictness analysis thus allowing flexibility in the choice of the strictness analysis used. In addition, we presented two possible methods of making use of the results of our analysis: stack frames, which allocates frames which are entirely transient on the stack; and partitioned frames, which nest a transient frame inside a persistent frame thus allowing the respective partitions to be reclaimed separately.

References

Argo, G.M. 1989. Improving the TIM. Proceedings of the 4th ACM conference on Functional Programming and Computer Architecture. London.

Fairbarn, J. and Wray, S. 1987. TIM: a simple abstract machine for executing supercombinators. Proceedings of the 3rd ACM conference on Functional Programming and Computer Architecture. Portland, Oregon.

Hughes, R.J.M. 1988. Backwards analysis of functional programs. Proceedings of the workshop of the Partial Evaluation and Mixed Computation (Bjorner and Ershov). North Holland.

Hudak, P. 1987. A semantic model of reference counting and its abstraction. Abstract interpretation of declarative languages (Abramsky and Hankin). Ellis Horwood.

Jones, S.B. and Le Metayer, D. 1989. Compile-time garbage collection by sharing analysis. Proceedings of the 4th ACM conference on Functional Programming and Computer Architecture. London.

Compiling Laziness by Partial Evaluation

Anders Bondorf *

DIKU, Department of Computer Science, University of Copenhagen

Universitetsparken 1, DK-2100 Copenhagen Ø, Denmark

e-mail: anders@diku.dk

December 5, 1990

Abstract

One application of partial evaluation is compilation: specializing an interpreter with respect to a source program yields a target program. And specializing the partial evaluator itself with respect to an interpreter yields a compiler (self-application).

Similix [3] [1] is a self-applicable partial evaluator for a higher order subset of the strict functional language Scheme [16]. It was demonstrated in [1] how Similix can be used to specialize interpreters for non-strict functional languages. Such interpreters implement non-strict argument evaluation by using the well-known suspension technique of wrapping an expression E into a lambda: (lambda () E). These suspensions give call-by-*name* reduction in the interpreters and in target programs obtained by partial evaluation.

Using delay/force [6], interpreters can also implement call-by-*need* (lazy) reduction. Unfortunately, delay is a side effecting operation that uses features not handled by existing self-applicable partial evaluators for higher order functional languages (such as Similix). In this paper we show that Similix is in fact strong enough to handle the limited use of side effects made by delay in interpreters. Correct target programs are generated because delay is a dynamic operation, because Similix guarantees against computation duplication and discarding, and because Similix preserves evaluation orders of evaluation order dependent expressions.

It is therefore possible to specialize interpreters for lazy languages. Using self-application, compilers (written in Scheme) from lazy languages into Scheme can be generated automatically from interpreters.

1   Introduction

Partial evaluation is a program transformation that *specializes* programs: given a *source* program and a part of its input (the *static* input), a partial evaluator generates a *residual* program. When applied to the remaining input (the *dynamic* input),

---

*This work was supported by ESPRIT Basic Research Actions project 3124 "Semantique"

the residual program yields the same result as the source program would when applied to all of the input. *Autoprojection* is a synonym for *self-applicable* partial evaluation, that is, specialization of the partial evaluator itself. It was established in the seventies that autoprojection can be used for automatic semantics directed compiler generation: specializing a partial evaluator with static input being (the text of) an *interpreter* for some programming language S yields a *compiler* for S [8] [7] [18]. Specializing the partial evaluator with static input being (the text of) the partial evaluator itself even yields a compiler generator (automatic compiler generator generation!).

The first successfully implemented autoprojector was *Mix* [11] [12]. The language treated by Mix was a subset of statically scoped first order pure Lisp, and Mix was able to generate compilers from interpreters written in this language. Since then, autoprojectors for several languages have been implemented, recently also for higher order functional languages (*Lambda-mix* [10], *Similix-2* [1], and *Schism* [5]).

Similix(-2) [3] [1] is an autoprojector for a higher order subset of Scheme [16]. Both source and residual programs are written in this Scheme subset. Similix handles side effecting operations on global variables, but otherwise it only treats a pure functional Scheme subset. In particular, Similix does not handle programs with set! operations on local variables.

It is well-known that call-by-name reduction can be achieved in otherwise strict languages by wrapping expressions into lambda's — in for instance Scheme by the *suspension* (lambda () E). Here E is not evaluated until the suspension is "forced", that is, applied to an empty argument list. One application of such suspensions is in interpreters for languages with call-by-name reduction. By partially evaluating such an interpreter, one can compile from a non-strict into a strict language [1]. Notice that the partial evaluator must be able to treat higher order constructs to handle the expression form (lambda () E).

Suspensions of the form (lambda () E) implement call-by-*name* reduction. However, lazy functional languages such as described in for instance [15] are based on call-by-*need* evaluation: a function argument is never evaluated more than once. It is possible also to implement call-by-need by using so-called "thunks" [6], local variables that memoize the value of the first application of the suspension. To do this, however, the side effecting operation set! is needed. This operation is not handled by existing autoprojectors for higher order functional languages (at least not by the ones we know of [10] [1] [5]), so how can we partially evaluate an interpreter that implements lazy evaluation by set!?

One could of course extend an existing autoprojector for a higher order functional language to be able to handle set! in general — but this would be cracking a nut with a sledge hammer. For our purpose, compiling laziness by partial evaluation, set! is only needed in a particular context, namely in interpreters to implement thunks. In this paper we show (informally) that Similix in its current form actually already is strong enough to handle this limited use of set!.

The consequence of this nice feature is that we can partially evaluate interpreters that implement call-by-need reduction by set!. And, using self-application, we can generate compilers (written in Scheme) from lazy functional languages into Scheme.

1.1 Outline

In section 2, we introduce a lazy example language $\mathcal{L}^{\mathcal{A}}_{\mathcal{Z}\mathcal{Y}}$. $\mathcal{L}^{\mathcal{A}}_{\mathcal{Z}\mathcal{Y}}$ is implemented by an interpreter written in Scheme. The interpreter uses thunks to implement laziness. In section 3, we argue that Similix in its current form already gives correct treatment of the thunk operation that uses set!. We give an example of specialization of the interpreter in section 4; this generates a quite readable target program which is shown in full. The performance is compared to Lazy ML and Miranda[1]. Finally, we conclude in section 5.

1.2 Prerequisites

Some knowledge about partial evaluation is desirable, e.g. as presented in [11] or [12]. Knowledge about Scheme is required (see e.g. [6]).

2 An Example Interpreter for the Language $\mathcal{L}^{\mathcal{A}}_{\mathcal{Z}\mathcal{Y}}$

To illustrate the use of delay we now present a lazy curried named combinator language $\mathcal{L}^{\mathcal{A}}_{\mathcal{Z}\mathcal{Y}}$ and an interpreter for $\mathcal{L}^{\mathcal{A}}_{\mathcal{Z}\mathcal{Y}}$ written in the Scheme subset treated by Similix [1]. A $\mathcal{L}^{\mathcal{A}}_{\mathcal{Z}\mathcal{Y}}$-program is a list of curried function definitions following the (abstract) syntax given in figure 1. An expression is a constant, a variable, a function name, a strict binary operation, a conditional, or a function application. For an example, the program in figure 2 computes a list of the first n even numbers; goal is the program's goal function.

```
P ∈ Program,  D ∈ Definition,  E ∈ Expression,
C ∈ Constant,  V ∈ Variable,  F ∈ FuncName,  B ∈ Binop

P  ::=  D*
D  ::=  (F V* = E)
E  ::=  C | V | F | (B E₁ E₂) | (if E₁ E₂ E₃) | (E₁ E₂)
```

Figure 1: Abstract syntax of $\mathcal{L}^{\mathcal{A}}_{\mathcal{Z}\mathcal{Y}}$

Some syntactic sugar, expanded by a parser, is used. First, if the body expression E of a function definition D is compound, the outermost parentheses are omitted. Second, $(E_1\ E_2\ \ldots\ E_n)$ abbreviates a nested application $(\ldots(E_1\ E_2)\ \ldots\ E_n)$.

```
(first-n n l  = if (= n 0)
                  '()
                  (cons (lazy-car l) (first-n (- n 1) (lazy-cdr l))))

(evens-from n = lazy-cons n (evens-from (+ n 2)))

(lazy-cons x y z = z x y)
(lazy-car x      = x 1st)
```

---

[1]Miranda is a trademark of Research Software Ltd.

```
(lazy-cdr x        = x 2nd)

(1st x y = x)
(2nd x y = y)

(goal input = first-n input (evens-from 0))
```

Figure 2: *evens source program written in $\frac{CA}{ZY}$*

2.1 $\frac{CA}{ZY}$-interpreter

The interpreter is given in figure 3. Syntax accessors (D-V*, Ecst-C, etc.), syntax predicates (isEcst?, isEvar?, etc.), and ext have been defined externally as primitive operations.

The interpreter is written in a compositional (denotational) way. To implement recursion, a recursive function environment is built using the usual applicative order fixed point operator (see function _P).

The function _D* traverses a list of function definitions. When the list is empty, _D* returns the empty function environment. Otherwise, it updates the function environment by binding the function name ((D-F D)) to its value (computed by _V*), and it recurses over the rest of the definitions.

_V* builds a curried Scheme function (possibly with zero arguments) that implements a curried $\frac{CA}{ZY}$-function. The environment r is initially empty and is updated for each function argument. When all arguments have been supplied, the function body is evaluated by calling _E.

_E evaluates a constant expression by simply returning its value (which is found by accessing the expression's abstract syntax, by (Ecst-C E)). Variables are looked up in the variable environment and are then "forced": to implement lazy evaluation, the values kept in the variable environment are suspensions rather than values. Functions are looked up in the function environment. Binary operations are implemented by the (external) primitive operation ext. Conditionals are implemented by Scheme conditionals. Applications are implemented by Scheme applications, but notice that the argument is "delayed" (generating a suspension).

```
;       Basic = Integer + Boolean + Basic* + ...
; v:    Value = Basic + (Suspension → Value)
; s:    Suspension = Unit → Value
; r:    VarEnv = Variable → Suspension
; phi:  FuncEnv = FuncName → Value

; Program × FuncName × Value → Value
(define (_P P F v)
  (((fix (lambda (phi) (_D* P phi))) F) (my-delay v)))

; Definition* × FuncEnv → FuncEnv
(define (_D* D* phi)
  (if (null? D*)
```

```
            (init-env)
            (let ((D (car D*)))
              (upd-env (D-F D)
                        (_V* (D-V* D) (D-E D) (init-env) phi)
                        (_D* (cdr D*) phi)))))

; Variable* × Expression × VarEnv × FuncEnv → Value
(define (_V* V* E r phi)
  (if (null? V*)
      (_E E r phi)
      (lambda (s)
        (_V* (cdr V*) E (upd-env (car V*) s r) phi))))

; Expression × VarEnv × FuncEnv → Value
(define (_E E r phi)
  (cond
   ((isEcst? E)
    (Ecst-C E))
   ((isEvar? E)
    (my-force (r (Evar-V E))))
   ((isEfct? E)
    (phi (Efct-F E)))
   ((isEbinop? E)
    (ext (Ebinop-B E) (_E (Ebinop-E1 E) r phi) (_E (Ebinop-E2 E) r phi)))
   ((isEif? E)
    (if (_E (Eif-E1 E) r phi)
        (_E (Eif-E2 E) r phi)
        (_E (Eif-E3 E) r phi)))
   ((isEapply? E)
    ((_E (Eapply-E1 E) r phi) (my-delay (_E (Eapply-E2 E) r phi))))
   (else
    (error ...))))

; Applicative order fixed point operator:
; (FuncEnv → FuncEnv) → FuncEnv
(define (fix f) (lambda (x) ((f (fix f)) x)))
```

Figure 3: $\frac{C\!A}{Z\!Y}$-interpreter written in Scheme

Environment initialization and updating are defined as syntactic extensions (macros) following the syntax of [14]:

```
(extend-syntax (init-env) ((init-env) (lambda (name) (error ...))))

(extend-syntax (upd-env)
  ((upd-env name value r)
   (lambda (name1)
     (if (equal? name name1)
         value
```

14

```
      (r name1)))))
```

Figure 4: Environment initialization and updating

In the interpreter, we have sloppily used the same syntactic extension `init-env` to initialize both variable and function environments. This plays no role in practice: the interpreter works on a parsed and scope checked program in which lookup errors cannot possibly occur. (The `error` call in `_E` is never reached in practice either.)

2.2 Delaying and forcing

`my-delay` builds and `my-force` applies suspensions. They are also defined as syntactic extensions; it is important that `my-delay` is non-strict, so it cannot be defined as a function.

```
(extend-syntax (my-delay)
  ((my-delay value) (save (lambda () value))))

(extend-syntax (my-force) ((my-force delayed-value) (delayed-value)))
```

Here `save` is a primitive operation implemented in Scheme as follows:

```
(lambda (s)
  (let ((thunk s))
    (lambda ()
      (let ((v (thunk)))
        (set! thunk (lambda () v))
        v)))))
```

The first time the saved lambda expression is applied (by `my-force`), the lambda expression is effectively overwritten by a new lambda expression (`lambda () v`). Here `v` is the value E evaluates to. This achieves lazy evaluation: all subsequent "forces" will apply the suspension (`lambda () v`) rather than (`lambda () E`), so E is evaluated at most once.

`my-delay` is a slightly modified version of the well-known `delay` described in [6] under "delayed evaluation". The difference is that we have put the part involving `set!` into the primitive strict operation `save`. A primitive strict operation is a syntactic form already known to the partial evaluator Similix, so by "hiding" `set!` inside a primitive, Similix need not be extended to handle an additional syntactic form. The remaining problem is that `save` involves side effects on the local variable `thunk`; Similix does not in general guarantee to handle such a primitive in a semantically correct way. However, as we shall see in section 3, the `save` primitive is actually handled correctly.

Notice that `save` does not depend on, nor does it change any externally observable state. We say that `save` is *evaluation order independent*. Each application of `save` creates a new local thunk variable which is independent of other thunks.

2.3 Memoization

`save` is a simple *memoization operator* (see for instance [9]) which memoizes a nullary function. Memoizing a pure function has no effect except efficiency: the memoized version *memo(f)* of a function *f* is *observationally equivalent* to (has the same input/output behavior as) *f*, but it may compute its result faster. Observationally, `save` is equivalent to the identity when applied to pure functions.

Memoizing an impure function does have an observational effect: only the first application of *memo(f)* may depend on or change a state. Subsequent applications will just return the value returned by the first application. *memo(f)* is thus not observationally equivalent to *f* if *f* is impure. Notice, however, that `save` itself is still evaluation order independent.

2.4 Optimizing the Interpreter

By investigating the interpreter text, it is simple to see that the program piece

```
((isEapply? E)
 ((_E (Eapply-E1 E) r phi) (my-delay (_E (Eapply-E2 E) r phi)))))
```

can be optimized. Optimizing the interpreter results in better target code when the interpreter is specialized with respect to source programs (written in $\frac{\mathcal{LA}}{2\mathcal{Y}}$).

First notice that there is no reason to use `save` when the argument of the application is a constant expression. A constant expression is evaluated by a single access (`Ecst-C E2`), and this operation is cheaper than performing the sequence

```
(let ((v (thunk)))
  (set! thunk (lambda () v))
  v))))
```

Therefore a constant argument can be delayed with the call-by-name delay `my-delay-cbname` defined by

```
(extend-syntax (my-delay-cbname)
  ((my-delay value) (lambda () value)))
```

`my-delay-cbname` can also replace `my-delay` in the function `_P`:

```
(define (_P P F value)
  ((((fix (lambda (phi) (_D* P phi))) F) (my-delay-cbname value)))
```

Second, when the argument is a variable,

```
(my-delay (_E (Eapply-E2 E) r phi))
```

reduces to

```
(my-delay (my-force (r (Evar-V (Eapply-E2 E)))))
```

which can be simplified to (r (Evar-V (Eapply-E2 E))). This is the new simplified piece of code in _E:

```
((isEapply? E)
 (let ((E2 (Eapply-E2 E)))
   ((_E (Eapply-E1 E) r phi)
    (cond
     ((isEcst? E2)
      (my-delay-cbname (Ecst-C E2)))
     ((isEvar? E2)
      (r (Evar-V E2)))
     (else
      (my-delay (_E E2 r phi)))))))
```

Figure 5: Optimized piece of interpreter code

3 Partial Evaluation of Programs with Thunks

We now argue that Similix handles save correctly.

3.1 Making save operations dynamic

We can simplify the problem of handling save by ensuring that save expressions always become residual (dynamic), that is, never get reduced at partial evaluation time. This has the consequence that functions memoized by save always become dynamic, that is, they are never applied at partial evaluation time.

We believe that this simplification is reasonable when considering interpreters: in these, save operations are typically used only for traditional run time (dynamic) operations, not for traditional compile time (static) operations such as syntax analysis and environment manipulation. This is at least the case for the $\frac{\mathcal{L}\mathcal{A}}{\mathcal{Z}\mathcal{Y}}$-interpreter: save is only used to memoize the function which suspends the argument to the dynamic (run time) application that implements application in the interpreted language. We do not expect this suspension to be reduced at partial evaluation (compile) time.

In Similix it is possible to specify that a primitive operation should always be considered dynamic [3], even when called with only non-dynamic arguments. By doing this for save, we are guaranteed that save expressions always become residual. Hence, expressions that apply memoized (saved) functions (for instance my-force expressions) always become dynamic too. Potential problems of performing side effects on thunk variables statically are thus eliminated: the code implementing memoization in save is never executed at partial evaluation time.

3.2 Pure functions

When applied to pure functions, save observationally acts like the identity operator, in source program expressions as well as in residual program expressions. Therefore observational equivalence between source and residual code is trivially preserved in this case.

Notice, however, that save was introduced for *efficiency*: preserving observational equivalence between source and residual code is *not* sufficient to ensure a "correct" treatment of save. Efficiency is a correctness issue here: if the memoization implemented by save in source programs is lost in residual programs, then we do not consider this a correct treatment of save.

Unfolding let-expressions and function calls is important in partial evaluation: it gives smaller and faster residual code. Unfolding may, however, make residual programs behave differently from the source programs. The reason is that unfolding in general may *duplicate* or *discard* (residual) expressions, and it may change the *evaluation order* of (residual) expressions. Similix has a property which is vital for the correct treatment of save from an efficiency point of view:

- No residual expression is ever duplicated nor discarded [3].

This property ensures that whenever the source program memoizes a function with save (whereby the function also becomes dynamic), the residual program is guaranteed to memoize the residual version of the (dynamic) function (no discarding), and it will do so only once (no duplication).

The important property is the "no duplication" one: duplicating a save expression (for instance by unfolding a let-expression with actual parameter expression being a save expression) would imply that a function was memoized more than once, thus losing efficiency.

3.3 Impure functions

When applied to impure functions, save is not observationally equivalent to the identity (cf. section 2.3). Similix allows impure functions that operate on global variables, so save might be applied to such functions in programs that are partially evaluated. Therefore save must be treated correctly by Similix, also when applied to impure functions.

When partially evaluating programs with impure functions, the "no duplication" and "no discarding" properties are necessary, not only for efficiency, but also to preserve observational equivalence between source and residual programs. In addition to this, preserving evaluation orders is necessary. This is described in detail in [3].

Two kinds of (dynamic) expressions need to be considered in connection to save: (*1) save expressions and (*2) expressions that apply memoized (saved) functions (for instance my-force expressions). Application expressions (*2) may now evaluate the body of an impure function, so they may neither be discarded nor duplicated, and their evaluation order must be preserved. save expressions (*1) may not be duplicated, not only because of efficiency (as in section 3.2), but, perhaps surprisingly, also to preserve observational equivalence.

Let us now address these points in more detail:

- *Discarding*

(*2) When applying an impure (possibly memoized) function, side effects may be performed if this is the first time the memoized function is applied. Such an application must not be discarded, even if the result is not used.

Similix never discards residual expressions.

- *Duplication*

  (*1) The impure operations in a function memoized by `save` are performed only once in the source program (the first time the memoized function is applied). The residual program must have exactly the same behavior. This requires that `save` expressions are not duplicated. If they were, we might generate several memoized versions of an impure function in the residual program.

  (*2) Since side effects may be performed when applying an impure (possibly memoized) function, such applications may in general not be duplicated.

  Similix never duplicates residual expressions.

- *Evaluation order*

  (*2) Applications of memoized impure functions are evaluation order dependent. Evaluation order dependent (dynamic) expressions are treated by Similix in the following way: as other dynamic expressions, they are never duplicated nor discarded; in addition to this, the order of evaluation of such expressions is always preserved.

  In binding time analysis, potentially evaluation order dependent dynamic expressions get a binding time value "X" which is greater (more conservative) in the lattice of binding time values than "D" (dynamic). Applications of impure functions get binding time value X. Applications of impure functions memoized by `save` also get binding time value X: applying a primitive (such as `save`) never lowers a binding time value in Similix. This means that the evaluation order of applications of memoized impure functions is preserved in residual programs.

To conclude, Similix preserves the semantics of `save` correctly, even when `save` is applied to impure functions. It does so because of its "no duplication", "no discarding", and evaluation order preserving properties.

4 Specializing the $\frac{\mathcal{LA}}{2y}$-Interpreter

Using Similix to specialize the $\frac{\mathcal{LA}}{2y}$-interpreter with respect to the *evens* program yields an efficient target program. Computing the list of the first 20 even numbers by the target program is around 14 times faster than by interpreting the source program using the interpreter. The text of the target program is given below (figure 6); function and variable names have been renamed by hand for readability, but otherwise the program was generated completely automatically. Notice that `(save (lambda () E))` corresponds to `(my-delay E)`, and that some applications `(E)` correspond to `(my-force E)`. `my-delay` and `my-force` are macros which are expanded before partial evaluation; therefore they do not occur in specialized programs.

```
(define (goal input)
   (((first-n) (lambda () input))
    (save (lambda () ((evens-from) (lambda () 0))))))

(define (evens-from)
   (lambda (n)
      (let ((result
               (save (lambda ()
                          ((evens-from) (save (lambda ()
                                                   (ext '+ (n) 2)))))))
            (lambda (z) (((z) n) result)))))

(define (first-n)
   (lambda (n)
      (lambda (l)
         (if (ext '= (n) 0)
             '()
             (ext 'cons
                  ((l)
                   (save (lambda () (lambda (x) (lambda (y) (x))))))
                  (((first-n) (save (lambda () (ext '- (n) 1))))
                   (save (lambda ()
                             ((l)
                              (save (lambda ()
                                        (lambda (x)
                                           (lambda (y) (y)))))))))))))
```

Figure 6: Machine produced evens target program written in Scheme

The program text corresponds closely to the source program (written in $\frac{\mathcal{L}\mathcal{A}}{z\dot{y}}$), the main difference being the many delays and forces (nullary applications).

By self-applying the partial evaluator, a stand-alone compiler is generated. Generating the target program using the stand-alone compiler is around 7 times faster than by applying the specializer to the interpreter. The size of the compiler is 10.6 Kbytes.

4.1 Comparing to other implementations

To get some idea of the efficiency of the target programs we generate, we have compared with Lazy ML (version 0.97) and Miranda (version 2.014). The Scheme system used is Chez Scheme (version 3.2). All runs are done on SPARC stations.

We have used a test program based on the *evens* program. Instead of returning a list of even numbers, the test program returns the sum of the first 1000 even numbers. This is done to avoid having the printing time being an important part of the run time.

Computing the sum 10 times takes around 0.9 seconds using Lazy ML, around 9 seconds using Miranda, and around 7 seconds using our Scheme target program. The Scheme program is thus faster than Miranda, but much slower than Lazy ML.

Notice, however, that the Scheme target program is far from being optimal. Firstly, arguments (for instance to `first-n`) may be *tupled* to avoid unnecessary currying. This can be done either by postprocessing target programs or by preprocessing $\frac{\mathcal{L}A}{2\mathcal{Y}}$-source programs to find tupled applications; the latter approach requires extending the interpreter to implement tupled applications.

Secondly, *strictness analysis* (see for instance [15]) may be used to avoid delaying and forcing arguments when this is not necessary. For instance, `first-n` is strict in its first argument n, so delaying and forcing this argument could be avoided. We could apply strictness analysis to source programs and then extend the interpreter to handle strict arguments differently from non-strict ones. This would then result in better, more reduced, target programs.

It should be noted that the test program cannot be typed by Lazy ML and Miranda (the problem is the recursive `evens-from` definition). To make the program run in Lazy ML, we simply switched off the type checking (this is possible to do in Lazy ML). This is not as bad as it sounds: we have not addressed compiling typed languages, so using an "untyped Lazy ML" seems reasonable for comparison. To get the program through the Miranda type checker, we redefined `lazy-cons`, `lazy-car`, and `lazy-cdr` to the built-in Miranda list operations `:`, `hd`, and `tl`. This makes the comparison less fair since Miranda presumably has efficient implementations of its built-in operations — and yet Miranda is still the slowest of the three.

5   Conclusion

We have demonstrated how to handle *dynamic* laziness: all (side effecting) computations involving `my-force`/`my-delay` were suspended till run time. We have not addressed *static* laziness; to handle this, it would be necessary to extend Similix to be able to execute `set!` operations statically.

The method presented in this paper could easily be used in other, more complex interpreters. For instance, one could write a self-interpreter for Scheme. This interpreter could then be changed to implement lazy evaluation; by specializing the lazy interpreter, one would compile from lazy Scheme into (standard) Scheme.

The idea can also be used to implement other lazy languages by partial evaluation into Scheme. Similix has already been used to compile a subset of an Orwell-like language into Scheme [13].

Acknowledgements

I would like to thank members of the "TOPPS/Semantics" group at DIKU, in particular Lars Ole Andersen, Jesper Jørgensen, Torben Mogensen, and Peter Sestoft. Also thanks to John Launchbury and John Hughes for their useful comments.

References

[1] Anders Bondorf. Automatic autoprojection of higher order recursive equations. *Science of Computer Programming*, 1991. Accepted for publication, to appear. Journal version of [2].

[2] Anders Bondorf. Automatic autoprojection of higher order recursive equations. In Neil D. Jones, editor, *ESOP'90, 3rd European Symposium on Programming, Copenhagen, Denmark. Lecture Notes in Computer Science 432*, pages 70–87, Springer-Verlag, May 1990.

[3] Anders Bondorf and Olivier Danvy. Automatic autoprojection of recursive equations with global variables and abstract data types. *Science of Computer Programming*, 1991. Accepted for publication, to appear. Journal version of [4].

[4] Anders Bondorf and Olivier Danvy. *Automatic autoprojection of recursive equations with global variables and abstract data types*. Technical Report 90-4, DIKU, University of Copenhagen, Denmark, 1990.

[5] Charles Consel. Binding time analysis for higher order untyped functional languages. In *1990 ACM Conference on Lisp and Functional Languages. Nice, France*, pages 264–272, June 1990.

[6] R. Kent Dybvig. *The SCHEME Programming Language*. Prentice-Hall, New Jersey, 1987.

[7] Andrei P. Ershov. On the partial computation principle. *Information Processing Letters*, 6(2):38–41, April 1977.

[8] Yoshihiko Futamura. Partial evaluation of computing process — an approach to a compiler-compiler. *Systems, Computers, Controls*, 2(5):45–50, 1971.

[9] John Hughes. Lazy memo-functions. In Jean-Pierre Jouannaud, editor, *Conference on Functional Programming Languages and Computer Architecture, Nancy, France. Lecture Notes in Computer Science 201*, pages 129–146, Springer-Verlag, 1985.

[10] Neil D. Jones, Carsten K. Gomard, Anders Bondorf, Olivier Danvy, and Torben Æ. Mogensen. A self-applicable partial evaluator for the lambda calculus. In *IEEE Computer Society 1990 International Conference on Computer Languages*, pages 49–58, IEEE, March 1990.

[11] Neil D. Jones, Peter Sestoft, and Harald Søndergaard. An experiment in partial evaluation: the generation of a compiler generator. In Jean-Pierre Jouannaud, editor, *Rewriting Techniques and Applications, Dijon, France. Lecture Notes in Computer Science 202*, pages 124–140, Springer-Verlag, 1985.

[12] Neil D. Jones, Peter Sestoft, and Harald Søndergaard. MIX: a self-applicable partial evaluator for experiments in compiler generation. *LISP and Symbolic Computation*, 2(1):9–50, 1989.

[13] Jesper Jørgensen and Lars Mathiesen. *Generating a compiler for a lazy functional language*. Student Report 90-5-16, DIKU, University of Copenhagen, Denmark, November 1990.

[14] Eugene E. Kohlbecker. *Syntactic Extensions in the Programming Language Lisp*. PhD thesis, Indiana University, Bloomington, 1986.

[15] Simon L. Peyton Jones. *The Implementation of Functional Programming Languages. Computer Science*, Prentice-Hall, 1987.

[16] Jonathan Rees and William Clinger. Revised report[3] on the algorithmic language Scheme. *Sigplan Notices*, 21(12):37–79, December 1986.

[17] David A. Schmidt. *Denotational Semantics, a Methodology for Language Development*. Allyn and Bacon, Boston, 1986.

[18] Valentin F. Turchin. Semantic definitions in Refal and the automatic production of compilers. In Neil D. Jones, editor, *Workshop on Semantics-Directed Compiler Generation, Århus, Denmark. Lecture Notes in Computer Science 94*, pages 441–474, Springer-Verlag, January 1980.

Strictness Analysis in 4D

Kei Davis
Philip Wadler

Dept. of Computing Science
University of Glasgow
Glasgow G12 8QQ
United Kingdom

Abstract

Strictness analysis techniques can be classified along four different dimensions: first-order vs. higher-order, flat vs. non-flat, low fidelity vs. high fidelity, and forward vs. backward. Plotting a table of the positions of known techniques within this space reveals that certain regions are densely occupied while others are empty. In particular, techniques for high-fidelity forward and low-fidelity backward analysis are well known, while those for low-fidelity forward and high-fidelity backward analysis are lacking. This paper fills in the gaps: the low-fidelity forward methods provide faster analyses than the high-fidelity forward methods, at the cost of accuracy, while the high-fidelity backward methods provide more information than the low-fidelity backward methods, at the cost of time.

1 Introduction

Strictness analysis is an important part of many compilers for lazy functional languages, and a wide variety of strictness analysis techniques have been proposed. It is not clear how all of the various techniques are related; this paper is in part an attempt to organise some of these methods, by determining their positions in a space of four properties. The second goal of the paper is to give analysis techniques for the heretofore unrepresented points in this space. The properties we consider are as follows.

First-order vs. higher-order. Analysis techniques may be applicable only to first-order languages, or more generally to higher-order languages. The ability to analyse higher-order expressions is important because higher-order programming is an essential part of the functional style.

Flat vs. non-flat. A flat semantic domain (e.g. the domain of integers or the domain of booleans) may be usefully abstracted to the two-point domain, since there are only two possible degrees of definedness: completely defined or completely undefined. This abstraction is too coarse for lazy data structures, for which it may be useful to differentiate between various degrees of definedness of the top-level structure (e.g. the spine of a list), and independently, between degrees of definedness of its subcomponents (e.g. the elements of a list). Analyses using only flat abstract domains will be called flat, while those using deeper domains will be called non-flat.

Low fidelity vs. high fidelity. The terms *low fidelity* and *high fidelity* are used to indicate how analyses are done with respect to either the free variables of an expression, or the formal parameters of a function definition. A low-fidelity analysis is one in which a separate analysis is done with respect to each free variable or formal parameter, and the results combined. In a high-fidelity analysis, all of the free variables or formal parameters are considered simultaneously, allowing possible relationships between their values to be considered. This means that a high-fidelity analysis can potentially detect *joint strictness* in two or more parameters, that is, that the result of the function may be defined if at least one of the arguments is defined, but is certainly undefined if all of the parameters are undefined. A low-fidelity analysis cannot detect joint strictness since it cannot consider two or more parameters being undefined simultaneously. (This should not be confused with the distinction between *independent* and *relational* analyses, with differ in the abstraction of products. All of the analyses presented here are independent in this sense.)

Forward vs. backward. The term *forward* is used to describe abstract interpretations in which the goal is to discover the definedness of an expression given the definedness of its free variables, while *backward* describes interpretations in which the required definedness of the free variables is to be determined given the required definedness of the entire expression. In operational terms, a backward analysis determines the demand (required degree of evaluation) of the free variables of an expression, given the demand on the entire expression.

		Forward		Backward	
		Flat	Non-flat	Flat	Non-flat
H.F.	F.O.	[Myc81]	[Wad87]	(this paper)	
	H.O.	[BHA85]			
L.F.	F.O.	(this paper)		[WH87]	
	H.O.			[Hug87]	

Figure 1: Four dimensions of strictness analysis

Historically, the development of strictness analysis started as first-order, flat, high fidelity, and forward [Myc81]. This theory was extended to higher-order by [BHA85]. This in turn was extended to non-flat abstractions of lazy data structures by [Wad87].

The development of backward strictness analysis was motivated in part by the need for a method that could detect, for example, *head strictness* on lists—that the head field of a cons cell is evaluated whenever the cons cell itself is evaluated. Hughes describes a first-order, low fidelity, non-flat backward analysis in [Hug85] based on a concept of *contexts*. The development in this paper derives from the more formal development in [WH87], in which the analysis is based on abstract domains of projections.

In first-order backward analysis, the abstract value of an expression of non-function type is a backward value, and the abstract value of a function definition or primitive function is a forward value—a function from backward values to backward values. Higher-order backward analysis is complicated by the necessity of abstract values having both forward and backward components. Consider an analysis of the call *length fs*, where *fs* is a list of functions. We expect *length* to take a backward value associated with *fs* and return a backward value, just as in the first-order case. However, in an analysis of *head fs x*, we expect a forward value to be extracted from the abstract value of *fs*, to be applied to the abstract value of x. Thus the abstract value of *fs* must have both forward and backward components.

As we show later, low-fidelity analysis of higher-order functions, both forward and backward, can be expected to give such poor information as to be useless. Presumably for this reason, the higher-order backward method outlined in [Hug87] is high fidelity in its higher-order components, but low fidelity in its first-order components.

Figure 1 summarises the development described thus far, and shows clearly an association of the high-fidelity property with the forward property, and the low-fidelity property with the backward property. On the basis of these associations, Hughes argues in [Hug87] that backward analysis is inherently faster than forward analysis. However, by giving low-fidelity forward and high-fidelity backward analysis techniques, we show that these associations are just artefacts of the historical development of the techniques, so that properly Hughes' argument is that low-fidelity analysis is faster than low-fidelity analysis.

This diagram is imperfect: ideally it would exclude low-fidelity analysis of higher-order higher-order functions (since it does not give useful analyses), and identify [Hug87] as a hybrid of low-fidelity first-order and high-fidelity higher-order backward analysis.

There is yet another dimension along which strictness analysis techniques may be characterised: monomorphic vs. polymorphic. This paper considers only techniques for the analysis of monomorphic languages. Techniques for polymorphic languages are described in [Abr85], [Hug88], and [Hug89b].

The rest of this paper is organised as follows. Section 2 defines the languages to be analysed. Section 3 describes first-order and higher-order low-fidelity forward analysis. Section 4 introduces projections and projection transformers, and recounts the essential properties of first-order low-fidelity and high-fidelity backward analysis. Section 5 describes higher-order high-fidelity backward analysis. Section 6 concludes.

2   Languages

This section defines the languages to analysed. The languages are assumed to be monomorphically typed. The language constructs and data types are representative of those in 'real' lazy functional languages: flat data types *Int* and *Bool* with strict operators + and =; a non-flat data type *List* with non-strict constructors [] and :, a **case** expression for decomposition of lists, and the conditional **if**. (Note the symbol : is also used to indicate type.)

In the domain equations, $\oplus$ denotes coalesced sum, and $\times$ denotes standard product. The constructions are standard, see e.g. [Sto77]. The symbol **1** is used to denote the one-point domain; its single element is denoted by (). Subscript $\perp$ denotes domain lifting.

2.1 A First-Order Language

Abstract Syntax

$x \in Var$	variables
$f \in FVar$	function variables
$e \in Exp$	expressions
$k \in Con$	numerals and boolean literals
$d \in Defs$	definition sets

$$
\begin{array}{lll}
e ::= & x & \text{variable} \\
& \mid k & \text{constant} \\
& \mid f\ e_1 \ldots e_n & \text{function application} \\
& \mid e_1 + e_2 & \text{sum} \\
& \mid e_1 = e_2 & \text{equality} \\
& \mid \textbf{if } e_0 \textbf{ then } e_1 \textbf{ else } e_2 & \text{conditional} \\
& \mid [\,] & \text{empty list} \\
& \mid e_1 : e_2 & \text{construct list} \\
& \mid \textbf{case } e_0 \textbf{ of } \{[\,] \rightarrow e_1; (x : xs) \rightarrow e_2\} & \text{list decomposition} \\
\end{array}
$$

$$
d ::= \{f_i\ x_{i,1} \ldots x_{i,n_i} = e_i \mid 1 \le i \le m\} \qquad \text{definition set}
$$

Semantic Domains

$$
\begin{array}{lll}
Bool & = \{true,\ false\}_\perp & \text{booleans} \\
Int & = \{\ldots, -1,\ 0,\ 1,\ \ldots\}_\perp & \text{integers} \\
List & = \mathbf{1}_\perp \oplus (Val \times List)_\perp & \text{lists} \\
Val & = Bool \oplus Int \oplus List & \text{values} \\
Fun & = \bigcup_{n=0}^{\infty} (Val^n \rightarrow Val) & \text{first order functions} \\
FEnv & = FVar \rightarrow Fun & \text{function environment} \\
VEnv & = Var \rightarrow Val & \text{variable environment} \\
\end{array}
$$

Semantic Functions

$$
\begin{array}{l}
\mathcal{E} : Exp \rightarrow VEnv \rightarrow FEnv \rightarrow Val \\
\mathcal{D} : Dfns \rightarrow FEnv \\
\mathcal{K} : Con \rightarrow Val \\
\end{array}
$$

The definitions of the semantic functions $\mathcal{E}$, $\mathcal{D}$, and $\mathcal{K}$ are standard, and are not repeated here. (See e.g. [Sto77].)

2.2 A Higher-Order Language

In the higher-order language, variables may have function values; given lambda abstractions, recursion equations are eliminated in favour of a fixed-point combinator.

Abstract Syntax

$x \in Var$ variables
$e \in Exp$ expressions
$k \in Con$ numerals and boolean literals

$e ::=$	x	variable
	$\mid k$	constant
	$\mid \lambda x.e$	lambda abstraction
	$\mid e_1\ e_2$	function application
	$\mid$ **fix** e	least fixed point
	$\mid e_1 + e_2$	sum
	$\mid e_1 = e_2$	equality
	$\mid$ **if** e_0 **then** e_1 **else** e_2	conditional
	$\mid []$	empty list
	$\mid e_1 : e_2$	construct list
	$\mid$ **case** e_0 **of** $\{[] \rightarrow e_1;\ (x : xs) \rightarrow e_2\}$	list decomposition

Semantic Domains

$$Bool = \{true,\ false\}_\perp \qquad \text{booleans}$$
$$Int = \{\dots,\ -1,\ 0,\ 1,\ \dots\}_\perp \qquad \text{integers}$$
$$Val = Bool \oplus Int \oplus List \oplus (Val \rightarrow Val) \qquad \text{values}$$
$$List = 1_\perp \oplus (Val \times List)_\perp \qquad \text{lists}$$
$$Env = Var \rightarrow Val \qquad \text{variable environment}$$

Semantic Functions

$$\mathcal{E} : Exp \rightarrow Env \rightarrow Val$$
$$\mathcal{K} : Con \rightarrow Val$$

Again, the definitions of $\mathcal{E}$ and $\mathcal{K}$ are standard.

3 Forward Analysis

In the first-order forward analysis described in [Myc81], and the higher-order forward analysis described in [BHA85], the abstraction maps flat concrete domains to the two-point domain **2** with elements $\perp$ and $\top$, with $\perp \sqsubseteq \top$. Non-$\perp$ concrete values are mapped to $\top$ in **2**, and $\perp$ is mapped to $\perp$. The abstraction of function types is induced by the abstraction of of the base types, so that, for example, if concrete function f has type $(Int \rightarrow Int) \rightarrow Int$, then the abstraction $f^\#$ of f has type $(\mathbf{2} \rightarrow \mathbf{2}) \rightarrow \mathbf{2}$. Extension to non-flat domains is described in [Wad87]. For all of the analysis techniques, we will use $^\#$ to indicate the mapping of concrete domains to abstract domains, and of values in concrete domains to values in abstract domains. We give enough of the first-order abstract semantics to be able to contrast the high-fidelity and low-fidelity analysis techniques.

Abstract Semantic Domains

$$
\begin{array}{llll}
Val^{\#} & = & Bool^{\#} \oplus Int^{\#} \oplus List^{\#} & \text{values} \\
List^{\#} & = & (Val^{\#}{}_{\bot})_{\bot} & \text{lists} \\
Fun^{\#} & = & \bigcup_{i=0}^{\infty}\,(Val^{\#^i} \to Val^{\#}) & \text{first order functions} \\
FEnv^{\#} & = & FVar \to Val^{\#} & \text{function environment} \\
VEnv^{\#} & = & Var \to Val^{\#} & \text{variable environment}
\end{array}
$$

Abstract Semantic Functions

$$
\mathcal{E}^{\#} : Exp \to VEnv^{\#} \to FEnv^{\#} \to Val^{\#}
$$
$$
\mathcal{D}^{\#} : Defs \to FEnv^{\#}
$$

$$
\mathcal{E}^{\#}[\![x]\!]\,\rho\,\sigma \;=\; \rho[\![x]\!]
$$

$$
\mathcal{E}^{\#}[\![k]\!]\,\rho\,\sigma \;=\; \top
$$

$$
\mathcal{E}^{\#}[\![f\;e_1\;\ldots\;e_n]\!]\,\rho\,\sigma \;=\; \sigma[\![f]\!]\,(\mathcal{E}^{\#}[\![e_1]\!]\,\rho\,\sigma)\;\ldots\;(\mathcal{E}^{\#}[\![e_n]\!]\,\rho\,\sigma)
$$

$$
\mathcal{E}^{\#}[\![e_1 + e_2]\!]\,\rho\,\sigma \;=\; v_1 \sqcap v_2
$$
$$
\text{where}
$$
$$
\begin{aligned}
v_1 &= \mathcal{E}^{\#}[\![e_1]\!]\,\rho\,\sigma \\
v_2 &= \mathcal{E}^{\#}[\![e_2]\!]\,\rho\,\sigma
\end{aligned}
$$

$$
\mathcal{E}^{\#}[\![e_1 = e_2]\!]\,\rho\,\sigma \;=\; v_1 \sqcap v_2
$$
$$
\text{where}
$$
$$
\begin{aligned}
v_1 &= \mathcal{E}^{\#}[\![e_1]\!]\,\rho\,\sigma \\
v_2 &= \mathcal{E}^{\#}[\![e_2]\!]\,\rho\,\sigma
\end{aligned}
$$

$$
\mathcal{E}^{\#}[\![\text{if } e_0 \text{ then } e_1 \text{ else } e_2]\!]\,\rho\,\sigma \;=\;
\begin{cases}
v_1 \sqcup v_2, & \text{if } v_0 = \top \\
\bot, & \text{if } v_0 = \bot
\end{cases}
$$
$$
\text{where}
$$
$$
\begin{aligned}
v_0 &= \mathcal{E}^{\#}[\![e_0]\!]\,\rho\,\sigma \\
v_1 &= \mathcal{E}^{\#}[\![e_1]\!]\,\rho\,\sigma \\
v_2 &= \mathcal{E}^{\#}[\![e_2]\!]\,\rho\,\sigma
\end{aligned}
$$

$$
\mathcal{D}^{\#}[\![\{f_i\;x_{i,1}\;\ldots\;x_{i,n_i} = e_i \mid 1 \le i \le m\}]\!]
$$
$$
= fix\,(\lambda\sigma.[(\lambda y_1 \ldots y_{n_i}.\mathcal{E}^{\#}[\![e_i]\!]\;[y_j/x_{i,j} \mid 1 \le j \le n_i]\;\sigma)/f_i \mid 1 \le i \le m])
$$

A prototypical example is:

$$
cond\;x\;y\;z = \text{ if } x \text{ then } y \text{ else } z.
$$

Then

$$
cond^{\#}\;\top\;y\;z = y \sqcup z,
$$

$$
cond^{\#}\;\bot\;y\;z = \bot.
$$

This analysis detects that *cond* is strict in its first argument and jointly strict in its second and third arguments. We call these analysis techniques *high fidelity* since, in general, every possible combination of abstract arguments must be considered to fully determine the value of the abstract function.

3.1 First-Order Low-Fidelity Analysis

In first-order low-fidelity analysis, strictness in each of a function's arguments is determined individually. Each function definition $f\ x_1\ \ldots\ x_n\ =\ e$ gives rise to n abstract functions $f^{(1)}, \ldots, f^{(n)}$ of a single argument, corresponding to the abstraction with respect to each of the arguments x_j. Then $f^{(j)} \perp = \perp$ implies that f is strict in its jth argument. The abstraction $f^{\#}$ of f is then taken to be

$$f^{\#} = \lambda x_1 \ldots \lambda x_n. f^{(1)}\ x_1\ \sqcap\ \ldots\ \sqcap\ f^{(n)}\ x_n.$$

The abstract semantic domains and equations for the low-fidelity analysis are the same as for the high-fidelity analysis, except for the definition of $\mathcal{D}^{\#}$, which becomes

$$\mathcal{D}^{\#}[\![\{f_i\ x_{i,1}\ \ldots\ x_{i,n_i}\ =\ e_i\ |\ 1 \le i \le m\}]\!]$$
$$= \textit{fix}\ (\lambda\sigma.[(\lambda y_1 \ldots \lambda y_{n_i}. \sqcap_{j=1}^{n_i} \mathcal{E}^{\#}[\![e_i]\!]\ \rho_{i,j}\ \sigma)/f_i\ |\ 1 \le i \le m]),$$

where $\rho_{i,j}$ is shorthand for

$$[\top/x_{i,k}\ |\ 1 \le k \le n_i,\ k \ne j][y_j/x_{i,j}].$$

This definition does not explicitly define each $f_i^{(j)}$, $1 \le j \le n_i$, $1 \le i \le m$; they are implicitly defined by

$$f_i^{(j)} = \lambda x. f_i^{\#}\ \top \ldots \top\ x\ \top \ldots \top,$$

where x appears in the jth argument position.

The advantage of the low-fidelity analysis is that for a function f of n arguments from abstract domains containing a_i elements each, $1 \le i \le n$, the abstraction of f is completely determined by only $\sum_{i=1}^n a_i$ combinations of argument values rather than $\prod_{i=1}^n a_i$ combinations for the high-fidelity analysis. The disadvantage is that joint strictness in two or more arguments cannot be detected. An example for which the low-fidelity analysis is as good as the high-fidelity analysis is

$$countdown\ x\ y\ =\ \textbf{if}\ y = 0\ \textbf{then}\ x\ \textbf{else}\ countdown\ x\ (y-1),$$

$$countdown^{\#}\ x\ y\ =\ ((\top \sqcap \top) \sqcap (x \sqcup countdown^{\#}\ x\ (\top \sqcap \top)))$$
$$\sqcap ((y \sqcap \top) \sqcap (\top \sqcup countdown^{\#}\ \top\ (y \sqcap \top)))$$

$$=\ x \sqcap y,$$

so low-fidelity analysis detects that $countdown$ is strict in both of its arguments. However, for $cond$ we have

$$cond^{\#}\ x\ y\ z\ =\ (x \sqcap (\top \sqcup \top))$$
$$\sqcap (\top \sqcap (y \sqcup \top))$$
$$\sqcap (\top \sqcap (\top \sqcup z))$$

$$=\ x,$$

so strictness in the first argument is still detected, but joint strictness in the second and third is not. It is not hard to show that the the high-fidelity analysis always gives results as good or better than the low-fidelity analysis.

3.2 Higher-Order Low-Fidelity Analysis

Low-fidelity analysis of higher-order functions can be expected to give very poor results. Consider *apply* as the simplest example of a function that takes as arguments both a function and a value to which that function is applied:

$$apply = \lambda f.\lambda x.f\ x.$$

The high-fidelity analysis gives

$$apply^{\#}\ f\ x\ =\ f\ x.$$

The low-fidelity analysis gives

$$
\begin{aligned}
apply^{\#}\ f\ x &= f\ \top \sqcap \top\ x \\
&= f\ \top \sqcap \top \\
&= f\ \top.
\end{aligned}
$$

All information about the second argument is lost. The same problem causes the analyses of functions such as *map* and *fold* to yield similarly poor results. For this reason, we expect higher-order low-fidelity analysis to generally give very poor information.

4 First-Order Backward Analysis

4.1 Projections

We review the approach of [WH87].

A domain *projection* is a continuous idempotent function that approximates the identity function. In this paper, γ and δ will always denote projections, and α and β will always denote projection-valued variables. Projections form a complete lattice under the domain ordering $\sqsubseteq$, with the identity function *ID* as the top element, and the function *ABS* that maps every element to $\bot$ as the bottom element. A technical detail: the greatest lower bound $\gamma \sqcap \delta$ of projections γ and δ is defined to be the greatest projection less than both γ and δ, since the greatest such function will not necessarily be a projection; for least upper bound, the function and projection coincide. The projections *FST* and *SND* are defined on pairs:

$$
\begin{aligned}
FST\ (u,v) &= (u,\bot), \\
SND\ (u,v) &= (\bot,v),
\end{aligned}
$$

for all values u and v. Then

$$
\begin{aligned}
FST \sqcup SND &= ID, \\
(FST \sqcap SND)\ (u,v) &= (\bot,\bot).
\end{aligned}
$$

Projections are used here to specify a degree of sufficient definedness of their arguments, by regarding those parts of their arguments which are mapped to $\bot$ as definitely not needed, and those parts left unchanged as possibly needed. For example, suppose that f is a function from pairs to pairs, and that for some particular application of f only the the first component of the result is needed. Then that instance of f may be safely replaced by $FST \circ f$. The terms *context* and *projection* are used interchangably; here f is said to be evaluated in context *FST*.

The particular context in which a function is evaluated may allow its argument to be less defined than in the general case. If

$$f(u,v) = (v,u),$$

then for f in context FST it is safe to apply SND to its argument, that is,

$$FST \circ f = FST \circ f \circ SND.$$

It is easy to show that for all projections γ and δ and functions f we have

$$\gamma \circ f = \gamma \circ f \circ \delta \text{ if and only if } \gamma \circ f \sqsubseteq f \circ \delta.$$

The projection δ is is not uniquely determined by f and γ, since for any f and γ, $\gamma \circ f \sqsubseteq f \circ ID$.

So far we have show how projections may be used to specify what part of a function's argument is not needed. Additionally, we wish to encode *necessity*: that some part of the argument is definitely required, or must be defined. To specify necessity with projections, all domains are extended by lifting. The new bottom-most element of each domain will be called $\lightning$, with domain D lifted written $D_{\lightning}$. We will interpret $\gamma u = \lightning$ to mean that γ *requires* a value more defined than u. Every function $f : D_1 \rightarrow D_2$ is extended to a function in $D_{1\lightning} \rightarrow D_{2\lightning}$ by making it strict in $\lightning$, that is, $f \lightning = \lightning$. The semantic function $\mathcal{E}$ is extended appropriately, with the additional condition that if its variable environment argument maps any variable to $\lightning$, then the result is $\lightning$. This ensures that functions such as $f\,x = 1$ with an argument that does not appear on the right-hand side of its definition are strict in $\lightning$. Thus the semantic domains become

$$
\begin{aligned}
Val &= Bool_{\lightning} \oplus Int_{\lightning} \oplus List_{\lightning} \quad &\text{values} \\
Fun &= \textstyle\bigcup_{n=0}^{\infty} (Val^n \rightarrow Val) \quad &\text{first order functions}
\end{aligned}
$$

Let the projection STR be defined by

$$
\begin{aligned}
STR\,\lightning &= \lightning, \\
STR\,u &= u,\ u \neq \lightning.
\end{aligned}
$$

Simple strictness may be defined using STR, since

$$STR \circ f \sqsubseteq f \circ STR \text{ if and only if } f \text{ is strict.}$$

Every projection must map $\lightning$ to $\lightning$, so the definition of ABS in the lifted domains is

$$
\begin{aligned}
ABS\,\lightning &= \lightning, \\
ABS\,u &= \bot,\ u \neq \lightning.
\end{aligned}
$$

The projection ID is similar extended. If a function f makes no use of its argument, then for all γ,

$$\gamma \circ f \sqsubseteq f \circ ABS.$$

We also have

$$\gamma \circ f \sqsubseteq f \circ \delta \text{ implies } (\gamma \sqcup ABS) \circ f \sqsubseteq f \circ (\delta \sqcup ABS).$$

The least projection *FAIL* is defined by

$$FAIL\ u\ =\ \text{\reflectbox{?}},\ \text{for all } u.$$

Then for all f, $FAIL \circ f \sqsubseteq f \circ FAIL$.

The discussion so far generalises to functions of several arguments, but using function composition to indicate the context of a function's argument, e.g. $f \circ \delta$, is not adequate.

If a projection maps $\perp$ to \reflectbox{?}, it is said to be *lift strict*. Thus *STR* and *FAIL* are lift strict, but *ABS* and *ID* are not. In fact, *STR* is the greatest lift-strict projection, *ABS* is the least projection that is not lift strict. Since $STR \sqcup ABS = ID$ and $STR \sqcap ABS = FAIL$, the projections *ID*, *STR*, *ABS*, and *FAIL* form a lattice; this lattice of projections will be denoted by the symbol $\Diamond$.

It is useful to think of the context of an expression as defining a *demand* on the expression, that is, specifying a degree of evaluation of the expression which is certain to be performed. If the context maps some component of the value of an expression to $\perp$ for every value of that component, then the evaluation required to generate that component need not be performed. If the context maps some value to \reflectbox{?}, then evaluation is certain to be performed at least far enough to guarantee that the result is not that value. Thus context *ABS* requires no evaluation. Context *STR* requires evaluation far enough to guarantee that the result is not $\perp$; for normal-order reduction, this means evaluation to WHNF. (For an expression of function type, it is not possible to determine that the expression does not denote the function $\perp$. Evaluation to WHNF is a safe degree of evaluation in context *STR*.) Context *ID* gives no information about how much evaluation will be performed. Context *FAIL* indicates that no degree of evaluation yields an acceptable value.

Other useful projections are those that require constructor values. For lists, define for all γ and δ

$$
\begin{array}{llll}
NIL\ \text{\reflectbox{?}} & = \text{\reflectbox{?}}, & CONS\ \gamma\ \delta\ \text{\reflectbox{?}} & = \text{\reflectbox{?}}, \\
NIL\ \perp & = \text{\reflectbox{?}}, & CONS\ \gamma\ \delta\ \perp & = \text{\reflectbox{?}}, \\
NIL\ nil & = nil, & CONS\ \gamma\ \delta\ nil & = \text{\reflectbox{?}}, \\
NIL\ (u:v) & = \text{\reflectbox{?}}, & CONS\ \gamma\ \delta\ (u:v) & = (\gamma\ u):(\delta\ v).
\end{array}
$$

Then, for example, the projection *CONS STR NIL* requires its argument to be a list containing exactly one element, and that that element not be $\perp$. Analogous projections may be defined for any sum-of-products type.

4.2 Projection Transformers

A unary function from projections to projections will be called a *projection transformer* (PT). For the remainder of this paper, τ will always denote a projection transformer. Given a function f of n arguments, we wish to determine for each argument x_i, $1 \le i \le n$, a corresponding PT τ_i such that for all γ,

$$\gamma\ (f\ x_1\ \dots\ x_n) \sqsubseteq f\ x_1\ \dots\ x_{i-1}\ (\tau_i\ \gamma\ x_i)\ x_{i+1}\ \dots\ x_n.$$

If this inequality holds for each τ_i, $1 \le i \le n$, then

$$\gamma\ (f\ x_1\ \dots\ x_n) \sqsubseteq f\ (\tau_1\ \gamma\ x_1)\ \dots\ (\tau_n\ \gamma\ x_n)$$

also holds.

More generally, given an expression e, we will say that τ *is a safe abstraction of* e *with respect to* x *at* σ if for all projections γ and variable environments ρ,

$$\gamma \, (\mathcal{E}[\![e]\!] \, \rho \, \sigma) \sqsubseteq \mathcal{E}[\![e]\!] \, \rho[(\tau \, \gamma \, (\rho[\![x]\!]))/x] \, \sigma.$$

Thus the analysis of an expression is with respect to a particular free variable. We will usually assume that σ is implicit, and omit the qualification "at σ". If this condition holds for all lift-strict γ not equal to *FAIL*, then it will hold for all γ if

$$\tau \; FAIL \qquad = \; FAIL,$$
$$\tau \; (ABS \sqcup \gamma) = \; ABS \sqcup \tau \, \gamma, \; \gamma \text{ lift-strict}.$$

Projection transformers satisfying these two equations will be said to have the *guard property*. We are only interested in PTs with the guard property, so PTs will be explicitly defined for arguments that are lift-strict and not equal to *FAIL*, with the understanding they satisfy these two equations. To indicate that PTs defined by lambda expressions have the guard property, the symbol $\bar{\lambda}$ is used instead of λ. So, for example

$$(\bar{\lambda}\alpha.ABS) \; FAIL \; = \; FAIL.$$

Following are some useful facts about safety.

Fact 1. The least safe abstraction of x w.r.t. x is $\bar{\lambda}\alpha.\alpha$. The formal verification is trivial.

Fact 2. A safe abstraction of y w.r.t. x is $\bar{\lambda}\alpha.ABS$. We may think of this as formalising the statement that in evaluating the expression y in any environment ρ, modifying ρ to map x to $\perp$ does not change the result. Note that $\bar{\lambda}\alpha.ABS$ is the least safe abstraction of y w.r.t. x, since if an environment ρ maps x to $\dagger$, then $\mathcal{E}[\![y]\!] \, \rho \, \sigma = \dagger$.

Fact 3. A safe abstraction of $x + y$ w.r.t. x is $\bar{\lambda}\alpha.STR$. Informally, this states that if $x + y$ must not be $\perp$, then x must not be $\perp$. In other words $x + y$ is strict in x.

Fact 4. The PT $\bar{\lambda}\alpha.ID$ is a safe abstraction of every expression w.r.t. every free variable. Note that $\bar{\lambda}\alpha.ID$ is the greatest PT with the guard property.

We will need PTs that map projections on constructor values to projections on their components. For lists we require PTs *HEAD* and *TAIL* such that for all u, v, and γ,

$$\gamma \, (u : v) \sqsubseteq (HEAD \; \gamma \; u) : (TAIL \; \gamma \; v).$$

The following definitions satisfy this requirement.

$$(HEAD \; \gamma) \, u \; = \; \bigsqcup\nolimits_{v \in List \; D} \; head \, (\gamma \, (u : v)),$$

$$(TAIL \; \gamma) \, v \; = \; \bigsqcup\nolimits_{u \in D} \; tail \, (\gamma \, (u : v)).$$

Then

$$HEAD \; (CONS \; \gamma \; \delta) \; = \; \gamma,$$

$$TAIL \; (CONS \; \gamma \; \delta) \; = \; \delta.$$

It will be convenient to define PTs by 'pattern-matching' lambda expressions, where the pattern is a projection constructor with variables in the argument positions. For lists we have

$$\bar{\lambda}NIL.e \;=\; \bar{\lambda}\alpha.\begin{cases} FAIL & \text{if } \alpha \; nil \;=\; \text{\textonehalf}, \\ e & \text{otherwise.} \end{cases}$$

$$\bar{\lambda}(CONS \; x \; y).f(x,y) \;=\; \bar{\lambda}\alpha.\begin{cases} FAIL, \text{ if } \bigsqcup_{u \in D} \bigsqcup_{v \in List \; D} \; \alpha \; (u:v) \;=\; \text{\textonehalf}, \\ f(HEAD \; \alpha, \; TAIL \; \alpha), \text{ otherwise.} \end{cases}$$

Intuitively, a PT defined in this way 'requires' that its argument accept some value or values, by returning $FAIL$ if it does not. For example, the PT defined by $\bar{\lambda}(CONS \; x \; y).f(x,y)$ yields $FAIL$ if its argument does not accept a cons node. This generalises to general sums-of-products in the obvious way.

The operators $\sqcup$ and $\sqcap$ are defined on PTs as follows. For all PTs τ_1 and τ_2,

$$\tau_1 \; \sqcup \; \tau_2 \;=\; \bar{\lambda}\alpha.\tau_1 \; \alpha \; \sqcup \; \tau_2 \; \alpha,$$

$$\tau_1 \; \sqcap \; \tau_2 \;=\; \bar{\lambda}\alpha.\tau_1 \; \alpha \; \sqcap \; \tau_2 \; \alpha.$$

Then PTs with the guard property form a lattice under the domain ordering $\sqsubseteq$.

Let e be an expression in which there are two instances of the free variable x. We will distinguish these two instances by substituting one instance of x by a new variable y, and call the resulting expression e'. Now suppose that for e' in context γ, we may safely apply projection δ_1 to x and projection δ_2 to y, that is, for all ρ,

$$\alpha \; (\mathcal{E}[\![e']\!] \; \rho \; \sigma) \;\sqsubseteq\; \mathcal{E}[\![e']\!] \; \rho[\delta_1 \; (\rho[\![x]\!])/x] \; \sigma,$$

$$\alpha \; (\mathcal{E}[\![e']\!] \; \rho \; \sigma) \;\sqsubseteq\; \mathcal{E}[\![e']\!] \; \rho[\delta_2 \; (\rho[\![y]\!])/y] \; \sigma.$$

In other words, for e in context α, δ_1 may be safely applied to one instance of x, and δ_2 to the other. Then a projection that may be safely applied to both instances of x is $\delta_1 \; \& \; \delta_2$, where for all γ and δ,

$$(\gamma \; \& \; \delta) \; u \;=\; \text{\textonehalf} \qquad \text{if } \gamma \; u \;=\; \text{\textonehalf} \text{ or } \delta \; u \;=\; \text{\textonehalf},$$
$$(\gamma \; \& \; \delta) \; u \;=\; (\gamma \; \sqcup \; \delta) \; u \quad \text{otherwise.}$$

The operator $\&$ is idempotent, commutative, associative, has ABS as identity, and distributes over $\sqcup$. Also, $\gamma \; \& \; FAIL \;=\; FAIL$ for all γ, and for all $\gamma, \delta, \gamma', \delta'$,

$$(CONS \; \gamma \; \delta) \; \& \; (CONS \; \gamma' \; \delta') \;=\; CONS \; (\gamma \; \& \; \gamma') \; (\delta \; \& \; \delta').$$

The idea may be extended to projection transformers. Let e and e' be as above. Then if τ_1 is a safe abstraction of e' w.r.t. x, and τ_2 is is a safe abstraction of e' w.r.t. y, then $\tau_1 \; \& \; \tau_2$ is a safe abstraction of e w.r.t. x, where

$$\tau_1 \; \& \; \tau_2 \;=\; \bar{\lambda}\alpha.\tau_1 \; \alpha \; \& \; \tau_2 \; \alpha.$$

4.3 Low-Fidelity Analysis

The low-fidelity first-order backward analysis is described in [WH87]. We briefly recount its essential properties. Given an expression e and free variable x, the abstract semantics yields a PT τ that is a safe abstraction of e w.r.t. x. The abstraction of a function definition $f\ x_1\ \ldots\ x_n\ =\ e$ is a collection of functions $f^{(1)}, \ldots, f^{(n)}$, each of a single argument. Each of these functions maps a PT to a PT, such that for each i, $1 \leq i \leq n$, and all ρ and γ,

$$\gamma\ (\mathcal{E}[\![f\ x_1\ \ldots\ x_n]\!]\ \rho\ \sigma)\ \sqsubseteq\ \mathcal{E}[\![f\ x_1\ \ldots\ x_n]\!]\ \rho[f^{(i)}\ \gamma\ (\rho[\![x]\!])/x]\ \sigma.$$

For $cond$ the analysis gives

$$\begin{aligned} cond^{(1)} &= \bar{\lambda}\alpha.STR \\ cond^{(2)} &= \bar{\lambda}\alpha.ID \\ cond^{(3)} &= \bar{\lambda}\alpha.ID \end{aligned}$$

This reveals that $cond$ is strict in its first argument, but tells nothing about strictness in its second and third arguments.

In general, the low-fidelity backward analysis, like the low-fidelity forward analysis, fails to detect joint strictness, and for a function of n arguments, requires only $\sum_{i=1}^{n} a_i$ combinations of abstract argument values to fully determine the abstraction of the function, where a_i is the size of the ith abstract argument domain.

4.4 High-Fidelity Analysis

The high-fidelity first-order backward analysis is described in [DW90]. Like low-fidelity analysis, the high-fidelity analysis maps expressions to PTs. The abstraction of a function, however, is a function from PTs to PTs. Let x be a free variable, f a function of n arguments, and τ_i a safe abstraction of expression e_i w.r.t. x, $1 \leq i \leq n$. Then the abstraction $f^\#$ of f has the property that $f^\#\ \tau_1\ \ldots\ \tau_n$ is a safe abstraction of $f\ e_1\ \ldots\ e_n$ w.r.t. x. For example,

$$cond^\#\ \tau_1\ \tau_2\ \tau_3\ =\ \bar{\lambda}\alpha.\tau_1\ STR\ \&\ (\tau_2\ \alpha\ \sqcup\ \tau_3\ \alpha).$$

To analyse $cond\ x\ y\ z$ w.r.t. x, take $\bar{\lambda}\alpha.\alpha$ as a safe abstraction of x w.r.t. x, and $\bar{\lambda}\alpha.ABS$ as safe abstractions of y and z w.r.t. x. Then

$$cond^\#\ (\bar{\lambda}\alpha.\alpha)\ (\bar{\lambda}\alpha.ABS)\ (\bar{\lambda}\alpha.ABS)\ =\ \bar{\lambda}.STR,$$

so $cond\ x\ y\ z$ is strict in x. To analyse $cond\ x\ y\ y$ w.r.t. y, take $\bar{\lambda}\alpha.ABS$ as a safe abstraction of x w.r.t. y, and $\bar{\lambda}\alpha.\alpha$ as a safe abstraction of y w.r.t. y. Then

$$cond^\#\ (\bar{\lambda}\alpha.ABS)\ (\bar{\lambda}\alpha.\alpha)\ (\bar{\lambda}\alpha.\alpha)\ =\ \bar{\lambda}\alpha.\alpha,$$

so $cond\ x\ y\ y$ is strict in y, that is, $cond$ is jointly strict in its second and third arguments.

In general, like high-fidelity forward analysis, the high-fidelity backward analysis can detect joint strictness in function arguments, and for a function of n arguments, requires $\prod_{i=1}^{n} a_i$ combinations of abstract argument values to fully determine the abstraction of the function, where a_i is the size of the ith abstract argument domain.

5 Higher-Order Backward Analysis

In the first-order analysis, the abstract value of an expression e relative to a given free variable x is a PT mapping a projection, the context of e, to a projection that may be safely applied to every instance of x in e. We will call this PT the *backward abstraction* of e with respect to x. In the first-order language, function definitions contain no free variables, so the values of functions and values of variables in an expression are completely independent. Given a function application, the function can only require particular definedness of a variable via its arguments, in which the variable may appear. Hence the abstract value of a function is just a function from the abstract values of its arguments to the abstract value of the application. We call this the *forward abstraction* of the function.

In the higher-order language, function definitions may contain free variables, so the evaluation of a function application may make some demand on a free variable, independent of the arguments. It may also make some additional demand on a variable via its arguments, as in the first-order case. For example, evaluation of the expression

$$(\text{if } b \text{ then } f \text{ else } g) \ b$$

requires that b be defined, independent of f and g. Application of f or g to b may also make some demand on b. This suggests that the abstract value of a function should encode two components: a backward abstraction giving demand on a given variable as a function of the surrounding context, independent of its arguments, and a forward abstraction, as in the first-order case. This is close to what we want.

5.1 Abstract Semantic Domains

The abstract value of every expression is a pair, consisting of a backward abstraction and a forward abstraction. The backward abstraction, as in the first-order case, is a projection transformer.

In the first-order analysis, the concept of a PT being a safe backward abstraction of an expression with respect to particular instances of a free variable was introduced. For informally explaining the higher-order analysis we introduce an operational element. Given a reduction rule—here normal order—and a specified degree of evaluation, e.g. to WHNF, suppose that for expression e in context γ, we may safely apply δ to those instances of the free variable x *referenced* during the reduction process. For example, for

$$\text{if } b \text{ then } (\lambda x.e_1) \text{ else } (\lambda x.e_2)$$

in context STR (indicating that the expression is certain to be evaluated to WHNF), we may safely apply STR to the instance of b immediately following **if**. We will not formalise the concept of 'reference during the reduction process'; it is for aiding intuition and will not be part of any formal definition.

We will say that τ is a safe backward abstraction of e with respect to x in reducing e to a given form if, for e in any context γ, we may safely replace those instances of x referenced during the reduction process by $\tau \ \gamma \ x$. For example, if no reduction of e occurs, then $\bar{\lambda}\alpha.ABS$ is a safe backward abstraction of e. In the first-order analysis, the backward abstraction of an expression corresponds to complete evaluation of the expression, that is, the resulting PT is a safe backward abstraction of the expression with respect to every instance of the relevant variable.

If τ is a safe backward abstraction of e in reducing e by some amount, then τ is also safe for any lesser amount of reduction. For the higher-order analysis we assume that expressions are reduced as far as possible, except for expressions or subexpressions of function type, which are reduced to WHNF. The resulting PT will then be safe for any lesser degree of reduction.

Let expression e have type T, and let $*$ be the type of free variable x. Then the type of any backward abstraction of e with respect to x is $|T| \rightarrow |*|$, where $|T|$ is the type of projections over T, and similarly for $|*|$.

Let A map the type of an expression to the type of its abstract value, and F map the type of an expression to the type of its forward abstraction. We have already decided that

$$A\,T \;=\; (|T| \rightarrow |*|) \;\times\; F\,T.$$

Since we intend to determine strictness using projections, the forward abstraction of an expression of base type needn't even come from a domain as rich as **2**, so we will take it from the one-point domain **1**, with sole element (). Thus

$$F\,K \;=\; \mathbf{1}.$$

The forward abstraction of an expression of function type is a function from abstract values to abstract values, so

$$F\,(U \rightarrow V) \;=\; A\,U \rightarrow A\,V.$$

We could take the forward abstraction of an expression of list type to be a list of forward abstractions. However, so that the abstract domains for any given program are finite (assuming the projection domains to be finite), we will represent this list by the least upper bound of all of its elements, so

$$F\,(List\;T) \;=\; F\,T.$$

5.2 Safety

The criteria for an abstract value $(\tau,\,\kappa)$ being a *safe* abstraction of an expression e with respect to x depend on the type of e:

Case $e : K$. For all ρ and γ we have

$$\gamma\,(\mathcal{E}[\![e]\!]\,\rho) \;\sqsubseteq\; \mathcal{E}[\![e]\!]\,\rho[(\tau\;\gamma(\rho[\![x]\!]))/x].$$

This is the same requirement as for the first-order case.

Case $e : U \rightarrow V$. Before giving the formal condition for safety we informally discuss the abstract semantics for application.

Intuitively, we may think of τ as being a safe abstraction of e in reducing e to WHNF. Let e_0 be an expression with safe abstraction σ_0 with respect to x. In applying e to e_0, e is first evaluated to WHNF, so the projection transformer mapping the context of $e\;e_0$ to the context of x in e is $\bar{\lambda}\alpha.\tau\;STR$. The resulting expression, with forward abstraction κ, is then applied to e_0, which has abstract value σ_0, giving some result with abstract value $(\tau_1, \kappa_1) = \kappa \, \sigma_0$. This result is in the same context as the application $e \, e_0$, so the two backward abstractions are &-combined:

$$(\bar\lambda\alpha.\tau \; STR) \; \& \; \tau_1 \;=\; \bar\lambda\alpha.\tau \; STR \; \& \; \tau_1 \; \alpha.$$

The forward abstraction of the result is then κ_1. Thus the rule for abstract application, which will be denoted by infix $\star$, is

$$\sigma_0 \; \star \; \sigma_1 \;=\; (\bar\lambda\alpha.\tau_0 \; STR \; \& \; \tau_2 \; \alpha, \; \kappa_2)$$
$$\text{where}$$
$$(\tau_0, \; \kappa_0) \;=\; \sigma_0$$
$$(\tau_2, \; \kappa_2) \;=\; \kappa_0 \; \sigma_1.$$

Formally, for all expressions e_0 with safe abstractions σ_0 with respect to x, the result of the abstract application $(\tau, \; \kappa) \; \star \; \sigma_0$ must be a safe abstraction of $(e \, e_0)$ with respect to x.

Case $e : List \; T$.   There are two pairs of conditions. Firstly, for all ρ,

$$NIL \; (\mathcal{E}[\![e]\!] \; \rho) \;\sqsubseteq\; \mathcal{E}[\![e]\!] \; \rho[(\tau \; NIL \; (\rho[\![x]\!]))/x],$$

$$(CONS \; ABS \; ABS) \; (\mathcal{E}[\![e]\!] \; \rho) \;\sqsubseteq\; \mathcal{E}[\![e]\!] \; \rho[(\tau \; (CONS \; ABS \; ABS) \; (\rho[\![x]\!]))/x].$$

Secondly, $head^\# \; \star \; (\tau, \; \kappa)$ and $tail^\# \; \star \; (\tau, \; \kappa)$ must be safe abstractions of $head \; e$ and $tail \; e$ with respect to x, respectively, where

$$head^\# \;=\; (\bar\lambda\alpha.ABS, \; \lambda(\tau, \; \kappa).(\bar\lambda\alpha.\tau \; (CONS \; \alpha \; ABS), \; \kappa)),$$

$$tail^\# \;=\; (\bar\lambda\alpha.ABS, \; \lambda(\tau, \; \kappa).(\bar\lambda\alpha.\tau \; (CONS \; ABS \; \alpha), \; \kappa)).$$

Intuitively, the first pair of conditions requires that τ be a safe backward abstraction of e with respect to x in evaluating e to WHNF. Note that the first of these is trivially satisfied when the value of e is cons, and the second when the value of e is nil. The second pair of conditions requires that the subcomponents—the head and tail of the list—be safely abstracted. This pair of conditions is trivially satisfied when the value of e is nil.

The definition of safety is recursively defined, firstly on the structure of the types expressions, and secondarily, because of the clause involving tails of lists, on the lengths of lists. Except for the case of infinite lists, the recursion is clearly well-founded. We conjecture that even in the case of infinite lists, the safety condition is still meaningful.

5.3   Abstract Semantic Function

The abstract semantic function $\mathcal{E}^\#$ must satisfy the following safety condition. If e is an expression with free variables z_i, $1 \le i \le n$, and e_i is an expression with safe abstraction σ_i with respect to x, $1 \le i \le n$, then $\mathcal{E}^\#[\![e]\!] \; [\sigma_i/z_i \mid 1 \le i \le n]$ is a safe abstraction of $e[e_i/z_i \mid 1 \le i \le n]$ with respect to x.

Abstract Semantic Domains

$$
\begin{aligned}
Val \quad &= Bool_{\uparrow} \oplus Int_{\uparrow} \oplus List_{\uparrow} \oplus \\
&\quad (Val \rightarrow Val)_{\uparrow} &&\text{values} \\
Proj \quad &\subseteq Val \rightarrow Val &&\text{projections} \\
BA \quad &= Proj \rightarrow Proj &&\text{backward abstractions} \\
FA \quad &= 1_{\perp} \oplus (Val^{\#} \rightarrow Val^{\#}) &&\text{forward abstractions} \\
Val^{\#} \quad &= BA \times FA &&\text{abstract values} \\
VEnv^{\#} \quad &= Var \rightarrow Val^{\#} &&\text{variable environment}
\end{aligned}
$$

Abstract Semantic Function. The type of the abstract semantic function is

$$\mathcal{E}^{\#} : Exp \rightarrow VEnv^{\#} \rightarrow Val^{\#}.$$

In the following explanation of the definition of $\mathcal{E}^{\#}$ we will implicitly use the fact that if τ is a safe backward abstraction of some expression e in reducing e to e', and τ' is a safe backward abstraction of e' in reducing e' to e'', then $\tau \mathrel{\&} \tau'$ is a safe backward abstraction of e in reducing e to e''.

All constants are of base type, so the forward abstraction of a constant is $()$. The backward abstraction is the same as for the first-order analysis, $\bar{\lambda}\alpha.ABS$, so

$$\mathcal{E}^{\#}[\![k]\!]\,\rho \;=\; (\bar{\lambda}\alpha.ABS, ()).$$

It is very easy to show that this definition satisfies the safety condition.

The abstract value of a variable is just its value in the enclosing environment:

$$\mathcal{E}^{\#}[\![x]\!]\,\rho \;=\; \rho[\![x]\!].$$

This definition trivially satisfies the safety condition.

The rule for application is

$$\mathcal{E}^{\#}[\![e_0\ e_1]\!]\,\rho \;=\; (\mathcal{E}^{\#}[\![e_0]\!]\,\rho) \star (\mathcal{E}^{\#}[\![e_1]\!]\,\rho).$$

If e_0 and e_1 are safely abstracted, then the definition trivially satisfies the safety condition.

A lambda expression is already in WHNF, so its backward abstraction is $\bar{\lambda}\alpha.ABS$. Some work is required to justify the the forward abstraction; intuitively, it is just like the rule for the ordinary lambda-calculus.

$$\mathcal{E}^{\#}[\![\lambda x.e]\!]\,\rho \;=\; (\bar{\lambda}\alpha.ABS,\ \lambda\sigma.\mathcal{E}^{\#}[\![e]\!]\,\rho[\sigma/x])$$

The abstraction of **fix** e is the least fixed point of the abstraction of e. Abstract application must be made explicit.

$$\mathcal{E}^{\#}[\![\mathbf{fix}\ e]\!]\,\rho \;=\; fix\ (\lambda\sigma.(\mathcal{E}^{\#}[\![e]\!]\,\rho) \star \sigma)$$

Addition is defined on integers, and equality is defined on integers and booleans. Assuming that e_1 and e_2 are safely abstracted, it is very easy to show that the following definitions satisfy the safety condition. The rule for addition has already been informally discussed; the same discussion applies to the rule for equality.

$$
\begin{aligned}
\mathcal{E}^{\#}[\![e_1 + e_2]\!]\,\rho \;=\;\; &(\bar{\lambda}\alpha.\tau_1\ STR \mathrel{\&} \tau_2\ STR,\ ()) \\
&\text{where} \\
&\quad (\tau_1, \kappa_1) \;=\; \mathcal{E}^{\#}[\![e_1]\!]\,\rho \\
&\quad (\tau_2, \kappa_2) \;=\; \mathcal{E}^{\#}[\![e_2]\!]\,\rho
\end{aligned}
$$

$$\mathcal{E}^{\#}[\![e_1 = e_2]\!] \rho = (\bar{\lambda}\alpha.\tau_1 \ STR \ \& \ \tau_2 \ STR, \ ())$$
$$\text{where}$$
$$(\tau_1, \kappa_1) = \mathcal{E}^{\#}[\![e_1]\!] \rho$$
$$(\tau_2, \kappa_2) = \mathcal{E}^{\#}[\![e_2]\!] \rho$$

In evaluating if e_0 then e_1 else e_2 in a lift-strict context, either e_0 is evaluated to WHNF, followed by evaluation of e_1 in the same context as the entire expression, giving backward abstraction $\bar{\lambda}\alpha.\tau_0 \ STR \ \& \ \tau_1 \ \alpha$, or, e_0 is evaluated to WHNF, followed by evaluation of e_2 in the same context as the entire expression, giving backward abstraction $\bar{\lambda}\alpha.\tau_0 \ STR \ \& \ \tau_2 \ \alpha$. Since either may occur, we take the least upper bound of these two backward abstractions as a safe for both alternatives. Similarly, assuming that κ_1 and κ_2 are safe forward abstractions of e_1 and e_2, respectively, then $\kappa_1 \ \sqcup \ \kappa_2$ is a safe abstraction of both. Thus

$$\mathcal{E}^{\#}[\![\text{if } e_0 \text{ then } e_1 \text{ else } e_2]\!] \rho = (\bar{\lambda}\alpha.\tau_0 \ STR \ \& \ (\tau_1 \ \alpha \ \sqcup \ \tau_2 \ \alpha), \ \kappa_1 \ \sqcup \ \kappa_2)$$
$$\text{where}$$
$$(\tau_0, \kappa_0) = \mathcal{E}^{\#}[\![e_0]\!] \rho$$
$$(\tau_1, \kappa_1) = \mathcal{E}^{\#}[\![e_1]\!] \rho$$
$$(\tau_2, \kappa_2) = \mathcal{E}^{\#}[\![e_2]\!] \rho.$$

Assuming that subexpressions e_0, e_1, and e_2 are safely abstracted, it is not hard to show that the definition satisfies the safety condition.

Evaluation of [] makes no demand on any variable, but the context must accept a nil value, so the backward abstraction is $\bar{\lambda}NIL.ABS$. The forward abstraction of a list is the least upper bound of the forward abstractions of its elements; [] has no elements and $\bot$ is the identity of $\sqcup$, so we take $\bot$ as its forward abstraction, so

$$\mathcal{E}^{\#}[\![[]]\!] \rho = (\bar{\lambda}NIL.ABS, \ \bot).$$

This definition is easily shown to satisfy the safety condition.

Intuitively, for $e_1 : e_2$ in context $CONS \ \alpha \ \beta$, e_1 is in context α and e_2 is in context β, so the backward abstraction of $e_1 : e_2$ is $\bar{\lambda}(CONS \ \alpha \ \beta).\tau_1 \ \alpha \ \& \ \tau_2 \ \beta$. If κ_1 is a safe forward abstraction of e_1, and κ_2 is a safe forward abstraction of every element of e_2, then $\kappa_1 \ \sqcup \ \kappa_2$ is a safe forward abstraction of every element of $e_1 : e_2$. Thus

$$\mathcal{E}^{\#}[\![e_1 : e_2]\!] \rho = (\bar{\lambda}(CONS \ \alpha \ \beta).\tau_1 \ \alpha \ \& \ \tau_2 \ \beta, \ \kappa_1 \ \sqcup \ \kappa_2)$$
$$\text{where}$$
$$(\tau_1, \kappa_1) = \mathcal{E}^{\#}[\![e_1]\!] \rho$$
$$(\tau_2, \kappa_2) = \mathcal{E}^{\#}[\![e_2]\!] \rho.$$

It is not hard to show that if e_1 and e_2 are safely abstracted, then this definition satisfies the safety condition.

Assuming that the subexpressions are safely abstracted, it is not too hard to show that the definition for **case** satisfies the safety condition:

$$\mathcal{E}^{\#}[\![\text{case } e_0 \text{ of } \{[] \ \rightarrow \ e_1; \ (x : xs) \ \rightarrow \ e_2\}]\!] \rho$$

$$= (\bar{\lambda}\alpha.(\tau_0 \ NIL \ \& \ \tau_1 \ \alpha) \ \sqcup \ (\tau_0 \ (CONS \ ABS \ ABS) \ \& \ \tau_2 \ \alpha), \ \kappa_1 \ \sqcup \ \kappa_2)$$
$$\text{where}$$
$$(\tau_0, \kappa_0) = \mathcal{E}^{\#}[\![e_0]\!] \rho$$
$$(\tau_1, \kappa_1) = \mathcal{E}^{\#}[\![e_1]\!] \rho$$
$$(\tau_2, \kappa_2) = \mathcal{E}^{\#}[\![e_2]\!] \rho[(head^{\#} \star (\tau_0, \ \kappa_0))/x, \ (tail^{\#} \star (\tau_0, \ \kappa_0))/xs].$$

Evaluation of the expression in a lift-strict context requires evaluation of e_0 to value nil followed by evaluation of e_1 in the same context as the entire expression, hence backward abstraction $\bar{\lambda}\alpha.\tau_0\ NIL\ \&\ \tau_1\ \alpha$, or, evaluation of e_0 is evaluated to a cons value followed by evaluation of e_2 in the same context as the entire expression, hence backward abstraction $\tau_0\ (CONS\ ABS\ ABS)\ \&\ \tau_2\ \alpha$. Since either of these may occur, we take the least upper bound as safely abstracting both. Similarly, we take as the resulting forward abstraction the least upper bound of the forward abstractions of the possible results, e_1 and e_2. The abstract environment for e_2 is the same as the environment of the entire expression, augmented by appropriate values for the newly introduced variables.

5.4 Example

Let

$$compose\ =\ \mathbf{fix}\ (\lambda compose.\lambda fs.\lambda x.\mathbf{case}\ fs\ \mathbf{of}$$
$$[]\ \ \to\ x$$
$$g:gs\ \to\ g\ (compose\ gs\ x)).$$

Our goal is to find a safe backward abstraction of *compose fs x* with respect to *fs*, under the assumption that every element of *fs* is strict. Choose the backward abstraction τ_f of *fs* to be safe with respect to *fs*, that is, $\bar{\lambda}\alpha.\alpha$. Choose the forward abstraction κ_{f_s} to be the greatest value such that each element of *fs* is strict, that is

$$\kappa_{f_s}\ =\ \lambda(\tau,\ \kappa).(\bar{\lambda}\alpha.\tau\ STR,\ \top).$$

Choose the backward abstraction τ_x of *x* to be safe with respect to *fs*, i.e. $\bar{\lambda}\alpha.ABS$. The forward abstraction κ_x of *x* does not affect the result. Then the first component of

$$\mathcal{E}^{\#}[\![compose\ fs\ x]\!]\ [(\tau_{f_s},\kappa_{f_s})/fs,\ (\tau_x,\kappa_x)/x]$$

is a safe backward abstraction *compose fs x* with respect to *fs*. The calculation is straightforward; the result is

$$\mu\tau.\bar{\lambda}\alpha.NIL\ \sqcup\ CONS\ STR\ (\tau\ STR)$$

$$=\ \bar{\lambda}\alpha.FIN\ STR$$

where for all α, $FIN\ \alpha\ =\ NIL\ \sqcup\ CONS\ \alpha\ (FIN\ \alpha)$. We conclude that if each element of *fs* is strict, then for the expression *compose fs x* in a strict context, it is safe to apply *FIN STR* to *fs*.

6 Conclusion

A new low-fidelity first-order forward analysis technique and high-fidelity higher-order backward analysis technique have been presented. Both appear to have potential for practical use. We have shown that low-fidelity higher-order forward analysis can be expected to give very poor results; we hypothesise similarly poor results from a low-fidelity higher-order backward analysis.

References

[Abr85]   Abramsky, S. "Strictness analysis and polymorphic invariance." In *Proceedings of the Workshop on Programs a Data Objects* (Copenhagen). H. Ganzinger and N. Jones, eds. LNCS 217. Springer-Verlag, Berlin, 1985.

[AH87]   Abramsky, S. and Hankin, C. (eds.). *Abstract Interpretation of Declarative Languages.* Ellis-Horwood, 1987.

[AH87b]   Abramsky, S. and Hankin, C. "An introduction to abstract interpretation." Chapter 1 of [AH87b]

[Bur90]   Burn, G.L. "A relationship between abstract interpretation and projection analysis." *POPL (San Francisco, January, 1990).*

[BHA85]   Burn, G., Hankin, C., and Abramsky, S. "The theory of strictness analysis for higher-order functions." In *Proceedings of the Workshop on Programs a Data Objects* (Copenhagen). H. Ganzinger and N. Jones, eds. LNCS 217. Springer-Verlag, Berlin, 1985

[CP85]   Clack, C. and Peyton Jones, S. "Strictness analysis—A practical approach." In *Proceedings of Functional Programming Languages and Computer Architecture* (Nancy, France). J.-P. Jouannaud, ed., LNCS 201. Springer-Verlag, Berlin, 1985.

[Dav89]   Davis, K. "Trading accuracy for efficiency in forwards strictness analysis." Unpublished report, 1989.

[DW90]   Davis, K. and Wadler, P. "Strictness analysis: Proved and improved." In *Functional Programming: Proceedings of the 1989 Glasgow Workshop, 21-23 August 1989, Fraserburgh Scotland.* K. Davis and J. Hughes, eds. Springer Workshops in Computing. Springer-Verlag, 1990.

[Hug85]   "Strictness detection in non-flat domains." *Proceedings of the Workshop on Programs a Data Objects* (Copenhagen). H. Ganzinger and N. Jones, eds. LNCS 217. Springer-Verlag, Berlin, 1985

[Hug87]   Hughes, R.J.M. *Backwards Analysis of Functional Programs.* Departmental Research Report CSC/87/R3, Department of Computing Science, University of Glasgow, 1987.

[Hug88]   Hughes, R.J.M. "Abstract Interpretation of First-Order Polymorphic Functions." *Proceedings of the 1988 Glasgow Workshop on Functional Programming.* August 2-5, 1988, Rothesay, Isle of Bute, Scotland. Department of Computing Science, University of Glasgow, Glasgow, Scotland.

[Hug89b]   Hughes, R.J.M. "Projections for polymorphic strictness analysis." In *Category Theory and Computer Science* (Manchester). D.H. Pitt, D.E. Rydeheard, P. Dybjer, A.M. Pitts, A. Poigne, eds. LNCS 389. Springer Verlag, Berlin, 1989.

[Myc81] Mycroft, A. *Abstract Interpretation and Optimising Transformations for Applicative Programs.* Ph.D. thesis, University of Edinburgh, 1981.

[Sto77] Stoy, Joseph E. *Denotational Semantics: The Scott-Strachey Approach to Programming Language Theory.* The MIT Press, Cambridge, Massachusetts, 1977.

[Wad87] Wadler, P. "Strictness analysis on non-flat domains by abstract interpretation over finite domains." Chapter 12 of [AH87].

[WH87] Wadler, P., and Hughes, J. *Projections for Strictness Analysis.* Report 35, Programming Methodology Group, Department of Computer Sciences, Chalmers University of Technology and University of Göteborg, Göteborg, Sweden, 1987.

An Algorithmic and Semantic Approach to Debugging

Cordelia Hall   Kevin Hammond   John O'Donnell

Abstract

This paper considers the problems of debugging large programs written in a pure functional style by experienced functional programmers. Several levels of debugging support are defined: specification, algorithmic, semantic, architectural and machine. We focus on the provision of tools for supporting algorithmic and semantic debugging. A significant feature of our work is that tools to support our approach may themselves be written in a pure functional language, and hence will be portable and easily modifiable.

1   Introduction

It is commonly claimed that functional programming makes designing and implementing large programs easy. It has even been claimed that the use of formal proof techniques for functional programs will make debugging unnecessary [Fis89]. In fact, to date there is little evidence to support either of these claims. Few functional programs of even medium size have been written by individuals, let alone teams of programmers (except perhaps the Alvey/ICL Flagship project). The most significant functional programs written to date have been compilers for functional languages. These programs have often been written by the language designers themselves, and rarely possess formal specifications.

This paper addresses the issue of debugging large programs at the semantic and algorithmic levels, that is locating and eliminating errors with regard to the meaning of a program. Our perspective is one of providing useful tools and techniques for use by experienced functional programmers working on large software projects. A link between our approach and formal methods of program development (as typified by e.g. Extended ML [San89]) is established at the algorithmic level.

2   Why Functional Debugging is Important

2.1   On the nature of errors

Many errors can be prevented by a good type system. However, no matter how strict a type-discipline is used, certain errors will still elude the type-checker. For example, the error which has rendered one mirror of the Hubble space telescope unusable is supposedly due to an incorrectly signed value in the software used to drive the mirror polisher, an error that no conceivable type-discipline could detect [Mih90]. It is insufficient (and bad software engineering practice) to assume that all errors can be caught automatically, or even by static proof techniques.

To provide maximum assistance to a programmer, it is necessary to consider all levels of error. From our perspective, statically detectable errors are not interesting: much work has been done on locating and presenting static errors in source programs, which applies equally to functional as to imperative languages. We therefore restrict our attention to the problem of locating and eliminating errors which cannot be easily detected by automatic static analysis of a program; that is, the kind of error which may have caused the failure of the Hubble space telescope.

2.2 Levels of abstraction in debugging

It is possible to visualise many levels at which debugging might be necessary:

- *specification:* errors in the problem specification;

- *algorithmic:* errors in the design of the algorithm used to implement the specification;

- *semantic:* errors in the implementation of the algorithm;

- *architectural:* errors in the implementation of the program for a given architecture;

- *machine*: where a machine imposes special constraints on a program.

Different techniques are suitable for these levels:

1. *Algorithmic debugging* concerns errors in the way the programmer reasons about the program. Tools for algorithmic debugging should fit in smoothly with reasoning and correctness proof techniques. For example, assertions about the relation between a function's arguments and result can be checked as the program executes, possibly exposing bugs in the program or its proof.

2. *Semantic debugging* concerns the values that are defined as a program executes. If the algorithm is correct but the program isn't, the programmer needs to know what is actually going on in the program — the values received and returned by functions, the choices made during pattern matching and conditionals, etc.

3. *Performance debugging* concerns how the values are computed; i.e. the operational properties of a program. This includes architectural and machine debugging. Examples of performance bugs include loss of sharing, demand for computation due to excessive strictness, too much or too little opportunity for parallelism, and premature demand for input by interactive programs. Such errors can be very serious and may render a program unusable.

A programmer uses different ways of reasoning about these classes of bug, and debugging tools for the levels must be implemented differently. Thus a performance debugger must examine the state of the graph at run time, while it is unnecessary and even undesirable for a semantic or algorithmic level debugger to do so. Although we do not deny the importance of performance debugging, we choose to concentrate on the hitherto neglected algorithmic and semantic aspects of debugging functional programs. A program which is fast, but wrong, is often of less use than one which is correct, but slow.

2.3 Why is it difficult to debug functional programs?

Imperative programmers often assume that functional programs are easy to debug. This may be true in the sense that state dependencies can be entirely discounted when debugging a functional program at the semantic level. However, several new problems arise precisely because of the declarative nature of functional programming languages. A major problem encountered when debugging programs written in a functional language is that the order in which expressions are evaluated may be highly non-intuitive. Lazy evaluation causes expressions to be evaluated only when needed. The implications of this evaluation strategy can surprise even experienced functional programmers. One consequence of this is to make tracing less effective than it would be with programs in an imperative language, even if print statements involving side-effects are permitted in the language. Similar problems arise with parallel evaluation.

A further consequence of lazy evaluation is that running programs frequently contain references to expressions which have not yet been evaluated. This causes special problems, since the examination of unreduced expressions may not be possible (if the expression evaluates to $\perp$).

Access to the values of intermediate data structures is also difficult. Although functions may be extracted from a program and tested in isolation, this can be unpleasant when the input to a function is the result of massive computation, or is a complex data structure. In a pure functional language, it is impossible to output such intermediate values directly, because they must be returned as part of the function result if they are to be viewed by the programmer. This necessitates a considerable amount of programming effort in order to "plumb" the required result between function calls.

An approach suggested by Wadler uses monads to encapsulate this plumbing within calls to higher-order functions [Wad90]. This is a significant improvement over the basic scheme, but still has the disadvantage that a program using this technique must be rewritten entirely, or almost entirely, in terms of monads. Since a prime advantage of using a functional program is the elegance with which algorithms may be expressed, it seems undesirable to obscure the clarity of an algorithm where monads are not the most appropriate program structure.

2.4   Alternative approaches for functional debugging

There are two completely different methods for implementing debugging tools for a functional language:

1. Write the debugging tools in a functional language, integrating it into a functional programming environment. This approach supports algorithmic and semantic debugging, but it cannot directly implement performance debugging tools. (It would be possible to simulate a graph reducer in the functional language, but this would be very inefficient and seems unreasonable.)

2. Include the debugging tools (or at least their lowest level components) in the underlying implementation. The main advantage is that performance debugging tools are feasible, at the cost of portability.

Some almost-pure functional languages provide impure features for occasional use. For example, imperative print statements, nonfunctional exceptions, and explicit sequencing control have been added to various languages. Such features are potentially useful for debugging, and it would be perfectly legitimate to study them further. Nevertheless, pure functional debugging is interesting because:

1. Debugging with side effects in an otherwise pure functional language has many pitfalls and can seriously mislead the programmer (an earlier paper gives examples [O'DH88]).

2. Widely available languages such as Haskell and Miranda[1] lack side effects, and they need debugging tools. (Indeed, impure language extensions tend to belong with a particular language implementation rather than the language definition.)

3. Debugging a program with side effects forces the programmer to think about evaluation order and parallelism. One of the advantages of functional languages is precisely that they free the programmer from such concerns.

4. It is interesting to see how far we can develop our ideas within a pure language. The attraction of using impure features is that traditional imperative debugging can be used, but our purpose is to develop new debugging techniques better suited for functional languages.

Several debugging strategies can be followed entirely within a pure functional language, without resorting to lower level tools:

- *Built-in diagnostics.* The programmer can provide debugging facilities as part of the basic design of the program. This is good practice anyway, and can be very helpful during software maintenance. Generally the programmer must provide functions to display important data structures, along with a mechanism for including such displays in the output of the program.

---

[1]Miranda is a trademark of Research Software Ltd., Canterbury, UK.

- *The shadow variable transformation.* A program can be transformed (either automatically or by hand) to display internal information, such as an execution trace and internal data structure values [O'DH88]. The trickiest part of the transformation is the plumbing: changing the types of functions to propagate the debugging information.

- *Interactive debugger with metacircular interpreter.* An interactive debugger can execute the program under the programmer's control. The user may single step through the program, set breakpoints, evaluate expressions, inquire about types, examine and modify the values of variables, etc. [O'DH88]

All three of these methods belong in a functional programmer's repertory. Because of the essentially ad hoc nature of programmer-defined diagnostics, we will not consider them further. We will, however, take into account the debugging needs which these diagnostics make apparent.

3 Related research

Most research that claims to concern debugging functional programs has been carried out in almost-functional languages that support side effects (e.g. Scheme and Standard ML [ToAp90]). Unfortunately these debuggers are based entirely on using those side effects, and so they cannot be adapted for a pure functional language.

Comparatively little work has been done on debugging pure functional languages. O'Donnell and Hall designed and implemented the first semantic-level debugger for a pure functional language [O'DH88]. This debugger constituted one component of a complete programming environment [O'D85] implemented entirely in Daisy, a functional language with nondeterminism. The former paper contains a full survey of related work as of 1987.

In the last two years there has been explosive growth in research on debuggers for parallel computers. Several conference proceedings have been devoted to this topic. Essentially all of this research concerns how to deal with time-dependent behaviour in imperative languages (primarily C and Fortran). Specific topics include synchronization primitives, debugging synchronization errors, exploring alternative possible sequences of time-dependent events, and animating execution traces to make them more readable.

From the point of view of functional programming, the entire field of "parallel program debugging" concerns a non-problem. Parallel execution does not affect the semantics of a functional program, and this is also true for debuggers written in functional languages. However, because conventional debugging techniques do not interact well with a pure functional approach, we must adapt such techniques when designing a functional debugger.

4 Semantic debugging

Semantic debugging provides tools for examining the values defined by a program, without giving the programmer direct access to the program's execution graph. Semantic debugging is concerned with the values defined by the language's denotational semantics rather than the method by which the implementation computes those values.

Programmers generally want to debug at the semantic level. For example, a programmer may want to ask "what is the value of x in function f?" or "which function called f, and what were the parameters?" It is seldom necessary to ask "what value is represented at address 0C3B61D4?"

A semantic debugger can give the programmer several ways to examine the program's execution. These include:

- *Tracing.* The debugger prints the function applications performed during the program's execution, along with the values of selected variables.

- *Interactive control of execution.* Tracing tends to produce too much output. Usually it is better to control the execution interactively, running most of the program quietly while examining the crucial parts in great detail.

- *Breakpoints.* Bugs often occur after the program has been running for a long time. This makes it inconvenient for the programmer to single-step the execution to the point where the error occurs, and tracing is even worse. A breakpoint allows the interactive debugger to be entered when a predefined condition occurs.

Semantic debugging tools can be implemented entirely within a functional language, without resorting to lower level tools. This makes the debugger more portable and easier to modify.

The simplest method for implementing a debugger is to transform the target program into a debugging version. This method is particularly well suited for tracing. The transformed program returns debugging information from each function, as well as the function's intended output. This means, of course, that the *entire* program must be transformed; otherwise there will be type errors.

The most straightforward way to implement an interactive debugger is to use a metacircular interpreter. This allows the debugger to control the execution of the program according to the programmer's commands, and it also provides a way to implement breakpoints. There are two main disadvantages with using a metacircular interpreter:

- It is necessary to ensure that the semantics defined by the interpreter is identical to the semantics defined by the compiler; otherwise the debugger may give misleading information. For a complex language, it may be difficult to ensure that two different implementations (the compiler and the metacircular interpreter) always have the same behaviour.

- The metacircular interpreter will be much slower than compiled code. This is acceptable for small programs, but good debugging tools are needed more for large programs than for small ones.

Experience with these techniques shows that the debugger must be able to execute functions from compiled object code modules without loss of speed. See section 6.

5 Algorithmic debugging

Algorithmic debugging provides high-level tools to assist with reasoning about the correctness of a program.

Our approach to algorithmic debugging differs significantly from Shapiro's seminal work [Sha82] in not relying on program synthesis, but rather accepting the program as given. There are several justifications for this attitude. Firstly, Shapiro's approach seems applicable only to small programs – like many other approaches to debugging, too much information is presented to the programmer. Secondly, the approach fails to deal with the need to debug finely-tuned programs. Thirdly, it will often be necessary to debug existing, incorrect programs, and impractical to resynthesise these programs. Finally, example-checking assertions fulfil much the same purpose as Shapiro's technique, but in a more permanent fashion – this is important for verifying the correctness of the program transformation process.

5.1 Algorithmic assertions

Assertions about the correctness of a program can provide useful algorithmic information to a compiler. An assertion is essentially a condition that must be true if a program is to produce correct results. Such assertions may be provided as part of a formal method, or directly by the programmer. In imperative programs assertions are often time or state-dependent; in functional programs, however, they usually relate function arguments to results. Certain assertions may be verified at compile-time, but a significant advantage of the approach we advocate is that assertions may also be used to verify the correctness of a program *during execution*.

In [Ham90b], we present a simple scheme which builds on the basic notion of assertions to provide four higher-level mechanisms: range checks, state checks, reasonableness checks and example checks. Figure 1 shows the assertions we support. precondition and postcondition assertions provide the basic mechanism for implementing state checks and reasonableness checks within a function definition. test assertions specify example checks. There is no way to express range checks directly: these must be provided as a set of individual assertions. [Ham90b] demonstrates the compilation of these higher-level assertions into calls of the primitive assertion function.

Ramamoorthy and Ho [RaHo77] regard all assertions as software redundancy incorporated in order to improve program reliability. Our attitude is similar: we regard assertions as visible and executable documentation for an algorithm, which does not

```
assertion s a e = if a then e else error s
{-# precondition   (f.n) :- <expr>        -}
{-# postcondition  (f.n) :- <expr>        -}
{-# test           (f)   :-  <expr>       -}
```

Figure 1: The primitive assertion function and algorithmic assertions.

change the result of a computation, but may make the result more reliable.

6 Separate Compilation

In [HHO'D90] we describe a scheme for interfacing the interpreter used in the debugger with pre-compiled code. Solving this problem efficiently is crucial if we are to be able to debug large programs. Our design allows compiled code to be executed by the interpreter, and interpreted code to be called from within compiled code. It also allows the insertion of trace or breakpoints in the compiled code. Compiled code should be executed at normal speed, with no degradation in time or space due to debugging. This is especially important when debugging long-lived programs.

We assume that for previously compiled modules we have access to at least the following information: the compiled object code; the names and entry points for all compiled functions; the types and arities of all compiled functions. Types and arities of functions will usually be available from the module interface; names and entry points may need to be explicitly included in the object code file.

From the entry points, we construct a jump table for all functions, whether compiled or interpreted, which is used to locate functions in "memory". The memory is a functional language array of machine instructions, a datatype which includes at least the JUMP and CALL constructors. Our intention is that our logical memory should map directly onto real physical memory. By using appropriate monadic structures, and ensuring that our interpreter is single-threaded, it is possible to modify our jump table and memory in-place [Wad90]. This allows compiled functions to be "shadowed" by interpreted functions, with no overhead for the compiled function calls.

This approach has a definite time advantage for debugging compiled modules, if the proportion of interpreted functions is low. There should be no time or space degradation until the debugger is entered. This is a significant advantage for a large, long-running, program. For example, certain errors in the Flagship runtime system occurred only after *a few days* execution.

In comparison, the "time-travelling" approach recently suggested by Tolmach and Appel for Standard ML [ToAp90] worsens execution time by a factor of 2-4, increases code size by a factor of 3-11, and significantly increases the program's runtime memory requirements. This is for a debugger which is highly optimised for a particular implementation, in contrast with our high-level semantic and algorithmic approach. Such overheads would be unacceptable for large programs, such as the Flagship runtime system, and undesirable for smaller, but still significantly sized programs.

Compared with more operational approaches [ToAp90], this approach may be restricted in the facilities provided by the debugger. However, we feel the tradeoff in favour of debugging large programs to be justified by our objectives.

6.1 Contingent Types

If a function definition is modified so that its type is changed, then it will be necessary to recheck all functions which depend on the type of that function, and perhaps provide new interpreted versions of those functions. This process must be repeated until all types in the program stabilise.

Although it may seem easier to simply update those type variables whose type is affected by the change, the process is complicated by the unification mechanism usually used to implement type-inference, and also by the fact that the implementation of a function will often depend on its type.

7 Conclusion

This paper has considered the problem of debugging pure functional languages. In contrast to more conventional approaches, we have chosen to concentrate on debugging at the semantic and algorithmic levels. This has several advantages: our debugging scheme is universally applicable to all implementations of a functional language; interaction is entirely in terms of the programming language semantics, with no extraneous operational detail; we may freely intermix compiled code with interpreted code, with no efficiency loss for fully compiled code segments, and without unnecessary recompilation of pre-compiled modules; and the debugger may be written in the functional language itself.

The principal disadvantage of our approach is that we lose the ability to deal with performance issues, including explicit parallelism. Although this is an important loss, we feel that performance issues are best addressed by implementation-specific tools, rather than the higher-level tools we propose here.

8 References

References

[Fis89]   Fischer, R., "Functional Programming and FPCA '89," Dr. Dobb's Journal, pp. 97–102, (December 1989).

[Ham89]   Hammond, K., "Exception Handling in a Parallel Functional Language: PSML," *Proc. IEEE TENCON 89*, Bombay, India, pp. 169–173, (1989).

[Ham90a] Hammond, K., *Parallel SML: A functional language and its implementation in Dactl*, Pitman Press, London, 1990.

[Ham90b] Hammond, K., "The use of Assertions for Algorithmic Debugging in Haskell," University of Glasgow, *in preparation*, 1990.

[HHO'D90] Hall, C.V., Hammond, K. and O'Donnell, J.T., "Debugging Functional Languages in the Presence of Separate Compilation," University of Glasgow, *in preparation*, 1990.

[HO'D85] Hall, C.V. and O'Donnell, J.T., "Debugging in a side effect free programming environment," *1985 ACM SIGPLAN Symposium on Programming Languages and Programming Environments*, June 1985, pp. 60–68, (1985).

[Mih90] Dimitri Mihalas, "Hubble," *RISKS digest #10.14*, June 29th, 1990, moderated by Von Neumann, P.G., (1990).

[MTH90] Milner, R., Tofte, M. and Harper, R., *The Definition of Standard ML*, MIT Press, Cambridge, Mass., (1990).

[O'D85] O'Donnell, J. T., "Dialogues: a basis for constructing programming environments," *1985 ACM SIGPLAN Symposium on Programming Languages and Programming Environments*, June 1985, pp. 19–27, (1985).

[O'DH88] O'Donnell, J. T. and Hall, C. V., "Debugging in applicative languages," *Lisp and Symbolic Computation*, Vol. 1, No. 2, pp. 113–145, (1989).

[RaHo77] Ramamoorthy, C.V. and Ho, S.F., "Testing Large Software with Automated Software Evaluation Methods," in *Current Trends in Programming Methodology, Vol II*, Yeh, R.T. (ed.), Prentice-Hall, Englewood Cliffs, N.J., pp. 112–150, (1977).

[San89] Sannella, D. and Tarlecki, A. "Program Specification and Development in Extended ML," *Proc. 1985 ACM Symposium on Principles of Programming Languages*, pp. 67–77, (1985).

[Sha82] Shapiro, E.Y., *Algorithmic Program Debugging*, ACM Distinguished Doctoral Dissertation Series, MIT Press, (1982).

[ToAp90] Tolmach, A.P. and Appel, A.W. "Debugging Standard ML without Reverse Engineering," *Proc. ACM conf. on Lisp & FP 90*, Nice, France, June 1990, pp. 1–12, (1990).

[Wad90] Wadler, P.L., "Comprehending Monads," Proc. ACM Symposium on Lisp and Functional Programming, pp. 61–78, (1990).

Abstract Interpretation of Term Graph Rewriting Systems
(Extended Abstract)

Chris Hankin[1,2]

ABSTRACT

In this paper we present a framework for the abstract interpretation of term graph rewriting systems. The framework is based on the approach taken by the Cousots for flowchart programs. We give an example of the use of the framework by presenting an interpretation which performs a form of type inference.

1. Introduction

In a Graph Rewrite System (GRS), rewrite rules relate arbitrary graph structures and, since these are not necessarily rooted, the overwriting of nodes is made explicit on the right hand side of the rule. This leads to a powerful formalism that is capable of modelling imperative language features (i.e. assignment) as well as purely declarative languages. This flexibility has led to GRSs being identified as a strong candidate for adoption as the intermediate code for general purpose parallel computers. One example of using GRSs in this way is reported in [Gla88a].

In Term Graph Rewriting (TGR) [Bar87], graphs are rooted. TGR systems have roughly the same power as term rewriting systems [Klo85]. The main distinction is that sharing is explicitly captured by shared subgraphs and, since cyclic structures are permitted, finite term graphs can represent infinite terms. There is a strong correspondence between computation in a TGR system and in graph reduction machines.

Viewing a graph rewrite system as a program raises the question of compilation and thus optimisation. Many of the classical analyses of functional programs [AH87] appear to be applicable in this new context. There may be some advantage to performing analyses at this intermediate level because, as it is "closer" to the machine, some opportunities for optimisation may be exposed which are hidden at the source language level. In this paper we will be concerned with semantics-based compile-time analysis of rewrite systems. The sort of properties that we will be interested in include the following: Strictness/Neededness [Bar87a]; Store Usage [Hud87]; Complexity [GH85], [San90]; Relevant Rules [Mis84]; and Types [Ban89].

---

[1] Dept of Computing, Imperial College of Science Technology and Medicine, 180 Queen's Gate, LONDON SW7 2BZ.
[2] The author was partially funded by ESPRIT BRA 3074 : Semagraph

The rest of this paper is organised into three main sections. In the next section we introduce the necessary details of TGR systems; this work has been reported in [Bar87] and [Ken88] and the interested reader is referred to those sources for further information. Section 3 sets up a framework for abstract interpretation; we present a "collecting" semantics [Cou77] - the most precise semantics which records complete information about possible executions of a program. The final main section presents an approximation of the collecting semantics - an abstract interpretation - which provides information similar to that produced by the analysis of [Ban89]. Section 5 contains some conclusions and directions for future work.

2. Term Graph Rewriting

The definitions presented in this section are based on [Bar87]. We give an operational account of TGR; [Ken88] gives a categorical semantics for a similar system. The main objective of TGR is to explicitly capture sharing as part of the rewrite mechanism. In TGR, rewrite rules effectively relate pairs of term graphs. We start by formally defining what we mean by "term graph":

Definition 2.1 (Term Graphs)

A term graph is represented by the quadruple:

$$(N,lab,succ,r)$$

where N is a set of nodes

$lab : N \rightarrow Symbol$ is a partial labelling function (nodes corresponding to variables are not labelled, i.e. $lab(n) = \perp$ for those nodes)

$succ : N \rightarrow N*$ is the node successor function (_* forms sequences)

r is a distinguished node called the *root*

We write:

$$G \mid n$$

to denote the subgraph of G rooted at the node n.

◊

For example, the formal representation of the following term graph:

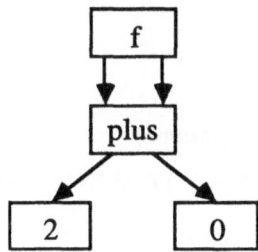

is:

$$(\{n_1,n_2,n_3,n_4\}, [n_1:=f, n_2:=plus, n_3:=2,n_4:=0],$$

$$[n_1:=n_2n_2, n_2:=n_3n_4, n_3:=\Lambda, n_4:=\Lambda], n_1)$$

where $[n_1:= \ldots]$ is a partial function which maps the specified nodes to the specified values and Λ represents the empty sequence.

Rules are defined as follows:

Definition 2.2 (Term Graph Rewrite Rules)

A term graph rewrite rule is a triple:

$$(g,n,n')$$

where g is a graph, i.e. a structure (N,lab,succ)

n is a node in g representing the root of the left hand side of the rule

n' is a node in g representing the root of the right hand side of the rule

such that all variable nodes appear in g|n.

◊

Thus, for example, the rule:

plus x 0 $\rightarrow$ x   (R1)

would be represented by:

$$(g,m_1,m_2)$$

where $g = (\{m_1,m_2,m_3\}, [m_1:=plus,m_3:=0], [m_1:=m_2m_3,m_2:=\Lambda,m_3:=\Lambda])$

In order to define a notion of reduction it is necessary to introduce a mechanism for identifying redexes in a graph. In order to do this, we have to introduce a number of definitions.

Definition 2.3 (Homomorphisms)

Given two term graphs, G and H, a mapping g : G $\rightarrow$ H (defined on the nodes of G and H) is homomorphic at a node n in G if:

either $lab_G(n) = \bot$

or $lab_H(g(n)) = lab_G(n)$

             $g(succ_G(n)_i) = succ_H(g(n))_i$ for all i, where $succ(n)_i$ is the i-th successor
                                                                                                                of n

◊

Definition 2.4 (Total Homomorphisms)

Given two term graphs, G and H, and a mapping g : G $\rightarrow$ H, g is a total homomorphism if it is homomorphic at *every node of G*.

◊

Definition 2.5 (Redex Occurrence)

A redex occurrence in some graph G is a total homomorphism from the left hand side of some rule to G.

◊

For example, there is an occurrence of (R1) in the example term graph such that the matching homomorphism is defined as:

$$[m_1 := n_2, \ m_2 := n_3, \ m_3 := n_4] \tag{O1}$$

Graph rewriting is a three phase process: the *build* phase, the *redirection* phase and the *garbage collection* phase.

During the build phase, copies of the nodes in the right hand side of the rule which do not appear in the left hand side are added to the graph; pointers to variable nodes are fixed up to point at the matching subgraph. We define the process more formally as follows ($N_{gln'}$ - N_{gln} are the nodes in the right hand side of the rule which are not shared with the left hand side - in particular, this excludes the variable nodes):

Definition 2.6 (The Build Phase)

Let H be the result of the build phase applied to a graph G, rewrite rule (g,n,n') and redex occurrence $f : g \rightarrow G$. We write:

$$H \quad = \quad G +_f (g,n,n')$$

and H is defined as follows:

$$N_H \quad = \quad N_G + (N_{gln'} - N_{gln}) \qquad \text{+ is disjoint union, - is set difference}$$

$$lab_H(m) = \quad \begin{array}{ll} lab_G(m) & m \in N_G \\ lab_g(m) & \text{otherwise} \end{array}$$

$$succ_H(m)_i = \quad \begin{array}{ll} succ_G(m)_i & m \in N_G \\ succ_g(m)_i & \text{both m and } succ_g(m)_i \text{ in } N_{gln'} - N_{gln} \\ f(succ_g(m)_i) & \text{m in } N_{gln'} - N_{gln} \text{ and } succ_g(m)_i \text{ in } N_{gln} \end{array}$$

$$r_H \quad = \quad r_G$$

◊

Performing the build phase at (O1) leaves the graph unchanged.

During the redirection phase all pointers to the root of the left hand side are redirected to point to the copy of the root of the right hand side. If the image of the root of the left hand side is the root of the whole graph, the root of the resultant graph will be the copy of the root of the right hand side of the rule; otherwise the overall root is unchanged. This is more formally defined in the following way:

Definition 2.7 (The Redirection Phase)

Define $H[a := b]$ to be the term graph $(N_H, lab, succ, r)$ such that:

$$lab(n) = lab_H(n) \qquad \text{for all nodes in } N_H$$

$$succ(n)_i = b \qquad \text{if } succ_H(n)_i = a$$

$$ succ_H(n)_i \qquad \text{otherwise}$$

$$r = b \qquad \text{if } r_H = a$$

$$ r_H \qquad \text{otherwise}$$

If H is the result of the build phase for an occurrence f and rule (g,n,n'), then:

$$J = H[f(n) := f(n')] \qquad \text{if } n' \in g|n$$

$$ H[f(n) := n'] \qquad \text{otherwise}^3$$

is the result of the redirection phase and we write:

$$J = H[f,(g,n,n')]$$

◊

For the example, the following graph results from the redirection phase:

$$(\{n_1,n_2,n_3,n_4\}, [n_1:=f, n_2:=plus, n_3:=2, n_4:=0],$$

$$[n_1:=n_3n_3, n_2:=n_3n_4, n_3:=\Lambda, n_4:=\Lambda], n_1)$$

The final phase is garbage collection which simply discards all nodes which are not accessible from the root of the graph.

Definition 2.8 (The Garbage Collection Phase)

For some term graph G the result of garbage collection, written GC(G), is defined as:

$$GC(G) = G \mid r_G$$

◊

Thus the final graph generated from our example is:

$$(\{n_1,n_3\}, [n_1:=f,n_3:=2], [n_1:=n_3n_3,n_3:=\Lambda], n_1)$$

3. A Collecting Semantics

A collecting semantics collects complete information about possible executions of a program [Cou77]. Abstract interpretations may be expressed as abstractions of, and proved correct with respect to, a collecting semantics. In the classical setting, the collecting semantics associates a context vector, a mapping from program points to sets of possible environments, with a program. The collecting semantics is defined in terms of a state transition function.

---

[3]This definition is slightly different from that given in [Bar87] which does not seem to handle selector rules correctly.

For flowchart programs, which is the application for the Cousots' original work, there is a clearly defined state transition function. Control flows from the entry points to the exits and is modified by tests. The situation is slightly more complicated for TGRSs. In our presentation, we make use of the following two sets:

Rule   the set of rules; elements are triples as presented in the last section

Graph   the set of graphs; elements are quadruples (N,lab,succ,r)

We use the notation:

$$\text{Graph} \rightarrow \text{Graph}$$

to represent the set of total graph homomorphisms. We define the next "state" for term graph rewriting by formalising the notion of reduction strategy. Following [Bar87], a strategy is a mapping from a graph to a set of reduction sequences; we will represent a reduction sequence as a sequence of pairs:

(Occurrence,Rule)

Thus the sequence:

$$(g_1,r_1)(g_2,r_2)\ldots(g_n,r_n)$$

associated with some graph, G_1, stands for a reduction sequence of n reductions steps:

$$G_1 \rightarrow_{g_1,r_1} G_2 \rightarrow_{g_2,r_2} \ldots G_n \rightarrow_{g_n,r_n} G_{n+1}$$

where g_i is an occurrence in G_i of the left hand side of r_i. The formal type of strategies is:

$$S \in \text{Strategy} = \text{Graph} \rightarrow 2^{((\text{Graph} \rightarrow \text{Graph}) \times \text{Rule})*}$$

We require that all sequences are nonempty [Bar87]. A strategy is *deterministic* if for all graphs, G, S(G) contains at most one element. S is a *one step strategy* (or *1-strategy*) if for all graphs, G, every member of S(G) has length 1^4. If G is in normal form, then S(G) will be empty.

Next we define our notion of state. To record the state of the system, it is sufficient to know the current state of the top-level graph. Thus we have:

$$\text{st} \in \text{State} = \text{Graph}$$

For now we will restrict our attention to 1-step, deterministic strategies and we will abuse notation by writing:

(f,r)   =   S(G)

to identify the single (Occurrence,Rule) pair when S(G) is nonempty. The next state function, nstate, is defined as follows:

nstate : State $\rightarrow$ State

nstate (G)   =   **let** seq = S(G)

         in   **if** seq = Ø

              then G

              else   **let** (f,r) = seq

---

[4] An example of a strategy which is not a 1 strategy is a strategy which reduces each redex to root-stable form (the graph analogue of weak head normal form)

$$\text{in GC}((G +_f r)[f,r])$$

We are now ready to define the collecting semantics; we follow [Jon87] in identifying program points with rules. We consider a set of m rules $\{(g_i,n_i,n'_i) \mid 0 < i \le m\}$ and an initial graph, Init, which we assume is not in normal form. We associate a "context" [Cou77] with each rule which is a set of pairs, where each pair specifies a graph and an occurrence of the left hand side of the rule in that graph:

$$C_r \in \text{Context} = 2^{\text{Graph} \times (\text{Graph} \to \text{Graph})}$$

$$C_r = \{(G,f) \mid n \ge 0, G = \text{nstate}^n(\text{Init}), (f,r) = S(G)\}$$

Thus a context specifies, for each use of the rule, which graph was being reduced and which redex within the graph was contracted. A context vector associates a context with each rule:

$$Cv \in \text{Context-vector} = \text{Rule} \to \text{Context}$$

and we define the vector associated with a program to be:

$$Cv = \lambda r.C_r$$

This semantics is similar to that presented in [Jon87] but, in contrast to Jones' semantics ours is more directly based on the Cousots' work using state transition functions and also takes the reduction strategy into account.

The set of context vectors forms a complete lattice. It is also possible to give a fixed point definition of the Context vector associated with a program. We define a function:

$$F : \text{Context-vector} \to \text{Context-vector}$$

in the following way:

$$
\begin{aligned}
F(Cv) = \quad &\bigcup\nolimits_{r \in \text{Rule}} \bigcup\nolimits_{(G,f) \in Cv(r)} (\\
&\quad \textbf{let } H = \text{nstate}(G) \textbf{ in} \\
&\quad\quad \textbf{if } S(H) = \emptyset \\
&\quad\quad \textbf{then } \bot \\
&\quad\quad \textbf{else } ([s := \{(H,h)\}] \textbf{ where } (h,s) = S(H))) \\
&\cup \; ([t := \{(\text{Init},k)\}] \textbf{ where } (k,t) = S(\text{Init}))
\end{aligned}
$$

note that the union operation is the operation from the lattice of context vectors.

It is straightforward to show that:

$$\text{fix } F = \lambda r.C_r$$

4. Approximating the Collecting Semantics

4.1 Banach's Analysis

The analysis in [Ban89] produces all possible (S,k,T) triples such that a node with label T can appear as the k-th successor of a node with label S during some reduction sequence. The analysis is guaranteed to be finite by ensuring that the set of symbols is finite; under the assumption that the only infinite subset of symbols is the integers, Banach does this by defining abstract graphs such that:

$$\underline{lab}\ n \quad = \quad lab\ n \quad \text{if (lab n) is not an integer}$$
$$\textbf{Int}\ \text{otherwise}$$
$$\underline{succ}\ n \quad = \quad succ\ n$$

The analysis is a form of type inference. It gives rather incomplete type information but it is sufficient to provide information to a more sophisticated analysis, presented in [Ban89], which allows atomicity conditions on rewrite rules to be relaxed. Thus the analysis is a vital component of an analysis which leads to efficient parallel implementations of graph rewriting languages.

4.2 Banach's Analysis as an Abstract Interpretation

The abstract interpretation will abstract a context vector by a set of triples:

$$SkT = (Symbol \times Integer \times Symbol)$$
$$Acontext\text{-}vector = 2^{SkT}$$

where Symbol is the finite set of node labels and elements in the set SkT are used to represent the same information as that produced by Banach's analysis. We ensure that Symbol is finite by using the same device as [Ban89] and assigning the symbol **Int** to any node labelled by an integer. The function $\underline{lab}$ maps each node to its associated abstract symbol (this is accomplished by the $\underline{lab}$ function). We will assume that symbols have a fixed arity, given by the following function:

$$\rho : Symbol \rightarrow Integer$$

These two constraints together ensure that the set SkT is finite. Acontext-vector is clearly a complete lattice.

In order to construct the abstraction and concretisation maps, we need to be able to abstract a single context with respect to a specified rule. This operation is achieved by the abs function:

$$abs : Graph \times (Graph \rightarrow Graph) \times Rule \rightarrow Acontext\text{-}vector$$

$$abs\ (G, f, r) = \bigcup_{m \in Glf(n)} \{ (\underline{lab}(m), i, \underline{lab}(m_i)) \mid 0 < i \leq \rho(\underline{lab}(m)), succ(m)_i = m_i \}$$
$$\text{where } r = (g, n, n')$$

The abstraction map is defined as follows:

$$\alpha : Context\text{-}vector \rightarrow Acontext\text{-}vector$$

$$\alpha(Cv) = \bigcup_{r \in Rule} \bigcup_{(G, f) \in Cv(r)} abs(G, f, r)$$

and concretisation is defined as follows:

$$\gamma : Acontext\text{-}vector \rightarrow Context\text{-}vector$$

$$\gamma(Av) = \bigcup \{ Cv \in Context\text{-}vector \mid \alpha(Cv) \leq Av \}$$

The abstract interpretation involves a fixed point computation over abstract context vectors. We will construct it in a way which should be reminiscent of the *nstate* function of Section 3. We need to introduce a number of definitions and auxiliary functions before we can define the abstract interpretation.

An assignment from an abstract contect vector is a mapping that maps variable nodes to symbols. Assignments are the abstract counterparts of occurrences. If a particular variable node is the i-th child of a node labelled S and there is an (S,i,T) triple in the vector, then the assignment can map the variable node to the symbol T. An assignment is *consistent* if, whenever the variable node is a child of more than one node, there are appropriate (S_j, i_j, T) triples in the abstract context vector (i.e. all of the triples contain the same symbol T). We define the predicate *is-assignment* which returns true when a consistent assignment exists:

is-assignment : Acontext-vector $\times$ Graph $\rightarrow$ Boolean

is-assignment(Av,G)

$\quad = \forall n \in G. \forall 0 < i \leq \rho(\underline{lab}(n)).$

$\quad\quad ((\underline{lab}(succ(n)_i) = \bot) \Rightarrow$

$\quad\quad\quad \exists T. \forall m \in G. \forall 0 < j \leq \rho(\underline{lab}(m)).$

$\quad\quad\quad\quad (succ(m)_j \neq succ(n)_i) \text{ or } (\underline{lab}(m),j,T) \in Av)$

$\quad\quad \text{and}$

$\quad\quad ((\underline{lab}(succ(n)_i) \neq \bot) \Rightarrow (\underline{lab}(n),i,\underline{lab}(succ(n)_i) \in Av)$

When consistent assignments do exist, the function *assignments* generates a function which maps the variable nodes to the set of possible symbols which might be assigned to them:

assignments : Acontext-vector $\times$ Graph $\rightarrow$ (Node $\rightarrow 2^{Symbol}$)

assignments(Av,G)

$\quad = \bigcup_{n \in G} \bigcup_{0 < i \leq \rho(\underline{lab}(n))}$

$\quad\quad \textbf{if } \underline{lab}(succ(n)_i) \neq \bot$

$\quad\quad \textbf{then } \emptyset$

$\quad\quad \textbf{else } \{[succ(n)_i =$

$\quad\quad\quad\quad \{T \mid \forall m \in G. \forall 0 < j \leq \rho(\underline{lab}(m)).(succ(m)_j \neq succ(n)_i)$

$\quad\quad\quad\quad\quad \text{or } (\underline{lab}(m),j,T) \in Av\}]\}$

Finally we need to apply the given assignment and generate the set of (S,k,T) triples present in the resultant graph; this is done by the function *triples,* it takes two parameters, a graph and an assignment:

triples : Graph $\times$ (Node $\rightarrow 2^{Symbol}$) $\rightarrow 2^{SkT}$

triples(G,f)

$\quad = \bigcup_{n \in G} \bigcup_{0 < i \leq \rho(\underline{lab}(n))}$

$$\textbf{if } \underline{\text{lab}}(\text{succ}(n)_i) \neq \perp$$

$$\textbf{then } \{(\underline{\text{lab}}(n),i,\underline{\text{lab}}(\text{succ}(n)_i))\}$$

$$\textbf{else } \{(\underline{\text{lab}}(n),i,S) \mid S \in f(\text{succ}(n)_i)\}$$

Armed with these definitions we can define abstract versions of the three phases of graph rewriting.

Definition 4.4 (The Abstract Build Phase)

Given an abstract context vector G, an assignment f and rule r (= (g,n,n')):

$$G \mathbin{\underline{\pm}_f} r = \quad G \cup \text{triples}(g|n',f)$$

◊

Definition 4.5 (The Abstract Redirection Phase)

Given an abstract context vector G, an assignment f and rule r (= (g,n,n')):

$$G\underline{[f,r]} = \quad G \cup \{(S,k,T) \mid (S,k,\underline{\text{lab}}(n)) \in G \text{ and}$$

$$(T=\underline{\text{lab}}(n') \text{ or } T \in f(n'))\}$$

◊

Definition 4.6 (The Abstract Garbage Collection Phase)

Given an abstract context vector G:

$$\underline{\text{GC}}(G) \quad = \quad G$$

i.e. abstract garbage collection is the identity function.

◊

Finally we define the function $\underline{F}$, which models the function F (defined in Section 3):

$$\underline{F} : \text{Acontext-vector} \rightarrow \text{Acontext-vector}$$

$$\underline{F}(Av) = \quad \bigcup_{r \in \text{Rule}} \quad (\textbf{if } \text{is-assignment}(Av,g|n)$$

$$\textbf{then } \underline{\text{GC}}((Av \mathbin{\underline{\pm}_f} r)\underline{[f,r]})$$

$$\textbf{else } Av$$

$$\textbf{where } r = (g,n,n')$$

$$\textbf{and } f = \text{assignments}(Av,g|n))$$

$$\cup \text{triples}(\text{Init},\lambda r.\emptyset)$$

$\underline{F}$ is clearly continuous and thus the abstract context vector associated with a program, which is the least fixed point of $\underline{F}$, may be found by iterating from $\emptyset$. Notice that our abstract interpretation takes no account of the reduction strategy or pattern matching; this is equivalent to Banach's analysis but there may be better analyses which do take some account of the strategy.

We finally have the safety theorem:

The Safety Theorem

$$\gamma \, (\textbf{fix } \underline{F}) \; \geq \; \textbf{fix } F$$

◊

5. Conclusions

We have sketched the development of a systematic approach to the static analysis of TGR systems and illustrated it in an application related to type checking. Our main contribution is that we have shown how the standard framework for abstract interpretation can be applied to Term Graph Rewriting Systems; the details of the particular abstract interpretation are secondary.

The style of the analysis presented in this paper is operational. [Ken88] presents a categorical semantics for graph rewriting in which the rewriting process is modelled by a pushout construction. This formalism allows elegant proofs for some standard results (e.g. Church Rosser properties) and may hold the key to a more algebraic approach to static analysis.

Acknowledgements

Thanks are due to Sebastian Hunt for his encouragement and constructive criticism of earlier drafts of this paper and to Muffy Thomas for her helpful comments. The author was partially funded by ESPRIT Basic Research Action 3074 : SemaGraph - The Semantics and Pragmatics of Generalised Graph Rewriting.

References

[AH87]   Abramsky S. and Hankin C. L.(eds) *Abstract Interpretation of Declarative Languages*, Ellis Horwood, 1987.

[Ban89]   Banach R. *Dataflow Analysis of Term Graph Rewriting Systems*, PARLE '89, Volume II, LNCS 366, Springer Verlag, pp 55-72.

[Bar87]   Barendregt H. P., Eekelen M. C. J. D., Glauert J. R. W., Kennaway J. R., Plasmeijer M. J. and Sleep M. R. *Term Graph Rewriting*, PARLE '87, Volume II, LNCS 259, Springer Verlag, pp 141-158.

[Bar87a] Barendregt H. P., Kennaway J. R., Klop J. W. and Sleep M. R. *Needed Reduction and Spine Strategies for the Lambda Calculus*, Information and Computation, **75** 3, pp 191-231.

[Cou77]   Cousot P. and Cousot R. *Abstract Interpretation: A unified lattice model for static analysis of programs by construction of approximations of fixed points*, 4th POPL, pp238-252, 1977.

[GH85]   Goldberg B. and Hudak P. *Serial Combinators: Optimal Grains for*

Parallelism, 2nd FPCA, LNCS 201, Springer Verlag, pp 382-399.

[Gla88a] Glauert J. R. W., Kennaway J. R. and Sleep M. R. *Final Specification of DACTL*, School of Information Systems, University of East Anglia, Norwich, UK.

[Hud87] Hudak P. *A semantic model of reference counting and its abstraction*, in [AH87], pp45-62.

[Jon87] Jones N. D. *Flow analysis of lazy higher-order functional programs*, in [AH87], pp103-122.

[Ken88] Kennaway J. R. *On "On Graph Rewritings"*, Theoretical Computer Science, **52**, pp37-58.

[Klo85] Klop J. W. *Term Rewriting Systems*, Notes for the seminar on graph reduction machines, Ustica, September 1985. A revised version to appear in the "Handbook of Logic and Computer Science", Oxford University Press, 1991.

[Mis84] Mishra P. and Keller R. M. *Static inference of properties of applicative programs*, 11th POPL, 1984.

[San90] Sands D. *Complexity Analysis for a Lazy Higher-order Language*, ESOP '90, LNCS 432, Springer Verlag, pp 361-376.

Compile-Time Garbage Collection by Necessity Analysis

G.W. Hamilton
S.B. Jones

Department of Computing Science,
University of Stirling,
Stirling FK9 4LA

September 1990

Abstract

This paper gives a brief overview of an analysis technique for determining at compile-time whether heap cells are still needed at a particular point in the execution of a functional program. This technique involves the analysis of necessity information. The analysis technique is used to determine at compile-time which heap cells can be deallocated, and also which of these deallocated cells can subsequently be reallocated.

1   Introduction

A substantial proportion of the execution time of functional programs is due to the large amount of heap storage management which must be performed (a figure of 10–30% is quoted in [1] for large LISP programs). Two apparent reasons why this should be the case are that more readable programs are often far from optimal, and that with a purely functional semantics the programmer is prevented from including explicit memory management operations.

To overcome the problem of sub-optimal programs, transformation techniques (such as those described in [2] and [3]) may be used to reduce their algorithmic complexity. To overcome the problem of the programmer being prevented from using explicit memory management operations, an efficient garbage collection method must be used. Transformation techniques are no substitute for an efficient garbage collector, since transformed programs may still have a large storage management overhead.

A technique for determining what heap storage management can be performed at compile-time within a functional program is described. This information can be used to generate more efficient compiled code and thus reduce the amount of execution time spent on heap storage management. The technique is based on the analysis of necessity information. Using this technique, certain heap cells may be collected earlier than in traditional garbage collection. These are those cells which are still accessible from the stack, but which will never be accessed by the computation.

This compile-time garbage collection also provides a good basis for further optimisations. The aim of these optimisations is to replace the allocation of new cells by the reuse of previously deallocated cells wherever possible. This technique is known as in-place updating. For example, consider the function:

f(x) = cons(head(x),tail(x))

The root cell of the list x can be deallocated after the execution of tail(x) if it is not needed for the evaluation of any other expressions. A new cell is also required immediately afterwards to build the result of cons. Instead of performing a deallocation and a subsequent allocation, the root cell of x can be reused for the cons operation. The implementation of f can therefore be optimised to reuse the root cell of its parameter for the cons operation.

The language for which these optimisations are to be performed is a simple first order functional language with lists which is executed using call-by-value with function arguments being evaluated from left to right.

Not all garbage collection can be performed at compile-time, so a traditional garbage collection method must still be used at run-time. However, compile-time garbage collection can serve to reduce the number of garbage collections which may be performed during the execution of a program (possibly to zero).

2 The Domain of Necessity Patterns

In order to determine necessity information at compile-time, some non-standard interpretations are defined. For space considerations, these interpretations are not given here, but full details can be found in [4]. The interpretations are defined on a domain of necessity patterns P. This domain is similar to the domain described in [5] and [6]. Elements of P indicate which parts of a list structure are required in an expression. These patterns may be evaluated at compile time and act as templates for the actual run-time structures in a program. P is defined as follows:

$$P = \{0,1\} + (\{0,1\} \times P \times P)$$

The elements of P are ordered as follows:

$0 < (x,y,z) < 1$
$(x_1,y_1,z_1) \leq (x_2,y_2,z_2)$ iff $x_1 \leq x_2$ and $y_1 \leq y_2$ and $z_1 \leq z_2$

The least element of the domain P is 0, which indicates that none of the structure it is associated with is required. The greatest element of the domain is 1, which indicates that all of the structure it is associated with is required. Between these two elements, there are elements denoting partial necessity of structures. These elements are represented by binary trees. Each node in a tree corresponds to a cell in the structure it represents. Branch nodes in this tree are represented by triples. The first element of this triple is either 0 or 1, indicating whether or not the root cell of the structure is required. The other two elements of this triple give the necessity patterns for the left and right substructures respectively of this cell. Leaf nodes in the tree are either 1 or 0 depending on whether or not a substructure is required.

The necessity patterns 1 and (1,1,1) both represent the same information (all of the associated structure is required). Similarly, the necessity patterns 0 and (0,0,0) both represent the same information (none of the associated structure is required).

Greater patterns represent lists with a higher degree of necessity and are thus "safer" as assumptions about the amount of the list which is needed. P is a complete lattice with the least upper bound of a subset being the union of its elements and the greatest lower bound the intersection. 0 is the least element of the lattice and 1 is the greatest.

Since P is an infinite domain, least fixpoint calculations of necessity patterns in P may not terminate. Finite domains which are approximations to P are therefore defined to guarantee termination of these calculations. The elements of these finite domains are defined to be greater than the corresponding elements of P and are thus "safe" approximations to them.

3 Necessity Based Garbage Collection

In this section a brief description is given of the analysis technique which is used to determine at compile-time which heap cells are garbage. A full description of the analysis technique is given in [4]. Normally, dereferenced cells are collected if they are not shared. The technique described here improves upon this strategy by collecting those dereferenced cells which are not needed for the evaluation of any further expressions, even if they are shared. Thus some heap cells may be collected earlier than in traditional garbage collection.

The analysis combines techniques used in *necessity analysis* and *path analysis*. Necessity analysis (as described in [5] and [6]) can be used to determine which parts of a list may be needed to evaluate an expression or appear in the result of the expression. Path analysis (as described in [7]) can be used to determine which expressions may be evaluated before or after the given expression. By combining the information obtained by these two analysis techniques, it is possible to determine which parts of a list may be needed for the evaluation of any expressions after a particular point in the execution of a program. Those parts of a list which are definitely not needed can be collected as garbage.

This analysis technique is used within an interpreter for a first order strict functional language to determine at which points of a program heap cells are no longer needed. By applying this interpreter to a particular program, it is possible to determine at which points in the program garbage is generated. The intermediate code produced by this interpreter could be used directly as the specifications of the actions to be compiled into the object code for the program. However, the output from the interpreter can be further optimised by determining which of the deallocated cells can be used for further allocations and performing in-place updates. This in-place updating can be performed where a cell deallocation is followed by an allocation. This kind of optimisation was first suggested in [8] in conjunction with a reference counting system.

For example, consider the reverse function:

```
reverse(l) = if null(l)
             then nil
             else append(reverse(tail(l)),cons(head(l),nil))
```

Using the described analysis, the part of the list l which is needed after the evaluation of head(l) is given by the necessity pattern (0,1,1). Thus the root cell of l is no longer required and can be reused to hold the result of the subsequent cons operation. Similarly, for the append function:

append(l1,l2) = **if** null(l1)
　　　　　　 then l2
　　　　　　 else cons(head(l1),append(tail(l1),l2))

The part of the list l1 which is needed after the evaluation of tail(l1) is given by the necessity pattern (0,1,1). Thus the root cell of l1 is no longer required and can be reused to hold the result of the subsequent cons operation. Thus all the allocations in the reverse program can be performed at compile-time, and no garbage collection needs to be done at run-time. Similarly, it can be shown that all the allocations in a quicksort program can be performed at compile-time.

4　Discussion

The work described here is very similar to the work described in [6]. In [6], a sharing analysis and a necessity analysis are defined on different interpretations of a domain of patterns. Thus the patterns resulting from these analyses cannot be combined in any way. A different domain of patterns is used in this work, which allows the the results of these analyses to be combined. This results in a simplification of the semantics describing the method.

Although necessity analysis is a backwards analysis technique, the method described here is essentially a forwards analysis technique, since it gives information about the necessity of an expression from necessity information about the variables in the expression. A backwards analysis technique for performing compile-time garbage collection is described in [9]. Using a backwards analysis technique, it is only possible to determine what sharing of the result of an expression will occur in the future, and not what sharing already exists in the expression. More work needs to be done to compare these two techniques.

More work needs to be done to determine how worthwile compile-time garbage collection is. Some preliminary studies have been performed in [10] and [11] which seem to indicate that only a low proportion of instructions may be optimised in this way. The method described is for a call-by-value semantics with function arguments evaluated from left to right. An extension of the method to a call-by-need semantics would be straightforward, but a loss of information would result from not being able to make any assumptions about the order of evaluation of expressions. Thus even less garbage collection could be performed at compile-time for lazy functional programs. However, if strictness analysis is also performed on the programs, more information can be obtained about the order of evaluation of expressions. It has already been shown in [5] how necessity analysis can be used to provide strictness information. An extension of the described method for higher order languages would be more difficult, and this has not been achieved yet.

70

References

[1] J. Cohen. Garbage collection of linked data structures. *Computing Surveys*, 13(3):341–367, September 1981.

[2] R.M. Burstall and J. Darlington. A transformation system for developing recursive programs. *Journal of the ACM*, 24(1):44–67, January 1977.

[3] P. Wadler. Deforestation: transforming programs to eliminate trees. *Lecture Notes in Computer Science*, 300:344–358, 1988.

[4] G.W. Hamilton and S.B. Jones. *Compile-Time Garbage Collection by Necessity Analysis*. Technical Report TR 67, Dept. of Computing Science, University of Stirling, 1990.

[5] S.B. Jones and D. Le Metayer. A new method for strictness analysis on non-flat domains. In *1989 Glasgow Workshop on Functional Programming*, pages 1–11, August 1989.

[6] S.B. Jones and D. Le Metayer. Compile-time garbage collection by sharing analysis. In *Proceedings of the Fourth International Conference on Functional Programming Languages and Computer Architecture*, pages 54–74, 1989.

[7] A. Bloss and P. Hudak. Variations on strictness analysis. In *Proceedings of the ACM Conference on LISP and Functional Programming*, pages 132–142, 1986.

[8] J.M. Barth. Shifting garbage collection overhead to compile time. *Communications of the ACM*, 20(7):513–518, July 1977.

[9] T.P. Jensen and T.A. Mogensen. A backwards analysis for compile-time garbage collection. *Lecture Notes in Computer Science*, 432:227–239, 1990.

[10] M. White. *Is Compile-Time Garbage Collection Worth the Effort?* Final Year Project Dissertation, Dept. of Computing Science, University of Stirling, April 1990.

[11] S.B. Jones and M. White. Is compile-time garbage collection worth the effort? In *Proceedings of the Third Annual Glasgow Workshop on Functional Programming*, August 1990.

Improving Full Laziness

Carsten Kehler Holst *

Abstract

The aim of transforming programs into fully-lazy form is to avoid recomputations by sharing as much computation as possible. In this paper we shall see how to improve programs, such that even more computation can be shared when the programs are transformed into fully-lazy form. This is done by treating control constructs specially. The idea is that when the condition in a conditional can be evaluated then the conditional should be reduced away (if True t e) should reduce to t even if t cannot be computed. We achieve this by transforming the conditionals such that the branches always can be evaluated when the condition can be evaluated. The results we achieve using this technique compares well with the results achieved by partial evaluation.

Keywords: Full Laziness, Partial Evaluation, Binding Times, Optimisations, Sharing.

1 Introduction

In functional programmming laziness is an aversion against recomputations. A lazy program has normal order reduction semantics but computes each argument at most once. Fully-lazy programs evaluate each expression at most once after its free variables become bound. Programs are transformed into fully-lazy form to achieve better sharing of computations. Section 2 review full laziness and describes how to transform programs to fully-lazy form.

This paper identifies a potentially sharable kind of computation, namely the computation of control. The problem with full laziness, as it is usually defined, is the view of control constructs, like conditionals and case-expressions, as expressions. This does not take account of the fact that these constructions can be computed independently of the values of the branches. Section 3 discusses this problem and propose a solution. The solution is a simple source-to-source transformation that improves the binding times of the control constructs and thereby the potential sharing exploited by the transformation into fully-lazy expressions.

The claim of this paper is that for a wide range of programs a significant part of the computation consists of "sharable" control and that the proposed transformation therefore is worthwhile. This claim is justified with two examples: the power function, and an interpreter both of which are speeded up with a factor of 2–3.

---

*Department of Computing Science, University of Glasgow, 17 Lilybank Gdns, Glasgow G12 8QQ. Supported by University of Copenhagen, The Danish Research Academy, Email: kehler@cs.glasgow.ac.uk

These two examples are found in sections 4, and 5. The results achieved in the interpreter example are compared with the results known from partial evaluation. Section 6 is the conclusion.

2 Full Laziness

We are considering a lazy HASKELL[1] -like language with let, and lambda expressions. The laziness ensures that let, and lambda bound expressions are evaluated at most once. In this section we consider how to share free expressions. The transformation, we consider, achieves what is known as full laziness.

Consider the following expression:

```
let f = \x -> \y -> fib x + fib y
    g = f 4
in g 5 + g 6
```

The subexpression (fib x) is evaluated twice after its free variable x is bound, x is bound by the application (f 4). To avoid this kind of recomputation expressions like (fib x) is moved out until they are in a position where they can be evaluated at most once. In this case (fib x) is moved to the outside of lambda-abstraction \y...

```
\x -> (let fx = (fib x) in \y -> fx + fib y)
```

To avoid the introduction of unnecessary bindings expressions like (fib x) are only moved out until they are no longer free. Consider the following function definition:

```
\x -> if (p x) (\y -> f x y) (\y -> g x y)
```

If the free expressions (f x), and (g x) are moved out as far as possible we get:

```
\x -> (let fx = (f x)
           gx = (g x)
       in if (p x) (\y -> fx y) (\y -> gx y))
```

One of the two let-bindings is in this example is unnecessary. A better solution is only to move the expressions out until there no longer is a risk of recomputation.

```
\x -> if (p x) (let fx = (f x) in \y -> fx y)
               (let gx = (g x) in \y -> gx y)
```

2.1 Staticness

When an expression like (\x -> \y -> \z -> e) is applied, x is bound before y which again is bound before z. We call the variables that are bound first *early* and the ones that are bound late *late* and we say that the early ones are more *static* than the late ones, which are more *dynamic* than the early ones. Concretely we assign binding times to variables, constants, and expressions. The constants get binding time 0, a variable gets as its binding time the number of lambdas surrounding its lambda-binding, so the outermost bound variable gets binding time 1. In this case x, y, and z have binding times 1, 2, and 3. We assign binding times to expressions by

---

[1]A non-strict functional language, Hudak and Wadler [3].

giving the expression the latest binding time of its free variables. So the expression (x + x) has binding time 1, and (y + x) has binding time 2.

An expression is *free* inside a lambda-abstraction if the binding time of the expression is smaller than the binding time of the variable abstracted by the lambda. A *free* expression might be evaluated several times after it's free variables are bound; once for each new binding of the variables with later binding times. Therefore, *free* expression should be floated out until they are no longer free. A *maximal free expressions* (MFE) is maximal in the sense that it is free and all the expressions of which it is a true subexpression are not free.

2.2 Algorithm

In this section we present an algorithm that transforms an expression into fully lazy form. The algorithm and the idea that full laziness is independent of lambda-lifting are due to Peyton Jones and Lester [9]. Originally the idea about floating out MFEs was combined with the idea of lambda-lifting, this is described by Hughes [4].

The algorithm is: repeat 1. and 2. below until all MFEs are trivial. A MFE is trivial if it is a constants or a variable.

1. Transform all the non-trivial MFE's to trivial let-expressions. A MFE, `mfe`, becomes (let v = mfe in v) where v is a unique new variable name.

2. Lift the let defined `mfe` out as far as possible by repeating the following transformations until the `mfe` is no longer free.

   (a) e (let n = mfe in e') $\Longrightarrow$ (let n = mfe in e e')

   (b) (let n = mfe in e') e $\Longrightarrow$ (let n = mfe in e' e)

   (c) \v -> (let n' = mfe in e) $\Longrightarrow$ (let n' = mfe in \v -> e)

   (d) let v = e' in (let n = mfe in e)
       $\Longrightarrow$ let n = mfe in (let v = e' in e)

3 Liberating Control

We begin with an aside about conditionals, then present what we claim is a problem and what we claim is the solution.

In functional languages conditionals are considered to be expressions. In a sense the introduction of an if-expression as opposed to an if-statement was what made it possible to write functional programs. In strict languages like LISP, if-expressions are special functions that evaluate their arguments in a special way. First the condition is evaluated; if it evaluates to NIL the third argument is evaluated, otherwise the second argument is. In lazy languages there is no need for this distinction since things are only ever evaluated if they are needed. But by regarding conditionals as mere expressions we lose part of our operational intuition about conditionals as control constructs.

The notion of MFEs is very nice, but it only tells part of the story. Consider the following expression:

    if (p x) (f x y) (g x y)

Suppose that x is an early variable and y a late variable. The problem is that the MFE becomes [if (p x)] and the expression as a whole depends on y. Intuitively we should be able to reduce (if True t e) to t, but since the conditional requires the *value* of its three arguments before it can be reduced, this cannot be done.

Our claim is that this is *bad*, the if-expression is a control construct, and that it can perform valuable computation given only the value of its first argument. This valuable computation ought to be shared. In the following we show how the if-expression can be transformed so its binding time is dependent only on the first argument, and prove by example that this is worth doing.

3.1 Moving from Values to Computations

One way of making the control facet of the if-expression more visible is to abstract the free variables out of the branches, thereby transforming them into constant combinators. Such combinators are descriptions of computations. Then the expression above becomes:

```
if :: Bool -> ((a,b) -> r) -> ((a,b) -> r) -> ((a,b) -> r)

(if (p x) (\(x,y) -> f x y) (\(x,y) -> g x y)) (x,y)
```

The binding time of the if-expression is now totally independent of the branches. To make the types fit we have to abstract the free variables in both branches. In general we need not abstract all the free variables to achieve the desired effect. Abstracting the variables with a later binding time than the condition will do, and will remove the need for transforming the if-expressions when the condition has a late binding time. This way we get:

```
if :: Bool -> (a -> r) -> (a -> r) -> (a -> r)

if (p x) (\y -> f x y) (\y -> g x y) y
```

Now the conditional has the same binding time as x and the control has become as static as possible.

3.2 Algorithm

The algorithm, which should be performed before the transformation to fully-lazy form described in section 2.2, transform the program as follows.

- For each conditional lift out the variables with later binding times than the condition from the two branches.

- Perform η-reductions where possible.

The algorithm is extremely simple, but should be enhanced with η-reductions since it often produces constructs of the form:

```
(\y -> e y)
```

where y does not occur in e. This occurs, for example, when conditionals are nested, as the example below shows. Assume y is a late variable occuring in t1, and t2.

```
if p1 t1 (if p2 t2 e2)
```

Which is transformed to:

```
(if p1 (\y -> t1) (\y -> (if p2 (\y -> t2) (\y -> e2)) y)) y
```

This expression should be η-reduced to:

```
(if p1 (\y -> t1) (if p2 (\y -> t2) (\y -> e2))) y
```

3.3 Other Control Constructs

The sketched transformation can be applied to other control constructs, like case-expressions. In general if we have an expression of the form

```
e1 e2  ... en
```

where e1 is any fully applied function of type $\alpha \to \alpha \to \ldots \to \alpha$, then the expression can safely be transformed into

```
(e1 (\y -> e2) ... (\y -> en)) y
```

This result follows from Theorems for Free! [12].

4 The Power Function

This section shows how the transformation described may substantially improve the sharing in a program and hence increase its efficiency. Consider the following definition of the well known power function.

```
power = \x -> \y -> if (zero x) 1
                    if (even x) (sqr (power (x div 2) y))
                                (y * power (x - 1) y)
```

The standard transformation to fully-lazy form, described in section 2, gives:

```
power = \x -> (let izx = if (zero x) 1
                   iex = if (even x)
                   pdx = power (x div 2)
                   pmx = power (x - 1)
           in
                   \y -> izx (iex (sqr (pdx y)) (y * (pmx y))))
```

Admittedly, this is not the best version. A common heuristics is: do not abstract partial applications. In this case it means: abstract (zero x), and (even x), but not the partially applied if. Since the difference is of little importance in this case, and that this kind of heuristics apply equally well to the standard transformation and the improved transformation, this kinds of heuristics wont be considered here. Compare the result of the standard transformation with the result of our improved transformation:

```
power = \x -> if (zero x) (\y -> 1)
              if (even x) (let pdx = power (x div 2) in
                                \y -> pdx y)
                          (let pmx = power (x - 1) in
                                \y -> y * (pmx y)))
```

4.1 Analysis

To get an understanding of the differences between these three versions of the power function, we examine the value of (power 5) for the three different versions of power.

In this analysis we assume that the program has been lambda lifted and we examine the combinator expressions corresponding to (power 5). We present the combinator expressions in normal form except for the parts that are never evaluated. The parts that are never evaluated (*i.e.*, the dead code) is written in angle brackets, such as <if (even 0)>.

The Original Power Function. After lambda lifting the original power function requires two arguments before any evaluation takes place so the expression is already in normal form:

```
(power 5)
```

The Fully-Lazy Power Function. After the transformation into fully-lazy form a lot of computation can take place when power is applied to its first argument. The normal form of the closure looks like:

```
($p (if False 1)
    (if False)
    <power (5 div 2)>
    ($p (if False 1)
        (if True)
        ($p (if False 1)
            (if True)
            ($p (if False 1)
                (if False)
                <power (1 div 2)>
                ($p (if True 1)
                    <if (even 0)>
                    <power (0 div 2)>
                    <power (0 - 1)>))
            <power (2 - 1)>)
        <power (4 - 1)>))
```

```
$p izx iex pdx pmx y = izx (iex (sqr (pdx y)) (y * (pmx y)))
```

$p is the combinator arising from lambda lifting the body of the let-expression. Examining the expression we can see that no further simplification can take place, so we are left with all the conditionals.

The Improved Fully-Lazy Power Function. Again we assume that fully-lazy lambda lifting has been performed and name the generated combinators $p1, $p2, and $p3.

```
(power 5) => ($p3 ($p2 ($p2 ($p3 $p1))))
```

```
$p1 y = 1
$p2 p y = sqr (p y)
$p3 p y = y * (p y)
```

Several things spring to the eye. The expression is much smaller. We have got rid of all the unevaluated closures. The control, which we knew was static, has been eliminated. By unfolding the combinator expression we can see that this is an almost optimal description of the remaining computation.

```
\y -> y * (sqr (sqr (y * 1)))
```

Results The table below shows the results of running the different versions of the power function on input 5 and 2. In the first run the power function is just applied to its two arguments. In the second run the partial application (power 5) has been evaluated. The difference between the two runs illustrate the amount of computation that can be performed given only the first parameter. power is the original power function, lpower is the fully-lazy power function, and ilpower is the improved fully lazy power function. The figures (the number of reductions / the number of cells claimed) are as given by the Orwell system. A reduction is the substitution of a left-hand-side with the corresponding right-hand-side.

run	power5 2	lpower5 2	ilpower5 2
1	47/116	52/131	52/107
2	47/116	21/44	12/15

These figures suggest that the fully-lazy, and the improved fully-lazy versions perform slightly worse on the first run, the improved fully-lazy version having the best storage performance. On the second run, when the closure has been evaluated the fully-lazy version outperforms the original version by a factor of two (half of the computation has been shared), and the improved fully-lazy version outperforms the original by a factor of four (twice as good as the ordinary fully-lazy version). Our conclusion is that both full laziness, and improved full laziness cost a bit when there is nothing to share, and that improved full laziness may be substantially better if there is a possibility of sharing.

These conclusions should not be taken as the final word in this case. A similar experiment has been carried out in LML and there a slight decrease in efficiency was observed. The reason seems to be that LML implements strict functions like power extremely efficient and partial applications extremely (relatively) inefficient.[2]

5   An Interpreter

This example is included to show how the proposed transformation makes it possible to achieve results comparable to the results achieved by partial evaluation Jones [5]. As is often the case in partial evaluation we make some small transformations, by hand, of the interpreter in order to achieve the desired binding times.

Let the following little interpreter be our example.

```
expr ::= Num num | Var [char] | Mul expr expr | Pred expr |
         If expr expr expr | Call [char] [expr]
```

---

[2]It is difficult to estimate the importance of the LML experiment. Using (+ 1) instead of (power 127) gave the same runtime.

```
run prog vals = snd (phi!0) vals
             where phi = [(n,eval phi ns e)| (n,(ns,e)) <- prog]

eval phi ns (Num n)     vs = n
eval phi ns (Var n)     vs = getval ns n vs
eval phi ns (Mul e1 e2) vs = eval phi ns e1 vs * eval phi ns e2 vs
eval phi ns (Pred e)    vs = eval phi ns e vs - 1
eval phi ns (If c t e)  vs = if (eval phi ns c vs = 0)
                                (eval phi ns e vs)
                                (eval phi ns t vs)
eval phi ns (Call n a)  vs = (let fun = (assoc phi n)
                                  ev  = (eval phi ns)
                              in \vs -> fun (map (\e -> ev e vs) a))
```

phi is our function environment. As in partial evaluation we have split the environment up into a namelist ns, and a value list **vs**. getval fetches the value of n in **vs**.

We will not show the fully lazy version of this interpreter but go directly to the improved fully lazy version.

```
eval phi ns (Num n)     = (\vs -> n)
...
eval phi ns (If c t e)  = (let c1 = (eval phi ns c)
                               c2 = (eval phi ns t)
                               c3 = (eval phi ns e)
                           in \vs -> if (c1 vs = 0) (c2 vs) (c3 vs))
eval phi ns (Call n a)  = (let fun = (assoc phi n)
                               arg = map (eval phi ns) a
                           in \vs -> fun (map (\c -> c vs) arg))
```

As is often the case in partial evaluation we have made some small transformations, by hand, of the interpreter in order to achieve the desired binding times. Besides splitting the environment in two, the original interpretation of function calls, seen below, has been transformed.

```
eval phi ns (Call n a) = assoc phi n (map (\e -> eval phi ns e vs) a)
```

Without this transformation the result would have been

```
eval phi ns (Call n a) = (let fun = (assoc phi n)
                              ev  = (eval phi ns)
                          in \vs -> fun (map (\e -> ev e vs) a))
```

But the static expression arg, which results from the transformed version, is much better than ev, which results from the untransformed version. In **ev** the staticness is completely destroyed. The following transformations, or laws were used to achieve the improved binding time properties of the interpreter:

```
(\e -> ev e vs) = (\c -> c vs) . (\e -> ev e)
map (f . g) = map f . map g

map (\e -> ev e vs) a = map (\c -> c vs) (map (\e -> ev e) a)
```

This is a particular example of a general transformation whose aim is to improve the binding time properties of programs found in Holst and Hughes [2].

5.1 Analysis

This analysis examines what happens when the two versions of our interpreter are used to interpret the classical fac program shown below.

```
fac n = if (n = 0) 1 (n * (fac (n - 1)))

facProg = [("f",(["n"],
                If (Var"n")
                   (Mul (Var"n") (Call "f" [(Pred (Var "n"))]))
                   (Num 1))
          )]
```

First we have a look at the evaluated closure for (run facProg). The original interpreter of course just generates (run facProg). But a look at the closure generated by the improved fully lazy interpreter justifies the claim that our transformation makes it possible to achieve results comparable to those achieved by partial evaluation. Again we assume that fully-lazy lambda lifting has been performed on the interpreter, and we examine the combinator expression corresponding to the closure. We have given the combinators generated for "if", and "call" but left out the rest. The hd occuring in the closure is the result of (getval ns n), it fetches the value of x.

```
(run facProc) =>  +-> ($if hd ($k 1)
                  |             ($mul hd ($call * [($pred hd)]))))
                  |_____|

$if c1 c2 c3 vs = if ((c1 vs) = 0) (c2 vs) (c3 vs)
$call fun arg vs = fun (map (\a -> a vs) arg)
...
```

The first impression is that the evaluated closure has a structure very similar to the original fac program, just as residual programs generated by partial evaluation of self-interpreters have a structure very similar to the original programs. It is particularly nice to see how the recursion in the original program is represented as a cycle in the closure.

Results   The table below shows the results of: Running the fac program directly on 5, (fac 5), running the unimproved interpreter on the fac program and input 5 (run facProg 5), and running the improved fully-lazy interpreter on the fac program and input 5 (run' facProg 5). The figures in the table are for evaluated versions of the partially applied interpreter, which is what we called the second run in the power example.

fac 5	run facProg 5	run' facProg 5
28/58	179/442	66/94

It is nice to see that the improved fully-lazy interpreter applied to fac runs only 2.4 times slower than the fac program itself and that it uses less than twice as much store. Furthermore these results (the slowdown with a factor of aprox. 2.4) compare well with the results obtained by partial evaluation without variable splitting in Sestoft [10], and Holst [1].

Looking at the speedup there is a speedup of 2.7 going from the unimproved interpreter to the improved fully-lazy interpreter. The same figures for partial evaluation are aprox. 20. The reason for this impressive speedup is the inefficiency of the interpreters normally used in the partial evaluation community. The interpreters are very inefficient because the object language used is very simple, and uses nested if-expressions instead of case-expressions.

6 Conclusion

We have described a very simple transformation that improves the staticness of control constructs, and thus improves the sharing properties. The transformation described makes it possible to achieve results comparable to the results achieved by partial evaluation. Producing closures with a structure resembling the structure of the residual programs from partial evaluation. Though no systematic examination of the effect of the proposed transformation has been made, the preliminary experiments suggest that substantial improvements (speedup factors between 2 and 4) can be obtained.

The transformation described in this paper is very simple compared with partial evaluation. Furthermore, this transformation is completely local, whereas partial evaluation is a global transformation. Nevertheless, it seems to achieve much the same effect.

6.1 Related Work

Very little work on improving binding times has been done in the functional language community. A lot of the lazy functional languages in use are not even fully lazy, for example Orwell[3] , and LML are not fully-lazy. On the other hand some work on improving binding times has been done by the partial evaluation community most notably Mogensen [7], and Nielsons [8].

6.1.1 Future Work

- In the near future we intend to include the suggested transformation in an existing compiler and make a better performance analysis. The analysis should also evaluate the improvements obtained by full laziness.

- We are trying to develop a more systematic approach to program transformations that improve binding times, such the transformation used in the interpreter example. Some work in that direction is presented in Holst and Hughes [2].

- This transformation of conditionals presented here mimics the reduction of conditionals in partial evaluation. There are other reductions used in some partial evaluators that can be mimiced in much the same way. For example, (* 1 f) can be reduced to f. The transformations needed to obtain the effect of such reductions are more complicated than the transformation of conditionals described in this paper and it is not clear that anything can be achieved

---

[3]A non-strict functional language related to Miranda[4] , Wadler and Miller [13].

except in special cases. This kind of reductions has also been abandoned in most partial evaluators. An exception is Mogensens partial evaluator [6] that was used to partial evaluate ray-tracers.

Should "optimisations", such as the transformation of programs into lazy, fully-lazy, or improved fully-lazy form, be a part of language design? I believe so. Nobody, for example, would be satisfied with a HASKELL implementation that used normal order reduction and was not lazy. The fact that improved full laziness makes certain programming techniques viable, for example, the interpreter example in section 5, suggest that such transformations should be part of future language designs, so that programmers could rely on this behavior. A language implementation should guarantee some "worst" runtime behavior, so programmers can reason about their programs complexity.

Acknowledgements

Thanks goes to Neil D. Jones who introduced me to partial evaluation, and to my supervisor John Hughes who is still convincing me that functional programming is a good thing. The idea presented in this paper was spawned in the twilight of dawn on the border between these two areas.

References

[1] Carsten Kehler Holst. Program specialization for compiler generation. Master's thesis, Department of Computer Science, University of Copenhagen (DIKU), Denmark, May 1989.

[2] Carsten Kehler Holst and John Hughes. Towards improving binding time for free! In *3rd Glasgow Functional Programming Workshop*, Ullapool, Scotland, 1990. Springer-Verlag.

[3] Paul Hudak and Philip Wadler (editors). Report on the programming language Haskell. Tecnical report, Yale University and Glasgow University, April 1990.

[4] John Hughes. *The Design and Implementation of Programming Languages.* PhD thesis, Oxford, 1983.

[5] Neil D. Jones, Peter A. Sestoft, and Harald Søndergaard. Mix: A self-applicable partial evaluator for experiments in compiler generation. *Lisp and Symbolic Computation*, 2(1):9–50, 1989.

[6] Torben Æ. Mogensen. The application of partial evaluation to ray-tracing. Master's thesis, DIKU, University of Copenhagen, Denmark, 1986.

[7] Torben Æ. Mogensen. Separating binding times in language specifications. In *Functional Programming Languages and Computer Architecture*, pages 14–25, London, England, September 1989. ACM, ACM Press and Addison-Wesley.

[8] Hanne Riis Nielson and Flemming Nielson. Eureka definitions for free! or disagreement points for fold/unfold transformations. In Neil D. Jones, editor, *ESOP '90 3rd European Symposium on Programming*, volume 432 of *Lecture Notes in Computer Science*, pages 291–305, Copenhagen, Denmark, May 1990. Springer-Verlag.

[9] Simon L. Peyton Jones and David Lester. A modular fully-lazy lambda lifter in Haskell. CS Report CSC 90/R17, Department of Computing Science, University of Glasgow, June 1990.

[10] Peter Sestoft. The structure of a self-applicable partial evaluator. In Harald Ganzinger and Neil D. Jones, editors, *Programs as Data Objects*, volume 217 of *Lecture Notes in Computer Science*, pages 236–256, Copenhagen, Denmark, 1986. Springer-Verlag.

[11] David Turner. An overview of Miranda. *Sigplan Notices*, 21(12):158–166, December 1986.

[12] Philip Wadler. Theorems for free! In *Functional Programming Languages and Computer Architectures*, pages 347–359, London, September 1989. ACM.

[13] Philip Wadler and Quentin Miller. An introduction to Orwell, 1985. Programming Research Group, Oxford.

Towards Binding-Time Improvement for Free

Carsten Kehler Holst   John Hughes *

Abstract

We show how application of commutative-like laws can improve binding
time properties. The quality of residual programs obtained by partial evaluation depends crucially on the binding time properties of the source program.
Likewise does the sharing obtained by full laziness depend on the binding time
properties of the program. This paper suggest that the commutative-like laws,
derivable from the types of polymorphic functions using the "free theorems"
approach, gives rise to a large set of non-trivial binding time improving transformations. The paper runs through a number of examples and shows how
these laws can be applied in a rather systematic way to achieve binding time
improvements. Ultimately it is our hope to automate the derivation and application of these binding time improving transformations.

Keywords: Binding Times, Polymorphism, Category Theory, Partial Evaluation, Full Laziness.

1   Introduction

Consider the function definition

$$f = \lambda x.\lambda y.(x + 1) + y$$

The sub-expression $(x + 1)$ is rather special, in that it depends only on f's first
parameter. Consequently, if a function g is defined by partially applying f:

$$g = f\ 3$$

then, in principle at least, no matter how many times g is called it is only necessary
to compute $(x+1)$ once. We call such expressions *static*.

Sharing the results of static expressions can potentially lead to large savings in
computer time. An implementation which does so is called a *fully lazy evaluator*, and
an efficient mechanism for fully lazy evaluation was outlined by Hughes [2]. Static
expressions play an even more important role in *partial evaluation* (see, for example, Jones *et. al.* [4]), whereby partial applications are automatically transformed by
evaluating their static expressions. It is because static expressions have already been
evaluated that the programs generated by a partial evaluator run faster than those
supplied as input.

---

*Dept. of Computing Science, University of Glasgow, Emails: `kehler@cs.glasgow.ac.uk`,
`rjmh@cs.glasgow.ac.uk`

Programs intended for partial evaluation must be written carefully to maximise the amount of static computation. For example, if the function f above had been written equivalently as

$$f = \lambda x.\lambda y.(x + y) + 1$$

then there would have been no static computation to share between the calls of g. As a less trivial example, consider a partial application of the function

$$h = \lambda xs.\lambda g.map\ (g\ \circ\ f)\ xs$$

to a value for xs. Here there is no static sub-expression, but if h is re-expressed as

$$h = \lambda xs.\lambda g.map\ g\ (map\ f\ xs)$$

then the entire computation of ($map\ f\ xs$) becomes static.

In partial evaluation the notion of static depends on the strength of the partial evaluator. As an example, the splitting of an environment into a static namelist and a dynamic value list is not necessary in Mogensen's [5] partial evaluator that is capable of handling partially static structures. Mogensen's partial evaluator can express binding times such as, a value is a static list of pairs whose first component is static and whose second component is dynamic. Partial evaluators like LambdaMix, Jones *et. al.* [3], are capable of handling function types like: ($Dynamic \rightarrow Dynamic$), and ($Static \rightarrow Dynamic$). In this paper we shall assume the simplest possible version of binding times. An expression is dynamic if it has an occurrence of a dynamic variable, otherwise it is static.

Researchers into partial evaluation commonly resort to rewriting programs to improve their staticness. For example, when Jones' group partially evaluated an interpreter for pure Lisp, they replaced the environment (a non-static, or *dynamic* value) with two separate parameters: a static list of names in scope, and a dynamic list of their values (see Jones *et. al.* [4]). Similarly, when Consel and Danvy [1] showed that Knuth-Morris-Pratt pattern matchers could be generated by partial evaluation, their first step was to rewrite a simple-minded pattern matcher to make more computations static.

There has been some work on performing such "binding-time improvement" automatically. Mogensen [6] showed how, given binding-time information (about the staticness of expressions), values such as the environment in Jones' interpreter can be split automatically into their static and dynamic parts. Nielsons [7] have shown how a similar splitting can be performed by synthesizing appropriate "Eureka!" definitions and using a fold-unfold program transformer to simplify them. Neither of these approaches, however, could improve the examples given above: transforming the first definition of h into the second, or the second definition of f into the first.

In both of these examples, the transformation depends on quite deep properties of the functions involved: the associativity and commutativity of addition; the distributivity of map over composition. In this paper, we study the possibility of automatically improving binding times using laws such as these. Because of the huge numbers of candidate laws, we restrict our attention to the "free theorems" derivable from a function's polymorphic type (Reynolds [8], and Wadler [10]), and the basic categorical properties of functions such as map. Thus we address the improvement of h above, but not f. Our work is at a preliminary stage: in particular, we have not yet built an automatic transformer based on these ideas.

As already mentioned an alternative approach to these transformations is a stronger partial evaluator. But, a stronger partial evaluator means a more complex patial evaluator. This results is slower partial evaluation and, if partial evaluation is used to generate compilers, slower compilers. The extra sophistication built into the partial evaluator is used to handle the structure of the interpreter not the program being compiled. By moving the sophistication into a pre-phase, *i.e.*, perform binding time improving transformations on the interpreter, and then use a simple and fast partial evaluator, we get faster compilers with the same quality of target code. This is why binding time improving transformations are a strong alternative to stronger partial evaluators, apart from being a way of utilising existing partial evaluators more efficiently.

The rest of the paper is organised as follows. In the next section we introduce some more categorical notation and restate the problem in this setting. In section 3 we explain how free theorems are derived from types. In sections 4, 5, and 6 we show how the free theorems can be applied, in the first and second order case, to improve binding-times. In section 7 we discuss a sub-problem — factoring out "elementwise" components of functions — and show that free theorems can help with this too. In section 8 we apply the techniques developed to transform a tiny interpreter into a compiler, and in section 9 we draw some tentative conclusions.

2 Moving to Categorical Notation

We believe it is helpful to reexpress the functions to be transformed in a more categorical notation. We will do so by expressing their bodies as functions of the static parameters, built up using categorical combining forms. For example, we will express the body of f above as a function of x, as follows:

$$+y \circ +1$$

(where +n denotes the function that adds n to its argument). Similarly, we express the body of h as

$$map \ (g \circ f)$$

The expressions to be transformed are thus combinations of smaller functions, some of which (such as $+y$ and g in these examples) may make reference to the dynamic variables. We will call functions that refer to dynamic variables *dynamic functions*, and the others *static functions*.

The transformations that improve f and h can now be concisely stated:

$$+1 \circ +y = +y \circ +1$$
$$map \ (g \circ f) = map \ g \circ map \ f$$

In each case, the result of the transformation is a composition of a dynamic function with a static one. And indeed, our goal will be to factor function bodies into this form, with as large a static component as possible, for when such a composition $d \circ s$ is applied to the function's static parameters (call them x), then the result is $d \ (s \ \mathbf{x})$ in which the entire computation of $(s \ \mathbf{x})$ is static.

We'll now introduce a little notation and sketch how terms written in this notation can be factorised into static and dynamic parts. In addition to function composition, we'll use the categorical functor notation whereby an operator on types is also considered to be an operator on functions. In general, if F is an operator on types (a *functor*), then it is also considered to be a polymorphic operator on functions, with the type

$$F : (a \to b) \to (Fa \to Fb)$$

Functors are generalisations of the well-known function map. Two functors we'll be particularly interested in are *product* and *list*. We define their action on functions as follows:

$$(f \times g)\,(x,y) \;=\; (f\ x,\ g\ y)$$
$$[f]\ xs \;=\; map\ f\ xs$$

The action of more complex functors built up from these can be inferred by using these definitions repeatedly, with the rule that constant functors (mapping every type to the same type) map every function to the appropriate identity function. For example, if

$$F\alpha = [string \times \alpha]$$

then F's action on functions is

$$F\ h = [id \times h]$$

We'll also need another useful combining form related to product, known as *construction*:

$$\langle f,g \rangle\ x = (f\ x,\ g\ x)$$

These constructs are sufficient to express any function body (not containing embedded lambda-expressions) as a function of its static parameters. The following rules show how this can be done. Here $s = (s_1, \ldots, s_n)$ is the tuple of static parameters, and $[\![e]\!]^S$ denotes the result of expressing e as a function of s.

$$[\![e]\!]^S \;=\; K_e \quad \text{if no } s_i \text{ occurs in } e$$
$$[\![s_i]\!]^S \;=\; sel_i$$
$$[\![e_1\ e_2]\!]^S \;=\; ap \circ \langle [\![e_1]\!]^S, [\![e_2]\!]^S \rangle$$

where K_x is the constant function returning x, sel_i is the function that selects the i'th component of a tuple, and ap is function application. While these three rules suffice, more concise results can be obtained by using the following optimisation as well:

$$[\![e_1\ e_2]\!]^S = e_1 \circ [\![e_2]\!]^S \quad \text{if no } s_i \text{ occurs in } e_1$$

Now let s_1, s_2 be static functions, and d_1, d_2 be dynamic functions. Once their component functions have been split into static and dynamic parts, we can factorise the various constructs introduced above as follows:

$$(d_1 \circ s_1) \times (d_2 \circ s_2) \;=\; (d_1 \times d_2) \circ (s_1 \times s_2)$$
$$[d_1 \circ s_1] \;=\; [d_1] \circ [s_1]$$
$$\langle d_1 \circ s_1, d_2 \circ s_2 \rangle \;=\; (d_1 \times d_2) \circ \langle s_1, s_2 \rangle$$
$$(d_1 \circ s_1) \circ (d_2 \circ s_2) \;=\; (d_1 \circ s_1 \circ d_2) \circ s_2$$

Unfortunately this last rule, for composition, gives a very poor result. If only s_1 and d_2 commuted, we could achieve the much better factorisation

$$(d_1 \circ s_1) \circ (d_2 \circ s_2) = (d_1 \circ d_2) \circ (s_1 \circ s_2)$$

Thus our attention is focussed on laws that enable us to commute static and dynamic operations. It is such laws that "free theorems" gives us.

3   Theorems for Free

We have several times referred to "free theorems". These are instances of the *abstraction theorem*, due to Reynolds [8], which states a type-dependent property that all functions definable in the polymorphic lambda-calculus satisfy. Wadler [10] reproved the result, and pointed out that this seemingly rather abstract property simplified to useful and well-known theorems in specific cases. He suggested that these theorems, which are essentially proved by the type-checker, could be used as convenient short cuts by program transformation and automated proof systems — hence, "theorems for free". Our paper is an attempt to pursue that idea in one direction.

To state the abstraction theorem, we will have to introduce *relations* on types. We'll consider a relation to be a set of pairs, and a function just to be a special case of a relation which relates its arguments to its results. We can extend our functors, which already operate on functions, to operate on general relations in a straightforward way: if $r : A \leftrightarrow B$ and $s : C \leftrightarrow D$ are relations, then we can define $r \times s$ and $[r]$ as follows:

$$(a,c)\ (r \times s)\ (b,d) \quad \text{iff} \quad a\ r\ b \text{ and } c\ s\ d$$
$$[a_1,\ldots,a_n]\ [r]\ [b_1,\ldots,b_m] \quad \text{iff} \quad m = n \text{ and for all } i,\ a_i\ r\ b_i$$

These definitions are consistent with the definitions given earlier for functions. However, the move to relations allows us to define similarly a *function-space* functor: given functions $f : A \to C$ and $g : B \to D$, we define

$$f\ (r \to s)\ g \quad \text{iff} \quad \forall a,b : a\ r\ b \Rightarrow (fa)\ s\ (gb)$$

That is, related arguments map to related results. Notice that this definition could not be made in the restricted world of functions, for while $r \times s$ and $[r]$ are functions whenever r and s are, $(r \to s)$ may be a many-to-many relation even if r and s are both functions.

Now let f be any polymorphic object of type $F(\alpha, \beta, \gamma \ldots)$, where $\alpha, \beta, \gamma, \ldots$ are type variables. The abstraction theorem states that, for *any* relations $r, s, t, \ldots$, the object f satisfies

$$f\ F(r, s, t, \ldots)\ f$$

In the next section we'll look at what this means in specific examples.

Technical Note: If general recursion is permitted in the programming language, then the abstraction theorem needs a side-condition — that $r, s, t, \ldots$ are "strict" relations in the sense that they relate $\bot$ to $\bot$. Although we permit general recursion, we will ignore this side condition, assuming that an automated implementation would either use strictness analysis to verify it, or detect instances of primitive recursion to avoid it. This point needs to be addressed more carefully in the future.

4 Using the Abstraction Theorem — the First-Order Case

Let's consider the case of a first-order polymorphic function

$$f : F\alpha \to G\alpha$$

where F and G do not involve function types. In this case, the functors F and G map relations that happen to be functions, to functions. The abstraction theorem says that, for any relation r,

$$f \ (Fr \to Gr) \ f$$

That is, for all arguments x and y,

$$x \ (Fr) \ y \Rightarrow fx \ (Gr) \ fy$$

But if r is a function, and so Fr and Gr are also functions, then this can be rewritten as

$$y = (Fr) \ x \Rightarrow fy = (Gr) \ (fx)$$

or, substituting for y,

$$f((Fr) \ x) = (Gr) \ (fx)$$

Since this is true for any x, the abstraction theorem in this case says

$$f \ \circ \ Fr = Gr \ \circ \ f$$

for any function r.

For example, for the three basic list-processing functions, the free theorems are

$$
\begin{aligned}
h \ \circ \ hd \ &= \ hd \ \circ \ [h] \\
[h] \ \circ \ tl \ &= \ tl \ \circ \ [h] \\
null \ &= \ null \ \circ \ [h]
\end{aligned}
$$

for any function h.

These free theorems are "commutative" laws of exactly the kind we need for binding time improvement. They can be exploited in two different ways: we can either move an elementwise dynamic operation leftwards through a static polymorphic function, or move an elementwise static operation rightwards through a dynamic polymorphic function. An example of the first kind might be

$$reverse \ \circ \ [d]$$

where d is a dynamic function; this can be improved, using the free theorem for reverse, as follows:

$$reverse \ \circ \ [d] = [d] \ \circ \ reverse$$

An example of the second kind might be

$$sq \ \circ \ (!i)$$

where sq is the (static) squaring function, $(!i)$ is the function that extracts the i'th element of a list, and i is a dynamic natural number. Since the type of $(!i)$ is

$$!i : [\alpha] \rightarrow \alpha$$

we can use the corresponding free theorem to optimise

$$sq \circ (!i) = (!i) \circ [sq]$$

Although we have clearly moved static computation rightwards, at first sight the optimised version appears to be the less efficient, since it squares *all* the elements of the static list it is applied to, while the original version squares only the selected element. However, a fully lazy evaluator running the second program would square only the elements actually selected, thanks to lazy evaluation, and would of course square each element at most once. A partial evaluator would indeed square all the elements of the static list supplied, but this computation is now entirely static, and so would take place during partial evaluation. The generated programs would contain a precalculated table of squares and fetch results from that as they were needed.

A good example of this last optimisation can be found in several partial evaluators. When the partial evaluator is being partially evaluated the program it specialise is *static* and the data with respect to which this program is being specialised is *dynamic*. So specialization of a function in the program has the form.

$$specialize \circ lookup\ fn$$

The program is represented as a list of function name, function body pairs. *specialize* takes a function definition and some data, and specialize the function with respect to the data. The data is dynamic, but the function could be static if it were not for the dynamic *lookup fn*, *fn* is dynamic because it depends on the data which functions that are going to be specialized. By commuting *specialize* with *lookup*, *specialize* works on static data, *i.e.*, *specialize* is specialised with respect to the different functions in the program.

$$lookup\ fn \circ [(id \times specialize)]$$

In partial evaluators for first-order languages this definition is then unfolded, so we end with a special version of lookup that apply *specialise* to the static elements before it makes the dynamic choice between them.

5 Using the Abstraction Theorem — the Higher-Order Case

In the case of higher-order polymorphic functions, the abstraction theorem does not reduce to a simple equation. Instead, Wadler derived from it *conditional equations*, which we can use to improve binding times provided we can satisfy the conditions.

Let's consider a polymorphic function Φ of type

$$\Phi : Fa \rightarrow Ga \rightarrow Ha$$

where G and H do not involve function types. We'll assume that we're interested in transforming partial applications of Φ, *i.e.*, that Φ is being used as a combining form. For example, we might want to transform a term

$$Hf \circ \Phi p$$

to move an elementwise static computation f to the right.

The free theorem for Φ states that, for all relations r,

$$\Phi \ (Fr \to Gr \to Hr) \ \Phi$$

That is, for all arguments p and q,

$$p \ (Fr) \ q \Rightarrow \Phi p \ (Gr \to Hr) \ \Phi q$$

Since G and H don't involve function types, then by the same reasoning as in the previous section we can rewrite the right hand side as

$$Hr \circ \Phi p = \Phi q \circ Gr$$

under the assumption that r is a function. So the free theorem gives us a conditional equation which we can use to transform terms such as

$$Hf \circ \Phi p$$

provided we can solve conditions of the form $p \ (Fr) \ q$ for r and q. If Φ is a second order function, so that Fa involves no nested function types, then the conditions to be solved are themselves equations. This is the case we will consider. In the next section we'll solve a number of examples by hand, which will illustrate a possible solution strategies.

5.1   A Useful pre-order

Before looking at the examples, it will be helpful to define a *pre-order* on functions. We say

$$f \le g \Leftrightarrow \exists h : f = h \circ g$$

The $\le$ relation is reflexive, transitive, has a maximal element (id), and satisfies

$$
\begin{aligned}
f &\le_{fst} \langle f, g \rangle \\
g &\le_{snd} \langle f, g \rangle \\
f \circ g &\le_f g
\end{aligned}
$$

We have sub-scripted the relation with the hidden function h. A nice property of $\le$ is that it is easy to construct the hidden function, h, from a proof of $f \le g$. We can just subscript the relation with the hidden function, and it is generated along with the proof.

$$
\begin{aligned}
f &\le_{id} f \\
f &\le_f id
\end{aligned}
$$

$$(f \le_v g \land g \le_w h) \Rightarrow f \le_{vow} h$$

We'll be particularly interested in cases where the function h is cheap to compute, since then we can interpret $f \leq g$ as "f can be defined efficiently in terms of g".

It will often turn out to be case that the equations we need to solve take the form

$$f_1 \leq g, \ f_2 \leq g, \ldots$$

in which g is unknown, and the mediating functions (the 'h's) are otherwise unconstrained. Such constraints can be solved easily by defining

$$g = \langle f_1, f_2, \ldots \rangle$$

and the taking the 'h's to be the appropriate selector functions.

An "free theorem" give us a rule that allow us to move some static computation a right under some conditions. When matching the "free theorem" against the concrete term we infer the constraint $s \leq a$, where s is a part of the concrete term. The idea is that if s fails to meet the conditions we split into $h \circ a$, where a meet the conditions, and move a right leaving h behind.

5.2 A Strategy

In the next section we shall see five examples of application of the abstraction theorem to improve binding times. We are going to use the following general strategy to solve the problem of generating a suitable rewrite rule from an instance the abstraction theorem.

- Given the term to be rewritten we first generate the "free theorem" from it's type. The theorem can be read a a rewrite rule with some preconditions.

$$p \ (Fr) \ q \Rightarrow Hr \circ \Phi p = \Phi q \circ Gr$$

- The term is matched against rewrite rule, and a set of conditions of the form $f \leq a$ is generated, where f is static and a is the function the rule allows us to commute. If f isn't static we must strengthen the constraint to $id \leq a$, or if f is of the form $d \circ s$, where s is static and d dynamic, to $s \leq a$.

- We rewrite the set of pre-conditions, which in the second-order case are equations, to a set of constraints. Where this is impossible, because the conditions are recursively defined we set the function in question to the identity.

- The constraints are solved and the resulting instance of the "free theorem" is used to rewrite the term.

While this isn't an algorithm, it is quite a systematic approach.

6 Five Second-Order Examples

The following five examples are all solved using the general strategy proposed in the previous section. In that sense the example can be seen as a justification for the strategy.

6.1 Factoring $map\ (d \circ s)$

As a first example, we consider factoring the term above into its static and dynamic parts — one of the problems in the introduction to this paper. Of course, if we know that map is the list functor by another name, we can factorise it at once as

$$map\ d \ \circ \ map\ s$$

But let's assume that all we know about map is its type:

$$map : (\alpha \to \beta) \to [\alpha] \to [\beta]$$

The free theorem is therefore

$$b \circ f = g \circ a \Rightarrow [b] \circ map\ f = map\ g \circ [a]$$

Since the term we wish to factor is just an application of *map*, it seems we should take b to be the identity. Now, to factorise

$$map\ (d \circ s)$$

we must solve the condition

$$d \circ s = g \circ a$$

for g and a, with the constraint that a should be static. One strategy for solving such equations is simply to look for obvious solutions! In this case, we can clearly take $g = d$ and $a = s$. The resulting factorisation is

$$map\ (d \circ s) = map\ d \circ [s]$$

6.2 Factoring $filter\ (d \circ s)$

For our next example, we'll factor a similar call of *filter*, whose type is

$$filter : (\alpha \to bool) \to [\alpha] \to [\alpha]$$

The corresponding free theorem is

$$p = q \circ a \Rightarrow [a] \circ filter\ p = filter\ q \circ [a]$$

Comparing the left hand side of this equation against the term to be factored suggests that a should be chosen to be the identity, but this would force p and q to be equal and result in a trivial factorisation. So this is an oversimplistic strategy. Instead, we shall constrain a so that $id \leq a$, or in other words, to have a left inverse. This will allow us to re-express the term to be factored as

$$filter\ (d \circ s) = [h] \circ [a] \circ filter\ (d \circ s)$$

for some h, and so to use the free theorem.

Now, if there were no other constraints on a (as in the case of map), we could choose $a = id$ as our solution. But in this case the condition of the free theorem can be stated as $p \leq a$ (and q is otherwise unconstrained). In the term to be factored, p is $d \circ s$, and so we require $d \circ s \leq a$. Since we want a to be static, we'll strengthen this requirement to $s \leq a$. Now the solution for a is obvious — it's just $\langle id, s \rangle$ — and the resulting factorisation is

$$filter\ (d \circ s) = [fst] \circ filter\ (d \circ snd) \circ [\langle id, s \rangle]$$

The effect of this factorisation in an implementation would be to build a precalculated table containing the values of the static parts of the filtering predicate.

6.3 Commuting $[s] \circ$ *filter* d

In this example, we wish to move a static elementwise computation $[s]$ to the right of the dynamic filtering. Comparing the term to be transformed against the left-hand-side of the free theorem suggests that a should be bound to s, but again this is too strong and we require only $s \leq a$ until we discover any other constraints on a. Such a constraint appears in the condition of the free theorem, which in this case states that $d \leq a$. Since we wish a to be static, we strengthen this to $id \leq a$ (since $d \leq id$, it follows that $d \leq a$). Now the constraints can be solved by taking a to be $\langle s, id \rangle$, with the resulting factorisation

$$[s] \circ \text{filter } d = [\text{fst}] \circ \text{ filter } (d \circ \text{snd}) \circ [\langle s, id \rangle]$$

We have succeeded in moving the static computation to the right of the filter.

6.4 Transforming $\text{foldr } (\text{add} \circ (sq \times id))\ 0 \circ \text{take } n$

This is a more complicated example, in which the solution cannot found quite as simply as in the cases above. The function $(\text{take } n)$ here returns the first n elements of a list, and has type

$$\text{take} : \text{int} \rightarrow [\alpha] \rightarrow [\alpha]$$

We assume that n is dynamic. The function *foldr* combines the elements of a list with a given binary operator and zero element: its type is

$$\text{foldr} : (\alpha \times \beta \rightarrow \beta) \rightarrow \beta \rightarrow [\alpha] \rightarrow [\beta]$$

The effect of the whole function is to find the sum of the squares of a dynamically chosen initial prefix of a static list. As it stands, no computation can be performed statically, since the very first function applied is dynamic. We'll see how this program can be transformed into one which performs all the squaring operations statically.

First let's examine the free theorem for foldr:

$$(b \circ f = g \circ (a \times b) \wedge w = b\ z) \Rightarrow b \circ \text{foldr } f\ z = \text{foldr } g\ w \circ [a]$$

Comparing the left hand side of the equation against the call of *foldr* to be transformed suggests that we require $id \leq b$ as before. But looking at the condition of the theorem, we see that b occurs on *both* sides of the equation we have to solve. We therefore cannot rewrite this equation as an inequality constraint on b, and indeed our only hope of finding a non-trivial solution is to use some law to commute b and f. Since the only laws we use are free theorems, and since in this particular case f has a monomorphic type, there is no hope of doing so. We therefore set b to be the identity, and try to solve the simpler constraint

$$f = g \circ (a \times id)$$

Since in this case f is $(\text{add} \circ (sq \times id))$ there is an obvious solution. We can simply take a to be sq and conclude that

$$\text{foldr } (\text{add} \circ (sq \times id))\ 0 = \text{foldr add } 0\ \circ\ [sq]$$

Substituting this into the original expression produces a subterm $[sq] \circ take\ n$, which can be further transformed using the (first-order) free theorem about take:

$$[sq] \circ take\ n = take\ n \circ [sq]$$

So the final result of the transformation is

$$foldr\ add\ 0 \circ take\ n \circ [sq]$$

in which the calculation of squares has been made entirely static.

A better solution would be

$$!n \circ scan\ (add \circ (id \times sq))\ 0$$

but, this result depends on deep knowledge about *take*, and the commutativity of *add*. $scan\ f\ u\ [x_1, x_2, \ldots] = [u, f\ u\ x_1, f\ (f\ u\ x_1)\ x_2, \ldots]$.

6.5 Factoring $s \circ if\ d\ q\ r$

Finally we consider a rule for optimising conditionals that has been previously used by Romanenko [9]. Here the function if, with type

$$if : (\alpha \to bool) \to (\alpha \to \beta) \to (\alpha \to \beta) \to \alpha \to \beta$$

is defined by

$$
\begin{aligned}
(if\ p\ q\ r)\ x &= q\ x \quad \text{if } p\ x \text{ is true} \\
&= r\ x \quad \text{otherwise}
\end{aligned}
$$

We assume that s, q and r are static functions, and aim to factor the term above into static and dynamic parts.

The free theorem for if is

$$(d = d' \circ a \ \wedge\ b \circ q = q' \circ a \ \wedge\ b \circ r = r' \circ a) \Rightarrow b \circ if\ d\ q\ r = if\ d'\ q'\ r' \circ a$$

Comparing the left hand side of this equation with the term to be transformed, we constrain b such that $s \leq b$. Looking at the condition of the free theorem, we constrain a so that $d \leq a$, $b \circ q \leq a$, and $b \circ r \leq a$. Since we want a to be static, we strengthen the first contraint to $id \leq a$. Solving the constraints, we set

$$
\begin{aligned}
b &= s \\
a &= \langle id, s \circ q, s \circ r \rangle
\end{aligned}
$$

giving the transformation

$$s \circ if\ d\ q\ r \Longrightarrow if\ (d \circ sel_1)\ sel_2\ sel_3 \circ \langle id, s \circ q, s \circ r \rangle$$

Not only are the static branches of the conditional factored out to be performed statically, but the static operations on the *result* of the conditional can also now be performed statically.

Romanenko [9] suggested that a partial evaluator should perform this transformation of conditionals when both branches are static. It is pleasant that a binding time improver based on free theorems would automatically do so.

6.6 Summary of the Method

We have not presented here an algorithm for applying free theorems to transform higher-order function applications. Nevertheless, we have developed an informal method which appears to work quite well, and which may not be too hard to automate.

To transform a higher-order function application, we first derive a statement of the free theorem from its type, in the form of a conditional equation. We then choose appropriate values for the commuting functions that satisfy the conditions of the theorem. We try to re-express the conditions as inequalities involving these functions. Where this is impossible (because a function name appears on both sides of one of the equations) we set the offending functions to the identity: this is always safe, but may not be terribly useful. We compare the left hand side of the theorem to the actual term to be transformed to derive further inequalities on these functions, and then we solve the collected inequalities in a straightforward manner. The solution gives us an instance of the free theorem that can be used to transform the term we started with.

Apart from possible problems in automating this method, its most obvious weakness is the very conservative treatment of conditions in which the same unknown appears on both sides. Perhaps to get good results for larger programs it will be necessary to solve some of these, with further applications of the free theorems.

7 Factorising out Elementwise Operations

We have seen how free theorems enable us to swap polymorphic functions with elementwise operations, for example transforming

$$Gh \circ f = f \circ Fh$$

When transforming a term such as $g \circ f$, therefore, we will wish to express g in the form $g' \circ Gh$ (where h performs as much computation as possible) so that the free theorem will be applicable. In this section we look at the problem of factoring functions into this form. Analogously, when transforming $f \circ g$ we might wish to express g as $Fh \circ g'$. This problem is essentially the same, and so we will not discuss it explicitly.

So, consider the problem of expressing an arbitrary f in the form $g \circ Fh$. It is always possible to do so, as follows:

$$f = f \circ F\,id$$

While little is gained by this factorisation, it is important to be able to factorise *any* function, since we can then assume when factorising compound terms that the subterms have already been factorised.

The ideal situation, of course, is when the function to be factorised is already in the form Fh, for then

$$Fh = id \circ Fh$$

More commonly, F may be a composition of two functors:

$$F\alpha = G(H\alpha)$$

and we may need to factorise a function of the form Gf. In such a case, we first factorise f with respect to H:

$$f = g \circ Hh$$

and then conclude

$$Gf = Gg \circ G(Hh)$$

Given a construction, we first factorise each component yielding a term of the form

$$\langle f_1 \circ Fg_1,\ f_2 \circ Fg_2 \rangle$$

and then choose any g such that $g_1 \leq g$ and $g_2 \leq g$. There must then exist functions h_1 and h_2 such that the term above factorises into

$$\langle f_1 \circ Fh_1,\ f_2 \circ Fh_2 \rangle \circ Fg$$

The most interesting case is a composition such as $f \circ g$. We first factorise g:

$$g = g' \circ Fh$$

and can now of course factorise the composition as

$$f \circ g = (f \circ g') \circ Fh$$

But if g' is suitably polymorphic we may be able to do better. If g' has the type

$$g' : F\alpha \to G\alpha$$

then we can factorise f with respect to G,

$$f = f' \circ Gh'$$

and then use the free theorem about g' to derive a better factorisation of the original composition:

$$f \circ g = (f' \circ g') \circ F(h' \circ h)$$

We will see examples of this later.

Finally, consider a recursively defined function

$$f = E(f)$$

where $E(f)$ is a term involving f. We'll use the following fact: if we can find E' and g such that, for any function p,

$$E(p \circ g) = E'(p) \circ g$$

then the function h defined by

$$h = E'(h)$$

satisfies

$$f = h \circ g$$

The proof is by recursion induction: we show that $h \circ g$ satisfies f's defining equation, since

$$E(h \circ g) = E'(h) \circ g = h \circ g$$

So to factorise a recursively defined function into the form $f' \circ Fg$, we try to find a g such that $E(h \circ Fg)$ factorises into $E'(h) \circ Fg$ for any h.

7.1 Factorising sum-of-squares

Let's take an example: the sum-of-squares function defined by

$$ss \quad :: \quad [int] \to int$$
$$ss \quad = \quad if\ null\ K_0\ (add \circ \langle sq \circ hd, ss \circ tl \rangle)$$

We'll factorise ss as $ss' \circ [g]$, for some g. We therefore try to factor

$$if\ null\ K_0\ (add \circ \langle sq \circ hd, ss' \circ [g] \circ tl \rangle)$$

To factorise the conditional, we need to factorise the condition and the two branches similarly (the free theorem tells us this), but we have at once that

$$null \quad = \quad null \circ [u]$$
$$K_0 \quad = \quad K_0 \circ [v]$$

for any u and v, from the free theorems for $null$ and K_0. Similarly, we have

$$sq \circ hd \quad = \quad hd \circ [sq]$$
$$[g] \circ tl \quad = \quad tl \circ [g]$$

Now we can factor g out of the whole conditional, provided the following constraints are satisfied:

$$u \quad \leq \quad g$$
$$v \quad \leq \quad g$$
$$sq \quad \leq \quad g$$
$$g \quad \leq \quad g$$

The solution is simple: $g = u = v = sq$. The final factorisation is therefore

$$ss \quad = \quad ss' \circ [sq]$$
$$ss' \quad = \quad if\ null\ K_0\ (add \circ \langle hd, ss' \circ tl \rangle)$$

as we would expect.

It's interesting that we needed to make no assumptions about the form of the recursive definition in order to factorise it, nor did we need to know more than the types of the functions occurring in the body. It's clear that factorisation would be no more difficult if tl were replaced by, say, *take* 3, *drop* 5, or even *reverse*. Free theorems give us a powerful tool for performing this kind of factorisation.

8 Transforming an Interpreter into a Compiler

In this section we describe the transformation of a fragment of an interpreter for a first-order functional language. Our aim is to make all the manipulation of the interpreted syntax tree static, so that after partial evaluation the remaining actions are just the essential run-time operations of the interpreted program. The transformed interpreter will therefore act in essence as a compiler. In fact, this example provided the initial motivation for this paper — it was the experimental discovery that improving the staticness of an interpreter was subtler than we expected that led us to try to systematize the transformations used.

We will need one more factorisation rule for this example. Let $\mathbf{d}$ be the tuple of dynamic variables, and let $E(\mathbf{d})$ be a term involving them. Define the function *supply* by

$$supply \; x \; y = y \; x$$

Then $E(\mathbf{d})$ can be factored as

$$E(\mathbf{d}) = supply \; \mathbf{d} \circ \lambda x.\lambda \mathbf{d}.E(\mathbf{d}) \; x$$

where x is a new variable name. The static part of this factorisation, given the static arguments, just constructs a function of the dynamic variables that invokes $E(\mathbf{d})$. The dynamic part takes this statically constructed function and passes the dynamic variables to it. For brevity, and because the name x introduced here is arbitrary, we will introduce a new $\underline{\lambda}$-notation to stand for lambda expressions of this form and write the rule as

$$E(\mathbf{d}) = supply \; \mathbf{d} \circ \underline{\lambda}\mathbf{d}.E(\mathbf{d})$$

The rule just given is always applicable, and at first glance might appear very powerful indeed — after all, the dynamic part is reduced to one function call, while the static part now includes all of $E(\mathbf{d})$. In fact, it is a very poor factorisation. Almost no static computation is possible when this term is applied to the static arguments, since the static part immediately returns another lambda expression which is in head normal form and needs no further evaluation. We may regard this head normal form as "code" for the term $E(\mathbf{d})$, and the corresponding $\underline{\lambda}$ expression as instructions to generate this code. Using the supply factorisation rule is effectively giving up the effort to find static computations, and just generating code for everything instead. Nevertheless, compilers must generate code occasionally, and for this reason the supply factorisation rule is necessary.

Now to the example. We'll consider a small fragment of the eval function, whose arguments are a (static) expression to evaluate, and a (dynamic) environment containing the values of the local variables. We'll suppose that the only kinds of expression to be interpreted are local variables and function calls. Then we might define eval in a Haskell-like language as follows:

$$eval \; x \; \rho \;\; = \;\; if \, (var? \; x) \; (lookup \; x \; \rho)$$
$$if \, (call? \; x) \; (invoke(fn \; x) \; (map \; (\lambda y.eval \; y \; \rho) \; (args \; x)))\ldots$$

where *var?* and *call?* recognise the two kinds of syntax tree node, *fn* and *args* extract the function name and list of parameters from a function call node, *lookup* finds the value of a local variable in the environment, and *invoke* interprets a function call.

Note that both *lookup* and *invoke* are, and must be, curried. This is important since in each case one parameter is static and the other dynamic, and we plan to simplify partial applications to the static one. Currying is an important transformation for improving staticness, as is splitting up partially static structures such as the environment into their static and dynamic parts. These transformations are important elements of previous work by Mogensen and the Nielsons, but are not addressed here. We shall just curry the necessary functions to begin with, leave the environment intact, and focus on the transformations of interest.

Now let us translate the definition of *eval* into our categorical notation. Note first that

$$\lambda x. f x \rho = supply\ \rho \circ f$$

Abstracting x from the left and right hand sides, and adopting a more readable notation for the conditional, we find

$$supply\ \rho \circ eval\ =\ \ var? \to supply\ \rho \circ lookup$$
$$call? \to ap \circ \langle invoke \circ fn, [supply\ \rho \circ eval] \circ args\rangle$$

If we could factor a (*supply* ρ) out of the right hand side, we could cancel it on both sides and derive a completely static definition of *eval*. We could of course use the supply factorisation rule above, but that would simply "generate code" to perform all the interpretation at run-time. Instead, let us try to factor the two arms of the conditional into their static and dynamic parts. Using the methods of the earlier sections, it is straightforward to arrive at the expression

$$var?\ \ \to\ \ supply \circ lookup\ f$$
$$call?\ \ \to\ \ ap \circ (id \times [supply\ \rho]) \circ \langle invoke \circ fn, [eval] \circ args\rangle$$

To get any further we have to factor a (*supply* ρ) out of the second branch, and the only way to do so is the supply factorisation rule. However, we need only supply ρ to the dynamic part of the expression, obtaining

$$var?\ \ \to\ \ supply\ \rho \circ lookup$$
$$call?\ \ \to\ \ supply\ \rho \circ (\underline{\lambda}\rho.ap \circ (id \times [supply\ \rho])) \circ \langle invoke \circ fn, [eval] \circ args\rangle$$

The "generated code" here is quite small — just

$$\underline{\lambda}\rho.ap \circ (id \times [supply\ \rho])$$

Indeed we can interpret it as sensible code for a function call — the *id* loads the address of the function to be called, the [*supply* ρ] calls the code to evaluate the parameters, and the *ap* actually enters the function.

Now (using the free theorem for the conditional!) we can at last factor (*supply* ρ) out of the whole expression, and conclude

$$eval\ =\ \ val? \to lookup$$
$$call? \to (\underline{\lambda}\rho.ap \circ (id \times [supply\ \rho])) \circ \langle invoke \circ fn, [eval] \circ args\rangle$$

The transformed eval performs all the interpretive operations — those that manipulate the syntax tree — statically. It is essentially a compiler, as desired.

9   Conclusions and Future Work

Our conclusions must be tentative because of the preliminary nature of the work described. However, we have demonstrated that the abstraction theorem, together with the standard properties of functors, suffice for hand transformations that can significantly increase the amount of static computation in programs. We claim, tentatively, that these transformations are suitable for automation because the hand transformations are fairly systematic and mechanical. In the future we hope to construct an automatic binding-time improver, and evaluate the increase in performance that results for more realistic programs. Construction of an automatic tool will oblige us to address the strictness condition in the abstraction theorem somehow, since otherwise it will not preserve correctness.

Binding-time improvement is a tricky, error-prone, and tedious activity to perform by hand. An automatic tool such as we envisage would be both useful in practice and a novel application of the "free theorems" idea.

References

[1] Charles Consel and Olivier Danvy. Partial evaluation of pattern matching in strings. *Information Processing Letters*, 30(2):79–86, January 1989.

[2] R. John M. Hughes. *The Design and Implementation of Programming Languages*. PhD thesis, Oxford, 1984.

[3] Neil D. Jones, Carsten K. Gomard, Anders Bondorf, Olivier Danvier, and Torben Æ. Mogensen. A self-applicable partial evaluator for the lambda-calculus. In *1990 Interational Conference on Computer Languages*. IEEE computer Society, 1990.

[4] Neil D. Jones, Peter A. Sestoft, and Harald Søndergaard. Mix: A self-applicable partial evaluator for experiments in compiler generation. *Lisp and Symbolic Computation*, 2(1):9–50, 1989.

[5] Torben Æ. Mogensen. Partially static structures in a self-applicable partial evaluator. In A.P. Ershov D. Bjørner and N.D. Jones, editors, *Partial Evaluation and Mixed Computation*, pages 325–347. North-Holland, 1988.

[6] Torben Æ. Mogensen. Separating binding times in language specifications. In *Functional Programming Languages and Computer Architecture*, 1989.

[7] Hanne Riis Nielson and Flemming Nielson. Eureka definitions for free! or disagreement points for fold/unfold transformations. In Neil D. Jones, editor, *ESOP '90 3rd European Symposium on Programming*, volume 432 of *Lecture Notes in Computer Science*, pages 291–305, Copenhagen, Denmark, May 1990. Springer-Verlag.

[8] John C. Reynolds. Types, abstraction, and parametric polymorphism. In R. E. A. Mason, editor, *Information Processing 83*, pages 513–523, Amsterdam, 1983. North-Holland.

[9] S.A. Romanenko. A compiler generator produced by a self-applicable specializer can have a surprisingly natural and understandable structure. In A.P. Ershov D. Bjørner and N.D. Jones, editors, *Partial Evaluation and Mixed Computation*, pages 445–463. North-Holland, 1988.

[10] Philip Wadler. Theorems for free! In *Functional Programming Languages and Computer Architectures*, pages 347–359, London, September 1989. ACM.

Towards Relating
Forwards and Backwards Analyses

John Hughes and John Launchbury
Glasgow University

Abstract

In this paper we take steps towards a unified framework in which both forwards
and backwards analyses may be discussed. We present natural deduction style
rules, instances of which may be used to define analyses in either direction. Some
insights resulting from the approach are drawn out, together with a conjecture that
non-relational forwards analysis is unable to discover head-strictness.

1 Introduction

Program analysis has been an active area for research, especially in the last decade. In
particular, strictness analysis has received a great deal of attention due to its implications
for the code quality of compiled lazy functional languages. Broadly speaking, the various
methods of analysis may be divided into two camps: forwards and backwards. Forwards
analyses begin with information about the input to a program or function, propagate that
information forwards through the program, and derive information about the result. In
contrast, a backwards analysis begins with information about the result of a computation
and, by propagating the information backwards through the program, derives information
about the input.

For some while, it has been clear that the two methods of analysis are intimately
related, but so far this relationship has not been made precise. There are a number of
obstacles to be overcome before a clear expression of the relationship may be obtained.
For example, even a fairly cursory glance at papers giving equations for either forwards or
backwards analyses is enough to realise that the equations look very different. Contrast,
for example, the equations presented in Chapter 1 of [AH87] with those of Chapter 4. In
addition, with few exceptions, the two analyses tend to manipulate very different kinds
of objects.

The aim of this paper is to take some steps towards a common framework in which
both forwards and backwards analyses may be discussed. For the purposes of this paper, we work with domain projections. The reason for this is that both forwards and
backwards analyses involving these have already been published. The backwards analysis
is a strictness analysis described in [WH87], and the forwards analysis is a binding-time
analysis which appears in [Lau89]. Both analyses use the same safety criterion so are
obvious candidates for inclusion into a common setting.

The work reported in [Burn90] is in some sense complementary to the work here. Whereas Burn relates the *results* of forwards abstract interpretation with backwards projection analysis (each so called smash projection corresponds to a certain Scott closed subset, and vice versa), we attempt to relate the analyses themselves. That this paper is only "towards" our ultimate goal reflects the fact that there are a number of shortcomings and limitations in what follows. Of these, the most significant is a restriction to a non-relational treatment of tuples. That is, the components of a pair (or n-tuple) are considered independently rather than in combination. A second limitation is our use of domain projections together with a concrete safety condition. A more general formulation is essential to obtain an all-encompassing structure. Nonetheless, even with these restrictions, there are some interesting observations that may be drawn.

2   Projections and Safety

A domain *projection* is an idempotent, continuous function which approximates the identity function. In strictness analysis, projections are used to represent demand. For example, consider the function $BOTH$ defined by

$$\begin{aligned} BOTH\ (x,y) &= (\bot,\bot) \quad \textit{if } x = \bot \textit{ or } y = \bot \\ &= (x,y) \quad \textit{otherwise} \end{aligned}$$

If $f \circ BOTH = f$, for some function f, then it is clear that if f needs either of its arguments, then it needs both of them. We say that f is $BOTH$-strict. The addition function is an example of a function which is $BOTH$-strict. When a strict function is $BOTH$-strict, then not only may the pair-structure be evaluated, but so may the two components.

More generally, we may wish to take the demand for the result of f into account. For example, it is not the case that $swap \circ BOTH = swap$ (where $swap\ (x,y) = (y,x)$) as only one component of the result may be required by the outer context. If, however, both components are required by the outer context, then it is safe to evaluate them both before executing $swap$. Semantically, we may characterise this by the equation, $BOTH \circ swap = BOTH \circ swap \circ BOTH$. This gives us the general form of the safety condition: we say that f is β-strict in a α-strict context if $\alpha \circ f = \alpha \circ f \circ \beta$ where α and β are projections. This should be read as meaning that if α's worth of output is demanded then it is safe to demand β's worth of the input. Notice that information flows backwards. We start with an initial demand on the output of the program, and propagate this demand through the other functions, until eventually we obtain a demand for the input to the program.

Two projections that will arise frequently are $ID\ (= \lambda x.x)$, and $BOT\ (= \lambda x.\bot)$. Their pervasiveness stems from the fact that they are respectively the greatest and least projections over every domain.

The safety condition *per se* contains nothing that makes it inherently more suited to backwards rather than forwards analysis. Indeed, precisely the same condition is used in binding-time analysis [Lau89]. The purpose of this analysis is to determine which parts of the result of a computation depend solely on specified parts of the input. The analysis is, therefore, forwards: we start with a description of the argument to a function and derive a description of the result. Projections may be used to specify parts of values. For example, the projections $LEFT$ and $RIGHT$ defined by $LEFT\ (x,y) = (x, \bot)$ and $RIGHT\ (x,y) = (\bot, y)$ may be used to specify the left and right components of the pair, respectively. If we wish to show that the left component of the result of $swap$ depends solely on the right component of its argument, then we have to show that $LEFT \circ swap = LEFT \circ swap \circ RIGHT$.

As it can be interpreted both forwards and backwards, we shall use this safety condition when we provide the adirectional analysis rules that follow. There is an equivalent formulation of the safety condition which is proved in [WH87], namely that the equation $\alpha \circ f = \alpha \circ f \circ \beta$ holds if and only if the inequality $\alpha \circ f \sqsubseteq f \circ \beta$ also holds. We use this alternative formulation in the proofs that follow.

3   The Object Language

We shall present analysis rules, instances of which may be used to define either a forwards or a backwards analysis. Consequently, we use a language which is symmetric with respect to input and output. The language is expressed in a categorical notation (resulting in an FP-like notation), and is restricted to be first-order only (extending projection analysis to the higher order case is still a research issue that we will not address here).

If f and g are terms in the language, and if $E(f)$ is a term depending on f, then the following are all terms in the language.

$f \circ g$	composition
$<f, g>$	product construction
$[f, g]$	sum decomposition
$\mu f.E(f)$	recursion

Furthermore, we assume the existence of various primitives. In particular, the product projections π_1 and π_2, and the sum injections in_1 and in_2 are present. This language is very much like the "machine-code" used in the Categorical Abstract Machine. It is not expected that anyone would actually write programs in the language, but that first-order functional programs may be translated into terms in the language.

The semantics of the language are given by a domain-theoretic model. We interpret terms as continuous functions, product as domain product, sum as separated sum, and recursion by least fixed point. Product construction and sum decomposition are defined as follows.

$$<f, g> x \ \cdot \ = \ (f\ x, g\ x)$$

$$[f, g]\ (in_1\ x) \ = \ f\ x$$
$$[f, g]\ (in_2\ y) \ = \ g\ y$$
$$[f, g]\ \bot \ = \ \bot$$

Thus, while the product is true categorical product, the sum is not (due to the presence of the new $\bot$ introduced by separated sum). In particular, it is not always true that

$h \circ [f, g] = [h \circ f, \ h \circ g]$. Note, however, that if h is strict, the equation does hold. This fact is useful to us as all projections are strict.

Both product and sum are functors and so they act both on domains and on functions. As projections are functions we may combine them using both $\times$ and $+$. As a consequence of the functorial laws, the following properties hold:

$$(\alpha \times \beta) \circ <f, \ g> \ = \ <\alpha \circ f, \ \beta \circ g>$$
$$[f, \ g] \circ (\alpha + \beta) = [f \circ \alpha, \ g \circ \beta]$$

Handling projections in this way gives a convenient method for representing the abstract values of composite concrete values in terms of abstractions of their parts.

4 Analysis Rules

Our analysis rules are stated as inference rules that conclude a safety condition for a term from safety conditions on its subterms. The first two analysis rules are straightforward and their verification trivial.

$$\frac{\alpha \circ f \sqsubseteq f \circ \beta \quad \beta \circ g \sqsubseteq g \circ \gamma}{\alpha \circ (f \circ g) \sqsubseteq (f \circ g) \circ \gamma} \quad \textbf{Composition}$$

$$\frac{\alpha \sqsubseteq \beta \quad \beta \circ f \sqsubseteq f \circ \gamma \quad \gamma \sqsubseteq \delta}{\alpha \circ f \sqsubseteq f \circ \delta} \quad \textbf{Approximation}$$

The approximation rule makes it very clear that the information content of projections depends on the direction of analysis. In a backwards analysis, after having obtained a safe projection on the argument of a function, we may always replace it with a larger one and still satisfy the safety condition. Thus, the smaller a projection is, the more informative it is. Conversely, in a forwards analysis we derive projections for the results of functions which, according to the rule, we may freely approximate downwards. Therefore, in a forwards analysis, it is the larger projections that are the most informative.

The next rule deals with product. We provide a proof of its correctness.

$$\frac{\alpha \circ f \sqsubseteq f \circ \beta \quad \gamma \circ g \sqsubseteq g \circ \delta}{(\alpha \times \gamma) \circ <f, \ g> \ \sqsubseteq \ <f, \ g> \circ (\beta \sqcup \delta)} \quad \textbf{Product}$$

Proof
An easy calculation suffices.

$$
\begin{aligned}
(\alpha \times \gamma) \circ <f, \ g> \ &= \ <\alpha \circ f, \ \gamma \circ g> \\
&\sqsubseteq \ <f \circ \beta, \ g \circ \delta> \\
&\sqsubseteq \ <f \circ (\beta \sqcup \delta), \ g \circ (\beta \sqcup \delta)> \\
&= \ <f, \ g> \circ (\beta \sqcup \delta)
\end{aligned}
$$

as required. □

The natural dual of the product rule deals with sum, but because the sum is not categorical sum, we need two rules (the second to deal with the extra value introduced by the sum construction).

$$\frac{\alpha \circ f \sqsubseteq f \circ \beta \quad \gamma \circ g \sqsubseteq g \circ \delta}{(\alpha \sqcap \gamma) \circ [f, \, g] \sqsubseteq [f. \, g] \circ (\beta + \delta)} \quad \textbf{Sum (1)}$$

$$BOT \circ [f, \, g] \sqsubseteq [f, \, g] \circ BOT \quad \textbf{Sum (2)}$$

Proof

The second rule is obvious. The first may be shown by calculation.

$$
\begin{aligned}
(\alpha \sqcap \gamma) \circ [f, \, g] \;&=\; [(\alpha \sqcap \gamma) \circ f, \, (\alpha \sqcap \gamma) \circ g] \quad \{\alpha \sqcap \gamma \text{ is strict}\} \\
&\sqsubseteq\; [\alpha \circ f, \, \gamma \circ g] \\
&\sqsubseteq\; [f \circ \beta, \, g \circ \delta] \\
&=\; [f, g] \circ (\beta + \delta)
\end{aligned}
$$

as required.   □

The second rule is necessary for a forwards analysis (as BOT cannot be approximated by anything of the form $\beta + \delta$), and beneficial for a backwards analysis because, when applicable, it gives a more informative result than the first rule does (as smaller projections are more informative when going backwards).

To analyse recursive functions, it is usually necessary to find fixed points of abstract equations. This is reflected in the rule for recursion. In particular, it is not sufficient to deal with single projections, but an indexed family must be used instead. This allows the recursive invocations of the function to be applied to different projections. The rule does not specify which fixed point of the abstract equations is the one to choose, but demonstrates that any is safe. In any particular analysis, therefore, either the least or the greatest fixed point would be chosen depending on whether the analysis was backwards or forwards (and hence whether smaller or larger projections convey the most information). Note that the rule gives no guidance on how to compute the fixed point efficiently.

$$\frac{(\forall i \, . \, \alpha_i \circ f \sqsubseteq f \circ \beta_i) \;\Rightarrow\; (\forall i \, . \, \alpha_i \circ E(f) \sqsubseteq E(f) \circ \beta_i)}{\forall i \, . \, \alpha_i \circ \mu f.E(f) \sqsubseteq \mu f.E(f) \circ \beta_i} \quad \textbf{Recursion}$$

Proof

We prove the correctness of the rule by fixed point induction, using the standard equivalence between $\mu f.E(f)$ and $\bigsqcup_{n=0}^{\omega} E^n(\lambda x.\bot)$. For the base case we note that $\forall i \, . \, \alpha_i \circ (\lambda x.\bot) \sqsubseteq (\lambda x.\bot) \circ \beta_i$ as projections are strict. Inductively we assume that $\forall i \, . \, \alpha_i \circ E^n(\lambda x.\bot) \sqsubseteq E^n(\lambda x.\bot) \circ \beta_i$, but then by the assumption in the rule we may deduce $\forall i \, . \, \alpha_i \circ E(E^n(\lambda x.\bot)) \sqsubseteq E(E^n(\lambda x.\bot)) \circ \beta_i$, that is, $\forall i \, . \, \alpha_i \circ E^{n+1}(\lambda x.\bot) \sqsubseteq E^{n+1}(\lambda x.\bot) \circ \beta_i$. Finally, for the limit case we appeal to the standard result that predicates involving only continuous functions, composition, and the $\sqsubseteq$ relation are admissible, so this case follows immediately.   □

We claim that the rules presented above may be used equally well for either backwards or forwards analysis. This is clearly the case with the composition, approximation and recursion rules as they are completely symmetric. At first sight it seems as though the product and sum rules each favour one direction over the other. It might be argued, for example, that the product rule favours a backwards analysis as only here may the rule be used in its full generality. To use the rule forwards necessitates inventing a factorisation of an input projection η into the least upper bound of two others. An obvious possibility comes from the equation $\eta = \eta \sqcup \eta$. A version of the rule using this factorisation (and hence tailored to forwards analysis) would appear as

$$\frac{\alpha \circ f \sqsubseteq f \circ \eta \quad \gamma \circ g \sqsubseteq g \circ \eta}{(\alpha \times \gamma) \circ <f,\, g> \sqsubseteq <f,\, g> \circ \eta} \quad \textbf{Product (forwards)}$$

However, while this rule appears less general, it cannot be bettered in a forwards analysis, as the factorisation $\eta = \eta \sqcup \eta$ is the best possible for a forwards analysis (as both arguments to the $\sqcup$ are maximal). Thus, even with the full generality of the usual product rule we could not hope to do any better. Unsurprisingly, a corresponding argument works for sum, demonstrating that it has no inherent bias towards forwards analysis.

We can make this more formal by defining the best possible forwards and backwards analyses allowed by the rules. Assume that, for each type A, we have a finite lattice of projections $Proj_A$ over A for use in analysis[1]. Given a term $t : A \to B$ in the object language, forwards analysis takes a projection $\alpha \in Proj_A$ and returns a projection $\beta \in Proj_B$. So for each term t we will define $t^{\mathcal{F}} : Proj_A \to Proj_B$ by the following equations to give the best possible forward analysis obtainable from the rules above.

$$
\begin{aligned}
(f \circ g)^{\mathcal{F}} \, \alpha &= f^{\mathcal{F}} \, (g^{\mathcal{F}} \, \alpha) \\
<f,g>^{\mathcal{F}} \, \alpha &= f^{\mathcal{F}} \, \alpha \times g^{\mathcal{F}} \, \alpha \\
[f,g]^{\mathcal{F}} \, (\alpha + \beta) &= f^{\mathcal{F}} \, \alpha \sqcap g^{\mathcal{F}} \, \beta \\
[f,g]^{\mathcal{F}} \, BOT &= BOT \\
(\mu f.E(f))^{\mathcal{F}} \, \alpha &= (\sqcap \, (E^n(\lambda x.ID))^{\mathcal{F}}) \, \alpha
\end{aligned}
$$

Similarly we define the backwards analysis $t^{\mathcal{B}} : Proj_B \to Proj_A$ as follows.

$$
\begin{aligned}
(f \circ g)^{\mathcal{B}} \, \beta &= g^{\mathcal{B}} \, (f^{\mathcal{B}} \, \beta) \\
<f,g>^{\mathcal{B}} \, (\alpha \times \beta) &= f^{\mathcal{B}} \, \alpha \sqcup g^{\mathcal{B}} \, \beta \\
[f,g]^{\mathcal{B}} \, \beta &= f^{\mathcal{B}} \, \beta + g^{\mathcal{B}} \, \beta \qquad \{\beta \neq BOT\} \\
[f,g]^{\mathcal{B}} \, BOT &= BOT \\
(\mu f.E(f))^{\mathcal{B}} \, \beta &= (\sqcup \, (E^n(\lambda x.BOT))^{\mathcal{B}}) \, \beta
\end{aligned}
$$

We claim that these sets of rules are equally powerful in that anything an analysis based on one set can discover, so could an analysis based on the other. The reason for this is that each set of rules defines the other uniquely: they form a Galois connection. Recall that a pair of functions $\phi : X \to Y$ and $\psi : Y \to X$ form a Galois connection between the partial orders X and Y if $\phi \circ \psi \sqsubseteq ID_Y$ and $ID_X \sqsubseteq \psi \circ \phi$. Here, ϕ is the left component of the connection, and ψ is the right. Galois connections correspond to adjoint functors between partial orders, and so each component uniquely determines the other.

---

[1] The restriction to finiteness is common practice and is necessary in order to be able to guarantee that the analyser is actually able to find either the least or the greatest fixed point—the approximations necessary with an infinite lattice may cause the analyser to give other fixed points.

Theorem 1
For any term t the functions t^B and t^F form a Galois connection.

Proof
The proof is by induction on the depth of recursion nesting in t, and then on its structure. The case of composition is trivial. We give the proof for sum (product is almost exactly the dual), and for recursion.

Suppose the term is of the form $[f, g]$. Then

$$[f, g]^B ([f, g]^F \ BOT) = BOT$$

and

$$
\begin{aligned}
[f, g]^B ([f, g]^F (\alpha + \beta)) &= [f, g]^B (f^F \alpha \sqcap g^F \beta) \\
&\sqsubseteq f^B (f^F \alpha \sqcap g^F \beta) + g^B (f^F \alpha \sqcap g^F \beta) \\
&\sqsubseteq f^B (f^F \alpha) + g^B (g^F \beta) \\
&\sqsubseteq \alpha + \beta
\end{aligned}
$$

The other composition is similar.

Now for the case of recursion, suppose that the term is of the form $\mu f.E(f)$. Then

$$
\begin{aligned}
(\mu f.E(f))^B &\circ (\mu f.E(f))^F \\
&= (\bigsqcup (E^n(\lambda x.BOT))^B) \circ (\bigsqcap (E^n(\lambda x.ID))^F) \\
&= \bigsqcup ((E^n(\lambda x.BOT))^B \circ (\bigsqcap (E^n(\lambda x.ID))^F)) \qquad \{\bigsqcup \text{ is defined pointwise}\} \\
&\sqsubseteq \bigsqcup ((E^n(\lambda x.BOT))^B \circ (E^n(\lambda x.ID))^F)
\end{aligned}
$$

By induction (there is one less level of recursion nesting), each of the terms is weaker than the identity map on $Proj_B$, and so is the lub. The converse is identical except that the finiteness of the projection lattices is required to ensure that the greatest lower bound in the forward analysis may be calculated pointwise. $\square$

The import of the theorem stems from the fact that one component of a Galois connection determines the other. We conclude, therefore, that in an analysis based solely on the rules in this section, neither forwards nor backwards analysis is inherently superior to the other in any respect. Hence, the choice as to which one to use in a particular situation need depend only on which is most convenient, i.e. whether the initial information is about the argument or the result of a term. In the next section, however, we present stronger rules used in strictness analysis, and these turn out to have a definite bias towards backwards analysis.

5 Strictness Analysis within Data Structures

One of the major advantages of the backward strictness analysis presented in [WH87] is its ability to discover head-strictness. This has important implementation consequences, as a list that appears in a head-strict context may be constructed from cons-nodes that are strict in their first argument[2]. Furthermore, as the external demand on a program corresponds to a head-strict context—the stream output is evaluated item by item in order to print it—the ability to manipulate and propagate this context seems quite important. So far, no forward analysis has been presented that has been able to discover head-strictness. Initially this was due to the fact that the usual abstract values used in forward analysis (Scott closed sets) were unable to abstract the property. More recently, however, it has become clear that both projections and PERs [Hun90] may be used in a forwards manner, and as both are able to describe head-strictness it seems plausible that forward analyses may be able to discover head-strictness. In this section we will present a result which suggests that this is not the case.

The rules above may be used for strictness analysis but will give very poor results. The major reason for this is that the projections that are interesting for strictness analysis cannot be described using usual domain sum and product. For example, the projection *BOTH* appearing in Section 2 cannot. Related to this is the fact that the usual denotational semantics do not directly reflect the structure of expression evaluation within the machine. Indeed, for most purposes, it is eminently desirable that they should not, but in order to analyse strictness it is necessary to use a version of the semantics whose operations and intermediate values correspond more directly to the internal workings of the machine. In doing this we shall make more clear the need for lifting described in [WH87]. That the meaning of programs is unaltered will be clear by appealing to standard isomorphisms.

Machine evaluation may be thought of as fundamentally strict. In particular, the basic notion of function evaluation is strict (we use $A \looparrowright B$ to denote the space of strict functions from A to B), the only method of constructing tuples is strict (we use $A \otimes B$ to denote the smash product of A and B), and likewise sums are inherently strict (denoted $A \oplus B$). In order to implement non-strict semantics the notion of closures is almost universally adopted: instead of producing a value, a pointer is provided to a structure (a graph, or code/environment block etc.) which when evaluated will return the value. Denotationally, closures of a type A may be modelled by values of a type $A_\perp$. The new bottom element corresponds to the inability to construct a closure (as might happen if there is no heap space, for example), and elements of the form (*lift a*) correspond to closures which represent values of A. Note in particular that (*lift* $\perp$) (denoting the closure representing non-termination) is not equal to $\perp$.

When a function is applied, a closure for the argument is constructed prior to the reduction of the body of the function. Thus a (possibly) non-strict function is implemented by a strict function over a closure—note that if the construction of the closure failed to terminate, then no result would be obtained from the function. That this may correctly implement the semantics is a consequence of the isomorphism $A_\perp \looparrowright B \cong A \to B$. Of course, if it is known that a particular function is strict then no closure need be constructed for the argument.

Similarly, to construct a lazy pair, the machine actually constructs a pair of closures. If either of the closures cannot be constructed then neither can the pair. The relevant isomorphism is $(A \times B)_\perp \cong A_\perp \otimes B_\perp$—note that the implementation models a *closure* of a pair. The case of sums is even more obvious. Separated sum is commonly defined in terms of smash sum and lifting: $A + B \cong A_\perp \oplus B_\perp$. Thus, constructing an element

---

[2]Not to be confused with the far weaker property of first-element strictness presented in [Burn90], confusingly also called head-strictness.

of a sum corresponds to tagging a closure representing the value of the summand. If the closure cannot be constructed then neither can the element of the sum.

Because of all this, strictness analysis proceeds in two phases. First the term is transformed by lifting and the liftings are driven through the term. Secondly, projection analysis takes place on the transformed program.

5.1 Lifting

Terms will be converted from the original form into terms using strict product and sum. We shall form a strict product using $\ll f, g \gg$ with component selection primitives $\pi_1^\bullet$ and $\pi_2^\bullet$, and form components of strict sums by the strict injections $in_1^\bullet$ and $in_2^\bullet$ with decomposition $[\![f, g]\!]$. In order to translate a term from the original form into a form using these strict constructions we initially form its closure (by lifting), and then push the liftings through the term. Note that, like the other constructions, lifting is a functor. Thus is $f : A \to B$ is a function then $f_\perp : A_\perp \leftrightarrow B_\perp$ is the function

$$
\begin{aligned}
f_\perp \perp &= \perp \\
f_\perp (lift\ a) &= lift\ (f\ a)
\end{aligned}
$$

The translation of terms is as follows.

$$
\begin{aligned}
(f \circ g)_\perp &= f_\perp \circ g_\perp \\
<f, g>_\perp &= \ll f_\perp, g_\perp \gg \\
(\pi_i)_\perp &= \pi_i^\bullet \\
[f, g]_\perp &= [\![f_\perp, g_\perp]\!]_\perp \\
(in_i)_\perp &= (in_i^\bullet \circ lift)_\perp \\
(\mu f. E(f))_\perp &= \mu f'. (E(f)_\perp\ [(f' \sqcup BOT_\perp)/f_\perp])
\end{aligned}
$$

If the initial term had type $t : A \to B$, then the lifted term has type $t_\perp : A_\perp \leftrightarrow B_\perp$. The projection analysis may draw the projections from a corresponding larger space. We define the (polymorphic) projection $STR : \forall X. X_\perp \to X_\perp$ by

$$
\begin{aligned}
STR\ \ \ \perp &= \perp \\
STR\ \ (lift\ \perp) &= \perp \\
STR\ \ (lift\ x) &= lift\ x \ \ if\ x \neq \perp
\end{aligned}
$$

STR collapses the original bottom element down to the new bottom but leaves everything else unchanged. It is important for strictness analysis as $STR \circ f_\perp \sqsubseteq f_\perp \circ STR$ if and only if f is strict.

For any type A, the projections over $A_\perp$ are either of the form $\alpha_\perp$ or $STR \circ \alpha_\perp$ (where α is a projection on A). Following [WH87] we write ABS for the smallest of the former, namely $BOT_\perp$. Note that STR is the largest in the latter group (as $STR = STR \circ ID_\perp$). Thus we may neatly divide the projections over $A_\perp$ into those greater than ABS, and those less than STR.

An effect of lifting is that every construct is strict (in the new bottom element). Because of this, it is possible to use a stricter form of least upper bound to combine results. Indeed, as we shall see, without doing so the results are very poor. We define

$$
\alpha \& \beta = \sqcup \circ \ll \alpha, \beta \gg
$$

110

In effect, $(\alpha\&\beta)$ acts just like $(\alpha \sqcup \beta)$ except that if either of the projections returns $\perp$ (the new bottom) then so does the combination.

5.2 Products Are Better Backwards

As strictness analysis is performed on the transformed program, we need rules to handle strict products and strict sums. The strict-product rule resembles the original, but takes advantage of strictness in the new bottom element. Note the replacement of $\sqcup$ by $\&$ of the right of the consequence of the rule.

$$\frac{\alpha \circ f \sqsubseteq f \circ \beta \qquad \gamma \circ g \sqsubseteq g \circ \delta}{(\alpha \otimes \gamma) \circ \ll f,\ g \gg \sqsubseteq \ll f,\ g \gg \circ (\beta\&\delta)} \qquad \textbf{Strict Product}$$

Proof
Again a direct calculation is sufficient.

$$
\begin{aligned}
(\alpha \otimes \gamma) \circ \ll f,\ g \gg &= \ll \alpha \circ f,\ \gamma \circ g \gg \\
&\sqsubseteq \ll f \circ \beta,\ g \circ \delta \gg \\
&\sqsubseteq (f \otimes g) \circ \ll \beta,\ \delta \gg \\
&\sqsubseteq (f \otimes g) \circ \sqcup \circ \ll \beta,\ \delta \gg \\
&= \ll f,\ g \gg \circ (\beta\&\delta)
\end{aligned}
$$

as required. $\square$

This rule, and its use of $\&$, is crucial to strictness analysis. As we shall demonstrate by example, without it we would obtain very poor results indeed. Significantly, it is only a backwards analysis that can take full advantage of this rule, making it truly asymmetric.

Consider the first projection π_1^* from a strict product. It has the following properties.

(p1) $STR \circ \pi_1^* \sqsubseteq \pi_1^* \circ (STR \otimes \alpha)$ if $ABS \sqsubseteq \alpha$
(p2) $BOT \circ \pi_1^* \sqsubseteq \pi_1^* \circ (STR \otimes \alpha)$ if $\alpha \sqsubseteq STR$

We will perform a strictness analysis of the term $\pi_1 \circ <id,id>$ (which is just the identity, of course). Lifting this term gives us $\pi_1^* \circ \ll id,\ id \gg$. Proceeding by backwards analysis we get,

$$
\begin{aligned}
&STR \circ \pi_1^* \circ \ll id,\ id \gg \\
&\sqsubseteq \pi_1^* \circ (STR \otimes ABS) \circ \ll id,\ id \gg \qquad \text{\{rule (p1) above\}} \\
&\sqsubseteq \pi_1^* \circ \ll id,\ id \gg \circ (STR\&ABS) \qquad \text{\{strict-product rule\}} \\
&= \pi_1^* \circ \ll id,\ id \gg \circ STR \qquad \text{\{$STR\&ABS = STR$\}}
\end{aligned}
$$

Using backwards analysis, no information has been lost even though a data structure was constructed and dismantled. However, this relied crucially on the final step which used the equation $STR\&ABS = STR$. If instead of using $\&$ the rule had used $\sqcup$, the result would have been ID (as $STR \sqcup ABS = ID$) making the result very poor.

Now consider the same analysis, but this time performed forwards. We start with a projection η for the right hand side of the term. To use the rule, we must factorise η into the form $\beta\&\delta$. One way to do this is to make both β and δ equal to η. This is valid as $\eta\&\eta = \eta$, and gives the following specialised form of the strict product rule.

$$\frac{\alpha \circ f \sqsubseteq f \circ \eta \qquad \gamma \circ g \sqsubseteq g \circ \eta}{(\alpha \otimes \gamma) \circ \ll f,\ g \gg\ \sqsubseteq\ \ll f,\ g \gg \circ\ \eta} \qquad \textbf{Strict Product (forwards)}$$

Unfortunately, however, this rule gives poor results. The analysis of the term given above would proceed as follows.

$$\pi_1^\bullet \circ \ll id,\ id \gg \circ\ STR$$
$$\qquad \sqsupseteq\ \pi_1^\bullet \circ (STR \otimes STR) \circ \ll id,\ id \gg \qquad \{\text{strict-product rule (forwards)}\}$$
$$\qquad \sqsupseteq\ BOT \circ \pi_1^\bullet \circ \ll id,\ id \gg \qquad\qquad \{\text{rule (p2) above}\}$$

Recall that we want to end up with as large a projection as possible when performing a forwards analysis. The result of the analysis, therefore, is very poor. Furthermore, it is not hard to see where the failure arose. The forwards version of the strict-product rule arose from the original by means of the factorisation of η into the form $\eta\&\eta$. Unfortunately, this is not the best possible factorisation. Worst of all, there is *no* best factorisation in general. Consider factorising STR. While $STR = STR\&STR$, it is also the case that $STR = STR\&ABS$ and that $STR = ABS\&STR$. Both of these factorisations involve larger projections and so provide more information for a forwards analysis. However, as $STR \neq ABS\&ABS$ there is no greatest factorisation. A choice must therefore be made. Which factorisation should be chosen? Clearly, which choice will be best depends on which function is going to be applied to the result at a later date. Of course, this could be determined by a backwards analysis . . .

Using the strict product rule backwards corresponds to a function over projections as before, but this time it gives a function which does not form the left component of a Galois connection. As it does not have a right adjoint, it is therefore impossible to obtain a corresponding forwards version of the rule of equal strength.

5.3 Sums Are No Better Forwards

The natural duality between products and sums (despite not being reflected fully in domain theory) leads to the intuition that if analysis of products works better backwards, then the analysis of sums should work better forwards. However, the rule for strictness analysis of sums is as follows (there is only one rule as coalesced sum is the categorical sum in the category of domains and strict functions).

$$\frac{\alpha \circ f \sqsubseteq f \circ \beta \qquad \gamma \circ g \sqsubseteq g \circ \delta}{(\alpha \sqcap \gamma) \circ [\![\ f,\ g\ ]\!] \sqsubseteq [\![\ f,\ g\ ]\!] \circ (\beta \oplus \delta)} \qquad \textbf{Strict Sum}$$

This rule is almost identical to the original one. Note in particular the occurrence of $\sqcap$ on the left hand side of the conclusion. As before, it is possible to obtain a best $\sqcap$-factorisation of a projection, and so the "restricted" backwards version of the rule is just as powerful as the forwards version.

The duality argument failed because this whole section relates to strictness analysis. If, instead, we consider the dual problem, namely termination analysis, then the situation would be reversed. The & operator would not be needed and so the problem with forwards analysis would disappear. Furthermore, if the language provided any constructs that terminated whenever any one of its sub-terms did, then there would be the need for a dual to & to capture this. The rule using this new operator could be used effectively forwards, but not backwards. However, as is well known, termination analysis is a lot harder than strictness analysis. The root cause of this is the fact that computers calculate least fixed points and not, for example, greatest fixed points. Thus, a fundamental asymmetry in computing means that many duality arguments are liable to fail.

6 Conclusion

There is still much to do, and this paper represents a workshop report of work in progress. However, we believe that we have identified a key reason why an analysis in one direction may be superior to an analysis in the other, namely that it may not be possible to generate good factorisations of an abstract value when appropriate. The example in this paper centred on the & factorisation that would be needed for a forwards projection-based strictness analysis. The major question of course is whether the result holds purely for projection-based analyses or whether it is more generally applicable. What we did was to construct a calculus of abstract values (in our case, projections) that corresponded directly with the type structure of the terms, and which had two properties of note: first, that the head-strict projection H may be expressed in the calculus (see [Hug89] for a fuller account of this), and secondly that the calculus works best backwards. We know of no other corresponding calculus that includes H but does not require an operation corresponding to &. Thus we conjecture that head-strictness and the & operation are fundamentally related. If this is indeed the case, then a forward, non-relational analysis will be unable to discover head-strictness.

The restriction to the analysis being non-relational is essential to the above conjecture. It is well known that computation itself is equally well defined either forwards or backwards, as given any function $f : A \to B$ the Scott closure of the direct image of f,

$$\exists f \ X \ = \ \{f \ x \mid x \in X\}*$$

(where $Y*$ is the Scott-closure of Y) is adjoint to the inverse image of f,

$$f^{-1} \ Y \ = \ \{x \in A \mid f \ x \in Y\}$$

(the adjunction maps between the lower power domains of A and B). As f defines and is defined by the direct image of f, and the direct image in turn defines and is defined by the inverse image, then all three are equivalent. Thus it is only the processes of abstraction and of moving from a relational to an independent framework that introduces imbalances between the two directions. Hunt's PER-based forward analysis [Hun90] which can model head-strictness will be an interesting test case. We conjecture that, although Hunt's abstract domain can capture head-strictness, his analyser will be unable to discover it.

7   Acknowledgements

The work reported here was carried out under funding from the ESPRIT basic research action Semantique. We would like to offer thanks to Sebastian Hunt and Patrick Cousot for the relevant discussions we have had, along with the other members of the Semantique project and members of the Glasgow Functional Programming Group.

References

[AH87]   S. Abramsky and C. Hankin (editors). *Abstract Interpretation of Declarative Languages*. Ellis Horwood, Chichester, England, 1987.

[BEJ88]   D. Bjørner, A. Ershov and N. Jones (Editors). *Partial Evaluation and Mixed Computation*. Proceedings IFIP TC2 Workshop, Gammel Avernæs, Denmark, October 1987. North-Holland, 1988.

[Burn90]   G. Burn. *A Relationship Between Abstract Interpretation and Projection Analysis*. POPL 90, San Francisco, 1990.

[Hug88]   R.J.M. Hughes. *Backwards Analysis of Functional Programs*. In [BEJ88], pages 187-208, 1988.

[Hug89]   R.J.M. Hughes. *Projections for Polymorphic Strictness Analysis*. In Proc of Symposium on Category Theory and Computer Science, Manchester 1989.

[Hun90]   S. Hunt. *PERs Generalise Projections for Strictness Analysis*. This volume.

[Lau89]   J. Launchbury. *Projection Factorisations in Partial Evaluation*. Ph.D. Thesis, Glasgow University, 1989.

[WH87]   P. Wadler and R.J.M. Hughes. *Projections for Strictness Analysis*. FPCA 87, Portland, Oregan, 1987.

PERs Generalise Projections for Strictness Analysis (Extended Abstract)*

Sebastian Hunt
Department Of Computing
Imperial College
London SW7 2BZ

Abstract

We show how Wadler and Hughes's use of *Scott projections* to describe properties of functions ("Projections for Strictness Analysis", FPCA 1987) can be generalised by the use of *partial equivalence relations*. We describe an analysis (in the form of an *abstract interpretation*) for identifying such properties for functions defined in the simply typed λ-calculus. Our analysis has a very simple proof of correctness, based on the use of *logical relations*. We go on to consider how to derive 'best' correct interpretations for constants.

1 Introduction

In [WH87], Phil Wadler and John Hughes suggested a method of describing properties of functions using *projections*, and developed an analysis for identifying such properties for functions defined in a first-order functional language. (A projection is a continuous map on a cpo $\alpha : D \to D$, such that $\alpha \sqsubseteq \mathrm{id}_D$ and $\alpha \circ \alpha = \alpha$.)

For an example of [WH87]'s use of projections, let $\mathcal{L}$ be the domain of finite, partial and infinite lists of elements of some domain (the particular choice of element domain is not important for the purposes of the example) ordered in the usual way. The projection $H : \mathcal{L} \to \mathcal{L}$ is defined such that

$$
\begin{aligned}
H(\bot) &= \bot \\
H([]) &= [] \\
H(\bot : y) &= \bot \\
H(x : y) &= x : (H\ y) \quad \text{if } x \neq \bot,
\end{aligned}
$$

where $[]$ is the empty list and $(:)$ is the cons operation. Suppose we have a lazy functional language in which we form an expression, $e_1 \circ e_2$ with denotation $[\![e_1 \circ e_2]\!] = [\![e_1]\!] \circ [\![e_2]\!]$. With the analysis of [WH87], we may be able to establish that the function $[\![e_1]\!]$ satisfies the property

$$[\![e_1]\!] \circ H = [\![e_1]\!],$$

---

*The full version of this paper is available as Departmental Report DOC 90/14, Dept. of Computing, Imperial College.

so that $[\![e_1 \circ e_2]\!] = [\![e_1]\!] \circ (H \circ [\![e_2]\!])$. As is suggested in [WH87], we could then modify the code generation for the sub-expression e_2 such that every call to (:) which "contributes to the output" of e_2 is implemented by a 'head-strict' (i.e., left-strict) cons operation.

The analysis described in [WH87] is a backwards analysis, propagating information about the context in which a function is called to yield information about the way in which its arguments are used. Other forms of program analysis, in particular that using abstract interpretation as described in [Myc81, BHA86, Bur87], work in a forwards manner. The work presented here is motivated by the fact that each of the two methods has advantages over the other:

(i) The [WH87] analysis can detect cases where a function is 'head-strict' as in the above example, and cases where a function ignores its argument. The analyses of [Myc81, BHA86, Bur87] are unable to incorporate this kind of test.

(ii) The [BHA86] and [Bur87] analyses are defined for the typed lambda calculus. The [WH87] analysis is restricted to a first-order language and has proved difficult to extend to higher-order languages (but see [Hug87] for one approach).

In this paper we describe an analysis in the form of an abstract interpretation which aims to combine the advantages of both methods. Our approach depends on using *partial equivalence relations* to generalise [WH87]'s use of projections to describe properties of functions.

The rest of this paper is organised as follows. Section 2 recalls the form of the condition tested for by the [WH87] analysis and gives the generalised version of it. Sections 3 and 4 review the formalism and results we will be using from [Abr90]. Section 5 describes the basic form of the analysis and proves it correct. Section 6 is concerned with the existence of best possible interpretations for constants. In section 7 we extend the analysis to a richer language. In section 8 we consider the relationship between our analysis and the analyses of [WH87] and [BHA86, Bur87] in a little more detail. Section 9 concludes.

2 Projections and Partial Equivalence Relations

All forms of strictness analysis aim to infer *safe* information about the denotation of a term. For simple strictness analysis we require a sound and effective test for the condition that $[\![e]\!] \perp = \perp$. It is well known how to achieve this using the technique of abstract interpretation ([Myc81], [BHA86], [Abr90]).

In an analysis based on the use of projections, the condition tested for is slightly more involved. Returning to the example in the introduction, having established that $[\![e_1 \circ e_2]\!] = [\![e_1]\!] \circ (H \circ [\![e_2]\!])$ by analysing e_1, we may wish to analyse e_2. This time, however, we need not restrict ourselves to identifying a projection α such that $[\![e_2]\!] = [\![e_2]\!] \circ \alpha$, but can use our information about the context in which e_2 occurs and try to find a projection α such that $H \circ [\![e_2]\!] = H \circ [\![e_2]\!] \circ \alpha$. In general, for an expression (in a first-order functional language) denoting a function $f : D \to D'$, given projections $\alpha : D \to D$ and $\beta : D' \to D'$, the analysis technique of [WH87] can provide a sound and effective test for the condition that:

$$\beta \circ f = \beta \circ f \circ \alpha. \tag{1}$$

As is shown in [WH87], with a little inventiveness it is possible to describe ordinary strictness using projections. For a function $f : D \to D'$, let $f_\perp : D_\perp \to D'_\perp$ be the function defined by

$$f_\perp \ x = \begin{cases} \perp_{D'_\perp} & \text{if } x = \perp_{D_\perp} \\ \mathit{lift}(f\ y) & \text{if } x = \mathit{lift}(y) \end{cases}$$

where *lift* is the evident injection into a lifted domain. It is then easy to verify that

$$f \perp_D = \perp_{D'} \Longleftrightarrow \mathit{Str}_{D'} \circ f_\perp = \mathit{Str}_{D'} \circ f_\perp \circ \mathit{Str}_D,$$

where $\mathit{Str}_D : D_\perp \to D_\perp$ is the projection defined by

$$\mathit{Str}_D \ x = \begin{cases} \perp_{D_\perp} & \text{if } x = \perp_{D_\perp} \\ \perp_{D_\perp} & \text{if } x = \mathit{lift}(\perp_D) \\ x & \text{otherwise} \end{cases}$$

The use of projections is not restricted to descriptions of strictness. Another property which can conveniently be expressed using projections is that of a function being constant, i.e., of a function's result being independent of its argument. To do this we can simply use the projection $\lambda x.\perp$, since f is constant iff $f \circ \lambda x.\perp = f$.

2.1 Partial Equivalence Relations

A *partial equivalence relation* (per) on a set D, is a transitive and symmetric relation $S \subseteq D \times D$. If S is such a per, then $|S|$ is the set $\{x \in D \mid (x,x) \in S\}$. We will write $x : S$ if $x \in |S|$. For each $x \in |S|$, $[x]_S$ is the equivalence class of x by S. The set of pers on D is closed under arbitrary intersection.

Partial equivalence relations over various applicative structures have been used to construct models of the polymorphic lambda calculus (see, for example, [Asp90]). In [AP90], pers over a *domain* are used for the same purpose. We will be using pers to describe properties of functions over Scott domains, in such a way that abstract interpretation may be used to test whether the properties hold of functions defined in a simply typed lambda calculus. Although the relationship is not explored in this paper, it seems clear that there are strong connections between our use of pers and that described in [AP90].

Definition 2.1 For each projection, $\beta : D \to D$, the equivalence relation $E_\beta \subseteq D \times D$ is defined by: $x \ E_\beta \ y \Longleftrightarrow \beta(x) = \beta(y)$. □

Definition 2.2 For Scott domains D, D' relations $S \subseteq D \times D$ and $T \subseteq D' \times D'$, the relation $S \Rrightarrow T \subseteq [D \to D']^2$ is defined by:

$$f\ (S \Rrightarrow T)\ g \Longleftrightarrow \forall x, y \in D.\, x\ S\ y \Rightarrow (f\ x)\ T\ (g\ y)$$

where $[D \to D']$ is the Scott domain of continuous maps from D to D'. □

It is straightforward to show that if S and T are pers, then so is $S \Rrightarrow T$. (In fact, there is a CCC with pers as objects and the $S \Rrightarrow T$ as exponent objects. See, e.g. [Asp90].) Borrowing the types convention, we will write a per of the form $S_1 \Rrightarrow (S_2 \Rrightarrow (\ldots(S_n \Rrightarrow T)\ldots))$ as $S_1 \Rrightarrow S_2 \Rrightarrow \ldots S_n \Rrightarrow T$. Recalling that for a per P we write $x : P$ to mean $x \in |P|$, we note the following equivalence:

$$f : S_1 \Rrightarrow \ldots \Rrightarrow S_k \Rrightarrow T$$
$$\Longleftrightarrow$$
$$(x_1\ S_1\ x_1') \wedge \ldots \wedge (x_k\ S_k\ x_k') \Rightarrow (f\ x_1\ \ldots\ x_k)\ T\ (f\ x_1'\ \ldots\ x_k').$$

Proposition 2.3 For projections $\alpha : D \to D$, $\beta : D' \to D'$, and function $f \in [D \to D']$
$$\beta \circ f = \beta \circ f \circ \alpha \Longleftrightarrow f : E_\alpha \Rrightarrow E_\beta$$

□

Thus any test for a condition of form (1) can be re-expressed as a test for a condition of the form

$$f : S \Rightarrow T \tag{2}$$

where S and T are pers.

Clearly, since E_α and E_β in the above proposition are equivalence relations, we do not need pers if we simply wish to rephrase statements of form (1). However, there are two good reasons for allowing the generality of pers:

(i) With pers, we can use form (2) both to rephrase statements of form (1) and, without lifting domains, to describe ordinary strictness. For each domain D, let Bot_D be the per $\{(\perp_D, \perp_D)\}$. Then for any $f : D \to D'$

$$f \perp_D = \perp_{D'} \Leftrightarrow f : Bot_D \Rightarrow Bot_{D'}.$$

(ii) In general, even if P and Q are both equivalence relations on domains, $P \Rightarrow Q$ will be a *partial* equivalence relation (consider $E_{\lambda x. \perp} \Rightarrow E_{id}$, for example). As we shall see in what follows, this makes it natural to consider pers rather than just equivalence relations when analysing definitions of higher-order functions.

The analysis presented in [WH87] is a first-order backwards analysis implementing tests of form (1). Here we present a higher-order forwards analysis which implements tests of the more general form (2).

With the exception of sub-section 4.2, the next two sections are essentially a review of the first three sections of [Abr90].

3   The Typed Lambda Calculus

Given a set of base types $\{A, B, \ldots\}$ we build type expressions, $\sigma, \tau, \ldots$ as follows:

$$\tau ::= A \mid \tau_1 \to \tau_2$$

A *Language L* is specified by giving a set of base types and a set of *typed constants* $\{c_\sigma\}$. For each type σ, we assume an infinite set of typed variables $Var_\sigma = \{x^\sigma, y^\sigma, \ldots\}$. Then $\Lambda_T(L)$ consists of typed terms $e : \sigma$ built according to the usual rules for the simply typed λ-calculus.

An *interpretation I* of L is specified by $I = (\{D_A^I\}, \{c_\sigma^I\})$, such that for each base type A, D_A^I is a Scott domain, and for each c_σ, $c_\sigma^I \in D_\sigma^I$, where the D_A^I are extended to higher types such that $D_{\sigma \to \tau}^I = [D_\sigma^I \to D_\tau^I]$ We will write the least element of D_σ^I as $\perp_\sigma^I$.

An interpretation I determines the semantic valuation function

$$\llbracket \cdot \rrbracket^I : \Lambda_T(L) \to Env^I \to \cup D_\sigma^I$$

where $Env^I = \{Env_\sigma^I\}$, $Env_\sigma^I = Var_\sigma \to D_\sigma^I$.

Assume that for each type σ there is a constant $Y_{(\sigma \to \sigma) \to \sigma}$. Following [Abr90], we say that I is a *normal* interpretation if

$$Y_{(\sigma \to \sigma) \to \sigma}^I(f) = \bigsqcup_{n=0}^{\infty} f^n(\perp_\sigma^I).$$

4 Logical Relations

[Abr90] shows how logical relations can be applied to the proof of correctness of program analyses based on abstract interpretation.

A *binary logical relation* $R : I, K$ is a family $\{R_\sigma\}$, with $R_\sigma \subseteq D_\sigma^I \times D_\sigma^K$ such that for all σ, τ, for all $f \in D_{\sigma \to \tau}^I, h \in D_{\sigma \to \tau}^K$:

$$f \; R_{\sigma \to \tau} \; h$$
$$\Longleftrightarrow$$
$$\forall x \in D_\sigma^I, a \in D_\sigma^K . \; x \; R_\sigma \; a \Rightarrow (f \; x) \; R_\tau \; (h \; a).$$

While binary logical relations are sufficient for establishing correctness of analyses such as those of [BHA86, Bur87], they are not quite enough for our purposes. We wish to use a family of *ternary* relations $R = \{R_\sigma\}$ with $R_\sigma \subseteq D_\sigma^I \times D_\sigma^I \times D_\sigma^K$, such that each domain point $a \in D_\sigma^K$ is associated with a per given by $\big\{ (x, y) \in D_\sigma^I \times D_\sigma^I \mid R_\sigma(x, y, a) \big\}$. For this reason, in reviewing the results of [Abr90] we make the (routine) generalisation to the n-ary case.

A *logical relation* $R : I_1, \dots, I_n$ is a family $\{R_\sigma\}$, with $R_\sigma \subseteq D_\sigma^{I_1} \times \dots \times D_\sigma^{I_n}$ such that for all σ, τ, for all $f_1 \in D_{\sigma \to \tau}^{I_1}, \dots, f_n \in D_{\sigma \to \tau}^{I_n}$:

$$(f_1, \dots, f_n) \in R_{\sigma \to \tau} \tag{3}$$
$$\Longleftrightarrow$$
$$\forall a_1 \in D_\sigma^{I_1}, \dots, a_n \in D_\sigma^{I_n} . \; (a_1, \dots, a_n) \in R_\sigma \Rightarrow (f_1 \; a_1, \dots, f_n \; a_n) \in R_\tau.$$

Any family of relations on the base types extends uniquely to a logical relation by using (3) as a definition of R_σ at the higher types.

A property P of relations is *inherited* if for all logical relations $R : I_1, \dots, I_k$, whenever $P(R_A)$ holds for all base-types, A, then $P(R_\sigma)$ holds for all types σ.

4.1 Relating Interpretations of Terms

If $R : I_1, \dots, I_k$ is a logical relation, then for $\rho_i \in Env^{I_i}$ we will write $(\rho_1, \dots, \rho_k) \in R$, meaning that $\forall x^\tau . \; (\rho_1 \; x^\tau, \dots, \rho_k \; x^\tau) \in R_\tau$.

Proposition 4.1 ([Abr90]) Let $R : I_1, \dots, I_k$ be a logical relation. Suppose that for each constant c_τ, $(c_\tau^{I_1}, \dots, c_\tau^{I_k}) \in R_\tau$. Then for all $e : \sigma$, for all $\rho_i \in Env^{I_i}$

$$(\rho_1, \dots, \rho_k) \in R \Rightarrow (\llbracket e \rrbracket^{I_1} \rho_1, \dots, \llbracket e \rrbracket^{I_k} \rho_k) \in R_\sigma$$

$\square$

4.2 Concretisation maps

In what follows it will often be convenient to present a logical relation in an alternative form. Given a logical relation $R : I, K$, we may form the family of *concretisation maps* $\gamma^R = \big\{ \gamma_\sigma^R \big\}$ as follows:

$$\gamma_\sigma^R : D_\sigma^K \to \wp(D_\sigma^I)$$
$$\gamma_\sigma^R \; a = \big\{ x \in D_\sigma^I \mid (x, a) \in R_\sigma \big\}$$

where $\wp(D)$ is the power set of D. Clearly R and γ^R may be used interchangeably, since $(x, a) \in R_\sigma$ iff $x \in \gamma_\sigma^R \; a$. Now for $f : D \to D'$, $X \subseteq D$, and $Y \subseteq D'$, let $(X \Rightarrow Y) \subseteq [D \to D']$ be defined by

$$f \in (X \Rightarrow Y) \Longleftrightarrow \forall x \in X. f \, x \in Y.$$

Then we may express the fact that R is logical purely in terms of γ^R:

Lemma 4.2 $R : I, K$ is logical iff for all σ, τ for all $f \in [D_\sigma^K \to D_\tau^K]$

$$\gamma_{\sigma \to \tau}^R f = \bigcap_{a \in D_\sigma^K} \gamma_\sigma^R a \Rightarrow \gamma_\tau^R(fa),$$

$\square$

We can make analogous definitions given a family of relations $R : I, I, K$. We form the concretisation maps as follows:

$$\gamma_\sigma^R : D_\sigma^K \to \wp(D_\sigma^I \times D_\sigma^I)$$
$$\gamma_\sigma^R a = \left\{ (x, y) \in D_\sigma^I \times D_\sigma^I \mid (x, y, a) \in R_\sigma \right\}$$

Again, R and γ^R may be used interchangeably. Furthermore, we may express the fact that R is logical purely in terms of γ^R:

Lemma 4.3 $R : I, I, K$ is logical iff for all σ, τ for all $f \in [D_\sigma^K \to D_\tau^K]$

$$\gamma_{\sigma \to \tau}^R f = \bigcap_{a \in D_\sigma^K} \gamma_\sigma^R a \Rrightarrow \gamma_\tau^R(fa)$$

$\square$

The analyses of [BHA86, Bur87] test for conditions of the form $f \in (X \Rightarrow Y)$ (in more familiar notation, $f(X) \subseteq Y$), where for $f : D \to D'$, $X \subseteq D$ and $Y \subseteq D'$ are Scott-closed sets. Both analyses use an abstract interpretation, say K, and can be proved correct using a binary logical relation $R : I, K$ where each $\gamma_\sigma^R a$ is a Scott-closed set[1].

We wish to test for conditions of the form $f : S \Rrightarrow T$ where S and T are pers. We will use an abstract interpretation J and prove correctness in terms of a ternary logical relation $P : I, I, J$ where each $\gamma_\sigma^P a$ is a per.

5 The Analysis

We assume a standard interpretation I which is normal, in which $D_{bool}^I = \{tt, f\!f\}_\perp$, the $\mathrm{cond}_{bool \to A \to A \to A}^I$ are conditionals, and all other first-order constants $c_{A_1 \to \cdots \to A_n \to B}$ are strict. Our analysis consists of two parts: an abstract interpretation (together with a logical relation) and a proof of correctness.

5.1 The Abstract Interpretation J

Our abstract interpretation has base domains

$$D_A^J = 3 = \{\textsc{bot}, \textsc{id}, \textsc{all}\}, \text{ with } \textsc{bot} \sqsubseteq \textsc{id} \sqsubseteq \textsc{all}.$$

The values in the abstract domains are related to those in the standard domains by the logical relation $P : I, I, J$, where:

(i) $\gamma_A^P \, \textsc{all} = \left\{ (x, y) \mid x, y \in D_A^I \right\}$

---

[1] The development of [BHA86, Bur87] preceded that of [Abr90] and correctness was actually proved without using logical relations.

(ii) $\gamma_A^P \text{ ID} = \left\{ (x,x) \mid x \in D_A^I \right\}$

(iii) $\gamma_A^P \text{ BOT} = \left\{ (\bot_A^I, \bot_A^I) \right\}$

It is straightforward to verify that for each $a \in D_A^J$, $\gamma_A^P \, a$ is a per, and using lemma 4.3, that this property is inherited at the higher types. Hence:

Proposition 5.1 For all σ, for each $a \in D_\sigma^J$, $\gamma_\sigma^P \, a$ is a per. □

(For the points ID and ALL, the pers correspond to projections, with $\gamma_A^P \text{ ID} = E_{id}$ and $\gamma_A^P \text{ ALL} = E_{\lambda x.\bot}$.)

J is a normal interpretation with:

- $\text{cond}_{bool \to A \to A \to A}^J \, X \, a \, b \ = \ \begin{cases} \text{BOT} & \text{if } X = \text{BOT} \\ a \sqcup b & \text{if } X = \text{ID} \\ \text{BOT} & \text{if } X = \text{ALL and } a \sqcup b = \text{BOT} \\ \text{ALL} & \text{if } X = \text{ALL and } a \sqcup b \neq \text{BOT} \end{cases}$

- $c_{A_1 \to \cdots \to A_n \to B}^J \, a_1 \ldots a_n \ = \ \begin{cases} \text{ID} & \text{if } n = 0 \\ \text{BOT} & \text{if } \exists 1 \leq i \leq n. \, a_i = \text{BOT} \\ \displaystyle\left(\bigsqcup_{i=1}^{n} a_i\right) & \text{otherwise} \end{cases}$

Intuitively, we may think of the abstract domain points as describing different degrees of "fixedness", where decreasing in the abstract domain ordering corresponds to an increasing degree of "fixedness". For example, we may think of BOT as meaning "fixed at bottom", ID as meaning "fixed at an unknown value", and ALL as meaning "varying". The definition of cond^J can then be understood in the following terms. If we fix the first argument to cond^I at bottom, then the result is fixed at bottom. If we fix the first argument to cond^I at an unknown value, then the result is at least as fixed as the most variable of the other two arguments. If we allow the first argument to cond^I to vary, then the result may vary unless both of the other arguments are fixed at bottom, in which case the result will be fixed at bottom.

Proposition 5.2 For each c_σ, $(c_\sigma^I, c_\sigma^I) \in \gamma_\sigma^P \, c_\sigma^J$. □

5.2 Correctness of J

We will say that J is *correct* iff for all terms $e : \sigma_1 \to \ldots \to \sigma_n \to B$, for all $a_i \in D_{\sigma_i}^J$, $1 \leq i \leq n$, and environments $\rho \in Env^J$, $\rho' \in Env^J$ such that $(\rho, \rho) \, P \, \rho'$:

$$(\llbracket e \rrbracket^J \rho' a_1 \ldots a_n = b) \Rightarrow (\llbracket e \rrbracket^I \rho) : \gamma_{\sigma_1}^P a_1 \twoheadrightarrow \ldots \twoheadrightarrow \gamma_{\sigma_n}^P a_n \twoheadrightarrow \gamma_B^P b \qquad (4)$$

Theorem 5.3 J is correct. □

5.3 Example

We conclude this section with an example application of the analysis. In the following we suppress the types for the sake of clarity. Consider the following function definition:

$$\text{pfac} = Y(\lambda f.\lambda x.\lambda y. \, \text{cond} \, (x = 0)$$
$$1$$
$$x * (f \, (x - 1) \, (y + 1)))$$

The standard interpretation of pfac is a 'perverse' factorial function which takes two arguments, the second of which is never needed. The interpretation under J is the function pfac^J, where for all $a, b \in \mathbf{3}$, $\text{pfac}^J\ a\ b = a$. Our correctness result allows us to infer the following about the standard interpretation pfac^I:

(i) pfac^I is strict in its first argument, since $\text{pfac}^J\ \text{BOT}\ \text{ID} = \text{BOT}$, hence:

$$\forall(x_1, x_2) \in \gamma^P\ \text{BOT}.\forall(y_1, y_2) \in \gamma^P\ \text{ID}.\,(\text{pfac}^I\ x_1\ y_1, \text{pfac}^I\ x_2\ y_2) \in \gamma^P\ \text{BOT}$$
$$\Rightarrow \forall y.\,\text{pfac}^I \perp y = \perp$$

(ii) pfac^I ignores its second argument, since $\text{pfac}^J\ \text{ID}\ \text{ALL} = \text{ID}$, hence:

$$\forall(x_1, x_2) \in \gamma^P\ \text{ID}.\forall(y_1, y_2) \in \gamma^P\ \text{ALL}.\,(\text{pfac}^I\ x_1\ y_1, \text{pfac}^I\ x_2\ y_2) \in \gamma^P\ \text{ID}$$
$$\Rightarrow \forall x.\forall y_1, y_2.\,\text{pfac}^I\ x\ y_1 = \text{pfac}^I\ x\ y_2$$

In the full paper we show how J can be used to test for strictness and constancy at all types.

6   Abstraction Maps and Best Interpretations

While we have presented a correct analysis, we have not yet dealt with a language incorporating list types. It is possible to extend the analysis to a richer language, but to do so we have to construct correct interpretations of higher type constants. This is less straightforward than for the first-order constants we have so far considered and it would be helpful to have some systematic way of deriving such interpretations.

6.1   Left Adjoints for Concretisation Maps

We will say that a logical relation $R : I, I, K$ satisfies property (M) if each γ_σ^R preserves meets, i.e., for each subset $X \subseteq D_\sigma^K$

$$\gamma_\sigma^R(\sqcap X) = \bigcap_{a \in X} \gamma_\sigma^R a$$

Note that this implies monotonicity of the γ_σ^R.

Proposition 6.1 When each D_A^K (hence each D_σ^K) is finite, property (M) is inherited. $\square$

Freyd's Adjoint Functor Theorem ([Lan71]), immediately gives us the following:

Corollary 6.1.1 If each D_A^K is a finite lattice, then each γ_σ^R has a left adjoint iff each γ_A^R preserves meets. $\square$

In the remainder of this section we will assume that each γ_σ^R has left adjoint, α_σ^R. The left adjoint of γ_σ^R can be constructed as:

$$\alpha_\sigma^R X = \sqcap\left\{a \in D_\sigma^K \mid X \subseteq \gamma_\sigma^R\ a\right\}$$

However, it is more useful to have an 'iterated' construction for the family $\alpha^R = \left\{\alpha_\sigma^R\right\}$:

Proposition 6.2 For each σ, τ, subset $F \subseteq [D_\sigma^I \to D_\tau^I]^2$, for each $a \in D_\sigma^K$:

$$\alpha_{\sigma \to \tau}^R\ F\ a = \alpha_\tau^R\left\{(f\ x, f'\ x') \mid (f, f') \in F, (x, x') \in \gamma_\sigma^R\ a\right\}$$

$\square$

We will say that c_σ^K is a *correct interpretation* for c_σ if $(c_\sigma^I, c_\sigma^I) \in \gamma_\sigma^R \, c_\sigma^K$. We will say further that c_σ^K is the *best* interpretation for c_σ if it is the minimum correct interpretation, since this guarantees that the set $\gamma_\sigma^R \, c_\sigma^K$ is as small as possible.

We can use the α_σ^R to derive best interpretations for the c_σ by defining:

$$abs_\sigma^R : D_\sigma^I \times D_\sigma^I \to D_\sigma^J$$
$$abs_\sigma^R(x, y) = \alpha_\sigma^R \{(x, y)\}$$

Proposition 6.3 For all σ, for all $x, y \in D_\sigma^I$, for all $a \in D_\sigma^K$

$$(x, y) \in \gamma_\sigma^R \, a \iff abs_\sigma^R(x, y) \sqsubseteq a$$

Proof: We observe that $(x, y) \in \gamma_\sigma^R \, a$ iff $\{(x, y)\} \subseteq \gamma_\sigma^R \, a$ and hence that $(x, y) \in \gamma_\sigma^R \, a \Longleftarrow \Longrightarrow \alpha_\sigma^R \{(x, y)\} \sqsubseteq a$, since α_σ^R left adjoint to γ_σ^R. $\qquad\square$

Thus $abs_\sigma^R(c_\sigma^I, c_\sigma^I)$ is the best interpretation for c_σ.

Observing that the α_σ^R preserve joins, it is straightforward to derive the following iterated construction for abs^R from that for α^R (proposition 6.2):

$$abs_{\sigma \to \tau}^R(f, g) \, a = \bigsqcup \left\{ abs_\tau^R(f\,x, g\,y) \mid abs_\sigma^R(x, y) \sqsubseteq a \right\}$$

We note that there is a striking similarity between our abs^R maps and the abs^S of [Abr90], but also that the abs^R are less well behaved than the abs^S in that in general they are not monotone.

7 Extending the Analysis

In this section we sketch how the analysis described in section 5 can be extended to a language including list types.

We extend the language L introduced in section 4 by adding the type *Alist* for each existing base type A (in what follows A, B will continue to range over the original base types) and by adding the constant $case_{B \to (A \to Alist \to B) \to Alist \to B}$ for each A, B.

We assume that the standard interpretation is extended so that D_{Alist}^I is the domain of finite, partial and infinite lists of elements of D_A^I, ordered in the usual way. The standard interpretation of a case constant is:

$$case_{B \to (A \to Alist \to B) \to Alist \to B}^I \, b \, f \, l = \begin{cases} \bot_B^I & \text{if } l = \bot_{Alist}^I \\ b & \text{if } l = [\,] \\ f\,x\,y & \text{if } l = x : y \end{cases}$$

There are numerous ways in which J might be extended, we consider a particularly simple example by way of illustration. The extension to list types is:

$$D_{Alist}^J = \{\text{BOT}, \text{ID}, \text{H}, \text{ALL}\} \text{ with BOT} \sqsubseteq \text{ID} \sqsubseteq \text{H} \sqsubseteq \text{ALL}.$$

The relation P is extended such that $\gamma_{Alist}^P \, \text{H} = E_H$, where H is the projection defined in the introduction.

The case constants are interpreted as follows:

$$case^J \, b \, h \, \text{BOT} = \text{BOT}$$
$$case^J \, b \, h \, \text{ID} = b \sqcup (h\,\text{ID}\,\text{ID})$$
$$case^J \, b \, h \, \text{H} = \begin{cases} b \sqcup (h\,\text{ID}\,\text{H}) & \text{if } h\,\text{BOT}\,\text{ID} = \text{BOT} \\ \text{ALL} & \text{otherwise} \end{cases}$$
$$case^J \, b \, h \, \text{ALL} = \begin{cases} \text{BOT} & \text{if } b = \text{BOT and } h = \bot_{A \to Alist \to B}^J \\ \text{ALL} & \text{otherwise} \end{cases}$$

Lemma 7.1 P satisfies property (M). $\qquad\square$

Proposition 7.2 Let σ range over types of the form $B \to (A \to Alist \to B) \to Alist \to B$. Then for each σ, case_σ^J is correct; i.e. $\text{case}_\sigma^J \sqsupseteq abs_\sigma^P(\text{case}_\sigma^I, \text{case}_\sigma^I)$. $\qquad\qquad$ □

Note: it is disappointing that we have been unable to show that the *case*^{J} are best rather than just correct. The proof of proposition 7.2 would go through with the inequality strengthened to equality in the case that for all σ, in addition to property (M) we had $\alpha_\sigma^P \circ \gamma_\sigma^P = id$ (equivalently, γ_σ^P injective). Although the property that $\alpha_\sigma^R \circ \gamma_\sigma^R = id$ is *not* inherited for arbitrary meet-preserving γ^R, the question of whether it holds for γ^P is still open.

7.1 Example

We will say that a function $f \in [D_{Alist}^I \to D_B^I]$ is *head-strict* if $f = f \circ H$, or equivalently, if $f : \gamma_{Alist}^P \text{ H} \Rightarrow \gamma_B^P \text{ ID}$.

The following example illustrates that our analysis can detect head-strictness. The standard interpretation of the following definition is czero^I, a function which tests whether or not a list of integers contains a 0:

$$czero = Y(\lambda f.\lambda l.\, \text{case false}$$
$$\lambda x.\lambda y.\, \text{cond } (x = 0)$$
$$\text{true}$$
$$(f\ y)$$
$$l\,)$$

The interpretation under J is the function czero^J, where:

$$czero^J\ a\ =\ \begin{cases} \text{ID} & \text{if } a = \text{H} \\ a & \text{otherwise} \end{cases}$$

Thus czero^I is head-strict.

8 Relationship to Other Analyses

In this section we consider the relationship between our analysis and the analyses of [WH87] and [BHA86, Bur87] in a little more detail.

8.1 Comparing PER and Projection Analyses

It is fairly easy to compare the kinds of questions which may be asked using pers with those which may be asked using projections. Proposition 2.3 shows that any question about a function f which can be asked using projections in form $\beta \circ f = \beta \circ f \circ \alpha$, can also be asked using pers in form $f : P \Rightarrow Q$. Since there are pers which do not correspond to projections, there are questions which can be asked using pers (and answered using abstract interpretation) which cannot be asked using projections.

On the other hand, it is difficult to compare a per-based *analysis* with a projection-based analysis. Our analysis is not restricted to a first-order language and so may be said to be more general than that of [WH87]. But the analysis of [WH87] is a backwards analysis, whereas ours is a forward analysis. This makes it hard to reason about the relative quality of the answers which may be obtained in the cases where both analyses are applicable. It is beyond the scope of this paper to attempt such a comparison (but see the paper "Towards Relating Forwards and Backwards Analyses" by John Hughes and John Launchbury, in this proceedings).

8.2 Comparing PER and Set Analyses

The analyses of [BHA86, Bur87] use abstract interpretation and can be proved correct in terms of logical relations of the form $R : I, K$, so that each $\gamma_\sigma^R a$ is a set. (Recall from section 4.2 that for $R : I, K$ the concretisation maps are defined by $\gamma_\sigma^R a = \left\{ x \in D_\sigma^I \mid R_\sigma(x, a) \right\}$.) Such analyses may be called set-based, in that they test for conditions of the form $f(X) \subseteq Y$, where X and Y are subsets of the domain and co-domain of f respectively. It is clear that questions such as whether f is constant, cannot be asked in this way. (We can ask whether f is the *particular* constant function which always returns e, for example, by asking whether $f(D) \subseteq \{e\}$, but we cannot just ask if f is constant.) We have seen that a per-based analysis *can* be used to ask such questions, posed in the form $f : P \Rightarrow Q$.

We now wish to establish that any set-based analysis using abstract interpretation can be expressed as one based on pers, thus demonstrating what is intuitively clear, that the use of pers gives us at strictly more power than the use of sets. To show this in a simple way, we concentrate on set-based analyses in which correctness is given by what [Abr90] calls a $\top$-*universal* logical relation, where $R : I, K$ is $\top$-universal iff for each type σ, D_σ^K has a greatest element $\top_\sigma^K$, and $\gamma_\sigma^R \top_\sigma^K = D_\sigma^I$. ($\top$-universality is an inherited property.)

If K and I are interpretations, related by a logical relation $R : I, K$, we define the logical relation $P(R) : I, I, K$ at the base types such that for all $x, y \in D_A^I$, and $a \in D_A^K$:

$$P(R)_A(x, y, a) \Longleftrightarrow (x = y) \wedge R_A(x, a).$$

Equivalently, we may define $P(R)$ at the base-types via the concretisation maps thus:

$$\gamma_A^{P(R)} a = \Delta(\gamma_A^R a),$$

where for any set X, $\Delta(X) = \{(x, x) \mid x \in X\}$.

Proposition 8.1 If $R : I, K$ is a $\top$-universal logical relation, then for all types σ, for all $a \in D_\sigma^K$

$$\gamma_\sigma^{P(R)} a = \Delta(\gamma_\sigma^R a).$$

□

Corollary 8.1.1 If $R : I, K$ is a $\top$-universal logical relation, then for all types σ, for all constants c_σ, c_σ^K is correct with respect to R iff c_σ^K is correct with respect to $P(R)$.   □

9   Conclusions

We have shown how partial equivalence relations can be used to describe properties of functions in a way that subsumes both the use of projections in [WH87] and the use of sets in [BHA86, Bur87].

In its relation to the use of projections, our work has three main advantages over [WH87]. Firstly, the use of pers fits in naturally with the use of logical relations, thus allowing us to develop an analysis in the form of an abstract interpretation with a very simple proof of correctness. Secondly, the use of pers extends smoothly to the higher order case (this is really another aspect of the first advantage). Lastly, we are able to formulate a test for strictness which does not involve lifting the domains (if nothing else, this has the attraction of relative simplicity).

The development of the material in this paper is far from complete. There are two areas in particular which we hope to be able to improve upon:

- Our failure to derive best interpretations for the $case_\sigma$ constants in section 7 highlights the fact that we have been unable to show that the γ_σ^P are injective. This implies that there may be 'redundant' points in the D_σ^J at higher types.

- The development of section 6.1 is lacking, in that it does not directly address the per structure inherent in the abstract interpretation. The use of the power set for the γ_σ^P also seems unsatisfactory since it ignores the domain structure of the D_σ^J. This raises the question of whether there is a class of pers which takes account of the underlying domain structure and which is appropriate to static program analysis (the class of 'good' pers of [AP90] is one possibility).

It seems likely that an investigation of the latter area will shed light on the former.

Acknowledgements

Thanks to Dave Sands and Thomas Jensen for the many hours of their time spent discussing the ideas presented in this paper. Thanks also to all those who reviewed this paper (particularly John Hughes), for their numerous constructive criticisms.

References

[Abr90]   S. Abramsky. Abstract interpretation, logical relations and Kan extensions. *Journal of Logic and Computation*, 1(1):5–39, 1990.

[AP90]   M. Abadi and G. Plotkin. A per model of polymorphism and recursive types. In *Logic in Computer Science*. IEEE, 1990.

[Asp90]   A. G. Asperti. *Categorical Topics in Computer Science*. PhD thesis, Università di Pisa, 1990.

[BHA86] G.L. Burn, C.L. Hankin, and S. Abramsky. Strictness analysis of higher-order functions. *Science of Computer Programming*, 7:249–278, November 1986.

[Bur87]   G.L. Burn. *Abstract Interpretation and the Parallel Evaluation of Functional Languages*. PhD thesis, Department of Computing, Imperial College of Science and Technology, University of London, 1987.

[Hug87]   R. J. M. Hughes. Backwards analysis of functional programs. DoC Research Report CSC/87/R3, University of Glasgow, March 1987.

[Lan71]   Saunders Mac Lane. *Categories for the Working Mathematician*. Springer-Verlag, Berlin, 1971.

[Myc81]   A. Mycroft. *Abstract Interpretation and Optimising Transformations for Applicative Programs*. PhD thesis, University of Edinburgh., 1981.

[WH87]   Philip Wadler and R.J.M. Hughes. Projections for strictness analysis. In *LNCS 274. Functional Programming Languages and Computer Architectures, Oregon, USA*, 1987.

Functional Programming with Relations

Graham Hutton
Department of Computing Science
Glasgow University, Scotland

December 1990

Abstract

While programming in a relational framework has much to offer over the
functional style in terms of expressiveness, computing with relations is less
efficient, and more semantically troublesome. In this paper we propose a
novel blend of the functional and relational styles. We identify a class of *causal
relations*, which inherit some of the bi-directionality properties of relations,
but retain the efficiency and semantic foundations of the functional style.

1 Introduction

In his ACM Turing Award Lecture, Backus presented a new style of programming,
in which programs are built piecewise by combining smaller programs [Backus78]. In
[Sheeran83], Sheeran showed how the same approach could be used to good effect in
VLSI design. In keeping with the special constraints of hardware, many designs have
a regular structure, with components communicating, often bi–directionally, only
with their immediate neighbours. With function composition as the main combining
form however, circuits with bi–directional data flow patterns tend to have rather
contorted descriptions in the functional style. This problem lead Sheeran to use
binary relations rather than functions as the underlying model of circuitry, thereby
removing the distinction between input and output which causes the problem in the
first place. An overview of the relational language *Ruby* is presented in Section 2.

Unfortunately, the many benefits of relations do not come for free. While relations have much to offer over functions for specification and refinement of a program
(see Section 2.4), when it comes to execution time, functions are clear winners. In
particular, with no inherent notion of data–flow, computing with relations is generally speaking much less efficient than computing with functions. Furthermore,
relational languages are not so semantically well behaved as their functional counterparts. For example, it is known that the standard fixed–point approach to recursion
does not naturally extend to the relational world.

In this paper, we propose a novel blend of the functional and relational styles. In
Section 3, we identify a class of functional or *causal* relations. Informally speaking,
a relation is causal if we can identify an "input" part of the relation, which uniquely

determines the remaining "output" part. Unlike functions however, the input part of a causal relation is not restricted to its domain, nor output part to the range; indeed, inputs and outputs may be interleaved throughout the domain and range. Furthermore, a causal relation may have many such functional interpretations. The intention is that a causal language brings some of the expressive power of a truly relational language, without incurring semantic and implementation problems. It is clear that many hardware style programs fall naturally into the causal class.

When two causal relations are composed, it is reasonable to expect that inputs on one side join with outputs on the other, and vice–versa. In Section 3.2 we find that this (and one other) restriction is in fact necessary to ensure that causal relations have the expected properties. Finally, in Section 4 we describe a simple system in which we may capture the functional ways in which a causal program may be used.

2 Programming in Hardware

In this section, we present an overview of the Ruby style of relational programming. The language is developed incrementally, beginning with a functional framework in 2.1, introducing streams in 2.2, structural recursion in 2.3, and finally, moving to relations in 2.4. Ruby itself is explained more fully in [Jones90b], where it is used in the stepwise derivation of many interesting hardware style programs.

2.1 Constructive programming

In the Miranda[1] style of functional programming, functions are commonly defined using abstraction (e.g. $f\,x = x+1$ defines a function which increments a number). In the FP [Backus78] style however, functions are built indirectly by combining other functions in various ways. Examples of such constructions include composition, defined by $f \circ g \triangleq \lambda x.\, f(g\,x)$, and product, defined by $f \times g \triangleq \lambda(x,y).\,(f\,x, g\,y)$. Later on in this section, concerns with the shape of a program lead us to use backward composition " ; ", defined by $f\,; g \triangleq g \circ f$, rather than the more usual forward composition " $\circ$ ".

Languages in which larger programs are built piecewise from smaller ones are sometimes known as *constructive* or *combinatory* languages. Similarly, the higher–order functions from which programs are built are often referred to as *combining forms*, or *combinators*[2] for short. Appart from FP itself, perhaps the most well known example of the constructive paradigm is the Bird–Meertens formalism [Bird88], also known as the "theory of lists".

It is well known that programming in the constructive style is a great aid to formal manipulation. In particular, the combining forms from which programs are built satisfy many useful algebraic laws, which can be used to derive and prove properties of programs. For example, it is easy to show that $(A\,; B) \times (C\,; D) = (A \times C)\,; (B \times D)$. In fact, many such theorems do not actually require an explicit

---

[1] Miranda is a Trademark of Research Software Ltd.
[2] Our informal use of this term is consistent with the standard λ–calculus meaning.

128

Figure 1: snd (fst not ; or) ; and

proof, their validity following from the types of the combining forms, under the observation that (parametric) polymorphism corresponds precisely to the notion of *naturality* in Category Theory. The idea that polymorphic type inference derives "free theorems" is developed in [Wadler89], and applied in the specific context of Ruby in [Sheeran89].

In the constructive style, it is quite natural to consider the *shape* of a program; the combining forms have both a behavioural and a pictorial interpretation [Sheeran81]. An example picture is given in Figure 1, with respect to the standard abbreviations fst $F \triangleq F \times id$ and snd $F \triangleq id \times F$. The identity for composition "id" corresponds to a notional wire in pictorial terms. Because information flow is most often from left to right in pictures, forwards composition " ; " is used rather than backwards composition " ∘ " in Ruby. Generalising from pictures, it is often useful to view a constructive program as a description of a process network or data flow graph, with primitive components communicating over channels.

2.2 Recursion and streams

Consider the factorial function. In a language like Miranda, where functions are most often built using abstraction, it may be defined recursively by:

$$
\begin{aligned}
fac \quad 0 \quad &= \quad 1 \\
fac \ (n+1) \quad &= \quad (n+1) * fac\ n
\end{aligned}
$$

In the constructive language FP, the corresponding program is:

$$fac \ = \ eq0 \rightarrow \overline{1} \ ; \ * \circ [id, fac \circ sub1]$$

where $eq0 = eq \circ [id, \overline{0}]$ and $sub1 = - \circ [id, \overline{1}]$. There is a however a problem with this style of recursion in our context. In FP, we may think of a program as the description of a *dynamic* network, in the sense that components may be freely created and destroyed at run–time. More formally (and in terms of pictures), the factorial program denotes an infinite network, corresponding to an infinite unwinding of the recursion.

While dynamic networks are fine for general purpose programming, in hardware we are restricted to entirely *static* networks. The reason is quite simple, the network is fixed once and for all when a circuit is fabricated on silicon. Components are not able to move around, duplicate or destroy themselves; explicit circuitry must be included for all eventualities which may arise.

In terms of programming style, the restriction to static networks means that *data dependent* recursion as used in the factorial example is not acceptable in our language. This restriction is the primary difference between "programming in hardware" and "programming in software".

Although infinite networks are not acceptable in a static language, there is nothing to stop us using *cyclic* networks. Consider a simple cyclic network – an and operator with its upper input driven from its own output. This may be cast as loop (and ; split) in Ruby notation. Assuming that all primitives are functional, it is clear that this program will deadlock, since the output is directly dependent upon itself. More formally, the constructive expression is equivalent to the recursive function $f = \lambda x.(x \wedge fx)$ in λ–style, which under least fixed-point semantics (and assuming strict conjunction) is in turn equivalent to $\lambda x.\bot$.

To allow programs involving cyclic networks to terminate, a notation of time is introduced into the language, through the use of *streams*. A stream has the same behaviour as a lazy list (i.e. only a prefix need be evaluated at any instant to allow computation to proceed), except that its elements are normally accessed by subscript, rather than by structural decomposition. A stream may be formally viewed as a mapping, with the natural numbers (representing time) as the domain.

To avoid deadlock in feedback programs, the first step is to lift all the primitives to the stream level, so that they operate pointwise over the components. For example, an and operator will now take a stream of booleans to a stream of their conjunctions. Now all we need do is ensure that at any moment, the output of feedback programs depends only upon their own value at strictly earlier instances in time. This is achieved by the introduction of a single sequential primitive, a unit delay, which returns its input value at time t as its output at time $t + 1$. Rather than filling the gap in the output at $t = 0$ with an undefined or fixed value such as $\bot$, we write D_s for a delay element whose first output is s. This gives us a direct form of control over the start–up phase in feedback programs.

Introducing a delay into our feedback example results in little change in the text of the constructive program, which now takes the form loop (snd D_T ; and ; split), where T denotes boolean *true*. However, the jump to streams results in a marked change to the analogous λ–style expression:

$$f\ x = \lambda t. \begin{cases} x_0 & \text{if } t = 0 \\ x_t \wedge f\ x\ (t-1) & \text{otherwise} \end{cases}$$

where x and the result of the function are streams of (i.e. mappings to) booleans. Note that T was carefully chosen as the starting value for the delay, such that $x_0 \wedge T$ simplifies to x_0 in the base case. Assuming strict conjunction again, this function clearly has least fixed point $\lambda x.(\lambda t. \bigwedge_{i=0}^{t} x_i)$. Thus, through the introduction of streams, and hence the delay primitive, the feedback program which previously denoted a non–terminating function now denotes a well defined boolean function which holds T until its input drops to F, after which it remains F for ever more, independent of subsequent input values.

From the programmer's point of view, the presence of streams means that combinational (time independent) and sequential (clocked) design is cast in a uniform framework. In particular, we can use the sequential primitive D as a buffer between combinational components, thereby introducing pipeline parallelism into our programs, in addition to the explicit parallelism of the "×" combining form.

2.3   Generic primitives

Many interesting hardware style (i.e. static) algorithms have a regular structure. For example, correlation (one of the most important signal processing algorithms) may be cast as a 2-dimensional array of simple binary components [Jones90b]. Since our language at present is itself entirely static, we would have to choose a particular size, and build such a grid explicitly using combining forms which stack components beside and above one another. While this approach would allow us to experiment with regular programs, it is far from satisfactory. Having multiple occurrences of the same combining forms and primitive cells would certainly hinder transformation and proofs. Furthermore, there is a danger in reasoning about fixed sized arrays; a theorem which holds for a particular instance (e.g. 3×3) may extend to some cases (e.g. odd-sized arrays), but not to the general case.

If the constructive style is to be practical, we must introduce some means to capture and manipulate regular structures, without reference to any particular size. How is this possible if all our programs must denote static networks? The key is to note that they need only be static at run-time, when the program is actually executed. It is perfectly acceptable to have dynamic primitives at compile-time, so long as we ensure that all programs are indeed of a fixed size when they come to be executed. At present, all our primitives are entirely static at compile-time.

A *generic* combining form denotes a family of fixed-sized networks, one for each instance of a regular pattern. For example, map in Ruby is a generalisation of the product construction "$\times$", such that (map R) denotes the infinite familily $\{R^n \mid n \in \mathbb{N}\}$, where R^n stands for the n-way product of R with itself. Generic plumbing such as zip (which interleaves two lists) are used to route data between generic components. In fact, inverse plumbing such as unzip is also useful. While generic plumbing and their inverse would normally have to be defined separately, in a relational language such as Ruby (see next section), one may be defined directly in terms of the other using relational inverse.

To ensure that generic programs are static at run-time, we introduce a new stage between compilation and execution. At *silicon-time*, the programmer will choose a particular size for the program, such that it may then be physically expanded to a fixed sized network. Thus, while $R \times R$ is static at compile-time, (map R) cannot be guaranteed to be static until run-time.

Since the compiler must now work with generic programs, the analysis phases during compilation have the opportunity to produce more general information. For example, we have devised a simple type system in which size information about generic programs is included in their types. Consider the program (tail ; halve), which knocks off the first element of a list, and splits the remainder into two equal length parts. In our system, the derived type $*^{2n+1} \rightarrow (*^n, *^n)$ captures precisely that this program only works properly with odd length lists.

Not surprisingly, generic primitives are defined recursively, on the structure (i.e. shape rather than content) of streams. Proofs involving generics naturally proceed by induction. For example, it is easy to show that (map R ; map S) = map (R ; S), a generalisation of the example theorem in Section 2.1. Just as for the simple static primitives, the validity of many theorems involving generics follows directly from their polymorphic types [Sheeran89].

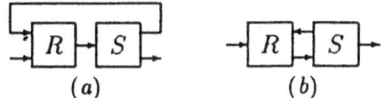

(a)　　　　(b)

Figure 2: Bi–directional communication between R and S

2.4 Relations

In keeping with the special constraints of hardware, many regular circuits make extensive use of bi–directional communication between components. For example, the systolic correlator in [Jones90b] has data flowing both rightwards and leftwards. While bi–directional communication can be achieved in the manner of Figure 2a, this breaks with the convention that constructive programs capture both shape and behaviour. In this sense, it would clearly be preferable to have components communicating directly, as in Figure 2b. Working in a functional language however, this is not directly possible, due to the uni–directional flow of data inherent in function composition.

While the data flow problem could be worked around by introducing a few special combining forms to capture bi–directional communication, a much more acceptable solution is to weaken the normal functional constraint, and allow inputs and outputs to be distributed throughout the domain and range of a program. In this manner, the standard composition operator " ; " may be used to combine any two components, regardless of whether they communicate bi–directionally or not. It is this observation which originally led Sheeran to consider using relations rather than functions, thereby removing the distinction between input and output entirely.

Not surprisingly, the jump to relations brings much more than bi–directionality properties. Since they are not biased towards a particular direction of data flow, relational combining forms tend to be more symmetric, and hence a single Ruby law often replaces a number of μFP laws. Furthermore, unlike in the (total) functional world, where only bijective functions may be inverted, every relation R has an inverse R^{-1}, defined[3] by $a \ R^{-1} \ b \triangleq b \ R \ a$. In terms of pictures, relational inverse corresponds to reflection of a program about the vertical axis.

The ability to invert programs means that many constructions which would normally have to be defined inductively may be defined quite naturally in terms of other related primitives. For example, the generic combining forms row and col tile components beside and above one another respectively; using inverse, one may be defined in terms of the other: col $R \triangleq (\text{row } R^{-1})^{-1}$. Defining components in this way also reduces the burden of proof. For example, any row theorem may be transformed into an analogous col theorem, without repeating the steps of the proof. It is interesting to note the similarity to the powerful notion of "duality" in Category Theory [Barr90], under which one proof yields two theorems.

Relational inverse has also proved useful in capturing abstraction and refinement steps in program derivation [Jones90a]. For example, given an initial word–level design, we can formally move down to a bit–level version by pushing the "refinement relation" bits (which relates numeric values to bit vectors) in from the left hand side of the program, and the "abstraction relation" bits^{-1} in from the right.

---

[3]In relational notation, a R b is simply a shorthand for $(a, b) \in$ R.

132

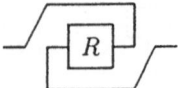

Figure 3: $R^{-1} \; \hat{=} \;$ left ; fst (snd R) ; right

While it is clear that many simple combining forms like fst may be defined in terms of others, it is perhaps surprising to find that in a relational framework, even such powerful constructs as loop and relational inverse may be defined in terms of simpler components. For example, Figure 3 shows how inverse may be defined using the plumbing relations[4] given by x left $((y,y),x)$ and $((x,y),y)$ right x. In fact, all (non–generic) components can be defined in terms of 4 basic constructs — composition " ; ", product "×", the delay element D, and a "spread" construction which allows us to represent combinational primitives and plumbing relations. This approach is developed in more detail in [Rossen90].

Since a function may be viewed as a restricted kind of relation, Ruby naturally admits a larger class of programs than μFP. For example, ignoring streams for simplicity, the program loop (and ; split) which was not acceptable in the functional framework of Section 2.2, has a perfectly well defined meaning as $\{(x,y) \mid y \equiv x \wedge y\}$ in Ruby, which simplifies to the relation $\{(F,F),(T,F),(T,T)\}$. Such programs are sometimes referred to as having non–deterministic behaviour, in the sense that a set of results may be produced for a given input value. In this case for example, T in the domain relates to both F and T in the range.

3   Causal Relations

Moving to relations is perhaps the most natural way to allow bi–directional communication over composition, but causes implementation and semantic problems. In particular, while relations are useful for specification and refinement of a design, the end product is normally functional, even though inputs and outputs may be distributed throughout the domain and range. With no inherent notion of data–flow, computing with relations is generally speaking much less efficient than computing with functions, even though most programs will in fact be used functionally. Furthermore, relational languages are not so semantically well behaved as their functional counterparts. For example, it is known that the standard fixed–point approach to recursion does not naturally extend to the relational world.

In this section, we consider how to get some of the expressive power of relations, without incurring the implementation and semantic problems. Our solution lies with what we shall call *causal relations*, a novel blend of the functional and relational styles. The intent is that we may use the full power of relations during program derivation, with the satisfaction of knowing that a final causal design has a functional style semantics, and may be implemented in an efficient manner.

[4]As shown in left/right, it is usual to omit " $\hat{=}$ T" from plumbing definitions.

3.1 Causality

We define a relation to be *causal* if we may identify an 'input part' of the relation, which totally and uniquely determines the remaining 'output part'. Unlike functions however, the input part is not restricted to the domain (left side) of a causal relation, nor output part to the range (right side); indeed, inputs and outputs may be interleaved throughout the domain and range.

For example, not = $\{(F, T), (T, F)\}$ is a causal relation, since the first component of each pair uniquely determines the second. Moreover, the second component also determines the first. This is perfectly acceptable; a causal relation may have many such functional interpretations. Conversely, $(or^{-1} ; and) = \{(F, F), (T, F), (T, T)\}$ is not causal, since no part of the relation uniquely determines the remainder. In particular, T in the domain relates to both F and T in the range; similarly for F in the reverse direction.

To capture precisely what me mean by causality, we use a slight modification of the "equivalence of spans" construction of binary relations [deMoor90]. We start by reviewing the standard construction of relations in terms of binary products.

Given sets A and B, their *cartesian product* is the set

$$A \times B \triangleq \{(a, b) \mid a \in A \land b \in B\}$$

together with *projection functions* $\pi_A : A \times B \to A$ and $\pi_B : A \times B \to B$, defined by

$$\pi_A \triangleq \lambda(a, b).a$$
$$\pi_B \triangleq \lambda(a, b).b$$

The construction is universal, in that given any other set W, together with total functions (we assume from now on that all functions are total) $f : W \to A$ and $g : W \to B$, there exists a unique *span*[5] $\langle f, g \rangle : W \to A \times B$, defined by

$$\langle f, g \rangle \triangleq \lambda x.(f x, g x)$$

such that $\langle f, g \rangle ; \pi_A = f$ and $\langle f, g \rangle ; \pi_B = g$, as shown in the diagram below.

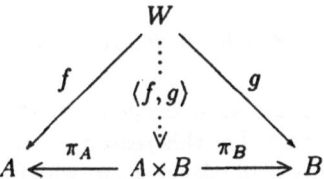

From the universality of the product, we deduce the useful law

$$h ; \langle f, g \rangle = \langle h ; f, h ; g \rangle$$

which we shall use without comment to simplify expressions involving spans. In this framework, a binary relation of type $A \leftrightarrow B$ is normally defined as a subset of $A \times B$.

---

[5] Normally, a span is defined as a pair of functions (f, g) with common domain, while $\langle f, g \rangle$ is called a *product function*. In this paper, for reasons of brevity, we prefer to call each $\langle f, g \rangle$ a span, citing the one-to-one correspondence between product functions and spans in our defense.

Since we are interested in functional relations however, we take a different route, modelling relations in terms of spans. The connection between the two is that the image of a span $\langle f, g \rangle : W \to A \times B$ is a relation of type $A \leftrightarrow B$, defined by

$$\{f, g\} \triangleq \{(f\,x, g\,x) \mid x \in W\}$$

Think of each $x \in W$ as a *witness* that $f\,x \in A$ is related by $\{f, g\}$ to $g\,x \in B$. While spans allow us to model relations in terms of functions, the representation is clearly not unique. We now proceed to define an equivalence relation "$\equiv$" on spans, such that if $\langle f, g \rangle : W \to A \times B$ and $\langle f', g' \rangle : W' \to A \times B$, then

$$\langle f, g \rangle \equiv \langle f', g' \rangle \quad \Leftrightarrow \quad \{f, g\} = \{f', g'\}$$

Given $R \triangleq \langle f : W \to A, g : W \to B \rangle$ and $R' \triangleq \langle f' : W' \to A, g' : W' \to B \rangle$, a *span morphism* $m : R \to R'$ is a function $m : W \to W'$, such that $\langle f, g \rangle = m ; \langle f', g' \rangle$.

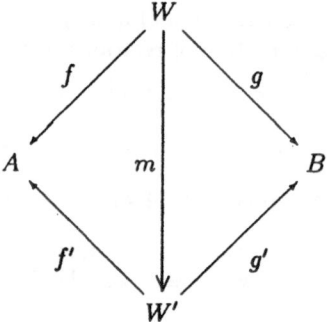

Span morphisms induce a pre–ordering "$\preceq$" on spans, defined by

$$R \preceq R' \triangleq \exists m : R \to R'$$

It is easy to see that $\{f, g\} \subseteq \{f', g'\}$ follows from $\langle f, g \rangle \preceq \langle f', g' \rangle$. Because "$\preceq$" is a pre–order, it can be extended to an equivalence relation on spans, defined by

$$R \equiv R' \triangleq R \preceq R' \wedge R' \preceq R$$

It follows immediately that two spans generate the same relation precisely when they are equivalent under "$\equiv$". For this reason, we model a relation not by a single span $\langle f, g \rangle$, but by its entire equivalence class, which we shall denote $[f, g]$.

Before considering causal relations in full, let us start with a simple case. Given a function $f : A \to B$, the span $\langle id_A, f \rangle$ determines the corresponding relation, $\{(a, f\,a) \mid a \in A\}$. In this manner, a relation $[f, g] : A \leftrightarrow B$ is functional from A to B precisely when there exists an $h : A \to B$, such that $\langle f, g \rangle \equiv \langle id_A, h \rangle$.

Causal relations are a generalisation of these functional relations, in that inputs are not restricted to the domain, nor outputs to the range. We start by defining what it means for a relation to be generated by a function.

Definition: Let $\langle s,t \rangle : I \to A \times B$ and $[f,g] : A \leftrightarrow B$, such that $\langle s,t \rangle \in [f,g]$. The span $\langle s,t \rangle$ is called a *functional interpretation* of the relation $[f,g]$ precisely when $\langle s,t \rangle = \langle id_I, h \rangle \,;\, \iota^{-1}$, where $h : I \to O$ is a total function, and $\iota : A \times B \to I \times O$ is a unique isomorphism.

In diagramatic form, everything fits as follows.

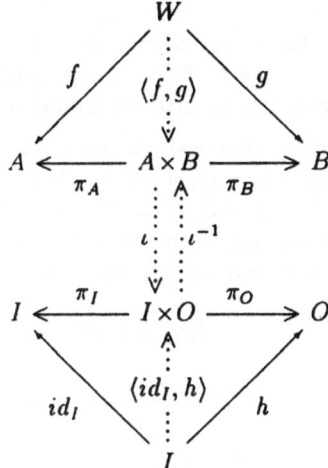

While the projections π_A and π_B decompose the product $A \times B$ into domain and range parts, the functions $\iota \,;\, \pi_I$ and $\iota \,;\, \pi_O$ allow us to decompose the relation into input and output parts, such that the first uniquely determines the second, as witnessed by the function $h : I \to O$. More precisely, it follows from definition of the span $\langle s,t \rangle$ and the universality of the product $I \times O$ that

$$\langle s,t \rangle \,;\, \iota \,;\, \pi_I \,;\, h = \langle s,t \rangle \,;\, \iota \,;\, \pi_O$$

The restriction to $I \times O$ being uniquely isomorphic to $A \times B$ ensures that the decomposition is purely structural. In particular, the familiar isomorphisms

$$A \times B \;\cong\; B \times A$$
$$A \times (B \times C) \;\cong\; (A \times B) \times C$$

confirm our intuition about how a relation may be permuted such that all the input parts are in the domain, and output parts in the range. The less well known $A \cong A \times 1$, where 1 is any singleton set, tells us that the unique $h : A \times B \to 1$ forms part of a functional interpretation of the full relation on $A \times B$.

Returning to our original motivation for functional interpretations, each such $\langle s,t \rangle$ allows us to generate the relation, just by looking at the input part, in that

$$\langle s,t \rangle \equiv \iota \,;\, \pi_I \,;\, \langle s,t \rangle \tag{1}$$

where $\iota \,;\, \pi_I$ picks out the input part of any pair in $A \times B$. The span morphisms which verify the equivalence are $\langle id_I, h \rangle \,;\, \iota^{-1}$ in the $I \to A \times B$ direction, and $\iota \,;\, \pi_I$ in the reverse direction. Naturally, $\langle s,t \rangle$ preserves the input part we supply, in that

$$\iota \,;\, \pi_I = \iota \,;\, \pi_I \,;\, \langle s,t \rangle \,;\, \iota \,;\, \pi_I$$

which follows immediately from the definition of $\langle s, t \rangle$. It is a useful exercise at this point to show that the $h : I \to O$ part of a functional interpretation is uniquely determined by the isomorphism ι. In other words, for each input/output decomposition, there is at most one function which precisely generates the relation.

While general relations may be modelled by an equivalence of spans, we will model a causal relation by a *non–empty equivalence of functional interpretations*. The fact that there may be many such interpretations just means that there may be many ways to generate the complete relation just by looking at some part of it; many ways to "drive the relation". Non–causal relations have no such functional interpretations, and hence do not fit into our model of causality.

To clarify our construction of causal relations, let us consider a simple example. Suppose we assert that the relation $[f, g] : X \leftrightarrow Y \times Z$ is really a function $h : X \times Z \to Y$ in disguise. If we take $I \triangleq X \times Z$, $O \triangleq Y$, and $\iota \triangleq \lambda\,(x, (y, z)) \,.\, ((x, z), y)$, our informal statement of the underlying functionality of the relation may be properly cast as the following equivalence of spans, where $\langle s, t \rangle \triangleq \langle id_I, h \rangle \,;\, \iota^{-1}$.

$$\langle f, g \rangle \equiv \langle s, t \rangle$$

Since $\langle s, t \rangle$ is a functional interpretation, it follows from property (1) that

$$\langle f, g \rangle \equiv \iota \,;\, \pi_I \,;\, \langle s, t \rangle$$

Using this equivalence, we can generate elements of the relation using the function h; given any $(x, (\perp, z))$ in $X \times (Y \times Z)$, where the value of $\perp$ is not important, we may produce an $(x, (y, z)) \in \{f, g\}$ as follows, where $y \triangleq h\,(x, z)$.

$$(x, (\perp, z)) \overset{\iota}{\longmapsto} ((x, z), \perp) \overset{\pi_I}{\longmapsto} (x, z) \overset{\langle id_I, h \rangle}{\longmapsto} ((x, z), y) \overset{\iota^{-1}}{\longmapsto} ((x, y), z)$$

3.2 Causality is not enough

While causality ensures that we only work with "functional relations", it is not the end of the story in itself. First of all, causal relations are not closed under composition. For example, both or^{-1} and and are causal, but $(\text{or}^{-1} \,;\, \text{and})$ is not, as we saw at the start of Section 3.1. Secondly, there are causal programs which involve non–functional data flow. For example, $(\text{and}^{-1} \,;\, \text{and})$ is equivalent to the identity relation on booleans (certainly a causal program), but operationally has non–functional flow of information between the two primitives. To ensure that causal programs are closed under composition, and have a functional semantics, we must restrict the way in which they are built. In particular, we require that programs are *well–directed*, and have no *unbroken loops*.

The composition $(R \,;\, S)$ is well–directed if all information flow is functional, in the sense that outputs in the range of R match with inputs in the domain of S, and vice–versa. For example, $(\text{and} \,;\, \text{not})$ is well–directed, since the output from the first component matches with the input of the second. Conversely, both $(\text{or}^{-1} \,;\, \text{and})$ and $(\text{and} \,;\, \text{and}^{-1})$ are ill–directed, due to a clash of inputs in the first case, and outputs in the second. In other words, both components in a composition must be used functionally in their own right, in addition to the functionality of the composition as a whole. In the next section, we describe a simple system in which it is possible to capture all the well–directed ways in which a causal program may be used.

While the direction constraint filters out most non–causal programs, some programs involving feedback slip through the net. For example, loop (and ; split) is well–directed, but as mentioned in Section 2.4, corresponds to the non–causal relation $\{(F,F), (T,F), (T,T)\}$. This problem is solved by insisting that all feedback loops must be broken by a delay element. For example, as we saw in Section 2.2, loop (snd D_T ; and ; split) is a perfectly valid causal program.

4 Directions

A relational program is causal if we can identify input and output parts. If internally, inputs and outputs match over composition, it is also well–directed. In the functional style, programs are automatically well–directed, since inputs are restricted to the domain, and outputs to the range. In moving to causal relations, we have removed the normal contextual distinction between input and output, so we now have an obligation to check that programs are indeed well–directed. In this section we describe a system in which it is possible to capture all the functional ways in which a causal program may be used. Examining directions provides considerable insight into the expressive power of causal relations.

4.1 Notation

Whereas types tell us what kind of data are expected, *directions* specify which parts of the data are inputs, and which are outputs. In general, since a causal relation R may have many functional interpretations, it has a *set* of directions, which we shall denote R^*. For example, we write not$^* = \{(\text{in}, \text{out}), (\text{out}, \text{in})\}$ to mean that the not relation is functional from domain to range, and range to domain.

In this setting, ill–directed programs such as (and;or^{-1}) correspond to the empty set of directions $\emptyset$. Following the terminology for types, a program with more than one direction will be called *polydirectional*.

4.2 What are directions?

While the directions for simple cases like and and not are intuitively obvious, it is important to understand precisely where such sets come from, and what they actually mean. We use the simple order–theoretic notion of a *lattice*; a set A, equipped with a partial-ordering "$\sqsubseteq$", least/greatest elements $\perp_A$ and $\top_A$, and binary meet and join operations, denoted by "$\sqcap$" and "$\sqcup$" respectively.

Under the ordering out $\sqsubseteq$ in, the primitive directions $\{\text{out}, \text{in}\}$ form a 2–point lattice, which we shall call D. It is easy to see that the lattice structure is closed under the product construction. For example, $D \times D$ is a lattice, with $\perp_{D \times D} = (\text{out}, \text{out})$ and $\top_{D \times D} = (\text{in}, \text{in})$, under the ordering $(a, b) \sqsubseteq (c, d) \triangleq a \sqsubseteq c \wedge b \sqsubseteq d$.

Just as $\perp$ and $\top$ are often used without subscript to denote the least and greatest elements in any lattice, so we will sometimes use out and in to denote the least and greatest elements of any product lattice constructed from D.

Recall from Section 3.1 that a causal relation $[f,g] : A \leftrightarrow B$ is modelled as an equivalence of functional interpretations $\langle s,t \rangle \in [f,g]$, such that each $\langle s,t \rangle$ has the form $\langle id_I, h \rangle \,;\, \iota^{-1}$, where $h : I \to O$ is a total function, and $\iota : A \times B \to I \times O$ a unique isomorphism. In this context, it is clear that directions have the same shape as the type of a causal relation, in that

$$[f,g]^* \subseteq [\![A \times B]\!]$$

where $[\![\cdot]\!]$ is a function which converts arbitrary products into direction lattices, such that for example $[\![X \times (Y \times Z)]\!] = D \times (D \times D)$. If we extend each ι to an isomorphism $[\![\iota]\!] : [\![A \times B]\!] \to [\![I \times O]\!]$ in the natural manner, it is clear that each functional interpretation $\langle s,t \rangle$ corresponds to a single direction, given by

$$\langle s,t \rangle^* \triangleq [\![\iota]\!]^{-1}\,(\top_{[\![I]\!]}, \perp_{[\![O]\!]})$$

Returning to our example at the end of Section 3.1, where $\langle s,t \rangle$ is a functional interpretation of a relation of type $X \leftrightarrow Y \times Z$, with $\iota = \lambda\,(x,(y,z))\,.\,((x,z),y)$, we obtain a direction corresponding to the span $\langle s,t \rangle$ as follows.

$$
\begin{aligned}
\langle s,t \rangle^* &= [\![\iota]\!]^{-1}\,(\top_{[\![I]\!]}, \perp_{[\![O]\!]}) \\
&= [\![\iota]\!]^{-1}\,(\top_{[\![X \times Z]\!]}, \perp_{[\![Y]\!]}) \\
&= [\![\iota]\!]^{-1}\,(\top_{D \times D}, \perp_D) \\
&= [\![\iota]\!]^{-1}\,((\mathsf{in}, \mathsf{in}), \mathsf{out}) \\
&= ((\mathsf{in}, \mathsf{out}), \mathsf{in})
\end{aligned}
$$

4.3 Composition

In lattice terminology, two elements a and b are said to be *complementary* if $a \sqcup b = \top$ and $a \sqcap b = \perp$. For example, $(\mathsf{in}, \mathsf{out})$ is the complement of $(\mathsf{out}, \mathsf{in})$ in $D \times D$. It is not hard to see that every direction has a unique complement. In Section 3.2 we said that for the composition $(R\,;S)$ to be *well–directed*, outputs in range of R must match with inputs in the domain of S, and vice–versa. Clearly then, two directions are only compatible over composition if they are complementary. Using this insight, we may now state precisely all the well–directed ways in which $(R\,;S)$ may be used:

$$a\,(R\,;S)^*\,d \triangleq (a\,R^*\,b) \wedge (c\,S^*\,d) \wedge (b \sqcup c = \mathsf{in}) \wedge (b \sqcap c = \mathsf{out})$$

For example, although not has two possible directions in isolation, only the left–to–right orientation is acceptable in $(\mathsf{and}\,;\mathsf{not})^* = \{((\mathsf{in}, \mathsf{in}), \mathsf{out})\}$. In keeping with the fact that not is its own inverse, we have $(\mathsf{not}\,;\mathsf{not})^* = \{(\mathsf{in}, \mathsf{out}), (\mathsf{out}, \mathsf{in})\} = \mathsf{not}^*$.

4.4 Plumbing relations

Plumbing relations are (parametrically) polymorphic, in that they may be viewed as a collection of monomorphic instances which, in some sense, behave in the same way.

Not surprisingly, plumbing relations are also polydirectional. By way of example, let us consider id, the identity element for composition. We start with the simplest instance, id_A, where A is an atomic type such as the booleans or integers. While it may appear that $\text{id}_A{}^* = D \times D$, this is not in fact the case. Since id is the identity for composition, we have that $(\text{id} \,;\, \text{id}) = \text{id}$. Clearly this property should also hold for directions. However, working with $\text{id}_A{}^* = D \times D$, we find that $(\text{id}_A \,;\, \text{id}_A)^* = \{(\text{out}, \text{in}), (\text{in}, \text{out})\} \neq \text{id}_A{}^*$. This situation arises because the rule for (;) insists that inputs match with outputs. Thus, we conclude that $\text{id}_A{}^* = \{(\text{out}, \text{in}), (\text{in}, \text{out})\}$.

Consider a more complicated instance, $\text{id}_{A \times A}$. A simple calculation shows that the directions for this expression may be given in terms of those for its components:

$$
\begin{aligned}
\text{id}_{A \times A}{}^* &= (\text{id}_A \times \text{id}_A)^* \quad [\times \text{ is a functor}] \\
&= \text{id}_A{}^* \times \text{id}_A^* \quad [* \text{ distributes over } \times]
\end{aligned}
$$

Using this equivalence, and recalling the definition of product on relations, $(a, b)\, R \times S\, (c, d) \triangleq a\, R\, c \wedge b\, S\, d$, we find that there are 4 directions for $\text{id}_{A \times A}$. While $(\text{out}, \text{out}) \leftrightarrow (\text{in}, \text{in})$ and its complement are perfectly intuitive, $(\text{in}, \text{out}) \leftrightarrow (\text{out}, \text{in})$ and its complement may seem a little strange, since they allow data flow in opposite directions over id at the same time. In a relational setting however, this kind of behaviour is quite natural. For example, we could imagine $(T, \bot)$ id $(\bot, F)$ resolving to $((T, F), (T, F))$. In general then, it is not hard to see that id^* is precisely the pairs of complementary directions:

$$
\text{id}^* \triangleq \{(a, b) \mid a \sqcup b = \text{in} \,\wedge\, a \sqcap b = \text{out}\}
$$

In terms of hardware, the polymorphic identity relation id may be viewed as an arbitrary bus of wires. Under this interpretation, $a \sqcup b = \text{in}$ means that each component wire is driven at least once, $a \sqcap b = \text{out}$ means that each wire is driven at most once; together they ensure that each wire has precisely one value.

5   Further Developments

In this paper, we presented causal relations as a new programming paradigm, particularly well suited to the bi–directionality demands of "programming in hardware". We have given a model of causality, in terms the equivalence of spans construction of relations, and presented a simple system in which we may examine various functional interpretations of a causal relation. At the present moment however, it is not clear how to incorporate the direction and feedback constraints into our model, and hence give a proof of closure under composition. Although the mathematical aspects of causality are not yet complete, we have taken some steps towards a causal implementation of the Ruby language.

In Prolog, bi–directional communication may be achieved using logic variables. In particular, if two processes A and B wish to communicate in both directions, A may pass a stream of pairs to B, with one component of each pair being a message from A, and the other being an uninstantiated variable, in which B may reply. Just as direction inference is important for causal languages, so mode annotations (and to a lesser extent mode inference) is important in logic languages. It is clearly important to investigate the use of bi-directionality in logic programming, and bring out the differences and similarities to our causal relational approach.

Acknowledgements

This work was completed under the SERC *Relational Programming* project. Thanks are due to my supervisor Mary Sheeran, for direction and encouragement, and to Carsten Kehler Holst, Sebastian Hunt and David Murphy for comments.

References

[Backus78]   John Backus. *Can programming be liberated from the von Neumann style? A functional style and its algebra of programs.* CACM vol. 9, August 1978.

[Bird88]   Richard Bird. *Lectures on constructive functional programming.* Oxford University, 1988. (PRG-69)

[Barr90]   Michael Barr and Charles Wells. *Category Theory for Computing Science.* Prentice Hall, 1990.

[deMoor90]   Oege de Moor. *Categories, Relations and Dynamic Programming.* Programming Research Group, Oxford University 1990. (PRG–TR–18–90)

[Jones90a]   Geraint Jones and Mary Sheeran. *Relations and refinement in circuit design.* Proc. BCS FACS workshop on refinement (ed. Carroll Morgan), Hursley, January 1990.

[Jones90b]   Mary Sheeran and Geraint Jones. *Circuit design in Ruby.* Formal Methods for VLSI Design (ed. Staunstrup), Elsevier Science Publications (Amsterdam), 1990.

[Rossen90]   Lars Rossen. *Formal Ruby.* Formal Methods for VLSI Design (ed. Staunstrup), Elsevier Science Publications (Amsterdam), 1990.

[Sheeran81]   Mary Sheeran. *Functional geometry and integrated circuit layout.* M.Sc. dissertation, University of Oxford, 1981.

[Sheeran83]   Mary Sheeran. *μFP – an algebraic VLSI design language.* D.Phil. thesis, Oxford University, 1983. (PRG-39)

[Sheeran89]   Mary Sheeran. *Categories for the working hardware designer.* Hardware specification, verification and synthesis: Mathematical aspects (ed. Leeser et al), Springer LNCS, 1989.

[Wadler89]   Phil Wadler. *Theorems for Free!* Proc. Conference on Functional Programming and Computer Architecture, London, Springer 1989.

Abstract Interpretation *vs.* Type Inference A Topological Perspective.

Thomas P. Jensen[*]

Imperial College[†]

Abstract

The connection between abstract interpretation and type inference is investigated. A list of analyses is examined and a framework for comparing the two kind of analyses is sketched. The framework is based on the notion of Stone duality and Domain Logic.

1 Introduction

Abstract interpretation is a method of analysing the run-time behaviour of a program by interpreting the program over a domain of abstract values. The values in the abstract domain represent the properties which the analysis is intended to detect. The concrete values are related to the abstract values by means of an abstraction function such that a concrete value is mapped to an abstract value only if it has the property described by the abstract value. The *correctness* of the analysis amounts to show that the result of interpreting a program over the abstract domain is a property of the result obtained by interpreting the program over the concrete domain. Strictness analysis, which is aimed at detecting when *lazy* evaluation can be replaced by the less expensive *eager* evaluation, is an example of an analysis which has been expressed successfully as an abstract interpretation.

Type inference is the process of deducing a type for a program given a type system for the programming language. Originally, types were viewed as a means of ensuring the consistency of a program; in Milner's words: "Well-typed programs can't go wrong" and so the original purpose of type inference was to eliminate the need for run-time checking when executing programs. Recently, several program analyses have been formulated as type inference over a non-standard type system. This suggests a change in the view of types: Types are properties of values and type

---

[*]This work was supported by ESPRIT grant BRA 3124 SEMANTIQUE

[†]Author's address: Dept. of Computing, Imperial College, 180 Queen's Gate, London SW7 2BZ, U.K.

systems are axiomatisations of the rules for deducing properties about programs. Using this approach analyses such as usage-count analysis [8], binding-time analysis [4] and strictness analysis [7] have been developed. For this class of analyses, the question of correctness is that of *soundness* of the type system (*i.e.*, what can be deduced is correct with respect to the semantics of the language), whereas the quality of the analysis corresponds to the question of *completeness* (*i.e.*, can the formal system establish all facts, which are true in the semantic interpretation).

An obvious question is how the two analysis methods are related. Are there analyses that can be expressed in one framework but not the other? Can a proof of correctness for an analysis in abstract interpretation style be converted to account for a type-inference style analysis and *vice versa*? In order to relate the two approaches we need a means of establishing a connection between points in a domain and the properties they satisfy. Viewing properties as subsets of domains this leads us into topological considerations. As shown in [1] there is a natural way of associating points in a domain with Scott-open subsets of the domain known as Stone duality [5]. This kind of duality forms the basis for our developments reported here.

2 Program analysis via type inference

In this section we give a list of program analyses, that are formulated in type inference style and discuss the validity and implementation of this kind of analysis.

- *Strictness analysis.* Strictness analysis via type inference was presented in [7]. It defines a language of strictness types by:

$$\tau ::= \phi \mid \Box \mid \tau \rightarrow \tau$$

  where ϕ is the type of a non-terminating expression, $\Box$ is the type of all expressions and $\tau_1 \rightarrow \tau_2$ is the type of all functions mapping arguments of type τ_1 to results of type τ_2. Thus *e.g.*, the type $\phi \rightarrow \phi$ expresses that a function is strict. It is now possible to define a type system for inferring types of composite expressions from the types of their free variables.

- *Binding-time analysis.* Binding-time analysis is used in a partial evaluator to decide whether the value of an expression in a program will be known given some partial knowledge about the input to the program. A binding-time analysis for untyped λ-calculus using type inference is given in [6]. An expression can either have type *static* indicating that it is computable by the partial evaluator or type *dynamic* in which case it cannot be reduced.

- *Linear types.* Wadler in [8] describes an analysis for the λ-calculus that determines whether a value is used *exactly* once in a term. The language of linear types is given by:

$$\tau ::= {}_i K \mid K \mid \tau \multimap \tau \mid \tau \rightarrow \tau$$

where K stands for any base type. The type $_¡K$ is assigned to values that are used *exactly* once in the term. Similarly, the type $\tau \multimap \tau$ is assigned to functions that use their argument *exactly* once. The type inference scheme for linear types differs from normal type inference in that it is now necessary to take the union of the environments when combining terms rather than their unification. Linear types can be seen as information about how many times a value is used when evaluating an expression. This kind of information is of use in optimising the storage use of a program.

An analysis should always be *safe* with respect to the semantics of the language. For an analysis given by inference rules this means that only formulas valid in the semantics should be derivable. This is known as *soundness* of the inference system. The present work can be seen as a step towards developing a general framework for establishing the soundness of the above mentioned analyses.

An analysis should also be implementable. Part of the success for inference-like analyses is due to the fact that there is a reasonably efficient algorithm given in [3] that implements the inference system. We shall not discuss implementation any further, but just mention that an implementation of an inference system also requires a proof of soundness and completeness, which in this case means that the implementation finds exactly the formulas provable in the inference system. In [7] the implementation of the type system is proven correct in this respect, whereas the relation to the semantics is not treated.

3   Stone dualities and program logics

The question underlying the theory of Stone Duality is how a topological space X relates to its lattice of open subsets denoted by ΩX. As ΩX is closed under finite meets (= intersection) and arbitrary joins (= union) and furthermore is distributive, this naturally leads to abstract algebraic structures satisfying these three conditions. Such structures are called *frames* and form a category **FRM** where the morphisms are mappings distributing over finite meets and infinite joins. The above mentioned question is answered by setting up a contravariant adjunction between **TOP**, the category of topological spaces, and **FRM**.

$$\Omega : \textbf{TOP} \to \textbf{FRM}$$

$$\text{pt} : \textbf{FRM} \to \textbf{TOP}$$

where $\text{pt}(A)$ is the set of completely prime filters[1] over A. The set $\text{pt}(A)$ can be topologised by taking sets of completely prime filters of the form $U_a = \{x \in \text{pt}(A) \mid a \in x\}$ as open sets. This is all verified in [5] p. 39-42.

The adjunction involves a natural transformation

$$\eta_X : X \to \text{pt}(\Omega(X))$$

---

[1] A *filter* is a subset F of A, which is upwards closed. It is a *prime* filter if it is closed under finite meets. It is a *completely* prime filter if it is inaccessible by joins, *i.e.*, $\bigsqcup d_i \in F \Rightarrow \exists d_n : d_n \in F$

which relates an element x of X to the collection of opens that contains x. If the adjunction is an equivalence, then η_X is an isomorphism that to an arbitrary completely prime filter of opens assigns a point that determines that filter. Thinking of opens as properties this is the kind of correspondence we need in order to say that points are determined by the properties they satisfy. In other words we seek spaces where to every completely prime filter there exists a unique point such that the filter arises as the set of opens that contains this point. Spaces satisfying this requirement are called *sober*.

Domains are topological spaces when given the Scott topology. Algebraic domains are furthermore sober in their Scott-topology. SFP domains have the further property that the compact-opens $K\Omega(X)$ (= upwards closures of a finite set of finite elements) form a basis which is closed under intersection, *i.e.*, the space is coherent. The significance of this is that the equivalence reduces to

$$K\Omega : \mathbf{CohSp} \to \mathbf{DLat}$$

$$\mathbf{Spec} : \mathbf{DLat} \to \mathbf{CohSp}$$

where **DLat** is the category of distributive lattices and $\mathbf{Spec}(A)$ is the set of prime filters over a distributive lattice A. For domains this means that we have an isomorphism:

$$\eta_D : D \to \mathbf{Spec}(K\Omega(D))$$

where

$$
\begin{aligned}
\eta_D(d) &= \{O \in K\Omega(D) \mid d \in O\} \\
\eta_D^{-1}(\mathcal{F}) &= \bigsqcup\{d \mid \uparrow(d) \in \mathcal{F}\}
\end{aligned}
$$

Distributive lattices can be viewed as algebraic formulations of logical theories and based on this fact, Abramsky in [1] developed his Domain Logic where a (very rich) language, in addition to its usual denotational interpretation, is described via a program logic operating with formulas of the form

$$P \vdash \varphi$$

where P is a term of some type σ in the language and φ denotes an element of the lattice of compact-opens of the domain corresponding to type σ. The formula $P \vdash \varphi$ means that P satisfies property φ, or, in spatial terms, the denotation of P belongs to the open set corresponding to φ. The main result is that the two interpretations are equivalent in the sense that:

$$\eta_D^{-1}(\{\varphi \mid P \vdash \varphi\}) = [\![P]\!]$$

i.e., the denotation of P corresponds by Stone Duality to the set of properties we can prove to hold for P using the Domain Logic. This is a strengthened form of a "Soundness & Completeness" result for the program logic.

4 Perspective

The Stone duality described in the previous section operates on open sets. The open sets are usually identified with *observable* properties of programs, such as termination. Thus a termination analysis would fit into this framework. There are, however, analyses which are more oriented towards the negation of observable properties. The basic property in strictness analysis is non-termination so in this case it seems natural to base a comparison between the two kind of analyses on the complement of open sets *viz.* closed sets. This suggests that we use a slightly different duality result based on the lattice of closed sets.

Further work should also examine the possibility of using a simpler Stone duality than the one between distributive lattices and coherent, algebraic domains. As most abstract interpretations only use finite lattices it should be possible to profit from the duality between algebraic lattices and meet-semilattices, which should give a simpler (and perhaps more efficient?) program logic. This needs further study. Finally it would be interesting to describe the logical counterpart to the abstraction mappings relating concrete values in the standard domains to abstract values in the abstract domains.

References

[1] S. Abramsky. Domain theory in logical form. In *Symposium on Logic In Computer Science*, pages 47–53. Computer Society Press of the IEEE, 1987.

[2] G.L. Burn, C.L. Hankin, and S. Abramsky. The theory and practice of strictness analysis for higher order functions. *Science of Computer Programming*, 7:249–278, 1986.

[3] L. Damas and R. Milner. Principal type schemes for functional programs. In *Proc. ACM Symposium on Principles of Programming Languages*, pages 207–212, 1982.

[4] C. K. Gomard. Partial type inference for untyped functional programs. In *Lisp and Functional Programming '90*, pages 282–287. ACM, 1990.

[5] P. T. Johnstone. *Stone Spaces*, volume 3 of *Cambridge Studies in Advanced Mathematics*. Cambridge University Press, Cambridge, 1982.

[6] Neil D. Jones, Carsten K. Gomard, Anders Bondorf, Olivier Danvy, and Torben Mogensen. A self-applicable partial evaluator for the lambda calculus. In *International Conference on Computer Languages*. IEEE Computer Society, 1990.

[7] T-M Kuo and P. Mishra. Strictness analysis : A new perspective based on type inference. In *Proc. 4th. Int. Conf. on Functional Programming and Computer Architecture*. ACM Press, 1989.

[8] Philip Wadler. Linear types can change the world. Unpublished. Dept. of Computing, Univ. of Glasgow. 22 p., 1989.

Analysing Heap Contents in a Graph Reduction Intermediate Language

Thomas Johnsson*

Abstract

We present an algorithm to analyse graph reduction intermediate code, which gives a safe approximation to what kind of nodes (i.e. which constructors and/or unevaluated function applications) pointers might point to at different points in the program. The analysed language, called GRIN (Graph Reduction Intermediate Notation) is a procedural language with operations essentially the same as in the G-machine but in the form of three address instructions. The analysis uses a framework developed by Jones and Muchnick for dealing with the interprocedural flow of information.

The analysis is motivated by our work on transforming the intermediate code of a lazy functional program, in particular doing in-line substitutions of calls to EVAL. An example of this is presented.

1 Introduction

In this paper we present an algorithm to analyse graph reduction intermediate code, similar to G-machine code. The purpose is to find out what kind of nodes on the heap pointer might point to, at different point in the program. We call our analysis 'Constructor Analysis', because all objects of the heap, be they canonical or not, are like constructors in a functional language which can be subjected to case analysis by the graph reduction intermediate language. The analysis is done by abstract interpretation of the graph reduction code, using a finite approximation of the heap.

We think that the analysis is general enough to be useful in many contexts; our motivation for developing the analysis is our (so far tentative) ideas on transforming graph reduction intermediate code. We will therefore begin the paper by presenting these ideas, in section 2. In section 3 we develop the analysis, and in section 4 we discuss some implementation details of the analysis.

2 Background: transforming graph reduction code

Over the last half decade, substantial advances have been made in compiling lazy functional languages for conventional architectures: the G-machine [Joh84], the

---

*This work was done in Glasgow, supported by an SERC visiting fellowship. Author's current address: Department of Computer Science, Chalmers Univerity of Technology, S-412 96 Göteborg, Sweden. email: johnsson@cs.chalmers.se

Spineless G-machine [BPR88], the Spineless Tagless G-machine [PS89], the TIM [FW87], and the work done at Yale[BHY89]. We now have the situation where for many applications it is possible to write programs in a lazy functional language which execute almost as fast as the corresponding ones written in an imperative language.

However, it is still much more difficult to generate code for functional languages than for traditional imperative ones. The underlying reason is of course that there is a much closer match between imperative languages and conventional architectures — indeed, traditional languages have evolved from the machine languages, and the essential features of the machine language are thus present in conventional imperative languages: a memory location becomes a variable in the language, machine instructions become sequences of statements, etc.

Closer inspection reveals other reasons for the efficiency difference, however. In an imperative program where efficiency matters the bulk of the work is done in relatively big procedures, and calls and returns to and from other procedures are relatively rare. In such situations there are well-established techniques for generating good code making good use of the machine resources, e.g. keeping frequently accessed variables in machine registers.

On the other hand, a typical functional program consists of a large number of small functions; indeed, programmers are encouraged to write their programs that way. Therefore the code from such programs has a much higher call/return overhead.

A common 'trick' in dealing with the high call/return overhead[1] is to make function bodies bigger by doing in-line expansion of function calls, i.e., replace a function application by an instance of the body of the applied function. But alas this is straightforward only if the applied function has a 'known' body; this rules out functions passed as arguments, for instance.

An additional difficulty with this is caused by laziness: In addition to the calls visible in the source program, the intermediate code for lazy programs also has a lot of calls to EVAL, i.e. the run-time system routine that reduces an unevaluated function application (a closure) to its value. As a result, it is nearly impossible to make good use of machine registers, since so little happens between calls in the code.

In this section we present some ideas for doing in-line substitution of 'unknown' calls also, notably the ubiquitous calls of EVAL (which implies a call of unknown code since in general we do not know what closure we have at each EVAL call). The aim is to make the code for function bodies 'bigger', and make calls and returns occur less frequently; this will reduce the overhead of calls and returns, and in general improve the conditions for a code generator by doing more computations between calls, thus enabling the code generator to keep more entities in machine registers.

Once we have done an in-line substitution, other improving transformations present themselves. We will, for instance, be able to do a transformation which is analogous to what the Spineless Tagless G-machine does at run-time with its vectored return mechanism.

---

[1]Tail calls do not have the high cost of calls we are talking about here, since they can be implemented by jumps and no context information (i.e. register contents) needs to be saved/restored.

2.1 The intermediate language

The intermediate language dealt with in this paper, called GRIN (Graph Reduction Intermediate Notation), is essentially a procedural version of the G-machine code, with the G-machine instructions in the form of three-address code [ASU86] instead of stack operations, thus always binding the result of an operation to a new name.

A functional language compiler compiles a program in the form of supercombinators (global recursive functions) into GRIN code. We shall illustrate compilation and transformation of the following functional program, which produces a list of prime numbers using the sieve of Eratosthenes algorithm.

```
upto m n = if m>n then [] else m : upto (m+1) n
filter p l = case l in
             []     -> []
             (x:xs) -> if x 'mod' p = 0
                       then filter p xs
                       else x : filter p xs
sieve l = case l in
          []     -> []
          (x:xs) -> x : sieve (filter x xs)
result = sieve (upto 2 1000)
```

Apart from the GRIN code for each supercombinator, the compiler must also emit a procedure main which builds the graph for the expression being the value of the program and then calls print:

```
main(){ t1' = basicconst 2
        t1 = constr [Cint t1']
        t2' = basicconst 1000
        t2 = constr [Cint t2']
        t3 = constr [Fupto t1 t2]
        t4 = constr [Fsieve t3]
        call print(t4)
}
```

The values of the variables are either pointers to nodes on the heap, or basic values (integers or booleans); as a convention basic-values variables will end with a prime, e.g. t1'. The operation t1' = basicconst 2 binds t1' to the basic value 2. (In all other GRIN instructions the arguments must be variables.) A variable being bound means that it is in scope in the rest of the statement list; variables are never reassigned. The operation t1 = constr [Cint t1'] builds a constructor node with the tag Cint on the heap and binds a pointer to it to t1. In general, nodes on the heap consist of a tag (e.g. Cint, Fupto) and a sequence of fields of pointers or basic values. Nodes represent either canonical forms i.e. values (our convention will be that their tags begin with the letter C) or closures i.e. unevaluated function applications (with tags beginning with F).

As an aid in understanding GRIN code we can, if we like, give a procedure a functional reading in a strict first-order functional language. Thus main would then be the function:

```
main(theheap) = let t1' = 2  in
                let (t1,theheap) = constr theheap "Cint" [t1']  in
```

```
             let t2' = 1000  in
             let (t2,theheap) = constr Cint [t2']  in
             let (t3,theheap) = constr Fupto [t1,t2]  in
             let (t4,theheap) = constr Fsieve [t3]  in
                    print(theheap,t4)
```

The basic three address code form of the GRIN code as shown above is what the compiler and transformer manipulates, but mostly in this paper we will find it too cumbersome to write, so we will allow ourselves the use of some syntactic sugar. Thus we could write main as follows:

```
main(){ t = constr [Fsieve [Fupto [Cint 2] [Cint 1000]]]
        call print(t)
```

print is the top level procedure that prints the value of the program and thus drives the execution of the entire program:

```
print(l){
    call EVAL(l)
    case l of
    Cnil -> ;
    Ccons x xs ->
        call EVAL(x)
        split x [Cint x']; printint x'
        call print(xs)
}
```

For the sake of simplicity we have assumed that the value of a program is always a list of integers. The operation call EVAL(l) reduces the graph pointed to by the variable l to its value (the procedure EVAL will be given below). The case l statement inspects the node pointed to by l, and control is transferred to the corresponding point. If the node is a cons, the head and tail components of the cons node are bound to the variables x and xs respectively. The split statement is like a one-armed case, used when a node can only be of one form. The printint instruction prints an integer value.

The EVAL procedure emitted by the compiler scrutinizes a node; if the node is canonical then nothing is done (i.e. EVAL returns), and if noncanonical, calls the corresponding procedure that does the actual graph reduction work.

```
EVAL(N){
    case N in
    Cnil          -> ;
    Ccons x xs    -> ;
    Cint i'       -> ;
    Fupto m n     -> call upto(m,n,N)
    Ffilter p l   -> call filter(p,l,N)
    Fsieve l      -> call sieve(l,N)
}
```

The case statement in the EVAL procedure must enumerate all constructors of all data types of the original program, as well as all unevaluated function applications ever built.

150

The procedure for each supercombinator takes the arguments from the node and a pointer to the node itself, which will be updated eventually with its value.[2] Thus the GRIN code for upto is:

```
upto(m,n,N){
    call EVAL(m); split m [Cint m']
    call EVAL(n); split n [Cint n']
    if m'>n' then
        update N [Cnil]
    else
        update N [Ccons m [Fupto [Cint (m'+1)] n]]
}
```

Above, the line

```
        update N [Ccons m [Fupto [Cint (m'+1)] n]]
```

is syntactic sugar for

```
        t1' = basicconst 1
        t2' = basicop +(m',t1')
        t1 = constr [Cint t2']
        t2 = constr [Fupto t1 n]
        update N [Ccons m t2]
```

Note that above we compute the expression m+1 and build a Cint node for it directly, instead of building a closure for m+1. This is safe to do because m has been evaluated previously in the same procedure. Finally, the filter and sieve functions get translated into the following GRIN procedures.

```
filter(p,l,N){
    call EVAL(l)              (*)
    case l of
    Cnil ->
        update N [Cnil]
    Ccons x xs ->
        call EVAL(x); split x [Cint x']
        call EVAL(p); split p [Cint p']
        if x' mod p' = 0 then
            call filter(p,xs,N)
        else
            update N [Ccons x [Ffilter p xs]]
}
sieve(l,N){
    call EVAL(l)
    case l of
    Cnil        -> update N [Cnil]
    Ccons x xs -> update N [Ccons x [Fsieve [Ffilter x xs]]]
}
```

As an aid to our intuition, figure 1 shows the first few reduction steps of this program.

---

[2]This is exactly what is on the G-machine stack at the beginning of the G-code for a function.

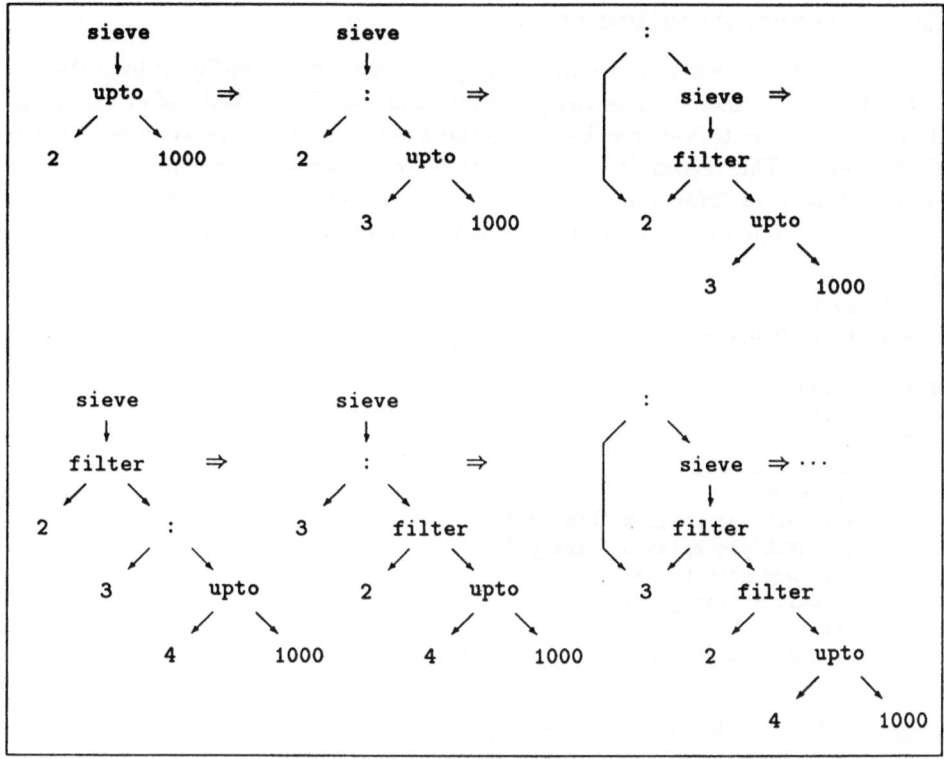

Figure 1: Some reduction steps in the execution of the primes program.

152

2.2 A transformation scenario

We we shall illustrate our transformation approach by doing in-line substitution of the call to EVAL marked (*) in the procedure filter above. But before doing the actual in-line substitution, we shall split the filter into two procedures, filter and filter2. The reason for this is that later on we will be copying the code following this call EVAL into many places, so replacing the code by a (tail) call prevents some code explosion during the transformations that follows.

```
filter(p,l,N){
    call EVAL(l)              (*)
    call filter2(p,l,N)
}
filter2(p,l,N){
    case l of
    Cnil ->
        update N [Cnil]
    Ccons x xs ->
        call EVAL(x); split x [Cint x']
        call EVAL(p); split p [Cint p']
        if x' mod p' = 0 then
            call filter(p,xs,N)
        else
            update N [Ccons x [Ffilter p xs]]
}
```

Let us now do the in-line substitution of the call marked (*). The procedure filter now looks like this:

```
filter(p,l,N){
    case l of{
    Cnil          -> ;
    Ccons x xs    -> ;
    Cint i'·      -> ;
    Fupto m n     -> call upto(m,n,l)
    Ffilter p2 l2 -> call filter(p,l2,l)
    Fsieve l2     -> call sieve(l2,l)
    }
    call filter2(p,l,N)                    *
}
```

The case statement in the procedure EVAL, being the general purpose evaluation dispatch procedure, must of course enumerate all constructors that could ever be subjected to EVAL. However, at the vast majority of calls to EVAL, only a subset of these constructors are can possibly occur. As should be obvious from figure 1, the only possible second argument of filter is an upto closure or another filter closure. So at this point we can actually remove all entries is the above case statement except the Fupto and Ffilter cases; however, for illustratory purposes we shall also keep the Cnil and the Ccons cases. Information about what possible constructors each variable might point to at different program points can be obtained from the analysis that is the main subject of this paper; see section 3.

To continue with our transformation example, we move the 'continuation' of the case statement in filter, the line marked with a * above, into each branch of of the case statement:

```
filter(p,l,N){
    case l of{
    Cnil            -> call filter2(p,l,N)        *
    Ccons x xs      -> call filter2(p,l,N)
    Fupto m n       -> call upto(m,n,l)
                       call filter2(p,l,N)
    Ffilter p2 l2 -> call filter(p2,l2,l)
                       call filter2(p,l,N)
    }
}
```

Let us now expand the call marked * above:

```
filter(p,l,N){
    case l of
    Cnil            -> case l of
                       Cnil ->
                           update N [Cnil]
                       Ccons x xs ->
                           call EVAL(x); split x [Cint x'];
                           call EVAL(p); split p [Cint p']
                           if x' mod p' = 0 then
                               call filter(p,xs,N)
                           else
                               update N [Ccons x [Ffilter p xs]]
    Ccons x xs      -> call filter2(p,l,N)
    Fupto m n       -> call upto(m,n,l)
                       call filter2(p,l,N)
    Ffilter p2 l2 -> call filter(p2,l2,l)
                       call filter2(p,l,N)
}
```

Now consider the two nested case statement above; they test on the same variable, 1. Obviously, we can simplify the whole thing to:

```
filter(p,l,N){
    case l of
    Cnil            -> update N [Cnil]
    Ccons x xs      -> call filter2(p,l,N)        *
    Fupto m n       -> call upto(m,n,l)
                       call filter2(p,l,N)
    Ffilter p2 l2 -> call filter(p2,l2,l)
                       call filter2(p,l,N)
}
```

Exactly the same thing can be made to happen at the line * above, to get:

```
filter(p,l,N){
    case l of
    Cnil            -> update N [Cnil]
    Ccons x xs      -> call EVAL(x); split x [Cint x'];
                       call EVAL(p); split p [Cint p']
                       if x' mod p' = 0 then
                           call filter(p,xs,N)
                       else
                           update N [Ccons x [Ffilter p xs]]
```

```
    Fupto m n      -> call upto(m,n,1)                              *
                      call filter2(p,1,N)
    Ffilter p2 12 -> call filter(p2,12,1)
                      call filter2(p,1,N)
}
```

What we have achieved so far is to remove the overhead of the call to EVAL when 1
is already canonical.

To continue our example, we shall now expand the call * to upto above.

```
filter(p,1,N){
    case 1 of
    ....
    Fupto m n      -> call EVAL(m); split m [Cint m']
                      call EVAL(n); split n [Cint n']
                      if m'>n' then
                          update 1 [Cnil]
                      else
                          update 1 [Ccons m [Fupto [Cint (m'+1)] n]]
                      call filter2(p,1,N)
    ....
}
```

We now move the call to filter2 into the two branches of the if, and then expand
the filter2 call in the then branch:

```
filter(p,1,N){
    case 1 of
    ....
    Fupto m n      -> call EVAL(m); split m [Cint m']
                      call EVAL(n); split n [Cint n']
                      if m'>n' then
                          update 1 [Cnil]
                          case 1 of                                *
                          Cnil ->
                              update N [Cnil]
                          Ccons x xs ->
                              call EVAL(x); split x [Cint x']
                              call EVAL(p); split p [Cint p']
                              if x' mod p' = 0 then
                                  call filter(p,xs,N)
                              else
                                  update N [Ccons x [Ffilter p xs]]
                      else
                          update 1 [Ccons m [Fupto [Cint (m'+1)] n]]
                          call filter2(p,1,N)
    ....
}
```

Consider the case statement at * above. Since 1 has just been updated to Cnil on
the previous line, the case statement simplifies to just the Cnil case:

```
filter(p,1,N){
    case 1 of
    ....
```

```
    Fupto m n    -> call EVAL(m); split m [Cint m']
                    call EVAL(n); split n [Cint n']
                    if m'>n' then
                        update l [Cnil]
                        update N [Cnil]
                    else
                        update l [Ccons m [Fupto [Cint (m'+1)] n]]
                        call filter2(p,l,N)
    ....
}
```

The same thing can also be done to the else branch:

```
filter(p,l,N){
    case l of
    ....
    Fupto m n    -> call EVAL(m); split m [Cint m']
                    call EVAL(n); split n [Cint n']
                    if m'>n' then
                        update l [Cnil]
                        update N [Cnil]
                    else
                        t = constr[Fupto [Cint (m'+1)] n]
                        update l [Ccons m t]
                        call EVAL(m); split m [Cint m']
                        call EVAL(p); split p [Cint p']
                        if m' mod p' = 0 then
                            call filter(p,t,N)
                        else
                            update N [Ccons m [Ffilter p t]]
    ....
}
```

It is possible to further simplify the above code. Firstly, the EVALs of m, n and p are not necessary, since they always point to Cint nodes; the analysis in section 3 should be able to determine this. Secondly, the inner split m [Cint m'] is redundant since the split has already been done earlier in the procedure. Thirdly, the update of the Fupto node with its value via the variable l is not necessary since it is not shared and thus cannot be used any further (this should be apparent from figure 1); this requires some kind of sharing analysis to discover [Hud87]. The result is:

```
filter(p,l,N){
    case l of
    ....
    Fupto m n    -> split m [Cint m']
                    split n [Cint n']
                    if m'>n' then
                        update N [Cnil]
                    else
                        split p [Cint p']
                        if m' mod p' = 0 then
                            call filter(p,t,N)
                        else
                            update N [Ccons m [Ffilter p [Fupto [Cint (m'+1)] n]]]
    ....
}
```

156

What goes on here is analogous to what happens in the Spineless Tagless G-machine at run-time: When an EVAL is followed by a case, in calling EVAL a vector of return addresses is passed, one for each constructor in the data type. When EVAL is about to return a cons, say, EVAL puts the head and tail components in predetermined registers and returns via the cons entry in the return vector. In our case, the code for the cons entry of filter follows directly after the update 1 [Ccons m t] (which was subsequently found to be redundant). What we gained by this was that some further simplification of the code was possible.

Our work on transforming graph reduction code in the manner described is so far only in its initial stages, and many questions are as yet unanswered. Possibly the most crucial question is: which calls shall we expand in-line, and which shall we leave unaltered? Obviously, undiscriminated in-line expansion leads to huge or infinite code expansion. But there is also no point in improving parts of the program which do not add significantly to the total running time of the program. An attractive possibility that we intend to investigate the feasibility of, is to let the transformation process be guided by run-time profiling from a previous run, so that effectively only the common and thus time-consuming parts of the program are improved.

3 The Constructor Analysis

We now come to the main subject of this paper: the constructor analysis. The purpose of the analysis is to give a safe approximation to what possible constructors pointers might point to, for all points in the program.

The GRIN language is an imperative one with procedures, so we must deal with the interprocedural flow of information, i.e., across calls and returns. In [JM82, section 3–] Jones and Muchnick presents a general framework for doing just this. So 'all we have to do' is to plug in our specific language into their framework. This framework requires the program to be in the form of a flow chart; section 3.1 presents the appropriate syntactic domains. Section 3.2 gives the semantics of GRIN in a form required by the framework. In section 3.3 we develop an approximate collecting interpreter using the Jones&Muchnick recipe.

A central problem we encounter is that we need to approximate the heap and pointers into the heap. In the exact semantics the heap is an arbitrarily big data object, and at each cons point in the GRIN program we can in principle get an arbitrary number of different pointers into the heap. In dealing with this problem we have borrowed ideas from [Hud87]. This is elaborated on further in section 3.3.

3.1 Syntactic domains

For the purpose of this analysis, the program is in the form of a flowchart, i.e., a directed graph where the nodes (called program points q) contain basic GRIN statements. In the statements the successor program points are embedded. The syntax we use is the following.

$$
\begin{array}{rcl}
x, f & \in & Var \qquad\qquad \text{(Variables)}\\
q & \in & Q \qquad\qquad \text{(Program points)}\\
K & \in & Con \qquad\quad\ \text{(Constructor names)}\\
op & \in & Op \qquad\qquad \text{(Basic operators +, - etc.)}\\
\pi & \in & Prog = Q \to Stmt \quad \text{(Programs)}\\
s & \in & Stmt \text{ where}
\end{array}
$$

$$
\begin{array}{rcl}
s & ::= & x = \mathtt{constr}\langle K\ x_1, \cdots, x_m\rangle; q'\\
& | & \mathtt{update}\, x\ \langle K\ x_1, \cdots, x_m\rangle; q'\\
& | & \mathtt{split}\, x\ \langle K\ x_1, \cdots, x_m\rangle; q'\\
& | & x = \mathtt{basicop}\, op_i\ x_1 \cdots x_m; q'\\
& | & x = \mathtt{basicconst}\, c; q'\\
& | & \mathtt{if}\, x\, \mathtt{then}\, q'\, \mathtt{else}\, q''\\
& | & \mathtt{case}\, x\, \mathtt{of}\ (K_1, q_1) \cdots (K_m, q_m)\\
& | & \mathtt{stop}\\
& | & \mathtt{call}\, q_p(\, x_1, \cdots, x_m)(f_1, \cdots, f_m); q'\\
& | & \mathtt{return}
\end{array}
$$

Programs to be analysed are on the form of a mapping π from program points to statements. The left column of the program in appendix A gives the primes program on this form. It should be noted that the **case** statement does not bind variables to components of the node; a separate **split** is required to do that. The second variable list in the **call** statement contains the names of the formal parameters (thus no procedure head is required, and it makes the semantics slightly simpler).

3.2 An interpreter for GRIN

Adhering to the Jones&Muchnick framework, we first give the (exact) semantics of GRIN code in the form of an interpreter. Our semantics domains are the following.

$$
\begin{array}{rcl}
l & \in & Loc \qquad\qquad\qquad \text{(Locations i.e. pointers into the heap)}\\
v & \in & Val = Bas + Loc\\
\rho & \in & Env = Var \to Val \quad \text{(Environments)}\\
\sigma & \in & Store = Loc \to Node\\
& & Node = Con \times Val^*
\end{array}
$$

The total state of the interpreter is a stack of triples

$$
S = \langle q_1, \rho_1, \sigma_1\rangle : \langle q_2, \rho_2, \sigma_2\rangle : \cdots : \langle q_n, \rho_n, \sigma_n\rangle : [\,]
$$

The current control point, current environment and the current store are q_1, ρ_1 and σ_1. The state associated with a certain point q is the state just before executing the statement at point q. The remainder of the stack contains saved stack pointers, environments and states; thus $\langle q_2, \rho_2, \sigma_2\rangle : \cdots : \langle q_n, \rho_n, \sigma_n\rangle : [\,]$ was the current (total) state just before the current procedure was entered.[3]

---

[3]It may seem a bit strange to save stores σ on the stack, but that is what the framework prescribes.

The semantics of the `constr` instruction is as follows (in what follows instructions will always be enclosed in $[\![\ ]\!]$).

$$\langle q, \rho, \sigma \rangle : S \text{ and } \pi q = [\![\, x = \text{constr}\langle K\ x_1, \cdots, x_m \rangle; q'\,]\!]$$
$$\Rightarrow \langle q', \rho[x \mapsto u], \sigma[u \mapsto \langle K\ \rho x_1 \cdots \rho x_m \rangle] \rangle : S \text{ where } u = unusedloc(\sigma)$$

where u is a previously unused location in the store, and the node $\langle K\ \rho x_1 \cdots \rho x_m \rangle$ is put there. (The notation $\cdots [x \mapsto \cdots]$ denoted updating of environments and stores.)

The semantics of `update` is:

$$\langle q, \rho, \sigma \rangle : S \text{ and } \pi q = [\![\, \text{update}\ x\ \langle K\ x_1, \cdots, x_m \rangle; q'\,]\!]$$
$$\Rightarrow \langle q', \rho, \sigma[\rho x \mapsto \langle K\ \rho x_1 \cdots \rho x_m \rangle] \rangle : S$$

The `split` instruction binds the component values $v_1 \cdots v_m$ of a node to variables $x_1 \cdots x_m$:

$$\langle q, \rho, \sigma \rangle : S \text{ and } \pi q = [\![\, \text{split}\ x\ \langle K\ x_1, \cdots, x_m \rangle; q'\,]\!]$$
$$\Rightarrow \langle q', \rho[x_1 \mapsto v_1, \cdots, x_m \mapsto v_m], \sigma \rangle : S \text{ where } \langle K\ v_1 \cdots v_m \rangle = \sigma(\rho x)$$

It is assumed that the node always has the right form (which it will if the compiler has emitted correct GRIN code).

The semantics of the `basicconst` and `basicop` are as follows.

$$\langle q, \rho, \sigma \rangle : S \text{ and } \pi q = [\![\, x = \text{basicop}\ op_i\ x_1 \cdots x_m; q'\,]\!]$$
$$\Rightarrow \langle q', \rho[x \mapsto \mathcal{B}[\![\, op_i\,]\!](\rho x_1, \cdots, \rho x_m)], \sigma \rangle : S$$

$$\langle q, \rho, \sigma \rangle : S \text{ and } \pi q = [\![\, x = \text{basicconst}\ c; q'\,]\!]$$
$$\Rightarrow \langle q', \rho[x \mapsto \mathcal{C}[\![\, c\,]\!]], \sigma \rangle : S$$

We assume that the semantics of the basic values operators and constants are given by semantic functions $\mathcal{B}$ and $\mathcal{C}$ which we do not specify further.

The remaining instructions have the following semantics.

$$\langle q, \rho, \sigma \rangle : S \text{ and } \pi q = [\![\, \text{if}\ x\ \text{then}\ q'\ \text{else}\ q''\,]\!]$$
$$\Rightarrow \langle \text{if}\ \rho x = True \text{ then } q' \text{ else } q'',\ \rho, \sigma \rangle : S$$

$$\langle q, \rho, \sigma \rangle : S \text{ and } \pi q = [\![\, \text{case}\ x\ \text{of}\ (K_1, q_1) \cdots (K_m, q_m)\,]\!]$$
$$\Rightarrow \langle q_i, \rho, \sigma \rangle : S \text{ where } \langle K_i\ \cdots \rangle = \sigma(\rho x)$$

$$\langle q, \rho, \sigma \rangle : S \text{ and } \pi q = [\![\, \text{stop}\,]\!]$$
$$\Rightarrow \langle q, \rho, \sigma \rangle : S$$

$$\langle q, \rho, \sigma \rangle : S \text{ and } \pi q = [\![\, \text{call}\ q_p(\ x_1, \cdots, x_m)(f_1, \cdots, f_m); q'\,]\!]$$
$$\Rightarrow \langle q_p, \rho[f_1 \mapsto \rho x_1, \cdots, f_m \mapsto \rho x_m], \sigma \rangle : \langle q, \rho, \sigma \rangle : S$$

$$\langle q_1, \rho_1, \sigma_1 \rangle : \langle q, \rho, \sigma \rangle : S \text{ and } \pi q_1 = [\![\, \text{return}\,]\!]$$
$$\Rightarrow \langle q', \rho, \sigma_1 \rangle : S \text{ where } \pi q = [\![\, \text{call}\ \cdots (\ \cdots)(\cdots); q'\,]\!]$$

3.3 An approximate collecting interpreter

Still instantiating our particular domains into the Jones&Muchnick framework, a state

$$S_1 = \langle q_1, \rho_1, \sigma_1 \rangle : \cdots : \langle q_n, \rho_n, \sigma_n \rangle : [\,]$$

in our interpreter will then be described (approximated) by a quadruple

$$\hat{S}_1 = \langle q_1, \hat{\rho}_1, \hat{\sigma}_1, t \rangle$$

where $\hat{\rho}_1$ represents ρ_1, $\hat{\sigma}_1$ represents σ_1, and $t = token(\hat{S}_2)$. Here $\hat{S}_2$ describes (approximates) the state just before entry to the current procedure, i.e.

$$S_2 = \langle q_2, \rho_2, \sigma_2 \rangle : \cdots : \langle q_n, \rho_n, \sigma_n \rangle : [\,]$$

Thus our *state descriptions* $\hat{S}$ are elements of

$$\hat{\Sigma} = Q \times \widehat{Env} \times \widehat{Store} \times T$$

The tokens $t \in T$ are the key to the approximation of the interprocedural flow of information, and by choosing different sets we can increase or decrease the precision (and the execution time) of the analysis.

The result of our analysis will be a *computation description* δ, a subset of $\hat{\Sigma}$, a safe description of all reachable program states.

State descriptions with the same program points q and tokens t will be merged to one state description, i.e., if $\hat{S}_1 = \langle q, \hat{\rho}_1, \hat{\sigma}_1, t \rangle \in \delta$ and also $\hat{S}_2 = \langle q, \hat{\rho}_2, \hat{\sigma}_2, t \rangle \in \delta$ then we replace $\hat{S}_1$ and $\hat{S}_2$ by $\langle q, \hat{\rho}_1 \sqcup \hat{\rho}_2, \hat{\sigma}_1 \sqcup \hat{\sigma}_2, t \rangle$ in δ.

Each of the simulation rules the we will give shortly will be of the form

> if $\langle q, \hat{\rho}, \hat{\sigma}, t \rangle \in \delta$ and $\pi q = [\![\cdots]\!]$ (and ...)
> then $\{\langle q', \hat{\rho}_1, \hat{\sigma}_1, t \rangle\} \sqsubseteq \delta$

This is a closure property. The computational implications of this is that if during the computation of δ we already have a quadruple $\langle q', \hat{\rho}_2, \hat{\sigma}_2, t \rangle$ in δ then we replace $\langle q', \hat{\rho}_2, \hat{\sigma}_2, t \rangle$ by $\langle q', \hat{\rho}_1 \sqcup \hat{\rho}_2, \hat{\sigma}_1 \sqcup \hat{\sigma}_2, t \rangle$ in δ. This process is iterated until a fixpoint is reached.

Much of the flexibility of the Jones&Muchnick framework lies in the wide choice of tokens available to us; almost any function $token(q, \rho, \sigma, t)$ will work. At one extreme, it is possible to get an *exact* description of the computation by choosing all the abstract domains to be equal to the concrete ones and by using the token function $token(q, \rho, \sigma, t) = (q, \rho, \sigma, t)$; the token will then be isomorphic to the rest of the stack, i.e., $\langle q_2, \rho_2, \sigma_2 \rangle : \cdots : \langle q_n, \rho_n, \sigma_n \rangle : [\,]$. In practice, however, one will do well by choosing something simple. We will use either of

$$token(q, \rho, \sigma, t) = 1$$
$$token(q, \rho, \sigma, t) = q$$
$$token(q, \rho, \sigma, t) = take\ N\ (q : t)$$

In the first case the analysis will not distinguish at all between the information from different calling points of procedures. In the second case this distinction will be made to one level of calls, and in the third case to N levels of calls. We avoid complications in the implementation of the analysis (see section 3.4) by not letting *token* depend on $\hat{\rho}$ or $\hat{\sigma}$.

We will now be more specific about our abstract domains. Using an idea from [Hud87], for abstract locations we will use a domain of bounded locations $\{1, 2, \cdots maxloc\}$ where *maxloc* is the total number of occurrences of constr GRIN code instructions. Each such occurrence of a constr instruction generates the same abstract location $\hat{l}$ every time it is executed. For convenience we will assume the constr instruction is annotated with the abstract location it generates, e.g., x = constr$_3$⟨Ccons y z⟩ generates 3. In fact we can use this annotation for the exact semantics as well, if in the exact semantics we have a location generator for *every* constr instruction. Then constr$_l$ would then generate the pair (l, i) where i is the next unused i for that particular constr. We can then conveniently write the *Abs* and *Conc* functions as

$$Abs(l, i) \equiv l$$
$$Conc\ l \equiv \{(l, i) | i \in Nat\}$$

The abstract domains we use are the following.

$$\hat{l} \in \widehat{Loc}$$
$$\widehat{Val} = \{BAS\} + \widehat{Loc}$$
$$\hat{v} \in \hat{V} = \mathrm{P}(\widehat{Val})$$
$$\hat{\rho} \in \widehat{Env} = Var \to \hat{V}$$
$$\hat{\sigma} \in \widehat{Store} = \widehat{Loc} \to \mathrm{P}(\widehat{Node})$$
$$\widehat{Node} = Con \times \hat{V}^*$$

Abstract stores contain *sets of* abstract nodes, where each component of an abstract node is a *set* of abstract values (which will be either $\{BAS\}$ or sets of abstract locations). In the store, for each location there will be only one node value for each particular constructor. That is, if we need to add the abstract node $\langle K\ \hat{v}_1 \cdots \hat{v}_m \rangle$ to a location that already has the node $\langle K\ \hat{v}'_1 \cdots \hat{v}'_m \rangle$ then we replace $\langle K\ \hat{v}'_1 \cdots \hat{v}'_m \rangle$ by $\langle K\ \hat{v}_1 \cup \hat{v}'_1 \cdots \hat{v}_m \cup \hat{v}'_m \rangle$.[4]

It will be useful to have an auxiliary function *addtostore* which to a set (list) of locations adds an abstract node (*addtostore* is used in the rules for constr and update):

$$addtostore(\hat{\sigma}, [\hat{l}_1, \cdots, \hat{l}_n], \langle K\ \hat{v}_1 \cdots \hat{v}_m \rangle) =$$
$$\hat{\sigma}[\ \hat{l}_1 \mapsto \hat{\sigma}\hat{l}_1 \sqcup \langle K\ \hat{v}_1 \cdots \hat{v}_m \rangle,$$
$$\vdots$$
$$\hat{l}_n \mapsto \hat{\sigma}\hat{l}_n \sqcup \langle K\ \hat{v}_1 \cdots \hat{v}_m \rangle$$
$$]$$

where

$$(ns \cup \langle K\ \hat{v}'_1 \cdots \hat{v}'_m \rangle) \sqcup \langle K\ \hat{v}_1 \cdots \hat{v}_m \rangle = (ns \cup \langle K\ \hat{v}_1 \cup \hat{v}'_1 \cdots \hat{v}_m \cup \hat{v}'_m \rangle)$$

---

[4] Another way to look at it would be that each location in the abstract store contains mappings $Con \to \hat{V}^*$, and for nodes that 'are not there' this mapping would return $[\emptyset, \cdots, \emptyset]$, i.e. a list of empty sets.

It will also be useful to have an auxiliary function to extract the argument list of the single abstract node value from S (coming from $\hat{\sigma}\hat{l}$) such that the node tag is K:

$$S \downarrow K = (\hat{v}_1, \cdots, \hat{v}_m)$$
$$\text{where}\{(\hat{v}_1, \cdots, \hat{v}_m)\} = \{ \ (\hat{v}_{i1}, \cdots, \hat{v}_{im_i})$$
$$\mid \ \langle K_i \ \hat{v}_{i1}, \cdots, \hat{v}_{im_i} \rangle \in S \text{ and } K_i = K \}$$

We have now developed sufficient machinery to formulate our specific simulation rules from the general recipe provided by the Jones&Muchnick framework.

First we shall look at intraprocedural actions with a single entry and a single exit – i.e., the sequential flow of control instructions. Let us just for the moment regard the ρ and σ components of a state description as a pair. Then for the intraprocedural action

$$q \longrightarrow \boxed{f} \longrightarrow q'$$

i.e. with a single exit, where f is a transfer function in $\widehat{Env} \times \widehat{Store} \to \widehat{Env} \times \widehat{Store}$ (this pattern matches the instructions constr, update, split, basicop and basicconst), we obtain the following (general) simulation rule (for further details on how this was obtained we refer the reader to [JM82]):

if $\langle q, (\hat{\rho}, \hat{\sigma}), t \rangle \in \delta$
then $\{(q', Abs\{f(\rho, \sigma) | (\rho, \sigma) \in Conc(\hat{\rho}, \hat{\sigma})\}, t)\} \sqsubseteq \delta$

from which we should be able to simply calculate the abstract rules for the sequential flow of control instructions. The approximation rules for the remaining instructions, i.e. if, case, call and return are straightforward adaptations of the rules given in [JM82].

if $\langle q, \hat{\rho}, \hat{\sigma}, t \rangle \in \delta$ and $\pi q = [\![x = \text{constr}_l \langle K \ x_1, \cdots, x_m \rangle; q']\!]$
then $\{(q', \hat{\rho}[x \mapsto [\hat{l}]], addtostore(\hat{\sigma}, [\hat{l}], \langle K \ \hat{\rho}x_1, \cdots, \hat{\rho}x_m \rangle), t)\} \sqsubseteq \delta$

if $\langle q, \hat{\rho}, \hat{\sigma}, t \rangle \in \delta$ and $\pi q = [\![\text{update } x \ \langle K \ x_1, \cdots, x_m \rangle; q']\!]$
then $\{(q', \hat{\rho}, addtostore(\hat{\sigma}, \hat{\rho}x, \langle K \ \hat{\rho}x_1, \cdots, \hat{\rho}x_m \rangle), t)\} \sqsubseteq \delta$

if $\langle q, \hat{\rho}, \hat{\sigma}, t \rangle \in \delta$ and $\pi q = [\![\text{split } x \ \langle K \ x_1, \cdots, x_m \rangle; q']\!]$
then $\{(q', \hat{\rho}[x_1 \mapsto \bigcup_{i=1}^n \hat{v}_{i1}, \cdots, x_m \mapsto \bigcup_{i=1}^n \hat{v}_{im}], \hat{\sigma}, t)\} \sqsubseteq \delta$
where $\quad \{\hat{l}_1, \cdots, \hat{l}_n\} \ = \ \hat{\rho}x$
$\qquad\quad (\hat{v}_{11}, \cdots, \hat{v}_{1m}) \ = \ \hat{\sigma}\hat{l}_1 \downarrow K$
$$\vdots$$
$\qquad\quad (\hat{v}_{n1}, \cdots, \hat{v}_{nm}) \ = \ \hat{\sigma}\hat{l}_n \downarrow K$

if $\langle q, \hat{\rho}, \hat{\sigma}, t \rangle \in \delta$ and $\pi q = [\![x = \text{basicop } op_i \ x_1 \cdots x_m; q']\!]$
then $\{(q', \hat{\rho}[x \mapsto \{BAS\}], \hat{\sigma}, t)\} \sqsubseteq \delta$

if $\langle q, \hat{\rho}, \hat{\sigma}, t \rangle \in \delta$ and $\pi q = [\![x = \text{basicconst } c; q']\!]$
then $\{(q', \hat{\rho}[x \mapsto \{BAS\}], \hat{\sigma}, t)\} \sqsubseteq \delta$

if $\langle q, \hat{\rho}, \hat{\sigma}, t \rangle \in \delta$ and $\pi q = [\![\, \mathtt{if}\, x\, \mathtt{then}\, q'\, \mathtt{else}\, q''\,]\!]$
then $\{\langle q', \hat{\rho}, \hat{\sigma}, t \rangle, \langle q'', \hat{\rho}, \hat{\sigma}, t \rangle\} \sqsubseteq \delta$

if $\langle q, \hat{\rho}, \hat{\sigma}, t \rangle \in \delta$ and $\pi q = [\![\, \mathtt{case}\, x\, \mathtt{of}\, (K_1, q_1) \cdots (K_m, q_m)\,]\!]$
then $\{\langle q_i, \hat{\rho}, \hat{\sigma}, t \rangle \mid i = 1 \cdots m$ and $\langle K_i\, \cdots \rangle \in \bigcup_{i=1}^n \hat{\sigma} \hat{l}_i\} \sqsubseteq \delta$
where $\{\hat{l}_1, \cdots, \hat{l}_n\} = \hat{\rho} x$

if $S = \langle q, \hat{\rho}, \hat{\sigma}, t \rangle \in \delta$ and $\pi q = [\![\, \mathtt{call}\, q_p(\, x_1, \cdots, x_m)(f_1, \cdots, f_m); q'\,]\!]$
then $\{\langle q_p, [f_1 \mapsto \hat{\rho} x_1, \cdots, f_m \mapsto \hat{\rho} x_m], \hat{\sigma}, token(S) \rangle\} \sqsubseteq \delta$

if $\langle q, \hat{\rho}, \hat{\sigma}, token(S_1) \rangle \in \delta$ and $\pi q = [\![\, \mathtt{return}\,]\!]$
  and $S_1 = \langle q_1, \hat{\rho}_1, \hat{\sigma}_1, t_1 \rangle$
  and $\pi q_1 = [\![\, \mathtt{call}\, \cdots (\, \cdots)(\cdots); q'\,]\!]$
then $\{\langle q', \hat{\rho}_1, \hat{\sigma}, t_1 \rangle\} \sqsubseteq \delta$

3.4   Implementation

In this section we discuss some issues pertaining to the implementation of the analysis in a lazy functional language (Haskell). This is an interesting functional programming exercise in its own right!

As a first step in implementing the analysis, we shall change the representation of analysed programs (i.e. GRIN code programs).

The basic GRIN code as hitherto described is on what one might call "go to form", since each instruction executes the operation and then "goes to" a successor program point. We shall now change the representation of the program to "come from form", which rather says "the state at (i.e. just before) point q is obtained by executing an I instruction *from* point q'". The reason for changing to this form is that it will enable us to use two different methods for accelerating convergence; one is a functional programming trick to counter otherwise inefficient handling of arrays, and one is a method from established compiler technology.

In the following clarifying examples we refer to appendix A. The left column of appendix A gives the "go to form" of the primes program, and the right column gives the "come from form" (with the statements written as constructor values as used in the analysis program to follow.) For instance, the instruction at point 2 of the "go to form" is the instruction t1 = constr [Cint t1'], hence in the "come from form" at point 3 the instruction is Constrfrom "t1" ("Cint", ["t1'"]) since the state at (i.e. just before) point 3 is obtained by executing said constr instruction from point 2 – the instruction in the "come from form" have shifted one step forwards. The situation is exactly similar for all the other sequential flow of control instructions. The situation is trickier for the non-sequential flow of control instructions. The if b' then 33 else 35 at point 32 in the "go to form" becomes Iffrom 32 at points 33 and 35 in the "come from form". The case 1 of (Cnil,43)(Ccons,45) at 42 becomes Casefrom "Cnil" 42 at 43 and Casefrom "Ccons" 42 at 45. The first instruction in each procedure in the "come from form" is a "Callfrom" instruction enumerating all point from which this procedure was called, and their corresponding actual arguments (the last argument of Callfrom is the names of the formal parameters). For instance, the Callfrom at point 41 says that filter is called from the two points 23 and 53. Finally, the statement at point 25 in the "go to form" is `call 58(1,N)(1,N)` (i.e. call `sieve`), hence at point 26 in the "come from form" the statement is `Returnfrom [61,65]` since control can be transferred from the two return statements at points 61 and 65.

In the abstract interpretation as described in section 3.3 computation descriptions δ were sets of state descriptions which were quadruples, i.e. members of $Q \times \widehat{Env} \times \widehat{Store} \times T$. Here we will represent a computation description *compdescr* by an array from program points q (we will use integers), to lists of triples (*env*, *st*, *tok*). Here *env* is an abstract local environment i.e. a mapping from variables to sets of abstract values (i.e. abstract pointers or the value *BAS*); we will ignore the issue of implementing environments, and simply write e.g. $env{\downarrow}i$ for environment lookups and e.g. $env{/\!/}(x,v)$ for environment updates. The second component *st* is the abstract store (heap); for lookups and updates we will use the same notation with $\downarrow$ and $/\!/$. (We will discuss the implementation of stores in section 3.4.2.)

We further assume that the program to be analysed is available as an array *prog* (formerly π) from program points to statements (constructor values) on "come-from form".

We now come to a function *one_iteration* which takes a computation description *compdescr* and returns a new computational description *compdescr'* by doing one iteration in the fix point finding. We can give *one_iteration* the following structure:

```
one_iteration compdescr =
  compdescr' where
    compdescr' =
      array(1, prog_size)
      [ i := case prog↓i of
              Init →                  ···
              Constr_from x l k xs →  ···
              Update_from x k xs →    ···
              Split_from x k xs →     ···
              Basicop_from →          ···
              Basicconst_from →       ···
              Print_from →            ···
              If_from q →             ···
              Case_from x q k →       ···
              Call_from fs xs →       ···
              Return_from qs →        ···
      | i ∈ [ 1 .. prog_size ]
      ]
```

That is, we construct and return a new *compdescr* using an array comprehension; the value at each index i depends on what $prog{\downarrow}i$ is. Thus each of the cases must return a list of triples (*env*, *st*, *tok*). For instance, the *Constr_from* case could then be written as follows.

```
Constr_from x l k (k,xs) →[ (env//(x,l), addtostore st [l] (k, [env↓x | x ∈ xs ]), tok)
                          | (env, st, tok) ∈ compdescr↓(i−1)
                          ]
```

We assume that the function *addtostore* implements the semantic function of the same name given in section 3.3.

There a problem with the above structure of *one_iteration*: The convergence towards the fixpoint is very slow. We now describe two methods for improving the speed of convergence.

3.4.1 Speeding up convergence

The problem above is that when we construct the next *compdescr*, in most points q the content of *compdescr* is unchanged, i.e., mostly the same sets of state descriptions are recomputed over and over again. To see this, consider the following very simple example:

$$\begin{cases} a \downarrow 1 = 1 \\ a \downarrow i = a \downarrow (i-1) + 1 \quad , i \in 1 \cdots N \end{cases}$$

The function *next* to compute the next value of the array a could then written as:

$$next\ a = array(1, N)([1 := 1] \mathbin{+\!\!+} [i := a \downarrow (i-1) + 1 \mid i \in [2 \cdots N]])$$

If we use a vector of ones as the initial a, subsequent values of the array a would have the values:

Initial value:	1	1	1	1	1	1	1
first iteration:	1	2	2	2	2	2	2
second iteration:	1	2	3	3	3	3	3
third iteration:	1	2	3	4	4	4	4

$$\vdots$$

Only one index in the array gets the correct value in each iteration, and it takes N iterations to reach the solution. Compare this to the straightforward imperative program which updates a single array a; the correct solution is obtained in one pass.

$$a \downarrow 1 = 1$$
$$\textbf{for } i = 2 \textbf{ to } N \textbf{ do}$$
$$\quad a \downarrow i := a \downarrow (i-1) + 1$$

We seem to have stumbled on a serious deficiency of functional languages, alas. But we can make the functional version converge after one iteration also, by using a recursively defined array, as follows.

$$solution = a'$$
$$\qquad \textbf{where}$$
$$\qquad a' = array(1, N)([1 := 1] \mathbin{+\!\!+} [i := a' \downarrow (i-1) + 1 \mid i \in [1 \cdots N]])$$

This works because although the definition of the array is 'circular' i.e. recursive, there are no circular data dependencies between the elements of the array (each element depends on its predecessor in the array). For our abstract interpretation problem the above correspond to programs with sequential flow of control instructions only. If in general we need to access the information at index k of the array during the computation of the ith element, we can use the following structure.

$$next\ a = a'$$
$$where$$
$$a' = array(1, N)\ [i := \cdots (\textbf{if}\ k < i\ \textbf{then}\ a' \downarrow k\ \textbf{else}\ a \downarrow k) \cdots$$
$$|\ i \in [1 \cdots N]]$$

This works well where the principal flow of control is forwards (as it is when most instructions are of the sequential flow of control flavour) with only an occasional backwards jump/call/return.

One further refinement of this idea is possible. A well-studied problem in data flow analysis theory is in what order we should visit the nodes in a data flow graph in order to reach a fixpoint in the fewest possible passes. A well-proven answer to this question is to use "depth-first ordering" of the nodes [ASU86]. That is, we compute an array $order$ of numbers such that $order \downarrow i < order \downarrow j$ is true if and only if node i should be visited before node j. We will not describe here how to compute $order$, but refer to [ASU86, pp 672–673,660–663] for the details of this.

Now back to our function $one\_iteration$! We pass as an additional argument the array $order$, and instead of using $compdescr$ and $compdescr'$ directly, we define a function $fcompdescr$ which uses the array $order$ to see whether it can use $compdescr'$ of this iteration or must resort to using $compdescr$ from the previous iteration.

```
one_iteration compdescr order =
   compdescr' where
     compdescr' =
       array(1, prog_size)
       [ i := case prog↓i of
             Constr_from x l (k,xs) → [ (env//(x,l),
                                          addtostore st [ l ] (k, [env↓x | x ∈xs ]),
                                          tok)
                                        | (env, st, tok) ∈ fcompdescr(i−1)
                                        ]
             Update_from x (k,xs) →  · · ·
                          ⋮
         where fcompdescr q = if order↓q < order↓i then compdescr'↓q else compdescr↓q
       | i ∈ [ 1 .. prog_size ]
       ]
```

3.4.2 The multiple stores problem

We now discuss efficient representation of the store values. A computation description will contain a lot of store values (each program point will have a set of them). The size of each store is in the same order as the analysed program itself (one element for each **constr** instruction). But we also note that most store values are small incremental updates of other store values in the same computation description. Thus the straightforward representation of stores using ordinary functional arrays is not only potentially expensive in terms of space, update operations would also be costly.

Let us review which operations that have to be done efficiently on store values.

↓ Store indexing.

∥ store updating.

merge Merge of stores, i.e. element-wise union (really, ⊔),

eq_store In checking if a fixpoint has been reached in the analysis, we compare computational descriptions for equality. Hence, all other things being equal, we also have to compare store values for equality pairwise in·the two computational descriptions.

The following representation using trees has the nice property that only the space needed to store the 'increment' for each store is needed, yet the indexing and the update is also reasonably efficient (order $\log n$).

The first idea is to use the (reverse of the) digits of the binary representation to describe the path down the tree where the element is found.

The second idea is to associate a name to each store value, the name being the the pair of the program point q and the token t where it was created. If we need a copy of a store value a from the place (q,t) we use $ST\_indir(q,t)\ a$ for the store instead. If we subsequently update this array then the ST_indir will 'bubble down' in the tree, to mark just where the difference between the original and the updated tree is.

The fast compare for equality relies on the fact that if in comparing two computation descriptions all the increments of the stores are pairwise equal, then all the stores themselves are pairwise equal.

The implementation of the the store functions is given below.

— Store indexing
$(ST\_node\ v\ a\ b)\!\downarrow\!1 = v$
$(ST\_node\ v\ a\ b)\!\downarrow\!i = \textbf{if}\ i\ `mod`\ 2 = 0$
$\qquad\qquad\qquad \textbf{then}\ a\!\downarrow\!(i/2)$
$\qquad\qquad\qquad \textbf{else}\ b\!\downarrow\!(i/2)$
$(ST\_indir\ n\ a))\!\downarrow\!i = a\!\downarrow\!i$
— Store updating
$(ST\_node\ v\ a\ b)\!/\!\!/(1,x) = ST\_node\ x\ a\ b$
$(ST\_node\ v\ a\ b)\!/\!\!/(i,x) = \textbf{if}\ i\ `mod`\ 2 = 0$
$\qquad\qquad\qquad\qquad \textbf{then}\ ST\_node\ (a/\!\!/(i/2,x))\ b$
$\qquad\qquad\qquad\qquad \textbf{else}\ ST\_node\ a\ (b/\!\!/(i/2,x))$
$(ST\_indir\ n\ (ST\_node\ v\ a\ b))/\!\!/(i,x) = (ST\_node\ v\ (st\_indir\ n\ a)(st\_indir\ n\ b))/\!\!/(i,x)$
— initial store
$st\_init\ v = a\ \textbf{where}\ a = ST\_node\ v\ a\ a$
— Merging stores
$merge\ (ST\_indir\ n1\ a1)\ (ST\_indir\ n2\ a2)\ |\ n1{=}n2 = ST\_indir\ n1\ a1$
$merge\ (ST\_indir\ n1\ (ST\_node\ v1\ a1\ b1))\ a2 = merge\ (ST\_node\ v1$
$\qquad\qquad\qquad\qquad\qquad\qquad\qquad\qquad (st\_indir\ n1\ a1)$
$\qquad\qquad\qquad\qquad\qquad\qquad\qquad\qquad (st\_indir\ n1\ a1))$

$$merge\ a1\ (ST\_indir\ n2\ (ST\_node\ v2\ a2\ b2)) = merge\ a1$$
$$\overset{a2}{(ST\_node\ v2}$$
$$(st\_indir\ n2\ a2)$$
$$(st\_indir\ n2\ a2))$$
$$merge\ (ST\_node\ v1\ a1\ b1)\ (ST\_node\ v2\ a2\ b2) = ST\_node\ (merge\_store\_values\ v1\ v2)$$
$$(merge\ a1\ a2)$$
$$(merge\ b1\ b2)$$

— *st_indir* avoids double *ST_indirs*

$st\_indir\ n'\ (ST\_indir\ n\ a) = (ST\_indir\ n\ a)$

$st\_indir\ n'\ a = (ST\_indir\ n'\ a)$

— Compare stores for equality

$st\_eq\ (ST\_indir\ n1\ a1)\ (ST\_indir\ n2\ a2) = n1 = n2 \lor st\_eq\ a1\ a2$

$st\_eq\ (ST\_indir\ n1\ a1)\ (ST\_node\ v2\ a2\ b2) = st\_eq\ a1\ (ST\_node\ v2\ a2\ b2)$

$st\_eq\ (ST\_node\ v1\ a1\ b1)\ (ST\_indir\ n2\ a2) = st\_eq\ (ST\_node\ v1\ a1\ b1)\ a2$

$st\_eq\ (ST\_node\ v1\ a1\ b1)\ (ST\_node\ v2\ a2\ b2) = v1=v2 \land st\_eq\ a1\ a2 \land st\_eq\ a1\ a2$

3.4.3 The *one_iteration* function

We can now sketch the function *one_iteration* that uses the machinery developed in sections 3.4.1 and 3.4.2.

```
one_iteration compdescr order =
  compdescr' where
    compdescr' =
      array(1, prog_size)
      [ i := case prog↓i of
          Init →                    [ (empty_env, empty_store, init_token) ]
          Constr_from x l (k,xs) →  [ (env//(x,l),
                                        addtostore (st_indir (i−1,tok) st)
                                          [ l ]
                                          (k, [env↓x | x ∈xs ]),
                                      tok)
                                      | (env, st, tok) ∈ fcompdescr(i−1)
                                    ]
          Update_from x (k,xs) →    [ (env,
                                        addtostore (st_indir (i−1,tok) st)
                                              (env↓x)
                                              (k, [env↓x | x ∈ xs ]),
                                      tok)
                                      | (env, st, tok) ∈ fcompdescr(i−1)
                                    ]
          Split_from x (k,xs) →     [ ( foldr (λ(y,vs)p→p//(y, foldr locs_union [] vs))
                                            env
                                            (zip xs (transpose [ vs | l ∈ env↓x,
                                                                 (k1,vs) ∈ st↓l, k1=k ])),
                                        st_indir (i−1,tok) st,
                                        tok )
                                      | (env, st, tok) ∈ fcompdescr(i−1)
```

]

$Basicop\_from\ x \rightarrow$ $[\ (env/\!/(x,[BAS]),\ st,\ tok)$
$|\ (env,\ st,\ tok) \in fcompdescr(i{-}1)$

$Bconst\_from\ x \rightarrow$ (same as above)

$If\_from\ q \rightarrow$ $[\ (env,\ st\_indir(q,tok)\ st),\ tok)$
$|\ (env,\ st,\ tok) \in fcompdescr\ q\ ]$

$Print\_from\ q \rightarrow$ $[\ (env,\ st\_indir(i{-}1,tok)\ st),\ tok)$
$|\ (env,\ st,\ tok) \in fcompdescr(i{-}1)]$

$Case\_from\ x\ q\ k \rightarrow$ $[\ (env,\ st\_indir\ (q,tok)\ st,\ tok)$
$|\ (env,\ st,\ tok) \in fcompdescr\ q,$
$[0|\ l \in env{\downarrow}x,\ (k1,\_) \in st{\downarrow}l,\ k1{=}k\ ] \neq [\ ]\ ]\ ]$

$Call\_from\ acs\ fs \rightarrow$ $merge\_states$
$[\ (mk\_env\ fs\ xs\ env,$
    $st\_indir\ (q,\ tok)\ st,$
    $token\ q\ (env,\ st,\ tok))$
$|\ (q,\ xs) \in acs,\ (env,\ st,\ tok) \in fcompdescr\ q$
]

$Return\_from\ qs \rightarrow$ $merge\_states$
$[\ (env1,\ st\_indir\ (q,\ tok2)\ st2,\ tok1)$
$|\ (env1,\ st1,\ tok1) \in fcompdescr(i{-}1),\ q \in qs,$
$(env2,\ st2,\ tok2) \in fcompdescr\ q,$
$token\ (i{-}1)\ (env1,\ st1,\ tok1) = tok2\ ]$

where $fcompdescr\ q = $ **if** $order{\downarrow}q < order{\downarrow}i$ **then** $compdescr'{\downarrow}q$ **else** $compdescr{\downarrow}q$
$|\ i \in [\ 1\ ..\ prog\_size\ ]$
]

The following functions used above have yet to be defined:

$merge\_states$ takes a list of state descriptions and merges those with the same token. Merging of two environments is done by

$$merge\_env\ [x_1 \mapsto v_1, \cdots, x_m \mapsto v_m]\ [x_1 \mapsto v'_1, \cdots, x_m \mapsto v'_m] =$$
$$[x_1 \mapsto v_1 \cup v'_1, \cdots, x_m \mapsto v_m \cup v'_m]$$

Merging of two stores is done by the function $merge$ defined in section 3.4.2.

$token$ was discussed in section 3.3.

mk_env constructs an environment needed at the beginning of a procedure:

$$mk\_env[f_1, \cdots, f_m][x_1, \cdots, x_m]\ env = [f_1 \mapsto env{\downarrow}x_1, \cdots, f_m \mapsto env{\downarrow}x_m]$$

4 Conclusion

Of course the proof of the pudding is in the eating. At the moment of writing this, the transformation techniques and the analysis outlined in this paper have not yet been tested in practice.

5 Acknowledgements

I am indebted to John Hughes for numerous discussions on program analysis in general and this work in particular, to Neil Jones for sorting out some misconceptions of mine about the Jones&Muchnick framework for interprocedural data flow analysis. Thanks are also due to the functional programming group in Glasgow for providing a stimulating environment and for making my stay there a pleasant one. This work was supported by an SERC visiting fellowship.

References

[ASU86] A. Aho, R. Sethi, and J. Ullman. *Compilers, Principles, Techniques and Tools.* Addison Wesley, 1986.

[BHY89] A. Bloss, P. Hudak, and J. Young. An optimising compiler for a modern functional language. *Computer Journal*, 32(2):152–161, April 1989.

[BPR88] Geoffrey L. Burn, Simon L. Peyton Jones, and John D. Robson. The spineless G-Machine. In *Proceedings of the 1988 ACM Conference on LISP and Functional Programming*, pages 244–258, 1988.

[FW87] Jon Fairbairn and Stuart Wray. Tim: A simple, lazy abstract machine to execute supercombinators. In *Functional Programming Languages and Computer Architecture*, volume 274 of *Lecture Notes in Computer Science*, pages 34–45. Springer-Verlag, 1987.

[Hud87] P. Hudak. A semantic model for reference counting and its abstraction. In Samson Abramsky and Chris L. Hankin, editors, *Abstract Interpretation of Declarative Languages*, pages 45–62. Ellis Horwood Ltd., 1987.

[JM82] N. Jones and S. Muchnick. A flexible approach to interprocedural data flow analysis and programs with recursive data types. In *Proceedings of POPL*, 1982.

[Joh84] Thomas Johnsson. Efficient compilation of lazy evaluation. In *Proceedings of the SIGPLAN '84 Symposium on Compiler Construction*, pages 58–69, 1984.

[PS89] Simon L. Peyton Jones and Jon Salkild. The Spineless Tagless G-machine. In *Functional Programming and Computer Architecture*, pages 184–201, 1989.

A Go-to and Come-from code for the primes program

	— go to form —	— come from form —
	————————— (main) —————————	
1	t1' = basicconst 2	Init
2	t1 = constr [Cint t1']	Basicconstfrom "t1'"
3	t2' = basicconst 1000	Constrfrom "t1" 1 ("Cint",["t1'"])
4	t2 = constr [Cint t2']	Basicconstrfrom "t2'"
5	t3 = constr [Fupto t1 t2]	Constrfrom "t2" 2 ("Cint",["t2'"])
6	t4 = constr [Fsieve t3]	Constrfrom "t3" 3 ("Fupto",["t1","t2"])
7	call 9(t4)(l)	Constrfrom "t4" 4 ("Fsieve",["t3"])
8	stop	Returnfrom [11,16]
	————————— (print) —————————	
9	call 17(l)(N)	Callfrom [(7,["t4"]),(15,["l"])] ["l"]
10	case l of (Cnil,11)(Ccons,12)	Returnfrom [18,19,20,22,24,26]
11	return	Casefrom "Cnil" 10
12	call 17(x)(N)	Casefrom "Ccons" 10
13	split x [Cint x']	Returnfrom [18,19,20,22,24,26]
14	printint x'	Splitfrom "x" ("Cint",["x'"])
15	call 9(xs)(l)	Printfrom
16	return Returnfrom [11,16]	
	————————— (EVAL) —————————	
17	case N of (Cnil,18)(Ccons,19)(Cint,20)	
	(Fupto,21)(Ffilter,23)(Fsieve,25)	Callfrom [(9,["l"]),(12,["x"]),(27,["m"]),(29,["n"]),
		(41,["l"]),(45,["x"]),(47,["p"]),(58,["l"])] ["N"]
18	return	Casefrom "Cnil" 17
19	return	Casefrom "Ccons" 17
20	return	Casefrom "Cint" 17
21	call 27(m,n,N)(m,n,N)	Casefrom "Fupto" 17
22	return	Returnfrom [34,40]
23	call 41(p,l,N)(p,l,N)	Casefrom "Ffilter" 17
24	return	Returnfrom [44,54,57]
25	call 58(l,N)(l,N)	Casefrom "Fsieve" 17
26	return	Returnfrom [61,65]
	————————— (upto) —————————	
27	call 17(m)(N)	Callfrom [(21,["m","n","N"])] ["m","n","N"]
28	split m [Cint m']	Returnfrom [18,19,20,22,24,26]
29	call 17(n)(N)	Splitfrom "m" ("Cint",["m'"])
30	split n [Cint n']	Returnfrom [18,19,20,22,24,26]
31	b' = basicop >(m',n')	Splitfrom "n" ("Cint",["n'"])
32	if b' then 33 else 35	Basicopfrom "b'"
33	update N [Cnil]	Iffrom 32
34	return	Updatefrom "N" ("Cnil",[])
35	t1' = basicconst 1	Iffrom 32
36	t2' = basicop +(m',t1')	Basicconstfrom "t1'"
37	t1 = constr [Cint t2']	Basicopfrom "t2'"
38	t2 = constr [Fupto t1 n]	Constrfrom "t1" 5 ("Cint",["t2'"])
39	update N [Ccons m t2]	Constrfrom "t2" 6 ("Fupto",["t1","n"])
40	return	Updatefrom "N" ("Ccons",["m","t2"])
	————————— (filter) —————————	
41	call 17(l)(N)	Callfrom [(23,["p","l","N"]),(53,["p","xs","N"])] ["p","l","N"]
42	case l of (Cnil,43)(Ccons,45)	Returnfrom [18,19,20,22,24,26]
43	update N [Cnil]	Casefrom "Cnil" 42
44	return	Updatefrom "N" ("Cnil",[])
45	call 17(x)(N)	Casefrom "Ccons" 42

46	split x [Cint x′]	Returnfrom [18,19,20,22,24,26]
47	call 17(p)(N)	Splitfrom "x" ("Cint","x‴")
48	split p [Cint p′]	Returnfrom [18,19,20,22,24,26]
49	b1′ = basicop mod(x′,p′)	Splitfrom "p" ("Cint","p‴")
50	b2′ = basicconst 0	Basicopfrom "b1‴"
51	b3′ = basicop =(b1′,b2′)	Basicconstrfrom "b2‴"
52	if b3′ then 53 else 55	Basicopfrom "b3‴"
53	call 41(p,xs,N)(p,l,N)	Iffrom 52
54	return	Returnfrom [44,54,57]
55	t1 = constr [Ffilter p xs]	Iffrom 52
56	update N [Ccons x t1]	Constrfrom "t1" 7 ("Ffilter",["p","xs"])
57	return	Updatefrom "N" ("Ccons", ["x","t1"])

———————————— (*sieve*) ————————————

58	call 17(l)(N)	Callfrom [(58,["l","N"])] ["l","N"]
59	case l of (Cnil,60)(Ccons,62)	Returnfrom [18,19,20,22,24,26]
60	update N [Cnil]	Casefrom "Cnil" 59
61	return	Updatefrom "N" ("Cnil",[])
62	t1 = constr [Ffilter x xs]	Casefrom "Ccons" 59
63	t2 = constr [Fsieve t1]	Constrfrom "t1" 8 ("Ffilter",["x","xs"])
64	update N [Ccons x t2]	Constrfrom "t2" 9 ("Fsieve",["t1"])
65	return	Updatefrom "N" ("Ccons", ["x","t2"])

Is Compile Time Garbage Collection Worth the Effort?

Simon B Jones, Michael White

Dept of Computing Science and Mathematics

University of Stirling, Scotland

Keywords Functional programming, optimization, garbage collection

1   Introduction

For some time one of us, Jones, has been studying the problem of the compile time garbage collection of dynamic data structures in functional languages; this work is in collaboration with Daniel Le Métayer (IRISA, Rennes, France), and has already been described in [1, 2]. The work described in these papers, and in others in the area (for example, [3]), is largely a *theoretical* study of the abstract interpretation techniques which might be applied to compile time garbage collection and related problems.

In this paper we report some preliminary *practical* studies aimed at assessing what gains there may be to be made, in execution time and/or storage use, through such optimization techniques.

2   The problem

The aim of [2] is twofold:

Compile time *deallocation* of heap cells: To detect, by static analysis, those operations in a functional program which dereference their operand(s), and which *on every execution* remove the last *useable* reference to an operand[1]. For such operations, code will be compiled which adds the dereferenced cell directly, and unconditionally, to the heap's free list, thus by-passing the usual garbage collection mechanism.

Compile time *reallocation* of heap cells: To detect, by static analysis, where a compiled deallocation can be coalesced with a subsequent allocation request ("cons"). In this case, no allocation nor deallocation code need be compiled, and the cell is safely *updated in place* by the subsequent code.

---

[1]**Note:** This may not be the last physical reference to a heap cell, since there may be extant references which *necessity analysis* has shown will *never be used* to access the cell

In [2] it is shown how *all* the allocations in naïve reverse can be coalesced with compiled deallocations. Hence a list can be reversed "in place" (provided that there is no other reference to it), and *no run time garbage collector is required.* Note that there is a simple criterion for elimination of the run time garbage collector: it is possible if *no allocate* requests remain in the optimized program.

Many simple list processing functions (for example, a large part of the Miranda prelude) are similarly optimizable. *But what about larger, more typical programs?* Can they have their garbage collection completely compiled — and hence be executed very cheaply? If not, to what extent can the garbage collection be compiled, and what are the potential gains? These are the questions that the work reported here addresses.

3   The apparatus

The approach that we took was to monitor the execution of real programs to discover which operations have "optimizable occurrences". These are operations which, on *every execution*, result in the removal of the last useable reference to their operand(s) (as described above). We chose several functional programs (quicksort and a simple compiler) and applied them to "typical" arguments (short list, an append program and the compiler itself). Each execution is then a "test" of the chosen program, which will yield results not necessarily valid for *all* executions of the chosen program, and not necessarily consistent with the predictions of a formal analysis carried out according to the techniques of [2]. Interpretation of the information collected is subject to two qualifications:

1. Since the analysis technique works by abstraction, it may not be able to predict *all* of the optimizable occurrences which will be found by monitoring.

2. Since we are only considering test executions of the functional programs, some operations may appear to be optimizable in the individual tests, when in fact they are not (because there may be other tests, not tried, in which the occurrences are not optimizable). In this case the formal analysis technique would correctly predict that these occurrences are *not* optimizable.

Notwithstanding these qualifications (which imply that the practical experiments will probably cause us to *over*estimate the potential optimizations), we may hope to obtain some indicative results.

The experiments are being carried out on an instrumented implementation of a simple functional language; details in [4]. It is based on Henderson's Lispkit Lisp and its SECD machine [5], augmented with a reference counted heap, additional abstract reference counts to track the reference counting model assumed in [2], monitoring of the degree of sharing of the operands of individual instructions, and collection of other statistics.

At present the monitored language is restricted to be first order, with no embedded LETs or LETRECs; these restrictions are to simplify the implementation, and are not fundamental problems. In addition, extra operations need to be added to provide some abstract usage information (some of which could be derived automatically if we improved the compiler). Also, currently we only monitor

174

for deallocation at operations such as CAR and CDR; we must add monitoring for deallocation at function entry and after selection of a conditional branch.

For example, here is a quicksort program which has been annotated with the additional monitoring operations SETUSES and DECRUSES (semantically (SETUSES 1 e) = e and (DECRUSES 1 e) = e):

```
(LETREC QSORT
  (QSORT LAMBDA (L)
    (SETUSES (4)
      (IF (EQ L (QUOTE nil))
        (DECRUSES (3) (QUOTE nil))
        (DECRUSES (0)
          (QS (CAR L)
            (SPLIT (CAR L) (CDR L) (QUOTE nil) (QUOTE nil)))))))))
  (QS LAMBDA (X L12)
    (SETUSES (1 2)
      (APPEND (QSORT (DECRARC (CAR L12))) (CONS X (QSORT (CDR L12))))))
  (APPEND LAMBDA (L1 L2)
    (SETUSES (3 2)
      (IF (EQ L1 (QUOTE nil))
        (DECRUSES (2 1) L2)
        (DECRUSES (0 1) (CONS (CAR L1) (APPEND (CDR L1) L2))))))
  (SPLIT LAMBDA (X L1 L2 L3)
    (SETUSES (3 6 3 3)
      (IF (EQ L1 (QUOTE nil)) (DECRUSES (3 5 2 2) (CONS L2 L3))
      (IF (LEQ (CAR L1) X)
        (DECRUSES (1 2 2 2) (SPLIT X (CDR L1) (CONS (CAR L1) L2) L3))
        (DECRUSES (1 2 2 2) (SPLIT X (CDR L1) L2 (CONS (CAR L1) L3)))))))))
)
```

4 The experiments and results

To date, the following experiments have been performed:

Expt	Program	Data	(a)	(b)	(c)	(d)
A	Quicksort	A short list	12	5	514	15
B	Compiler	Append	67	27	1489	29
C	Compiler	Compiler	74	28	34210	569

Key:

(a) Number of instances of CAR and CDR executed.

(b) Number of optimizable instances of CAR and CDR found.

(c) Total number of instructions executed.

(d) Total number of optimizable instructions executed.

Further obervations on the results of these experiments:

A All allocations can be coalesced with preceding optimizable deallocations.

B, C Most allocations can be coalesced with preceding optimizable deallocations; many optimizable deallocations cannot immediately be taken advantage of in this way, but they seem to be comparable in number with the residual allocations.

5 Analysis and conclusions

What can we conclude at this early stage?

At first sight we seem to have discovered that a (disappointingly?) low proportion of executed instructions may be optimized. However, the relevance of this depends on the kind of garbage collector that we intend to support our optimized programs with:

- A reference count garbage collector would seem to be a bad option, because we would only succeed in reducing the cost of storage management (incrementing, decrementing and testing reference counts) by a small fraction (by those operations for which we avoid compiling a decrement and test). To improve matters we would have to analyse programs to discover which operations always handle cells destined for a definite compiled collection — possibly a tough job.

- On the other hand, a mark/scan garbage collector has no overhead for those operations which we cannot optimize, and the effect of compiled collection is simply to defer the next mark/scan. So, the saving here depends on how many cells have optimized deallocations relative to the number of allocations that occur — if the proportion is high then we reduce the total number of garbage collection pauses considerably, and this is where we gain; this is *independent* of whether we succeed in coalescing deallocation and allocations at compile time. The information required to determine this is not gathered at present by our system, but it is an important extension which will allow us to estimate better the gains to be made.

Clearly more experiments need to be done. It is meaningless to talk about "typical" programs, so we will simply have to try a range of common applications and commonly used styles, and report back .....

6 References

[1] S. B. Jones, D. Le Métayer. "Optimization of storage management in functional languages by static analysis of programs (Extended abstract)" *Proceedings of the 1988 Glasgow Workshop on Functional Programming (Rothesay, August 1988)* Research Report 89/R4, Department of Computing Science, University of Glasgow. February 1989.

[2] S. B. Jones, D. Le Métayer. "Compile-time Garbage Collection by Sharing Analysis" In *Proceedings of the 4th International Conference on Functional Programming and Computer Architecture (Imperial College, London, September 1989)* ACM. September 1989.

176

[3] P. Hudak. "A semantic model of reference counting and its abstraction" In *Abstract interpretation of declarative languages*, eds. S. Abramsky, C. Hankin. Ellis Horwood. 1987.

[4] M. White. "Is compile time garbage collection worth the effort?" *Final year project dissertation* Dept of Computing Science and Mathematics, University of Stirling. April 1990.

[5] P. Henderson. *Functional programming: application and implementation* Prentice Hall International. 1980.

Generating a Pattern Matching Compiler by Partial Evaluation

Jesper Jørgensen *
DIKU, Department of Computer Science
University of Copenhagen
Universitetsparken 1, DK-2100 Copenhagen Ø
Denmark
e-mail: knud@diku.dk

December 6, 1990

Abstract

Partial evaluation can be used for automatic generation of compilers and was first implemented by Jones et. al. [9]. Since partial evaluation was extended to higher order functional languages, Jones et. al. [8] and Bondorf [2], it has become possible to write denotational semantics definitions of languages and implement these with very few changes in the language treated by partial evaluators.

In this paper we use this technique to generate a compiler for a small strict combinator language with pattern matching. First, a simple denotational specification for the language is written and a compiler is generated. This first compiler turns out not to generate too efficient code.

By changing the denotational specification, new compilers that generate more efficient code are obtained. This process can be described as generating optimizing compilers by changing specifications. The optimization concerns generation of object code for pattern matching and the final compiler does in fact generate very efficient code for this. Specifically, it treats non-uniform function definitions in a satisfactory way. The optimization performed can be viewed as being equivalent to the well-known compiler optimization called common subexpression elimination.

1 Introduction

1.1 Compiler Generation

One field in which partial evaluation have been used with considerable success is automatic compiler generation, i.e. generating compilers from interpreters [9]. Another is algorithms involving pattern or string matching, Emanuelson [6], Consel and Danvy [5]. Since many functional languages like Haskell [11] and Miranda[1] [16] use pattern matching, it is natural to ask if it is possible, using partial evaluation,

---

*This work was supported by ESPRIT Basic Research Actions project 3124 "Semantique"
[1]Miranda is a trademark of Research Software Ltd.

to generate a compiler that compiles function definitions with pattern matching into efficient matching code. This is the motivation for this work.

The partial evaluator used is Similix [4] [2], an autoprojector for a higher order subset of Scheme [12], including both lambda abstractions and side effects on global variables. The fact that the language is a member of the LISP family makes it well suited for directly implementing denotational semantic definitions. In this way compilers can be generated from specifications by expressing these as Scheme programs (interpreters).

The method of generating compilers from denotational specifications works, but the compilers do not always generate efficient code. Therefore one usually has to do some rewriting of the specification before generating the final compiler. This paper describes such a process for a compiler for a small strict combinator language with pattern matching.

One could say that the method is a way to construct optimizing compilers, but where all the work is done by changing the specification. This has some advantages compared to the usual methods:

- It is conceptually simpler.

- It is easier to prove correct.

- The optimizer gets integrated into the compiler (no separate optimization phase).

A key point in the rewriting process is to identify static information in the specification (interpreter) and use this to do more work at partial evaluation time. Partial evaluation in general represents not only one evaluation of a program, but many. At a given point in the process of partial evaluation there might be certain statically determinable information on dynamic variables that the specializer is not using. It is this information that should be identified and made visible to the specializer by incorporating it as static data in the interpreter.

The specification presented in this paper will be rewritten three times and the three versions of the compiler will be presented and the problems they solve will be described.

In the description of the specifications the focus is on the part concerning pattern matching. The first version is a fairly straightforward implementation with only few minor changes from the denotational definition.

The second version is obtained from the first by changing it to reuse results of tests on dynamic data, a method also used by Consel and Danvy in [5]. The naïve matching algorithm of the first version tries to match one alternative (list of patterns in a function definition) in turn. No information on failed attempts is reused when matching new alternatives. A way to describe results of previously performed test is devised and is used to achieve efficient matching code in target programs.

The third version solves a problem not present in [5], i.e. the decomposing of dynamic values into substructures. Programs should only decompose some dynamic value into its subparts at most once; a way to ensure this is to introduce occurrences as pointers to dynamic structures.

Finally a way to solve problems of code duplication is discussed. The problem occurs if definitions have overlapping alternatives. In that case the same code can be present many times in the target programs.

In terms of compiler optimization all these changes can be viewed as common subexpression elimination in the code generated from the first specification.

1.2 Outline of the Paper

The paper is organized as follows. After a short section on notation, we introduce the combinator language and its denotational semantics. In section 3 we develop the three versions of the compiler, we discuss how to solve the problem of code duplication, and we give some statistics on the compiler. In Section 4 we look at possible extensions of the work, and in section 5 we give a comparison with related work. Section 6 contains a conclusion.

1.3 Prerequisites

Knowledge of partial evaluation [9] and of denotational semantics [13] is required.

1.4 Notation

In denotational definitions v^* is an abbreviation of a sequence of v's. If D is the name of a syntactical domain then D^* is the domain of sequences of elements from D. Lists of values are written in a Prolog like style, e.g. [1,2,3] and $[h|t]$. Otherwise the notation follows Schmidt [13] where a conditional is written $\_ \rightarrow \_ [] \_$, $\underline{\lambda}$ is a strict lambda (i.e. $\underline{\lambda}v.e = \lambda v.v=\bot \rightarrow \bot[]e$) and function updating is written $[\_ \mapsto \_]\_$. ρ is a variable environment and ϕ a function environment. Continuations are written κ. Some specification of domains have been left out for the sake of simplicity. Thus, in the second version the specification domains of continuations are left out because these differ from valuation function to valuation function; S-cont and F-cont stand for any continuation.

Programs are written in the subset of Scheme handled by Similix [2]. Predicates on sorts always have prefix "is" and suffix "?" and functions decomposing structures into substructures are written "Structure-sort"-"Substructor-sort", e.g. Patcst-C returns the constant when applied to a constant pattern. Injection functions into sorts are written with prefix "in". The definition of these primitive operations are left out, but it should be clear from the context what they do. upd-env and init-env are syntactic extensions:

```
(extend-syntax (init-env) ((init-env) (lambda (v) (error ...))))

(extend-syntax (upd-env)
  ((upd-env v w r) (lambda (v1) (if (equal? v v1) w (r v1)))))
```

In the output from Similix, variable and function names have been renamed by hand in order to make the code more readable.

180

2 The Combinator Language

2.1 Syntax of the Language

The syntax of the language is shown in figure 1. The language is a strict version of the curried named combinator language described in [3] extended with pattern matching. A program consists of a list of function definitions d*, each of which consists of a name F and a list of alternatives a*. An alternative is a list of patterns and an expression. Patterns can be constants, variables, and compound patterns using the constructor :. Repeated variables in one alternative are not permitted. Alternatives may overlap and are matched from left to right. Expressions can be constants, variables, function names, the constructor : applied to two expressions, or the application of an expression to another. The constructor : is not curried.

Abstract Syntax:

pgm ∈ Program, d ∈ Definition, e ∈ Expression, c ∈ Constant
v ∈ Variable, f ∈ Function-name, a ∈ Alternative, p ∈ Pattern

$$
\begin{array}{lll}
\text{pgm} & ::= & d^* \\
d & ::= & (f\ a^*) \\
a & ::= & (p^* = e) \\
p & ::= & c \mid v \mid (p_1 : p_2) \\
e & ::= & c \mid v \mid f \mid (e_1 : e_2) \mid (e_1\ e_2)
\end{array}
$$

Figure 1: Syntax of the combinator language

Here is an example of a combinator program that will be used as source program to test the generated compilers:

```
(goal ((x : y)    = test x y))
(test (1  (2 : x) = test 1 x)
      (x  (y : 5) = x : y)
      (x  y       = y))
```

Some syntactic sugar is used here. A parser will insert parenthesis around compound right hand sides and in applications following the convention that functions associate to the left.

2.2 The Semantics of the Language

As mentioned, the intention is to construct the compiler from the denotational semantics of the language[2]. Figure 2 shows the semantics of the language. Since the focus is on pattern matching, the semantic definition for expressions has been

---

[2]When implementing a denotational semantics in a strict language like Scheme, one is faced with the problem of how to implementing the fixpoint operator. One way to do this is to use the applicative fixpoint operator: `(define (fix f) (lambda (x) ((f (fix f)) x)))` and otherwise just rewrite the semantics as a Scheme program (i.e. all lambda's become strict). This method was used to transform the semantics in this paper into Similix programs, but it is not the point of this paper to prove that this in fact gives a correct implementation of the semantics.

left out. The result of running a program is the value of a specified goal function (f_{goal}) applied to a value (v_{input}). The goal function can be any one-argument function in the program. a_f is the arity of the function f and should actually have been written arity$[\![f]\!]$. ϕ_{init} and ρ_{init} are initial environments.

Pgm defines the semantics of a program. ϕ is the function-environment and is the least fixed point over the recursively defined combinators.

There are several reasons for using continuation passing style [13] in the semantic functions for patterns. First, it is a simple way to handle backtracking. Second, it is useful to avoid using error tags. In this way all handling of error cases is left to the expression evaluation function E. An error can only occur when matching if no alternative matches the arguments (remember that the language is strict). Third, continuations can be used to return multiple results from functions in a nice way. This has two advantages; it makes specifications (interpreters) easier to read, and when specializing the interpreters values are not returned, but passed as arguments to continuations, which then gives *variable splitting*, Sestoft [14].

S-cont is the domain of success continuation and F-env the domain of failure continuation.

3 Generating the compiler

To get a compiler for the language we write an interpreter *Int* for the language. This is a straightforward process. From this interpreter the compiler is generated in the usual way, i.e. by specializing the specializer with respect to the interpreter:

Compiler = *Mix* Mix Int

or by using the compiler generator:

Compiler = *Cogen* Int

where Mix is the specializer. Program names written in *italics* designate the meaning of the program, while names in the normal font designates program texts.

The static input to the interpreter, which is also the input to the compiler, is a source program and a goal function. So we run the compiler like:

Target = *Compiler* Source f_{goal}

3.1 The First Implementation

Before showing the first interpreter we make a small change in the semantics. Thus we replace the list $[v_1,...,v_n]$ by an environment binding indices to their values (in fact we really bind $a_f - i$ to v_i, because it is simpler).

The reason for building up this environment has to do with the way Similix works; the idea is to achieve variable splitting for v* in the semantics. This is a general trick where one uses a higher order environments to represent structures of dynamic values. This will be explained by a small example where the structure is a list. Consider the expression:

```
(let ((1 (cons v1 (cons v2 '())))) (cadr 1))
```

Semantic domains:

$v \in$ Value $= ((\text{Value} \to \text{Value}) + \text{Basic})^{\cdot}\bot$

$\rho \in$ V-env $=$ Variable $\to$ Value

$\phi \in$ F-env $=$ Function-name $\to$ Value $\to$ Value

$\kappa_s \in$ S-cont $=$ V-env $\to$ Value

$\kappa_f \in$ F-cont $= Unit \to$ Value

Valuation functions:

Pgm: Program $\to$ Function-name $\to$ Value $\to$ Value

$\text{Pgm}[\![pgm]\!][\![f_{goal}]\!]\ v_{input} = \text{fix}\ (\lambda\phi.\text{D*}[\![pgm]\!]\phi)\ [\![f_{goal}]\!]\ v_{input}$

D*: Definition* $\to$ F-env $\to$ F-env

$\text{D*}[\![\ ]\!]\phi = \lambda f.\bot$

$\text{D*}[\![(fa^*)d^*]\!]\phi = [[\![f]\!] \mapsto (\underline{\lambda}v_1...\underline{\lambda}v_{a_f}.\text{A*}[\![a^*]\!][v_1,...,v_n]\phi)](\text{D*}[\![d^*]\!]\phi)$

A*: Alternative* $\to$ Value* $\to$ F-env $\to$ Value

$\text{A*}[\![\ ]\!]v^*\phi = \bot$

$\text{A*}[\![(p^*=e)a^*]\!]v^*\phi = \text{P*}[\![p^*]\!]v^*(\lambda v.\bot)(\lambda\rho.\text{E}[\![e]\!]\rho\phi)(\lambda().\text{A*}[\![a^*]\!]v^*\phi)$

P*: Pattern* $\to$ Value* $\to$ V-env $\to$ S-cont $\to$ F-cont $\to$ Value

$\text{P*}[\![\ ]\!]v^*\rho\kappa_s\kappa_f = \kappa_s\ \rho$

$\text{P*}[\![p\ p^*]\!][v|v^*]\rho\kappa_s\kappa_f = \text{P}[\![p]\!]v\rho(\lambda\rho'.\text{P*}[\![p^*]\!]v^*\rho'\kappa_s\kappa_f)\kappa_f$

P: Pattern $\to$ Value $\to$ V-env $\to$ S-cont $\to$ F-cont $\to$ Value

$\text{P}[\![v]\!]v\rho\kappa_s\kappa_f = \kappa_s\ ([\![v]\!] \mapsto v]\rho)$

$\text{P}[\![c]\!]v\rho\kappa_s\kappa_f = (\text{C}[\![c]\!]=v) \to \kappa_s\ \rho\ []\ \kappa_f\ ()$

$\text{P}[\![(p_1:p_2)]\!]v\rho\kappa_s\kappa_f = \textbf{case v of}$

$\qquad\qquad\qquad (v_1,v_2) \qquad : \text{P}[\![p_1]\!]v_1\rho(\lambda\rho'.\text{P}[\![p_2]\!]v_2\rho'\kappa_s\kappa_f)\kappa_f$

$\qquad\qquad\qquad \_ \qquad\qquad : \kappa_f\ ()$

E: Expression $\to$ V-env $\to$ F-env $\to$ Value (omitted)

C: Constant $\to$ Value (omitted)

Figure 2: Semantics of combinator language with patterns

If we specialize this when **v1** and **v2** are dynamic, we get the residual expression

```
(cadr (cons v1 (cons v2 '())))
```

But if we replace the list with an environment representing the list

```
(let ((r (upd-env 1 v1 (upd-env 2 v2 (init-env))))) (r 2))
```

it specializes to the residual expression **v2**.

In case of structures that are more general than lists one has to use something more general than indices to reference the values. We shall see an example of this in section 3.3. Here *occurrences* will be used to reference parts of structured values. Why we use the name O-env for the domain of these environments will also become clear then.

Semantic domains:

$\omega \in \text{Occ} = \text{Nat}$

$\varrho \in \text{O-env} = \text{Occ} \to \text{Value}$

$\kappa \in \text{Cont} = \text{O-env} \to \text{Value}$

Valuation functions:

$\text{D*: Definition*} \to \text{F-env} \to \text{F-env}$

$\text{D*}[\![\ ]\!]\phi = \lambda f.\bot$

$\text{D*}[\![(fa^*)d^*]\!]\phi = [[\![f]\!] \mapsto \text{L } a_f\ (\lambda\varrho.\text{A*}[\![a^*]\!]\varrho a_f\phi)]\ (\text{D*}[\![d^*]\!]\phi)$

$\text{L: } Nat \to \text{Cont} \to \text{Value}$

$\text{L } 0\ \kappa = \kappa\ \lambda\omega.\bot$

$\text{L } \omega\kappa = \underline{\lambda}v.\text{L } (\omega\text{-}1)\ (\lambda\varrho.\kappa([\omega \mapsto v]\varrho))$

$\text{A*: Alternative*} \to \text{O-env} \to \text{Occ} \to \text{F-env} \to \text{Value}$

$\text{A*}[\![\ ]\!]\varrho\omega\phi = \bot$

$\text{A*}[\![(p*\!=\!e)a^*]\!]\varrho\omega\phi = \text{P*}[\![p*]\!]\varrho\omega(\lambda v.\bot)(\lambda\rho.\text{E}[\![e]\!]\rho\phi)(\lambda().\text{A*}[\![a^*]\!]\varrho\omega\phi)$

$\text{P*: Pattern*} \to \text{O-env} \to \text{Occ} \to \text{V-env} \to \text{S-cont} \to \text{F-cont} \to \text{Value}$

$\text{P*}[\![\ ]\!]\varrho\omega\rho\kappa_s\kappa_f = \kappa_s\ \rho$

$\text{P*}[\![p\ p*]\!]\varrho\omega\rho\kappa_s\kappa_f = \text{P}[\![p]\!](\varrho\ \omega)\rho(\lambda\rho'.\text{P*}[\![p*]\!]\varrho(\omega\text{-}1)\rho'\kappa_s\kappa_f)\kappa_f$

Figure 3: Changes to the semantics for version 1

Figure 3 shows the changed parts of the semantics. ϱ is the argument environment and L the function building it. L also constructs the lambda abstractions of $(\lambda v_1...\lambda v_{a_f}.\text{A*} ...)$ from the first version of the semantics. Figure 4 shows a fairly straightforward implementation of the semantic. This is the only interpreter that will be shown in the paper. Only the parts relevant for the pattern matching are shown.

If we generate a compiler from the first version of the interpreter and compile the example program of section 2.1 we get the result shown in figure 5. In this figure only the function of the target program corresponding to the function test is shown.

There are a few peculiarities in this program that are due to Similix's way of working. The many superfluous parameters to _P1 are generated when Similix do variable splitting when generating residual calls; Similix's postprocessor could be extended to remove these.

Even apart from this it is clear that the code is not optimal; it may perform the same test several times. If the test (equal? 2 (car y)) fails, the first action of _P1 is the test (pair? val6) which is essentially the same test as the (pair? y) previously performed. The program also performs the same decomposing more than once; (car y) and (car val6) do same operation.

The problem lies in the way the semantics are written. The alternatives are matched one at a time and when matching a new alternative no results obtained by matching against earlier alternatives are reused.

```
(define (_D* D* phi)
  (if (null? D*)
      (init-env)
      (let* ((D (car D*))
             (occ (D-arity D)))
        (upd-env (D-F D)
                 (L occ (lambda (ro) (_A* (D-A* D) occ ro phi)))
                 (_D* (cdr D*) phi)))))

(define (L occ c)
  (if (zero? occ)
      (sc (lambda (w) '()))
      (lambda (v)
        (L (sub1 occ) (lambda (r) (sc (upd-env occ v r)))))))

(define (_A* A* occ ro phi)
  (if (null? A*)
      (error '_A* "No matching alternatives ~s" '-)
      (let* ((A (car A*)))
        (_P* P* occ ro (init-env)
             (lambda (r) (_E (A-E A) r phi))
             (lambda () (_A* (cdr A*) occ ro phi))))))

(define (_P* p* occ ro r sc fc)
  (if (null? p*)
      (sc r)
      (_P (car p*) (ro occ) r
          (lambda (r1) (_P* (cdr p*) (sub1 occ) ro r1 sc fc))
          fc)))

(define (_P p val r sc fc)
  (cond
    ((isPvar? p) (sc (upd-env (Pvar-V p) val r)))
    ((isPcst? p) (if (equal? (Pcst-C p) val) (sc r) (fc)))
    (else ; Pattern must be :-pattern!
     (if (pair? val)
         (_P (P:-P1 p) (car val) r
             (lambda (r1) (_P (P:-P2 p) (cdr val) r1 sc fc))
             fc)
         (fc)))))
```

Figure 4: A part of version 1 of the interpreter

3.2   The Second Implementation

The first problem that we treat is the one of redundant testing. What we need is some way to memorize what know we at a given time about the arguments we match against. For this purpose we introduce a new concept, a *description* which describes what we already know about an argument. We introduce a partial ordering on descriptions, saying that one description is less than another if the set of values it describes includes of the set of values the other describes. If we have

```
(define (test)
  (lambda (x)
    (lambda (y)
      (if (equal? 1 x)
          (if (pair? y)
              (if (equal? 2 (car y))
                  (((test) 1) (cdr y))
                  (_P1 x y x y x y x y))
              (_P1 x y x y x y x y))
          (_P1 x y x y x y x y)))))
(define (_P1 r7 val6 sc5 sc4 sc3 sc2 fc1 fc0)
  (if (pair? val6)
      (let ((val1 (car val6)))
        (if (equal? 5 (cdr val6)) (cons r7 val1) fc0))
      fc0))
```

Figure 5: Target program of the first version

two descriptions of some argument we can get a new description of the values by taking the least upper bound of the two descriptions. The set of values this new description describes is the intersection of the sets of values of the two original descriptions (assuming that the two descriptions do not conflict in which case it describes the empty set).

We now formalize descriptions. A description is an element in the domain Desc defined by:

$$\text{Desc} = \{\ \top, \bot\ \} \cup \text{Constant} \cup \{\ (d_1 : d_1) \mid d_1, d_1 \in \text{Desc}) \ \}$$
$$\cup \{\ \neg S \mid S \in \wp(\{\ :\ \} + \text{Constant})\}$$

where $\wp(S)$ indicates the powerset of S. In the following α and β are arbitrary elements in Desc. The ordering is:

$\alpha \sqsubseteq \top$
$\bot \sqsubseteq \alpha$
$\neg S \sqsubseteq c$ **if** $c \notin S$ **and** $c \in \text{Constant}$
$\neg S \sqsubseteq (\alpha_1 : \alpha_2)$ **if** $: \notin S$
$\neg S_1 \sqsubseteq \neg S_2$ **if** $S_1 \subseteq S_2$
$(\alpha_1 : \alpha_2) \sqsubseteq (\beta_1 : \beta_2)$ **if** $\alpha_1 \sqsubseteq \beta_1$ **and** $\alpha_2 \sqsubseteq \beta_2$

A description can be one of: A constant c, a pair-description $(\alpha_1 : \alpha_2)$[3], a nomatch description $\neg S$, the bottom element $\bot$ or the top element $\top$. The constant description says that the described value is the constant; the :-description says that the value is a pair with subdescriptions described by the two components of the pair. The nomatch description describes what the value is known not to match. : in this set means that the data is not a pair. There is no need for compound descriptions like (1:2) in the set of nomatch elements, because descriptions are supposed to describe results of tests. The only tests that are performed on values are equal? and pair? and therefore the only possible results of failed tests are that a value is not a

---

[3]Notice: : is here an constructor on descriptions

given constant or that it is not a pair. $\perp$ means "no information" about the value, and $\top$ describes a conflict. The least upper bound of descriptions is given by:

$$
\begin{array}{lll}
\perp \sqcup \alpha & = \alpha & \\
c \sqcup c & = c & \text{if } c \in \text{Constant} \\
c \sqcup \neg S & = c & \text{if } c \in \text{Constant and } \alpha \notin S \\
(\alpha_1{:}\alpha_2) \sqcup \neg S & = (\alpha_1{:}\alpha_2) & \text{if} : \notin S \\
\neg S_1 \sqcup \neg S_2 & = \neg(S_1 \cup S_2) & \\
(\alpha_1{:}\alpha_2) \sqcup (\beta_1{:}\beta_2) & = (\alpha_1 \sqcup \beta_1{:}\alpha_2 \sqcup \beta_2) & \text{if } (\alpha_1 \sqcup \beta_1) \neq \top \text{ and} \\
& & \quad (\alpha_2 \sqcup \beta_2) \neq \top \\
\alpha \sqcup \beta & = \top & \textbf{otherwise}
\end{array}
$$

together with the fact that $\sqcup$ is commutative.

We now change the semantics so that whenever a test is performed, the description is updated. If the result of a test can be decided entirely from the description, the test does not have to be performed at all.

A key point is that the modifications of the description depend only on the patterns. Therefore the description becomes static. This is an example where we have identified some static information and made it visible to the specializer.

The new semantics are shown in figure 6. Now L also builds up a list of bottom descriptions having a length corresponding to the arity of the function. This list is the initial description δ^* of the argument values.

The important point in the new version is that, before trying to match the next alternative, we test if the pattern list can match values with the given description. This is done by the operation inc? which returns true if the pattern and the description are incompatible. A pattern and a description are incompatible, if the pattern can not match any value in the set of values described by the description. To see why this is a good idea, let us look at this somewhat strange function:

```
(foo (x 2 7 = 1)
     (1 2 5 = 2)
     (x y z = 5))
```

If we fail to match the 2 pattern of the first alternative we should not consider the second alternative at all, and decide this before actually starting to match the patterns of the second alternative, because there is no need to first match against the 1 pattern and then fail when matching the 2 pattern, even if this failure is statically decidable from the description. If the language were lazy instead of strict, this optimization would be incorrect because it would change the semantics (e.g. evaluation of (foo bottom 1 1) would terminate, even if evaluation of bottom would fail to terminate).

If we write an interpreter from this second version of the semantics and generate a new compiler, we get the result shown in figure 7 when compiling the example program of section 2.1.

We see that the problem we set out to solve, the redundant testing, has disappeared. But the decomposition problem still remains.

Semantic domains:

$\delta \in$ Desc

Valuation functions:

D*:Definition* $\rightarrow$ F-env $\rightarrow$ F-env

$D^*[\![\ ]\!]\phi = \lambda f.\bot$

$D^*[\![(fa^*)d^*]\!]\phi = [[\![f]\!] \mapsto L\ a_f\ (\lambda\varrho.\lambda\delta^*.A^*[\![a^*]\!]\varrho\ a_f\delta^*\phi)](D^*[\![d^*]\!]\phi)$

L:$Nat \rightarrow$ Cont $\rightarrow$ Value

$L\ 0\ \kappa = \kappa\ \varrho_{init}\ [\ ]$

$L\ \omega\kappa = \underline{\lambda}v.L\ (\omega\text{-}1)\ (\lambda\varrho.\lambda\delta^*.\kappa\ ([\omega \mapsto v]\varrho[\bot_D|\ \delta^*])$

A*:Alternative* $\rightarrow$ O-env $\rightarrow$ Occ $\rightarrow$ Desc* $\rightarrow$ F-env $\rightarrow$ Value

$A^*[\![\ ]\!]\varrho\omega\delta^*\phi = \bot$

$A^*[\![(p^*=e)a^*]\!]\varrho\omega\delta^*\phi = inc?\ [\![p^*]\!][\![\delta^*]\!]\ \rightarrow A^*[\![a^*]\!]\varrho\omega\delta^*\phi$

$\qquad\qquad [\!]\ P^*[\![p^*]\!]\varrho\omega\delta^*(\lambda v.\bot)(\lambda\rho.E[\![e]\!]\rho\phi)(\lambda\delta^*_1.A^*[\![a^*]\!]\varrho\omega\delta^*_1\phi)$

P*:Pattern* $\rightarrow$ O-env $\rightarrow$ Occ $\rightarrow$ Desc* $\rightarrow$ V-env $\rightarrow$ S-cont $\rightarrow$ F-cont $\rightarrow$ Value

$P^*[\![\ ]\!]\varrho\omega\delta^*\rho\kappa_s\kappa_f = \kappa_s\ \rho$

$P^*[\![p\ p^*]\!]\varrho\omega[\delta|\delta^*]\rho\kappa_s\kappa_f =$

$\qquad P[\![p]\!](\varrho\ \omega)\delta\rho(\lambda\rho_1.\lambda\delta_1.P^*[\![p^*]\!]\varrho(\omega\text{-}1)\delta^*\rho_1\kappa_s(\lambda\delta^*_1.\kappa_f\ [\delta_1|\delta^*_1]))(\lambda\delta_1.\kappa_f\ [\delta_1|\delta^*])$

P:Pattern $\rightarrow$ Value $\rightarrow$ Desc $\rightarrow$ V-env $\rightarrow$ S-cont $\rightarrow$ F-cont $\rightarrow$ Value

$P[\![v]\!]v\delta\rho\kappa_s\kappa_f = \kappa_s\ ([[\![v]\!] \mapsto v]\rho)\ \delta$

$P[\![c]\!]v\delta\rho\kappa_s\kappa_f = isC?(\delta) \rightarrow \kappa_s\ \rho\ \delta$

$\qquad\qquad [\!]\ (C[\![c]\!]=v) \rightarrow \kappa_s\ \rho\ inD(C[\![c]\!])\ [\!]\ \kappa_f\ (\delta \sqcup inD(\neg\{C[\![c]\!]\}))$

$P[\![p]\!]v\delta\rho\kappa_s\kappa_f = isD:?(\delta) \rightarrow P:[\![p]\!]v\delta\rho\kappa_s\kappa_f$

$\qquad\qquad [\!]\ pair?(v) \rightarrow P:[\![p]\!]v\ inD(\bot_D:\bot_D)\rho\kappa_s\kappa_f\ [\!]\ \kappa_f\ (\delta \sqcup inD(\neg\{:\}))$

P::Pattern $\rightarrow$ Value $\rightarrow$ Desc $\rightarrow$ V-env $\rightarrow$ S-cont $\rightarrow$ F-cont $\rightarrow$ Value

$P:[\![(p_1:p_2)]\!](v_1,v_2)(\delta_1:\delta_2)\rho\kappa_s\kappa_f =$

$\quad P[\![p_1]\!]v_1\delta_1\rho$

$\quad (\lambda\rho_1.\lambda\delta'_1.P[\![p_2]\!]v_2\delta_2\rho(\lambda\rho_2.\lambda\delta'_2.\kappa_s\ \rho_2\ inD(\delta'_1:\delta'_2))(\lambda\delta'_2.\kappa_f\ inD(\delta'_1:\delta'_2)))$

$\quad (\lambda\delta'_1.\kappa_f\ inD(\delta'_1:\delta_2))$

Figure 6: Changes to the semantics for version 2

3.3 The Third Implementation

This section describes the idea behind the third version of the compiler, but without giving a detailed description of the semantics. The idea is to extend the argument environment also to hold values of subparts of the arguments. This new argument environment is updated with values of subparts of the values the first time these are found; they can then be retrieved whenever the subparts are used again. To point out the subparts, we define a concept called *occurrences*. An occurrence is a sequence of a's and d's pointing out a given subpart of some argument in such a way that the value of the subpart could be found by applying the corresponding sequence of car's and cdr's to the value. In order to know which argument the subpart belongs to the last element in the sequence will be the argument number.

```
(define (test)
  (lambda (x)
    (lambda (y)
      (cond
        ((equal? 1 x)
         (if (pair? y)
             (if (equal? 2 (car y))
                 (((test) 1) (cdr y))
                 (let ((val1 (car y)))
                   (if (equal? 5 (cdr y)) (cons x val1) y)))
             y))
        ((pair? y)
         (let ((val2 (car y)))
           (if (equal? 5 (cdr y)) (cons x val2) y)))
        (else y))))))
```

Figure 7: Target program of the second version

So an example of an occurrence could be [d a 2]. The environment that binds these occurrences to their values is called the *occurrence environment*.

Figure 8 shows a small part of the semantics for the last version. The central point in this version is that the decomposing of an argument into a given subpart has been moved to the point where the value of the subpart is first needed. When we need to know the value of some proper subpart of an argument, we first look at the description of this to see if this is $\perp$. If this is the case it means that the value has not been found before, so we have to force the computation of the subpart. For example, if the occurrence is [d a 2] the value is found by looking up the value of [a 2] in the occurrence environment and finding the right subpart of this value. The function FS is the function that finds the values of subparts.

Notice that the variable environment now binds variables to occurences. This means that updating a variable does not force any decomposing. The variable environment used in the evaluation of the right hand side of the alternative is not created until the match succeeds.

Similix's unfold strategy for let-expressions ensures that dynamic let-expressions only get unfolded when the let-variable is used exactly once. Therefore if we know that the specification (interpreter) only decomposes an argument into a given subpart at the most once and only when needed, then the same will be the case for the target programs.

If we write an interpreter from this third version of the semantics and generate a new compiler, we get the result shown in figure 9 when compiling the example program of section 2.1.

This code is now nearly optimal and looks much like the program one would write by hand. But one problem still remains to be solved.

This problem concerns the size of the code and is due to the fact that the two occurrences of cons both come from specialization of the _E function in the interpreter with respect to the expression of the second alternative in the source program. If this expression was not x:y, but some huge expression, we would get two, and in other cases more, huge copies of the specialized code.

Semantic domains:

$\rho \in$ VO-env $=$ Variable $\rightarrow$ Occ

$\kappa_s \in$ S-cont $=$ VO-env $\rightarrow$ O-env $\rightarrow$ Desc $\rightarrow$ Value

$\kappa_f \in$ F-cont $=$ O-env $\rightarrow$ Desc $\rightarrow$ Value

Valuation functions:

P:Pattern $\rightarrow$ O-env $\rightarrow$ Occ $\rightarrow$ Desc $\rightarrow$ VO-env $\rightarrow$ S-cont $\rightarrow$ F-cont $\rightarrow$ Value

$P[\![v]\!]\varrho\omega\delta\rho\kappa_s\kappa_f = \kappa_s\,([\![v]\!] \mapsto \omega]\rho)\,\varrho\,\delta$

$P[\![c]\!]\varrho\omega\delta\rho\kappa_s\kappa_f = \text{isC?}(\delta) \rightarrow \kappa_s\,\rho\,\varrho\,\delta$

$\quad\quad []\,(\delta=\perp_D) \rightarrow \text{let } v=\text{FS}\,\varrho\,\omega \text{ in}$

$\quad\quad\quad\quad (\text{C}[\![c]\!]=\text{v}) \rightarrow \kappa_s\,\rho\,([\omega \mapsto \text{v}]\varrho)\,\text{inD}(\text{C}[\![c]\!])$

$\quad\quad\quad\quad []\,\kappa_f\,([\omega \mapsto \text{v}]\varrho)\,(\delta\sqcup\,\text{inD}(\neg\{\text{C}[\![c]\!]\}))$

$\quad\quad []\text{let } v=\varrho\,\omega \text{ in}$

$\quad\quad\quad\quad (\text{C}[\![c]\!]=\text{v}) \rightarrow \kappa_s\,\rho\,\varrho\,\text{inD}(\text{C}[\![c]\!])\,[]\,\kappa_f\,\varrho\,(\delta\sqcup\,\text{inD}(\neg\{\text{C}[\![c]\!]\}))$

$P[\![p]\!]\varrho\omega\delta\rho\kappa_s\kappa_f = \text{isD:?}(\delta) \rightarrow P:[\![p]\!]\varrho\omega\delta\rho\kappa_s\kappa_f$

$\quad\quad []\,(\delta=\perp_D) \rightarrow \text{let } v=\text{FS}\,\varrho\,\omega \text{ in}$

$\quad\quad\quad\quad []\text{pair?}(\text{v}) \rightarrow P:[\![p]\!]([\omega \mapsto \text{v}]\varrho)\omega\,\text{inD}(\perp_D:\perp_D)\rho\kappa_s\kappa_f$

$\quad\quad\quad\quad []\,\kappa_f\,([\omega \mapsto \text{v}]\varrho)\,(\delta\sqcup\,\text{inD}(\neg\{:\}))$

$\quad\quad []\text{let } v=\varrho\,\omega \text{ in}$

$\quad\quad\quad\quad \text{pair?}(\text{v}) \rightarrow P:[\![p]\!]\varrho\omega\,\text{inD}(\perp_D:\perp_D)\rho\kappa_s\kappa_f\,[]\,\kappa_f\,\varrho\,(\delta\sqcup\,\text{inD}(\neg\{:\}))$

Figure 8: P function in the semantics for version 3

```
(define (test)
  (lambda (x)
    (lambda (y)
      (cond
       ((equal? 1 x)
        (if (pair? y)
            (let ((val1 (car y)))
              (cond
               ((equal? 2 val1) (((test) 1) (cdr y)))
               ((equal? 5 (cdr y)) (cons x val1))
               (else y)))
            y))
       ((pair? y)
        (if (equal? 5 (cdr y)) (cons x (car y)) y))
       (else y)))))
```

Figure 9: Target program of the third version

The reason why we get these identical pieces of code in the residual code is that they are the result of specializing the same code with respect to different values of some static arguments where the values had no influence on the result.

The static values in question are the values of the description and the occurrence environment. The problem is in fact that we have now collected static information (e.g. the description) that we might not need, but which still influences the specialization. One could solve this by removing superfluous parts of the description. This could be determined statically from the remaining patterns, but there is a simpler solution which is described in the next section.

3.4 Solving the Problem of Code Duplication

The code duplication problem can be solved in a simple way that gives an acceptable result where the code generated from the right-hand sides are shared. We replace the call to _E in _A* by a call to a new function rhs defined as follows:

```
(define (rhs e r phi)
  (_E e r phi))
```

We then force the specializer to make this function residual, i.e. not to unfold calls to it. Now the duplicated code becomes calls to specialized versions of rhs, and since the static arguments to rhs have the same values the code gets shared. Using this method we get the target program in figure 10.

```
(define (test)
  (lambda (x)
    (lambda (y)
      (cond
        ((equal? 1 x)
         (if (pair? y)
             (let ((val1 (car y)))
               (cond
                 ((equal? 2 val1) (((test) 1) (cdr y)))
                 ((equal? 5 (cdr y)) (rhs1 x val1))
                 (else y)))
             y))
        ((pair? y)
         (if (equal? 5 (cdr y)) (rhs1 x (car y)) y))
        (else y)))))
(define (rhs1 r1 r0) (cons r1 r0))
```

Figure 10: Target program with sharing of right hand sides

Now the code generated from the right-hand sides is shared, but some of the matching code, is still duplicated (e.g. (if (equal? 5 (cdr y)) ...)).

3.5 The Compiler

The structure of the part of the compiler involving the pattern matching is rather complex and will not be shown. The compiler has 43 functions and the size is 49552 bytes. The compiler was run on a Sun 3/160 using Chez Scheme Version 2.0.3, and the time used to compile the example from section 2.1 was 0.43 CPU seconds, not including garbage collection.

Running the first version of the interpreter 1000 times on the example of section 2.1 with input '(1 . (2 . (2 . (2 . (2 . 3)))) takes 18.1 sec, while running the target program on the same input 1000 times takes 0.73 sec. This gives a speedup of around 25 times.

The speedup gained by the optimazations can in general be made arbitrary large, but tests run on a few smaler examples has shown a speedup of around 2 times from version 1 to version 3.

4   Extensions

This section discusses some possible ways to extend the work presented.

4.1   Other Kinds of Patterns

Extending the pattern matching to handle other kinds of patterns poses no great problems. Repeated variables can be treated by keeping a list of variables encountered so far. When meeting a new variable one can easily decide if this is already bound and, if so, check the value. Wildcard variables can be treated as normal variables, except that no updating should take place. User defined constructors can also be handled, but is related more closely to typed languages. One needs some information about the constructors, at least the arity, to be able to generate good code.

4.2   Use of Type Information

The combinator language considered in this paper is untyped, but most of the languages it resembles are typed. One could consider using type information to get even better matching code. For example, the function append:

```
(append (()      ys = ys)
        ((x : xs) ys = x : (append xs ys)))
```

compiles to:

```
(define (append)
  (lambda (xs)
    (lambda (ys)
      (cond
        ((equal? () xs) ys)
        ((pair? xs) (cons (car xs) (((append) (cdr xs)) ys)))
        (else (error ...)))))))
```

But if the language were typed and there were type information making : and () the only two members of a family of constructors, then knowing that a program is well-typed and that some value is not equal to () would imply that the value must be of the form (v1,v2). In this case the matching algorithm should not update the description to be $\neg$ {()}, but $(\perp_D : \perp_D)$. Using this type information append now compiles to the "usual" Scheme definition:

```
(define (append)
  (lambda (xs)
```

```
(lambda (ys)
  (if (equal? () xs)
      ys
      (cons (car xs) (((append) (cdr xs)) ys)))))))))
```

A similar solution can be found to handle type declarations with more than two constructors. The final result for the append function was in fact produced by a compiler generated from an extended version of the third interpreter.

4.3 Lazy Pattern Matching

It has been shown by Bondorf [3] that it is possible to use partial evaluation to generate compilers for lazy languages and it is also fairly easy to change the interpreter for the combinator language to become lazy. This amounts to inserting "force" and "delay" operations at strategic places in the interpreter and, as mentioned above (section 3.2), to leave out the test inc? that was introduced in the second version. But leaving out the test inc? means that we also have to introduce a new test to check whether a constant pattern matches a constant description.

5 Related Work

To our knowledge, the first published work on matching and partial evaluation is Emanuelson [6]. He used partial evaluation to optimize pattern matching in text manipulation. The matching involved only one pattern. Since the partial evaluator he used was not self-applicable, no compiler was generated. Also, since he did no rewriting of the interpreter, his target programs have the same problems as those of our first version.

A work similar to ours is [5] where the matching problem is to find a given substring within another string. A general string pattern matcher is rewritten several times finaly leading to the Knuth, Morris and Pratt algorithm [10]. The difference between their work and ours is that while we treat many patterns and that these are trees with variables, they only treat one one constant pattern (the substring).

The first published description of a pattern matching compiler is Augustsson's description of the techniques used in the LML compiler [1]. A good description where Augustsson's work is pressented and extended is given by Wadler in [17]. The following example is taken from this, except that the right hand sides have been slightly changed:

```
(demo (f '()      ys       = ys)
      (f xs       '()      = xs)
      (f (x : xs) (y : ys) = (f x y) : (demo xs ys)))
```

Compiling this program with the final version of the compiler extended with type information on : and () gives the following target program:

```
(define (demo)
  (lambda (f)
    (lambda (xs)
```

```
(lambda (ys)
 (cond
  ((equal? () xs) ys)
  ((equal? () ys) xs)
  (else
   (cons ((f (car xs)) (car ys))
         ((((demo) f) (cdr xs)) (cdr ys)))))))))))
```

This result is actually better than the one Wadler gets. Wadler defines a restricted class of function definitions, that he calls *uniform definitions*. A definition is uniform if the patterns are such that the order of the alternatives does not matter (regardless of the right hand sides). The compilers of Augustsson or Wadler do not in general give good matching code for non uniform definitions, i.e the resulting code may examine some arguments more than once.

6   Conclusion

It has been outlined how optimizing compilers can be generated by changing specifications. The method is demonstrated on a combinator language using pattern matching where the development of a compiler for the language was described. This compiler generates very efficient matching code and the way in which the compiler was developed ensured that the target programs possesed certain properties. These are:

- An argument to a function is only tested at most once for a given property and only when needed.

- A compound argument to a function is only decomposed at most once, and only when needed.

- No code duplication of right hand sides.

- Could be extended to use type information.

These properties ensure that the compiler is capable of treating non uniform definitions in a satisfactory way.

One problem with the method is that it can give target code size that is exponential in the size of the patterns. This problem might be solved, if a method can be found that also gives sharing of matching code.

It is an interesting open problem whether the methods demonstrated in this paper can be made automatic. It should then be a part of the preprocess phase of the partial evaluater, because knowledge of binding time values is necessary to do the rewriting.

On the other hand it would be better if one could improve the process of partial evaluation in such a way that no rewriting is nessesary. Two methods generalizing the ideas used in partial evaluation look promising: Supercompilation by Turchin [15] and Generalized Partial Computation by Futamura and Nogi [7].

7 Acknowledgement

Many people have contributed in various ways; but I would especially like to thank Anders Bondorf, Torben Mogensen, Olivier Danvy and Neil D. Jones for valuable inspiration, help and comments. I would like to thank the referees: Carsten Kehler Holst, Duncan Sinclair, Rogardt Heldal and Geoff Hamilton for comments on how to improve the paper, and I also like to thank Jette Holm Broløs, Grethe Jørgensen and the members of the Topps group at DIKU.

References

[1] Lennart Augustsson. Compiling pattern matching. In J.-P. Jouannaud, editor, *Conference on Functional Programming Languages and Computer Architecture, Nancy, France. Lecture Notes in Computer Science 201*, pages 368–381, Springer-Verlag, 1985.

[2] Anders Bondorf. Automatic autoprojection of higher order recursive equations. In Neil D. Jones, editor, *ESOP'90, Copenhagen, Denmark. Lecture Notes in Computer Science 432*, pages 70–87, Springer-Verlag, May 1990.

[3] Anders Bondorf. Compiling laziness by partial evaluation. In *1990 Glasgow Workshop on Functional Programming, Ullapool, Computing Science Department, Glasgow University, Glasgow, Scotland*, 1990.

[4] Anders Bondorf and Olivier Danvy. *Automatic autoprojection of recursive equations with global variables and abstract data types*. Technical Report 90-4, DIKU, University of Copenhagen, Denmark, 1990.

[5] Charles Consel and Olivier Danvy. Partial evaluation of pattern matching in strings. *Information Processing Letters*, 30(2):79–86, 1989.

[6] Pär Emanuelson. From abstract model to efficient compilation of patterns. In M. Dezani-Ciancaglini and U. Montanan, editors, *International Symposium on Programming, 5th Colloquium, Turin, Lecture Notes in Computer Science 137*, pages 91–104, Springer-Verlag, April 1982.

[7] Yoshihiko Futamura and Kenroku Nogi. Genreralized partial computation. In Dines Bjørner, Andrei P. Ershov, and Neil D. Jones, editors, *Partial Evaluation and Mixed Computation*, pages 133–151, North-Holland, 1988.

[8] Neil D. Jones, Carsten K. Gomard, Anders Bondorf, Olivier Danvy, and Torben Æ. Mogensen. A self-applicable partial evaluator for the lambda calculus. In *IEEE Computer Society 1990 International Conference on Computer Languages*, IEEE, March 1990.

[9] Neil D. Jones, Peter Sestoft, and Harald Søndergaard. An experiment in partial evaluation: the generation of a compiler generator. In J.-P. Jouannaud, editor, *Rewriting Techniques and Applications, Dijon, France. Lecture Notes in Computer Science 202*, pages 124–140, Springer-Verlag, 1985.

[10] Donald E. Knuth, James H. Morris, and Vaughan R. Pratt. Fast pattern matching in strings. *Siam Journal on Computing*, 6(2):323–350, 1977.

[11] Paul Hudak and Philip Wadler, editors. *Report on the programming language Haskell*. Technical Report, Yale University and Glasgow University, April 1990.

[12] Jonathan Rees and William Clinger. Revised report[3] on the algorithmic language scheme. *Sigplan Notices*, 21(12):37–79, December 1986.

[13] David A. Schmidt. *Denotational Semantics, a Methodology for Language Development*. Allyn and Bacon, Boston, 1986.

[14] Peter Sestoft. The structure of a self-applicable partial evaluator. In Harald Ganzinger and Neil D. Jones, editors, *Programs as Data Objects, Copenhagen, Denmark. Lecture Notes in Computer Science 217*, pages 236–256, Springer-Verlag, October 1985.

[15] Valentin F. Turchin. The concept of a supercompiler. *Transactions on Programming Languages and Systems*, 8(3):292–325, 1986.

[16] David Turner. An overview of Miranda. *Sigplan Notices*, 21(12):158–166, December 1986.

[17] Philip Wadler. Efficient compilation of pattern-matching. In Simon L. Peyton Jones, editor, *The Implementation of Functional Programming Languages*, chapter 5, pages 78–103, Prentice-Hall, 1987.

An Experiment using Term Rewriting Techniques for Concurrency

Carron Kirkwood*
Department of Computing Science
University of Glasgow

November 14, 1990

Extended Abstract

Introduction

The purpose of this extended abstract is to report on a preliminary investigation into the use of term rewriting theorem proving to support verification of formal description techniques for concurrent systems. The RRL [1, 2] system, particularly Knuth-Bendix completion and equational proofs, is used to investigate verification of specifications written in the formal description language LOTOS. This work was completed as part of the SERC/IED ERIL project, which is investigating the use of Equational Reasoning for LOTOS. A more complete presentation of the results given here may be found in [3]. That paper also reports on complementary work, also undertaken as part of the ERIL project, using the LP theorem prover [4] for equational and inductive proofs about CSP [5].

The examples we present are all small ones, but are already at the level where hand verification is tedious and error prone. They execute immediately in RRL, and give hope that the same techniques can be used on much larger examples.

Experiments using LOTOS and RRL

LOTOS (Language of Temporal Ordering Specification) is based on the concept of specifying a system in terms of observable behaviour, i.e. events. Constraints may be expressed on the order of events, but there is no explicit representation of time. The communication and change of information within a system is expressed by the structure of the events.

LOTOS is made up of two distinct parts. The process part describes the behaviour of processes and is based on CCS, with some modifications drawn from other concurrency formalisms, such as CSP. The abstract data type part describes the observable behaviour of the data being exchanged by the processes. The application of term rewriting systems to abstract data types is a well researched area;

---

*Funded by SERC grant gr/f 35371/ 4/1/1477, Verification Techniques for LOTOS.

what is not so clear is how suitable such systems are for theorem proving in the process algebra of LOTOS.

The aim of our experiments was to generate a *complete* set of rewrite rules from the axioms of weak bisimulation congruence presented in appendix B.2.2 of the LOTOS standard.

For a set of rewrite rules to be *complete* two properties are required: the equational system must be *confluent* and *terminating*. These properties ensure that every term has a unique normal form and give us a decision procedure for equality of terms.

A set of rules with these properties can be used in a variety of ways. We have a decision procedure for the word problem specified by the original equational system. We have a check for consistency and completeness of algebraic data types. We can carry out proofs by inductionless induction, and proofs by refutation in First Order Predicate Calculus.

The Rewrite Rule Laboratory (RRL) was used to attempt to generate a complete set of rules. RRL can perform completion in the presence of a-c operators and has a limited form of order-sortedness.

The set of axioms used was built up incrementally, adding new axioms one by one, and rejecting those which cause the completion algorithm to fail or diverge. At present only a small subset of the axioms in appendix B.2.2 have been successfully run through the completion procedure. However, even this small set of rewrite rules can be useful.

Equational Proofs

With the complete set of rules obtained, simple equational proofs may now be carried out which were not possible before completion. Examples of these are:

$$(A \gg stop) \gg B \equiv A \gg stop$$
$$((A \gg exit) \gg exit) \gg B \equiv (A \gg exit) \gg B$$

For a more complex example, see figure 1.

This example shows that a two-way buffer is the same as two one-way buffers in parallel. Unfortunately, this example is a little forced as recursion is not part of our restricted LOTOS. This means that these buffers only handle one data element and then die.

The second statement in this example is far easier to read than the first, demonstrating that simply-defined processes in parallel are frequently easier to understand than large process written without parallelism.

The rules already generated are not enough to prove the buffer example; laws relating some of the higher level constructs (such as parallelism) to the basic constructs of action sequencing and choice are also required. These are known as the expansion laws. Any LOTOS process can be written using just action sequencing and choice. The expansion law required here is the following:

$$B \mid [A] \mid C = \quad [] \ \{b_i; (B_i \mid [A] \mid C) \mid name \ (b_i \notin A, i \in I\}$$
$$[] [] \ \{c_j; (B \mid [A] \mid C_j) \mid name \ (c_j \notin A, j \in J\}$$
$$[] [] \ \{a; (B_i \mid [A] \mid C_j) \mid a = b_i = c_j, name \ (a) \in A, i \in I, j \in J\}$$

$$
\begin{array}{l}
(x1; \quad (x2; \quad (y1; \ y2; \ \text{exit} \\
\qquad\qquad\qquad [] \ (y2; \ y1; \ \text{exit})) \\
\qquad\quad [] \ (y1; \ x2; \ y2; \ \text{exit})) \\
[] \ (x2; \quad (x1; \quad (y1; \ y2; \ \text{exit} \\
\qquad\qquad\quad [] \ y2; \ y1; \ \text{exit}) \\
\qquad\quad [] \ (y2; \ x1; \ y1; \ \text{exit})))
\end{array}
$$

is weak bisimulation congruent to

$$(x1; \ y1; \ \text{exit}) \ ||| \ (x2; \ y2; \ \text{exit})$$

Figure 1: Buffer example

This law cannot be entered straight into RRL because generalised choice is not a part of the restricted LOTOS used, so two useful instantiations of this expansion law are derived:

$$a; A \ ||| \ b; B \ == \ (a; (A \ ||| \ b; B)) \ [] \ (b; (B \ ||| \ a; A)))$$
$$a; A \ ||| \ \text{exit} \ == \ a; (A \ ||| \ \text{exit})$$

When these are added to the complete set of rules, the equivalence in figure 1 may be proved as an equational theorem.

Axioms causing Infinite Sequences of Rewrite Rules

As mentioned earlier, some axioms of appendix B.2.2 caused the completion procedure to diverge, generating an infinite sequence of rewrite rules. It would be useful if these rules could be generalised by producing a finite set of rules that subsume the infinite sequence of rules and are terminating and confluent. Further details of various techniques for generalising infinite sequences of rules may be found in [6, 7, 8].

Some attempts were made to generalise the particular sequences obtained. For example, the law distributing **hide** across $\gg$,

$$\textbf{hide A in } (B_1 \gg B_2) \equiv (\text{hide } A \text{ in } B_1) \gg (\text{hide } A \text{ in } B_2)$$

produces two distinct infinite sequences of rewrite rules. The generalisations for these are as follows.

$B_1 \gg B_2 \rightarrow B_1$
where B_1 has **stop** *as the rightmost argument*
and B_1 is built from applications of **hide** *and* $\gg$.

and

$(B_1 \gg B_2) \gg B_3 \rightarrow B_1 \gg B_3$
where B_2 is built from applications of **hide**, $\gg$ *and* **exit**,
and B_2 is a subterm of B_1.

The sequences generated by this rules can be eliminated by adding two new rules.

$$\text{hide } A \text{ in stop} \equiv \text{stop} \qquad\qquad since \ L\text{(stop)} = \emptyset$$
$$\text{hide } A \text{ in exit} \equiv \text{exit} \qquad\qquad since \ L\text{(exit)} = \emptyset$$

However, most of the infinite sequences generated by our experiments were not so easy to eliminate. For example:

The rules in the infinite sequence generated by the addition of the axiom for associativity of choice (A [] B) [] C == A [] (B [] C) follow this basic pattern:

$$A \,[]\, B \rightarrow B$$

This rule is of course undesirable as it makes choice totally unfair (it will always choose the second argument). Also it is not an exact generalisation (i.e. not every instantiation is a rule) and so adding it would imply unsound equivalences. We know that A is a subterm of B (by inspection of the rules generated), but there is a more complex relationship between these two terms, which deserves further investigation.

Other Results

It is expected that the weak bisimulation congruence laws in appendix B of the LOTOS standard will be sound. It was suspected that this was not true and our experiments revealed an inconsistency.

When deciding which laws to use we entered:

$$A \gg \text{stop} \equiv A \,|||\, \text{stop}$$

When taken with other rules in the rule set, this rule causes the following contradiction:

$$\text{i; stop} \equiv \text{stop}$$

Under weak bisimulation congruence this is false as the two equivalent processes are required to behave in the same way in all contexts. To test this condition it is necessary only to test the way in which the processes behave when part of a choice statement.

Conclusions and Further Work

We conducted an experiment in the application of term rewriting to the concurrency formalism, LOTOS. While the results we obtained were hopeful, we appreciate that there is still much work to be carried out in this area.

This preliminary investigation has been successful in that not only have we have shown that term rewriting is useful in reasoning about concurrency, we have also uncovered several areas for further development.

Acknowledgements

We should like to thank Deepak Kapur for letting us have RRL. We would especially like to thank Ursula Martin, Muffy Thomas and Phil Watson, our colleagues.

References

[1] D. Kapur and H. Zhang, RRL : Rewrite Rule Laboratory User's Manual, 1987, Revised May 1989.

[2] H. Zhang, D. Kapur, M.S. Krishnamoorthy: *A Mechanizable Induction Principle for Equational Specifications*, Proc. 9th Intl. Conference on Automated Deduction, LNCS 310 (1988).

[3] C. Kirkwood and K. Norrie, Some Experiments using Term Rewriting Techniques for Concurrency. Technical Report — Royal Holloway and Bedford New College, 1990.

[4] S.J. Garland, J.V. Guttag: *An Overview of LP, The Larch Prover*, Proc. Rewriting Techniques and Applications, 3rd Intl. Conference, LNCS 355 (1989), 137-151.

[5] C. A. R. Hoare, Communicating Sequential Processes, Prentice-Hall, 1985.

(September 1988)

[6] M. Thomas and K.P. Jantke, Inductive Inference for Solving Divergence in Knuth-Bendix Completion, Proc. Analogical and Inductive Inference '89, GDR, LNCS 367, Springer-Verlag, 1989.

[7] St. Lange, Towards a Set of Inference Rules for Solving Divergence in Knuth-Bendix Completion, Proc. Analogical and Inductive Inference '89, GDR, LNCS 367, Springer-Verlag, 1989.

[8] M. Thomas and P. Watson, Solving Divergence in Knuth-Bendix Completion by Enriching Signatures, in preparation, 1990.

TYPE REFINEMENT IN RUBY

DAVID MURPHY

UNIVERSITY OF GLASGOW

ABSTRACT. This paper is about refinement in *Ruby*. Ruby is a relational language whose main concern is structure; it describes how primitive relations are structured to form a larger relation. As such, it is admirably suited to the design of VLSI or highly parallel systems.

Design in Ruby usually proceeds by *calculation*. One starts with a high-level relational description of a system, and gradually refines it towards an implementation. Refinement is achieved by the use of laws, – every Ruby combinator has many laws describing how it can be manipulated, introduced and eliminated, – and by introducing more information. A refinement step, then, involves calculating a new relation from a old one. Most of the Ruby literature concentrates on refinement using 'built-in' laws; this paper, in contrast, will focus on the matter of adding new information from outside the system. (Such information will capture pragmatic engineering decisions, and should be articulated as formally as possible, so that the consequences of those decisions can be elucidated.)

Typically, a Ruby specification will involve user-defined types; in writing the specification of an arithmetic chip, for instance, we may well need to deal with various rings of integers. These types must eventually be implemented in whatever the target medium provides: bits in VLSI; more primitive data-types in some parallel software applications. Hence, at some stage in the design, the user-defined types will need to be refined; a ring of integers, for instance, will often be implemented using fixed size words of bits. We will be concerned with describing how such type refinement information can be used properly. In particular, the later a type refinement happens in a design, the more global we want the effects to be. Thus we will show how to drag type constructors thorugh 'plumbing' circuitry to achieve this effect.

1. INTRODUCTION

The relational language Ruby was initially introduced by Sheeran and Jones to describe the structure of calculations amenable to layout on silicon. A good introduction is [10] or [4]. These techniques had some success in describing and implementing systolic algorithms, [11], and latterly in deriving architectures used for digital signal processing, [7]. The paradigm is of 'design by calculation.' (It has been developed for (sequential) software applications by Bird, cf. [1].) In this section the notion of refinement in Ruby will be formalised, and some of the advantages of the Ruby style will be discussed.

Department of Computer Science, Glasgow, G12 8QQ. Email : dvjm@uk.ac.glasgow.cs.

1.1. REFINEMENT IN RUBY

Refinement in Ruby is treated in [5]. Here we give our own perspective. The basic idea is that the behaviour of a system, be it a circuit or a piece of software, can be thought of as a binary relation. The system relates pieces of data to pieces of data. Thus our behavioural calculus will be the calculus of (binary) relations.

When attempting to design a system, we start off with some notion of how the data will behave, some set of constraints on the inputs, if you like. Call this C. Under these conditions, we would like some behaviour to be manifest, some relation to hold, R say. Thus a specification is a set of constraints and a relation, and we want the system to ensure that if the constraints are met then the relation will hold, so a specification is a statement $C \vdash R$. A refinement step will usually involve noting more information about the data processed, additional constraints C' say, and using this information to obtain a new specification $C, C' \vdash R'$ involving a new relations R'. Thus a refinement step has the form

$$\frac{C \vdash R}{C, C' \vdash R'}$$

Often, no extra assumptions are made. In this case the derivation can be made both ways and we have

$$\frac{C \vdash R}{C \vdash R'}$$

(where we use a double line to indicate that the inference can be drawn both ways). In this latter case, where we can deduce C from the context, we often write just $R = R'$.

1.2. DESIGN BY CALCULATION

In the design-by-calculation tradition, the relation R' is obtained from R by calculation. In this sense Ruby can be said to be *constructive*. There are several advantages to the design-by-calculation approach: –

- The calculus is *homogenous*; both specifications and implementations are the same kind of object, namely relations. One can stop refining a specification when one reaches a suitable level; a library components in VLSI, for instance.
- Refinement steps are made because of design decisions. One cannot introduce a refinement without being aware of its consequences on the design. Thus Ruby offers a convenient way of articulating design decisions and of investigating their consequences cheaply.
- It is relatively easy, as we showed in [7], to turn a Ruby description of an algorithm into a simulation of that algorithm. Tools to propitiate the development of Ruby descriptions are being developed.
- There are various non-standard interpretations of Ruby programs; see [6]. These allow one to obtain various measures on the program, such as area consumed, maximum delay and so on. Such measures are vitally important if the target medium is silicon, for there many design decisions are taken for extra-algorithmic reasons; faster algorithms, for instance, are often rejected in favour of more regular, or lower-area ones.

- Design-by-calculation proceeds easily if there are lots of combinators and lots of laws about those combinators. Ruby uses generic combinators that correspond to commonly found ways of organising data-flow in algorithms. (These resemble the combinators of a functional language.) Using such generic combining forms has the advantage of separating *structural* information from *computational* information. Indeed, in contrast to VLSI verification techniques such as HOL, it might be claimed that the latter is much more implicit in Ruby while the former is clearly elucidated.

1.3. THE REMAINDER OF THE PAPER

The rest of the paper is organised as follows. The next section presents an introduction to the Ruby language and introduces most of the notation that will be used. Here some of the most useful refinement rules are given. The following section discusses polymorphism and presents some new results on type refinement and the conditions when it is allowed. The paper concludes with an abbreviated example of the use of type refinement. More comprehensive use of these ideas is made in [7].

2. RUBY

The design of circuits is an activity which spans many levels of abstraction, from specification to layout in a particular technology. Ruby is suitable for passage between the upper few levels of this hierarchy; it is useful for specification capture, algorithm design and, to a limited extent, abstract layout.

In this section the language Ruby will be briefly introduced. Some primitives and their associated transformation rules will be discussed; in general, we confine ourselves to the material that will be used later in the paper. These laws capture the semantics of Ruby in a useful form, indicating the valid ways of decomposing and reasonning about programs.

Before proceeding, one slightly unusual aspect of Ruby should be mentioned: each Ruby expression has an associated *picture*. These pictures or *abstract floorplans* show the connectivity or possible flow(s) of information, of signals, through the structure of a Ruby expression. They enable us to see the structural consequences of design decisions,* make the progress of a design more visible, and generally aid the intuition. However, we will never *reason* with pictures; they are not parts of the calculus.

2.1. RELATIONS AND CIRCUITS

Circuits in Ruby are described by binary relations. The basic idea is that a device is a *constraint* that holds between its ports. Thus, some device R with connections

---

*Abstract floorplans are useful for indicating *locality*; whether or not components are connected to components that are near to them. They also indicate the possibility of signal cross-over. Both of these factors are important factors in determining the cost of fabricating a circuit.

204

to the outside world x and y might be described as $(x, y) \in R$ or, more usefully,

$$x \, R \, y$$

This is an assertion about the behaviour of R.

The associated picture is

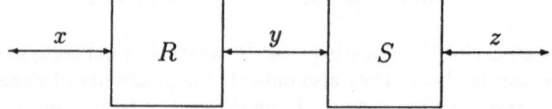

and the intention is for the reader to think of R as somehow constraining x and y.

Although Ruby is relational, we will often want to think of some signals as 'really' inputs and some as outputs. To that end, a convention governs pictures; the left-hand edge of a relation will be called its *domain* and will often contain 'inputs,' while the right-hand edge will be the relation's *range* and will often contain 'outputs.'

The fundamental notion, then, is of a circuit as a relation between its connections. We will not constrain ourselves to thinking of the domain and range of a relation as just electronic signals, – we may want to think of an entire circuit as a single relation, and thus consider relations that operate on complex data types. The issue of the Ruby *type system* will be dealt with later; merely notice now that we write

$$R :: \alpha \sim \beta$$

to indicate that R relates something of type α to something of type β, and annotate the picture as above.

Our first example of a relation will be the relation not $::$ **Bool** $\sim$ **Bool** defined thus;

$$x \text{ not } y \iff x = \neg y$$

Here a relation called "not" has been defined over the Booleans **Bool**. Two booleans x and y are related by not iff x is the negation of y.

Notice that we have not committed ourselves to the nature of *values* in Ruby; $x \, R \, y$ can be thought of as either relating a *single value* x to a single value y or a *stream* of values x to a stream of values y. Thus Ruby can describe combinatoric circuits or clocked synchronous ones with equal ease; see [2] for details.

2.2. COMPOSITION

Composition of relations is defined by

$$x \, (R \, ; \, S) \, z \iff \exists y. \; x \, R \, y \; \& \; y \, S \, z$$

The picture shows a connection of the range of R to the domain of S;

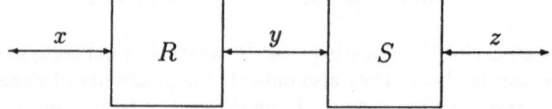

Relational composition is obviously associative;

$$(R \mathbin{;} S) \mathbin{;} T = R \mathbin{;} S \mathbin{;} T = R \mathbin{;} (S \mathbin{;} T)$$

and it often makes sense to define the *iterated composition* of a relation;

$$\begin{aligned} R^1 &= R \\ R^{n+1} &= R \mathbin{;} R^n \end{aligned}$$

(At this stage, we might go on to investigate some of the laws relating to composition a little further. For instance, if for some R and S it is the case that $R \mathbin{;} S = S \mathbin{;} R$, then, by induction, $R \mathbin{;} S^n = S^n \mathbin{;} R$. The reader should have no trouble in proving facts like these about the operators introduced as the need arises.)

2.3. INVERSE

The *inverse* of a relation R, written $R^{\leftharpoonup}$, just swaps the domain and the range;

$$y \, R^{\leftharpoonup} \, x \iff x \, R \, y$$

Pictorially, inverse is just reflection: the connections on the left of R appear on the right of $R^{\leftharpoonup}$ and vice versa.

If $R :: \alpha \sim \beta$ and $x \, R \, y$ then we can picture $R^{\leftharpoonup}$ as

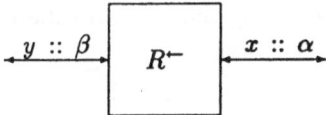

Since reflecting twice gets us back the original circuit, for any relation R the inverse of its inverse is the same circuit; $(R^{\leftharpoonup})^{\leftharpoonup} = R$.

A good example of Ruby's relational nature can be seen by reconsidering the relation not :: **Bool** $\sim$ **Bool**; Clearly, since $\neg\neg x = x$, not$^{\leftharpoonup}$ = not, and the picture of the relation not is rotation-invariant. By using the relational calculus, we have abstracted away from the notion of which port is the input and which the output of the not-gate.

Inverse and composition interact quite simply; you can reflect the picture of a composition by swapping the components and reflecting each of them, so keeping corresponding edges connected;

$$(R \mathbin{;} S)^{\leftharpoonup} = (S^{\leftharpoonup}) \mathbin{;} (R^{\leftharpoonup})$$

(Notice that this law has an implicit quantification; it should be read '*for all relations R and S, the inverse of R composed with S is ...*')

Notice too that we have used $R^{\leftharpoonup}$ for the inverse of R rather than the more usual R^{-1}. This is to stop one concluding that, since $R^{m+n} = R^m \mathbin{;} R^n$, it is the case that $R^{m-n} = R^m \mathbin{;} (R^{\leftharpoonup})^n$. This latter equation does *not*, in general, hold. Furthermore, given some relation R which relates things of type α to things of type α, written $R :: \alpha \sim \alpha$, it is also *not* always the case that the expression $R \mathbin{;} R^{\leftharpoonup}$ is the identity on α, which we will write id_α and deal with further in the discussion of the type system in the next subsection.

206

A circuit and its inverse often appear separated by another relation, as here;

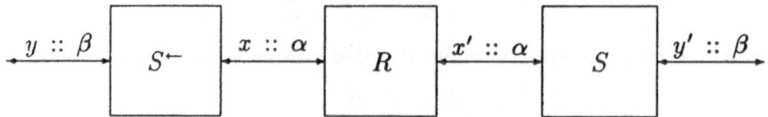

This is *conjugation* construction. The R conjugate of S, written $R \setminus S$, is defined as;

$$R \setminus S \stackrel{\mathrm{def}}{=} S^{\leftarrow} \,;\, R \,;\, S$$

It is easy to derive the composite behaviour of conjugation and composition; if we have $S \,;\, S^{\leftarrow} = \mathsf{id}_\beta$ then

$$(R \setminus S) \,;\, (T \setminus S) = (R \,;\, T) \setminus S$$

2.4. INTRODUCING THE RUBY TYPE SYSTEM

The reader should be warned before proceeding any further that the Ruby type system is under development; the definitive work will be [8].

There is clearly a need for a type system for Ruby; we would like to be able to impose types on our relations, and to have the added security and convenience of a type checker. Naïvely, we can just suppose that the domain and range of a relation are typed, that is, anything that appears there will be a member of some set, known as a type. When asserting

$$R :: \alpha \sim \beta$$

we mean that if $x \, R \, y$ then we will always be able to say that x is of type α and y is of type β. Any attempt to violate this, for instance by writing $x \, R \, y$ where x is not of type α is merely meaningless.

Each type α will come endowed with an *identity* relation id_α, defined thus; if x is of type α, (written $x :: \alpha$), then

$$x \, \mathsf{id}_\alpha \, x$$

always. A consequence of this, of course, is that $\mathsf{id}_\alpha = \mathsf{id}_\alpha{}^{\leftarrow}$ and $\mathsf{id}_\alpha{}^n = \mathsf{id}_\alpha$. (I.e. identities are reflexive, symmetric and transitive relations.)

If $R :: \alpha \sim \beta$ then we demand that[†]

$$
\begin{aligned}
R &= \mathsf{id}_\alpha \,;\, R \\
R &= R \,;\, \mathsf{id}_\beta
\end{aligned}
$$

The view of the type system given above enables us to understand conjugation a little better. We can see that $R \setminus S$ for $S :: \alpha \sim \beta$ is only defined if $R :: \alpha \sim \alpha$.

[†]We might be tempted to follow the spirit of [3] and *define* the type of a relation R as $\alpha \sim \beta$ if and only if $R = \mathsf{id}_\alpha \,;\, R \,;\, \mathsf{id}_\beta$ but this would be a mistake, since there that would not guarantee we had found the most general type (the 'smallest' α and β such that the above holds). Certainly, under those conditions R could be typed as $\alpha \sim \beta$, but we want to reserve $R :: \alpha \sim \beta$ for the assertion that α and β are the *smallest* types such that $R = \mathsf{id}_\alpha \,;\, R$ and $R = R \,;\, \mathsf{id}_\beta$. The existence of such a *principal* type will not be discussed here; see [8] for details.

We can think of conjugation as allowing us to perform *data reification*; if we have an operation defined in terms of an abstract data-type β then we can implement it in terms of a concrete operation R over a concrete data-type α, by using an *abstraction*, S.

As an example consider negation over Bits **Bit**. We have required that **true** not **false** and **false** not **true**. Assume as given a bit-level negation,

$$1 \quad invert \quad 0$$
$$0 \quad invert \quad 1$$

The relation "not" can then be implemented using the abstraction *abs* and *invert*;

$$1 \quad abs \quad \textbf{true}$$
$$0 \quad abs \quad \textbf{false}$$

since not $= invert \setminus abs$.

For this to work, of course, the abstraction mechanism must be faithful; we require that $abs \; ; \; abs^{\leftarrow} = \mathsf{id}_\beta$. This means that the abstraction *invabs* where

$$1 \quad invabs \quad \textbf{false}$$
$$0 \quad invabs \quad \textbf{true}$$

would have done as well, but

$$1 \quad nonabs \quad \textbf{true}$$
$$0 \quad nonabs \quad \textbf{true}$$

would not, since $nonabs \; ; \; nonabs^{\leftarrow} \neq \mathsf{id}_{\textbf{Bit}}$. If a relation $S :: \alpha \sim \beta$ is faithful over β, i.e. if $S^{\leftarrow} \; ; \; S = \mathsf{id}_\beta$, then we call S an *abstraction* over β. Notice that we do *not* require that $S \; ; \; S^{\leftarrow} = \mathsf{id}_\alpha$. Simplistically, we might say that not all concrete elements of α need represent abstract elements of β.

In Ruby we always assume that the type of the natural numbers, $\mathbb{N}$, and the type of Bits, **Bit**, always exist, possibly together with other basic types. More complex structured types are built using *type constructors* which will now be introduced.

2.5. PAIRS AND PARALLEL COMPOSITION

One standard type constructor is *pairing*. Given two separate pieces of data of types α and γ we can construct a composite piece of data of type $[\alpha, \gamma]$ by pairing. The pictorial interpretation is just the wire carrying things of type α below the one carrying things of type γ. Pairing can be thought of as forming the *product* type.

The analogous construction on relations is *parallel composition*. Given two relations $R :: \alpha \sim \beta$ and $S :: \gamma \sim \delta$, the parallel composition of R and S, $[R, S]$, is of type $[\alpha, \gamma] \sim [\gamma, \delta]$. If $x \, R \, y$ and $u \, S \, v$ then $(x, u) \, [R, S] \, (y, v)$.

The picture is

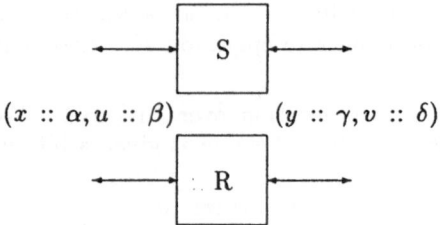

$$(x :: \alpha, u :: \beta) \qquad (y :: \gamma, v :: \delta)$$

The parallel composition of a circuit with an identity is often used, so a special notation is introduced for it. If $R :: \alpha \sim \gamma$ then

$$\text{fst } R \stackrel{\text{def}}{=} [R, \text{id}]$$

So

$$\text{fst } R :: [\alpha, *] \sim [\gamma, *]$$

The picture is obvious;

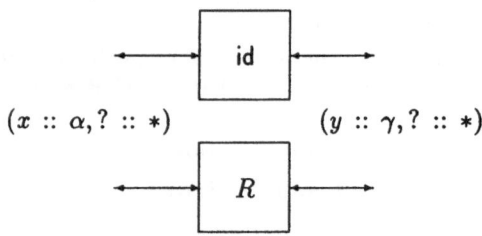

$$(x :: \alpha, ? :: *) \qquad (y :: \gamma, ? :: *)$$

Here $*$ represents some type; we do not have enough information to fully determine the type of ?; we merely say that it must be properly typed, or that ? :: $*$. This indicates that fst is *polymorphic*; for each type η, and relation $R :: \alpha \sim \gamma$ there is a fst R (or, rather, an *instance* of fst R) of type $[\alpha, \eta] \sim [\gamma, \eta]$.

It does not matter what type the second component of the domain of fst is; we can make the domain of fst R some $(x :: \alpha, ? :: \eta)$ for any η and the expression will remain properly typed. Many of the relations of interest to us, like id :: $* \sim *$, are polymorphic.[‡]

Similarly, we define snd $R \stackrel{\text{def}}{=} [\text{id}, R]$, so if $R :: \alpha \sim \gamma$ then snd $R :: [*, \alpha] \sim [*, \gamma]$.

Notice that fst and snd commute with each other and distribute through composition and inverse;

$$\text{fst } R \text{ ; snd } S = \text{snd } S \text{ ; fst } R$$
$$\text{fst } (R \text{ ; } S) = \text{fst } R \text{ ; fst } S$$
$$(\text{fst } R)^{\leftarrow} = \text{fst } (R^{\leftarrow})$$

We will often need to extract the components of a pair. To do this we use *projections*; π_1 projects out the first components, so that

$$(x, u) \; \pi_1 \; x$$

[‡]This is *parametric* polymorphism; a relation can only be polymorphic in an argument if it doesn't 'look too hard' at the type of the argument; see [9] for details. Notice, incidentally, that id is the *only* polymorphic relation of principle type $* \sim *$.

And so

$$\pi_1 \; :: \; [*_1, *_2] \sim *_1$$

Similarly, $[x, u]\,\pi_2\,u.$ and $\pi_2 \; :: \; [*_1, *_2] \sim *_2$. (Notice that here we need two type variables, $*_1$ and $*_2$, since the two components of the pair can be of different types; π_1 and π_2 are completely polymorphic.)

Notice that

$$[R, S] \; ; \; \pi_1 = \text{snd } S \; ; \; \pi_1 \; ; \; R$$
$$\text{fst } R \; ; \; \pi_1 = \pi_1 \; ; \; R$$

But, if S is, for instance, the empty relation,

$$[R, S] \; ; \; \pi_1 \neq \pi_1 \; ; \; R$$

A construction we will need in this paper is that of reconstructing a pair of a pair.

$$\text{swm} \; :: \; [[*_1, *_2], [*_3, *_4]] \sim [[*_1, *_3], [*_2, *_4]]$$

Suppose $w :: \alpha, x :: \beta$ and $y :: \gamma, z :: \delta$. Then

$$((w, x), (y, z)) \; \text{swm} \; ((w, y), (x, z))$$

The picture is

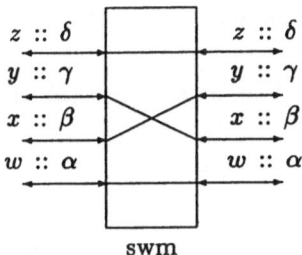

$$\text{swm}$$

2.6. Lists and Operations over Lists

Another common structured type is the *list*. Given an item of type α, we can build a one-element list of type lst α using the list constructor $\langle \_ \rangle$, often called 'giftwrap'.

The type of giftwrap is

$$\langle \_ \rangle \; :: \; * \sim \text{lst}_1*$$

so giftwrap takes something of any type and produces a list of that type, whose only element is its argument. Notice that we sometimes decorate lst with the length of the list, here one. When we want to refer to the ith element of a list a we sometimes write a_i.

The pictorial interpretation of lists is as a collection going up; the first element of the list appears at the bottom of the picture. We can append lists to other lists of the same type using the primitive *app*.

Suppose we have two lists $x :: \text{lst}_m \alpha$ and $y :: \text{lst}_n \alpha$; then we can construct a list of type $\text{lst}_{m+n} \alpha$ using append, written app.

The type and definition of app are straight-forward;

$$\text{app} \quad :: \quad [\text{lst}_m*, \text{lst}_n*] \sim \text{lst}_{m+n}*$$
$$(xs, ys) \text{ app } zs \quad \Longleftrightarrow \quad zs = xs \mathbin{+\!\!+} ys$$

A representative picture is

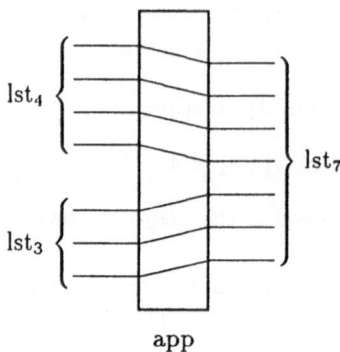

app

Lists are *homogeneous*; all elements have the same type. This means that if $x :: \text{lst}_n\alpha$ and $y :: \text{lst}_m\beta$ with $\alpha \neq \beta$, there is no z such that (x, y) app z.

We can append things to a list one at a time, either from the left, using *apl*

$$(x, xs) \text{ apl } y \quad \Longleftrightarrow \quad y = \langle x \rangle \mathbin{+\!\!+} xs$$

or from the right, using *apr*

$$(xs, x) \text{ apr } y \quad \Longleftrightarrow \quad y = xs \mathbin{+\!\!+} \langle x \rangle$$

The types are

$$\text{apl} :: [\alpha, \text{lst}_n\alpha] \sim \text{lst}_{n+1}\alpha \quad \text{apr} :: [\text{lst}_n\alpha, \alpha] \sim \text{lst}_{n+1}\alpha$$

Given a list of wires of types α say, we may want to apply a relation $R :: \alpha \sim \beta$ to all of them. The right constructor for this is *map*;

$$\text{map}_n R \quad :: \quad \text{lst}_n\alpha \sim \text{lst}_n\beta$$
$$\langle x \rangle \mathbin{+\!\!+} xs \text{ map}_n R \langle y \rangle \mathbin{+\!\!+} ys \quad \Longleftrightarrow \quad x \, R \, y \; \& \; xs \text{ map}_{n-1} R \; ys$$
$$\langle x \rangle \text{ map}_1 R \langle y \rangle \quad \Longleftrightarrow \quad x \, R \, y$$

Notice that map is parameterised by the length of the list concerned, and so should carry a subscript. (Be warned that [4] uses a different notational convention for the subcripts of map.)

Here is an instance of map, namely $\text{map}_3 R$:

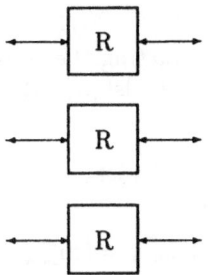

By induction on the width of the list, one can show that map distributes over sequential composition and inverse

$$\text{map}\,(R \,;\, S) \;=\; (\text{map}\,R)\,;\,(\text{map}\,S)$$
$$\text{map}\,(R^\leftarrow) \;=\; (\text{map}\,R)^\leftarrow$$

Consider a circuit that takes a pair of buses (i.e something of type $[\text{lst}\,\alpha, \text{lst}\,\beta]$) and applies a relation 'pointwise,' R say. We will clearly need to be able to extract the pairs so that we can apply map R to them; *zip* is the right function for this:

$$\text{zip} \quad :: \quad [\text{lst}_n \alpha, \text{lst}_n \beta] \quad \sim \quad \text{lst}_n[\alpha, \beta]$$
$$(\langle x \rangle + \!\!+\, xs, \langle y \rangle + \!\!+\, ys) \;\text{zip}\; \langle z \rangle + \!\!+\, zs \quad \Longleftrightarrow \quad z = (x, y) \;\&\; (xs, ys)\;\text{zip}\; zs$$
$$(\langle \rangle, \langle \rangle) \quad \text{zip} \quad \langle \rangle$$

The instance zip_2 can be thought of as much like swm; the picture is the same, but the typing is different.

A picture of zip_4 is

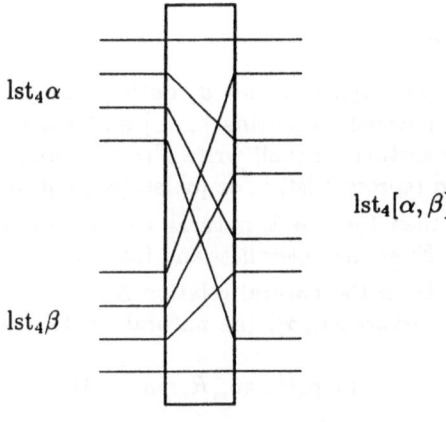

$$\text{zip}_4 \;::\; [\text{lst}_4 \alpha, \text{lst}_4 \beta] \sim \text{lst}_4[\alpha, \beta]$$

Our final constructor will be *transpose*, written trn. This is a generalisation of zip; it takes any number of buses and interleaves them together. Suppose x is a collection of buses each of the same type, α so that $x \;::\; \text{lst}_m\,\text{lst}_n \alpha$, and y is a bus of such collections, $y :: \mathrm{lst}_n \, \mathrm{lst}_m \alpha$. Then $\mathrm{trn}_{n,m}$ interleaves them in the obvious way;

$$x \; \mathrm{trn}_{n,m} \; y \; \overset{\mathrm{def}}{=} \; \forall i,j \, . \, x_{i,j} = y_{j,i}$$

(Remember the convention for extracting the components of lists; $x_{i,j} :: \alpha$ is the jth component of the ith list $x :: \mathrm{lst}_m \, \mathrm{lst}_n \alpha$, with $1 \leq i \leq m, 1 \leq j \leq n$.)

For trn we have the typing

$$\mathrm{trn}_{n,m} \; :: \; \mathrm{lst}_m \, \mathrm{lst}_n * \; \sim \; \mathrm{lst}_n \, \mathrm{lst}_m *$$

and the obvious law

$$\mathrm{trn}_{n,m} = \mathrm{trn}_{m,n}^{\leftarrow}$$

Before leaving this section, it should be mentioned that we haven't treated many of the higher-order functions that are often used, essentially because they won't be useful in our discussion of refinement.

3. TYPE REFINEMENT

When performing a refinement step in Ruby, it is convenient to allow *type refinement*; one may discover that some abstract type is best thought of as being a combination of simpler types. Integers in a given range will be implemented as buses (lists of bits), for instance. In this section we will investigate the calculus of type refinement in Ruby. Our general view will be that if in some context C we have $C \vdash R$, and if we refine a type α to that $\alpha \mapsto F(\beta)$ say, then we want to determine a new version of R, R' say, working with the new type.

Thus, in the paradigm of the introduction, we have a derivation like

$$\frac{C \vdash R}{C, \{\alpha \mapsto F(\beta)\} \vdash R'}$$

3.1. TYPE CONSTRUCTORS

We have seen that, given types α and β, both $[\alpha, \beta]$ and $\mathrm{lst}_n \alpha$ are types. For this reason we have referred to pairing $[\_,\_]$ and list construction lst_n as *type constructors*. In this section we shall write $F(\alpha)$ for some type constructed from α, so that $F(\alpha)$ could represent $\mathrm{lst}_n \alpha$, or $[\alpha, \mathrm{lst}_n(\mathrm{lst}_m \alpha)]$, but not $[\alpha, \mathrm{lst}_n(\mathrm{lst}_m \beta)]$.

If $R :: \alpha \sim \beta$ then there is a natural way to lift it to a relation of type $F(\alpha) \sim F(\beta)$ for any F; we map over lists and take parallel composition over pairs.

Thus if $F(\alpha) = \mathrm{lst}_n \alpha$ the natural relation $S :: \mathrm{lst}_n \alpha \sim \mathrm{lst}_n \beta$ is just $\mathrm{map}_n R$, whilst if $F(\alpha) = \mathrm{lst}_n([\mathrm{lst}_m \alpha, \mathrm{lst}_m \alpha])$ the natural relation derived from R of type $F(\alpha) \sim F(\beta)$ is

$$\mathrm{map}_n([\mathrm{map}_m R, \mathrm{map}_m R])$$

When we want to refer to the structure of the type constructed by F without applying it, we just neglect to write the type.

Thus, our first constructor is

$$F = \mathrm{lst}_n$$

While our second is

$$F = \mathrm{lst}_n([\mathrm{lst}_m, \mathrm{lst}_m])$$

For some constructor F we write $F(R)$ for its application to R, so that if $F = [\,,\,]$,

$$F(R) = [R, R]$$

while if $F = \mathrm{lst}_n([\mathrm{lst}_m, \mathrm{lst}_m])$,

$$F(R) = \mathrm{map}_n([\mathrm{map}_m R, \mathrm{map}_m R])$$

This notation is especially useful for conjugation; if we have $R :: F(\alpha) \sim G(\alpha)$ and an abstraction $S :: \alpha \sim \beta$, we write $R \ _F\backslash_G \ S$ for

$$F(S^\leftarrow) \,;\, R \,;\, G(S)$$

Thus if $R :: [\alpha, \alpha] \sim \mathrm{lst}_n([\alpha, \mathrm{lst}_m \alpha])$,

$$R \ _{[,]\backslash \mathrm{lst}_n([,\mathrm{lst}_m])} \ S \ \stackrel{\mathrm{def}}{=} \ [S^\leftarrow, S^\leftarrow] \,;\, R \,;\, \mathrm{map}_n([S, \mathrm{map}_m S])$$

Here we are exploiting the intuition that list construction and pairing are ways of *structuring independent* pieces of data, and it is nice to have a way of constructing relations that act *independently* over those structures. This notion of independence will be made more precise in the next subsection.

3.2. INDEPENDENCE

Naïvely, a relation $R :: F(\alpha) \sim F(\beta)$ is independent if it can be thought of as a relation $S :: \alpha \sim \beta$ "dragged up" to $F(\alpha) \sim F(\beta)$ by some plumbing. Thus if $T :: \alpha \sim \beta$, then

$$R \stackrel{\mathrm{def}}{=} \mathrm{map}_n T$$

is independent in F since it acts independently on each element of the list.

Similarly, if $U :: \mathrm{lst}_p \alpha \sim \beta$,

$$
\begin{aligned}
S \quad &:: \quad \mathrm{lst}_n([\mathrm{lst}_m \mathrm{lst}_p \alpha, \mathrm{lst}_p \alpha]) \sim \mathrm{lst}_n([\mathrm{lst}_m \beta, \beta]) \\
S \quad &\stackrel{\mathrm{def}}{=} \quad \mathrm{map}_n([\mathrm{map}_m U, U])
\end{aligned}
$$

is independent on $\mathrm{lst}_n \, [\mathrm{lst}_m \, \_, \_]$. Independent relations, then, can be made from plumbing together more primitive ones in canonical ways. This is the intuitive meaning of independence; a relation is independent over F if its type is $F(\alpha) \sim F(\beta)$ (for not necessarily atomic α and β) and it can be made from some $R : \alpha \sim \beta$ by doing the 'obvious' thing.

Our characterisation of independence is nonconstructive in the sense that no algorithm is given to determine whether or not a given relation is indepenent in a given type constructor.

(Notice that independence is rather weaker than polymorphism; all polymorphic relations are independent, but, as the examples above illustrate, not all independent relations are polymorphic. The notion of independence allows us to differentiate between structure and functionality.)

Our characterisation of independence will rely on exploiting the intuition that independent relations can be decomposed.

In particular,

$$R \; :: \; F([\alpha_1, \alpha_2]) \sim F([\beta_1, \beta_2])$$

is independent in F if there are relations

$$S_1 \quad :: \quad F(\alpha_1) \sim F(\beta_1)$$
$$S_2 \quad :: \quad F(\alpha_2) \sim F(\beta_2)$$

so that R can be expressed as $[S_1, S_2] \setminus \delta_{[,]}F$, where $\delta_{[,]}F$ is a piece of plumbing that depends only on F.

Suppose we have some $U \; :: \; F(\alpha) \sim F(\alpha)$ and we do the type refinement $\alpha \mapsto [\beta_1, \beta_2]$. If U is independent in F then we can drag the pair out to the outermost level, expressing it as $[V_1, V_2] \setminus \delta_{[,]}F$ where

$$V_1 \quad :: \quad F(\beta_1) \sim F(\beta_1)$$
$$V_2 \quad :: \quad F(\beta_2) \sim F(\beta_2)$$

Similarly, $R \; :: \; F(\mathrm{lst}_n \alpha) \sim F(\mathrm{lst}_n \beta)$ is independent in F if there is a relation $S \; :: \; F(\alpha) \sim F(\beta)$ such that R can be expressed as

$$\mathrm{map}_n S \setminus \delta_{\mathrm{lst}_n} F$$

All that remains is to define the plumbing relations like $\delta_{\mathrm{lst}} F$. Notice that we may sometimes be faced with deciding if $R \; :: \; F(\alpha) \sim G(\beta)$ is independent. It is just when there is a relation $S \; :: \; F(\alpha) \sim F(\beta)$ which is independent, and there is an instance of a polymorphic relation $T \; :: \; F(\beta) \sim G(\beta)$ so that $R = S \; ; \; T$.

3.3. CANONICAL PLUMBING

In this subsection we will generate the plumbing mentioned above. Suppose $F = F_1(F_2)$ for $F_1 = \mathrm{lst}$ or $[\,,\,]$. Then

$$\delta_{\mathrm{lst}_n} F \overset{\mathrm{def}}{=} \begin{cases} \mathrm{trn}_{n,m} \; ; \; \mathrm{map}_m(\delta_{\mathrm{lst}_n} F_2) & \text{if } F_1 = \mathrm{lst}_m \\ \mathrm{zip}_n \; ; \; [\delta_{\mathrm{lst}_n} F_2, \delta_{\mathrm{lst}_n} F_2] & \text{if } F_1 = [\,,\,] \end{cases}$$

$$\delta_{[,]} F \overset{\mathrm{def}}{=} \begin{cases} \mathrm{zip}_m \; ; \; \mathrm{map}_m(\delta_{[,]} F_2) & \text{if } F_1 = \mathrm{lst}_m \\ \mathrm{swm} \; ; \; [\delta_{[,]} F_2, \delta_{[,]} F_2] & \text{if } F_1 = [\,,\,] \end{cases}$$

The base cases are;

$$\delta_{\mathrm{lst}_n} \mathrm{lst}_m \overset{\mathrm{def}}{=} \mathrm{trn}_{n,m} \qquad \qquad \delta_{[,]} \mathrm{lst}_m \overset{\mathrm{def}}{=} \mathrm{zip}_m$$
$$\delta_{\mathrm{lst}_n} [\,,\,] \overset{\mathrm{def}}{=} \mathrm{zip}_n \qquad \text{and} \qquad \delta_{[,]} [\,,\,] \overset{\mathrm{def}}{=} \mathrm{swm}$$

Notice that all of these pieces of plumbing are suitably independent, so we can keep pulling independent relations 'inside out.'

As an example, consider the relation R independent in F where $F = \mathrm{lst}_n \, \mathrm{lst}_m$ and

$$R \; :: \; \mathrm{lst}_n \, \mathrm{lst}_m([\mathrm{lst}_p \alpha_1, \mathrm{lst}_p \alpha_2]) \sim \mathrm{lst}_n \, \mathrm{lst}_m([\beta_1, \beta_2])$$

Independence tells us that there are relations

$$S_i \; :: \; \mathrm{lst}_n \mathrm{lst}_m \mathrm{lst}_p \alpha_i \sim \mathrm{lst}_n \mathrm{lst}_m \beta$$

So that R is expressible as

$$[S_1, S_2] \setminus \delta_{[,]} F$$

And, since $\delta_{[,]} F = \delta_{[,]} \text{lst}_n \text{lst}_m = \text{zip}_n \; ; \text{map}_n \text{zip}_m$,

$$R = [S_1, S_2] \setminus (\text{zip}_n \; ; \text{map}_n \text{zip}_m)$$

3.4. The Structural Independence Theorem

In the section before last we had cause to deal with relations of type

$$F(\alpha) \sim G(\beta)$$

Recall that these are independent in F is there is an instance of a polymorphic relation $T :: F(\beta) \sim G(\beta)$ and a relation independent in F, $S :: F(\alpha) \sim G(\alpha)$ so that we have $R = S \; ; T$. In this case we will write R as $_{F(\alpha)} R_{G(\beta)}$.

There is an intimate relationship between independent relations and abstractions; if $_{F(\alpha)} R_{G(\alpha)}$ is a relation independent in F, and $S :: \alpha \sim \beta$ is an abstraction, then

$$F(S) \; ; {}_{F(\beta)} R_{G(\beta)} = {}_{F(\alpha)} R_{G(\alpha)} \; ; G(S)$$

This is called the *structural independence* theorem. It follows immediately from our characterisation of independence.[§]

This theorem is useful in combination with a conjugation; suppose $S :: \alpha \sim \beta$ is an abstraction over β and we have some $R :: F(\alpha) \sim G(\alpha)$. Then, if

$$R = {}_{F(\alpha)} T_{F'(\alpha)} \; ; U \; ; {}_{G'(\alpha)} V_{G(\alpha)}$$

(i.e. T and V are just plumbing and U does the work), we have $U :: F'(\alpha) \sim G'(\alpha)$ and, by the structural independence theorem,

$$R \;_{F \setminus G} S \; = \; {}_{F(\beta)} T_{F'(\beta)} \; ; (U \;_{F' \setminus G'} S) \; ; {}_{G'(\beta)} V_{G(\beta)}$$

so we can push the abstraction through the plumbing. As it is often $U \;_{F' \setminus G'} S$ that we know how to implement, this is often a useful thorem.

3.5. The Consequences of Type Refinement

Suppose we have some type α. At some stage of the design we notice that it is convenient to express α as $F(\beta)$ for some type constructor F. We now have the machinery to discuss how relations involving α can be re-expressed as relations involving β.

Let $_{F(\alpha)} R_{G(\alpha)}$ be a relation independent in F. Then if $\alpha \mapsto [\beta_1, \beta_2]$ we are guaranteed from the independence of R the existence of

$$S_1 :: F(\beta_1) \sim G(\beta_1)$$
$$S_2 :: F(\beta_2) \sim G(\beta_2)$$

with

$$R \; = \; (\delta_{[,]} F)^{\leftarrow} \; ; [S_1, S_2] \; ; \delta_{[,]} G$$

[§]This is proved in [8] where a semantic characterisation of independence is given.

Similarly, if $\alpha \mapsto \mathrm{lst}_n\beta$ we are guaranteed, from the independence of R, the existence of a relation

$$S :: F(\beta) \sim G(\beta)$$

with

$$R = \mathrm{map}_n S \setminus \delta_{\mathrm{lst}_n} F$$

This enables us to pull the refinement out to the outermost level.

4. EXAMPLE

The most widespread application of the theory discussed in this paper comes in circuits like the one discussed in the structural independence section. Recall that we had

$$R = {}_{F(\alpha)}T_{F'(\alpha)} \; ; \; U \; ; \; {}_{F'(\alpha)}V_{F''(\alpha)}$$

Here T and V are pieces of plumbing (instances of polymorphic relations) that just serve to give $U :: F'(\alpha) \sim F'(\alpha)$ with its data in a suitable form.

Suppose we do a type refinement $\alpha \mapsto \mathrm{lst}_n\beta$. We want to express R as map something. Suppose U is independent in F'. Then we can express it as

$$\mathrm{map}_n W$$

Thus we have

$$R = {}_{F(\mathrm{lst}_n\beta)}T_{F'(\mathrm{lst}_n\beta)} \; ; \; \mathrm{map}_n W \; ; \; {}_{F'(\mathrm{lst}_n\beta)}V_{F''(\mathrm{lst}_n\beta)}$$

From the independence of T and V it follows that ${}_{F(\mathrm{lst}_n\beta)}T_{F'(\mathrm{lst}_n\beta)} = \mathrm{map}_n({}_{F(\beta)}T_{F'(\beta)})$ and similarly for V. Then we have

$$R = (\mathrm{map}_n({}_{F(\beta)}T_{F'(\beta)})) \; ; \; \mathrm{map}_n W \; ; \; (\mathrm{map}_n({}_{F'(\beta)}V_{F''(\beta)}))$$

The plumbing $\delta_{\mathrm{lst}_n} F'$ is independent in F', so we get

$$R = (\mathrm{map}_n \; ({}_{F(\beta)}T_{F'(\beta)} \; ; \; W \; ; \; {}_{F'(\beta)}V_{F''(\beta)})) \setminus \delta_{\mathrm{lst}_n} F'$$

The reader is referred to [7] for further examples.

CONCLUDING REMARKS

We have presented a syntax for reasonning about relations, and hinted at its semantics. This calculus,—which can be seen as an extention of functional programming to the relational case,—is also a hardware design language. This analogy has been persued thoroughly.

Of particular interest to us, from the point of view of refining the descriptions of circuits, has been the calculus of type refinement. This has been presented using the notion of independence, and the technical machinery necessary to use it in Ruby has been elucidated.

My thanks are due to Graham Hutton and Geraint Jones for help, both typographical and mathematical, on many occasions, and to Mary Sheeran for suggesting, encouraging and criticising this work. This work was completed under IED project 1759, *High performance VLSI Architectures for DSP*; funding is gratefully acknowledged.

BIBLIOGRAPHY

1. R. Bird, *Lectures on constructive functional programming*, Tech. report, Programming Research Group technical monograph PRG–69, September 1988.
2. M. Sheeran G. Jones, *Timeless truths about sequential circuits*, Concurrent computations: algorithms, architecture and technology (S. Schwartz S. Tewksbury, B. Dickinson, ed.), Plenum Press, New York.
3. G. Jones, *Designing circuits by calculation*, Tech. Report PRG–TR–10–90, Oxford University Computing Laboratory, 1990.
4. G. Jones and M. Sheeran, *Circuit design in Ruby*, Formal Methods for VLSI Design (J. Staunstrup, ed.), North–Holland.
5. _____, *Relations and refinement in circuit design*, Refinement, Hursley 1990 (C. Morgan, ed.), Springer-Verlag Workshops in Computing Series.
6. W. Luk, *Analysing parametrised designs by non-standard interpretation*, Application Specific Array Processesors, IEEE Computer Press.
7. D. Murphy, *Arithmetic on the A110*, Tech. report, Department of Computing Science, University of Glasgow, 1990.
8. D. Murphy and G. Hutton, *Programming with relations*, In preparation.
9. A. Mycroft, *Polymorphic type schemes and recursive definitions*, International Symposium on Programming, LNCS 167, Springer-Verlag, pp. 217–239.
10. M. Sheeran, *Describing and reasoning about circuits using relations*, Proceedings of the workshop on theoretical aspects of VLSI design (J. Tucker et al., ed.), CUP.
11. G. Jones W. Luk, *From specification to parametrised architectures*, The fusion of hardware design and verification (G. Milne, ed.).

Normal-Order Reduction Using Scan Primitives

William D. Partain*
Computing Science Department, Glasgow University

December 10, 1990

Abstract

A parallel computer with fast scan primitives allows an unusual approach
to the normal-order reduction of the λ-calculus. For such machines, this
approach runs contrary to some common notions of what are "expensive" and
"cheap" aspects of the reduction process.

In my thesis work [1], I described a method for the normal-order tree reduction[1]
of the pure λ-calculus that has worst-case time and space efficiency comparable to
Wadsworth's classical graph reducer [2]—*assuming* a machine model with suitable
primitive operations. In this paper, I present the core algorithms of my tree reducer
and sketch its overall operation.

1 Introduction

Graph reduction is the dominant implementation technique for lazy functional languages. Conceptually, program and data are represented by a graph of linked nodes,
and the reduction process manipulates and changes the graph directly. The essential
virtue of graph reduction is that any piece of the program/data graph may be *shared*
by aiming many pointers at that piece's root node.

Graph reduction becomes problematic when one considers its implementation
on highly parallel computers with thousands or millions of processors. It is hard
to throw many processors at a single reduction and gain any speedup—sequential
hopping from one node to another via a pointer is inherent in the graph reduction
model. Also, any node may point to any other in the graph. One cannot make
strong claims about locality in the graph; this is most unfortunate, because highly

---

*This work was done at the University of North Carolina at Chapel Hill and was supported
mainly by an Army Science and Technology Fellowship (grant number DAAL03-86-G-0050) ad-
ministered by the U. S. Army Research Office. My e-mail address is partain@cs.glasgow.ac.uk.

[1]I prefer the term "tree reduction" over "string reduction" when the techniques used are strongly
biased to strings that are flattened representations of trees. When manipulating lists of arbitrary
symbols, "string reduction" is the better term.

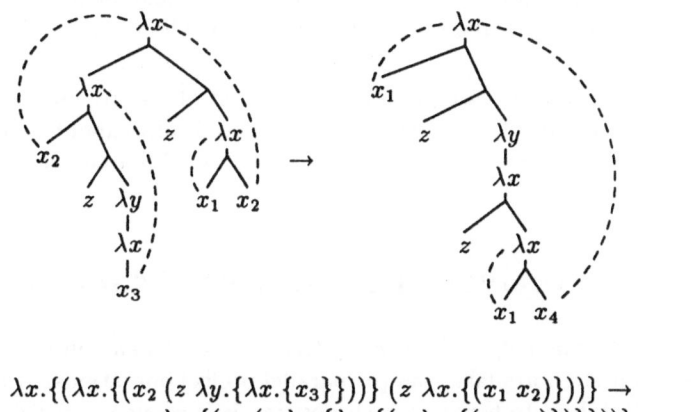

$$\lambda x.\{(\lambda x.\{(x_2\,(z\,\lambda y.\{\lambda x.\{x_3\}\})))\}\,(z\,\lambda x.\{(x_1\,x_2)\}))\} \rightarrow$$
$$\lambda x.\{(x_1\,(z\,\lambda y.\{\lambda x.\{(z\,\lambda x.\{(x_1\,x_4)\})\}\}))\}$$

Figure 1: A β-reduction with de Bruijn numbers

parallel machines (of which the Connection Machine is an example [3]) depend on locality for good performance.

The problem considered in this paper is artificial, confined to basics, and follows Wadsworth [2]:

- I do β-reduction of the pure λ-calculus (variables, lambdas, and applications).

- I reduce to full normal form, including inside lambdas.

- I do simple leftmost-first normal-order evaluation. Given that this sequentializes the reductions, I am mainly interested in parallelism that can be applied to a single reduction step.

- The reducer is purely interpretive. The practical use of graph reduction breaks the reduction process into smaller steps, and then does as much as possible at compile time to avoid wasted interpretive effort. The Chalmers G-Machine is a standard example [4].

- I am only interested in implementations on highly parallel machines of the kind suggested above.

I make *no claims* about the direct practical use of the methods described in this paper. At best, they would be a starting point for a real implementation.

2 λ-calculus with de Bruijn numbers

One may use a pure λ-calculus with variables represented by *binding indices*, commonly called "de Bruijn numbers" [5; 6; 7]. If you walk up a λ-term in tree form from a variable to its binder (a lambda node), a count of the binders met along the way is the variable's de Bruijn number. Figure 1 shows two terms with de Bruijn numbers given as subscripts. Dashed arcs highlight where some variables are bound. I *omit* subscripts for bindings outside the λ-term of interest, as for z in Figure 1.

The scopes of λ-expressions are shown explicitly in textual form by *braces*. Applications are fully *parenthesized* in textual form; they are shown as unadorned two-child nodes in tree form.

Figure 1 shows a de Bruijn-style β-reduction of the top redex; observe how de Bruijn numbers anywhere in the term may need adjustment. This systematic adjustment takes the place of full-blown α-conversion;[2] I like the de Bruijn approach because it fits the FFP Machine model (next section).

3   Scan primitives and the FFP Machine

The efficacy of the main algorithms in my tree reducer depend on an underlying machine model that supports fast *scan* (or parallel prefix) operations. A scan produces a "fold" or a "total-up-to-here" at each position in a sequence of values. More formally, a left-to-right scan operates on a *sequence* of values $(i_1, i_2, \ldots, i_n)$ to produce a *sequence* of results $(o_1, o_2, \ldots, o_n)$

$$o_j = i_0 \bullet i_1 \bullet i_2 \cdots i_{j-2} \bullet i_{j-1}, 1 \leq j \leq n;$$

where i_0 is the identity value for the associative binary operation $\bullet$. Here is an example of an integer-addition left-to-right scan (0 is the identity value):

$$\begin{array}{ll}
\text{scan input:} & 2 \;\; 7 \;\; \text{-4} \;\; 1 \;\; \text{-2} \\
\text{scan result:} & 0 \;\; 2 \;\; 9 \;\; 5 \;\; 6
\end{array}$$

Right-to-left scans may also be used. Another minor variant is segmented scans, in which the input sequence is broken up into disjoint segments and a scan takes place within each segment. Right-to-left scans and segmented scans (either direction) take the same amount of time as the more common left-to-right scans.

Much of the most effective programming on Connection Machines, MasPar MP-1s, etc., is built around fast scan operations. John O'Donnell's APSA machine is an SIMD design specifically for functional programming; fast scans are important for it, too [8]. Blelloch advocates an entire "model of computation" built around scans [9].

The FFP Machine is a highly-parallel small-grain MIMD computer architecture to support functional programming, notably that of the Backus FP camp [10]. Magó and Stanat's 1989 paper is the best recent description [11]. The basic model is that in Figure 2: a linear array of small cells, each capable of independent computation and communication and having a small fixed-size memory. Symbols are laid out in a fully-parenthesized linear representation, one symbol per processing cell. Figure 2 shows the λ-term $\lambda y.\{\lambda x.\{((x_1 \; y_2) \; (y_2 \; y_2))\}\}$. Lambda symbols need not appear, so I put the associated variable names next to the left braces; remember, the names serve no purpose in the de Bruijn λ-calculus other than user-friendliness. As a λ-term changes during reduction, symbols move from cell to cell along the lateral connections, making room for new symbols and closing up gaps.

The main point about an FFP Machine is that its "communication networks" support scan operations (all flavors) that work in $O(\log A)$ time at hardware speeds,

---

[2]A pre-reduction pass to give unique names to all the variables in an initial λ-term is not sufficient to avoid runtime renaming (or the avoidance thereof).

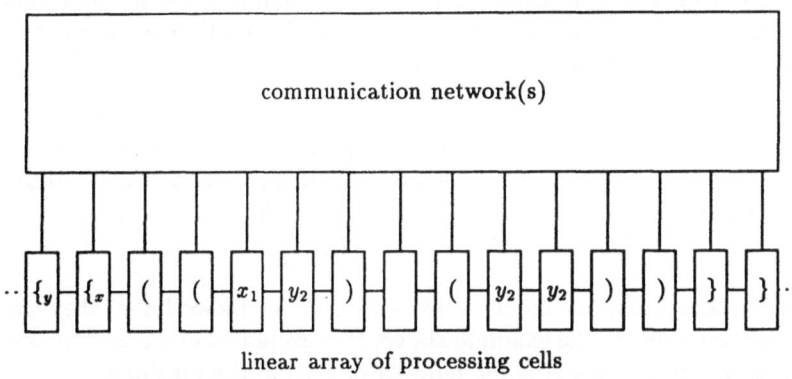

Figure 2: The FFP Machine model

where A is the number of cells in a Machine. Such operations are directly comparable to shared-memory accesses across a multi-stage network in a conventional multiprocessor; when you see "$O(\log A)$," you may safely read "non-outlandish constant."

The most important scan operations used in my tree reducer are those that calculate a nesting level for each symbol, indicating how deeply nested each symbol is inside a particular λ-term. One scan calculates it: cells with opening delimiters contribute a $+1$, cells holding closing delimiters contribute -1, other cells contribute 0. An example:

$$(\quad \{_x \quad (\quad x_1 \ z \quad) \quad \} \quad \{_y \ y_1 \quad \} \quad)$$

scan input:	+1	+1	+1	0	0	-1	-1	+1	0	-1	-1
scan result:	0	1	2	3	3	3	2	1	2	2	1
nesting level:	0	1	2	3	3	2	1	1	2	1	0

A post-decrement by cells holding closing delimiters gives the final nesting levels.

Binding levels are a slight variant in which only binder delimiters (braces) "count". They are not too exciting for this example:

$$(\quad \{_x \quad (\quad x_1 \ z \quad) \quad \} \quad \{_y \ y_1 \quad \} \quad)$$

scan input:	0	+1	0	0	0	0	-1	+1	0	-1	0
scan result:	0	0	1	1	1	1	1	1	1	1	0
nesting level:	0	0	1	1	1	0	0	1	0	0	

4 Detecting bound or free variables

The core algorithms for a normal-order tree reducer—finding the free or bound variables in a λ-term—are simple on an FFP Machine, and they illustrate how the tradeoffs change with scan-based underlying machinery. An example should suffice, beginning with the bound-variable problem.

Consider the λ-term below, with indices (a left-to-right enumeration—one scan) and binding levels already calculated (one scan, as above) for each symbol.

We want to identify all the bound variables of the lambda whose delimiting braces are marked by $\Downarrow$; call those two cells L (left) and R (right). Our aim is to find the bound variables of λy in cells marked by $\uparrow$.

$$
\begin{array}{c}
\Downarrow \qquad\qquad\qquad\qquad\qquad\qquad\qquad\qquad\qquad\qquad \Downarrow \\
\{_x\ (\ \{_y\ (\ (\ x_2\ y_1\ )\ (\ \{_z\ (\ y_2\ z_1\ )\ \}\ a\ )\ )\ \}\ z\ )\ \}
\end{array}
$$

index:	1	2	3	4	5	6	7	8	9	10	11	12	13	14	15	16	17	18	19	20	21	22
binding-level:	0	1	1	2	2	2	2	2	2	2	3	3	3	3	2	2	2	2	1	1	1	0
		$\uparrow$							$\uparrow$												

1. Cell L broadcasts its index; cells with smaller index know they are not a bound variable. In the example above, this excludes cells 1–2. This step takes $O(\log A)$ time, where A is the number of cells in the machine.

2. Cell R broadcasts its index; cells with larger index know they are not a bound variable. This excludes cells 20–22. This takes $O(\log A)$ time.

3. Cell L broadcasts its binding level, '1' in the example; call it **top_bl**. This takes $O(\log A)$ time.

4. A cell holding a variable with de Bruijn number **db** = binding-level − **top_bl** is a bound variable. In the example, cells marked $\uparrow$ meet this condition. This step takes constant time.

Intuitively, a binding level counts binders downwards from the root of the overall λ-term to its leaves. Subtracting **top_bl** adjusts the count to start from the binder in question instead of the root of the whole λ-term. A de Bruijn number, on the other hand, is counting binders upwards from a variable's leaf position toward the root. Where the two counts are equal—a bound variable.

To find free variables, change the test in step 4 to: **db** > binding-level − **top_bl**.

Overall, it takes $O(\log A)$ time (and no extra space) to detect a binder's bound or free variables, no matter the size of the λ-term. These are cheap operations!

5 Sketch of a fast tree reducer

In my thesis, to make my tree reducer for the λ-calculus work very much like Wadsworth's classical graph reducer, I used considerable exotic FFP Machine hackery, and the result is certainly impractical as its stands. The basic ideas are not difficult, though.

β-reduction is the heart of λ-calculus evaluation. Figure 3 shows one β-reduction step in various guises. The top redex in the λ-term at the top left is to be reduced. The top right shows the reduction done by naive tree reduction; one can already see the potential for abominable space consumption. At the bottom left is the same thing done by graph reduction. The bottom right shows my approach: replace the redex with what amounts to a let-expression (a square-brackets node $[f]$ in the figure): "let $f = \lambda x.\{(x_1\ y_3)\}$ in $(\hat{f}_1\ (\hat{f}_1\ (\hat{f}_1\ \hat{f}_1)))$". The $[f]$ structure is a new kind of binder for de Bruijn numbers; I put hats on the bound $\hat{f}_1$'s to show they are bound at a let, not a lambda.

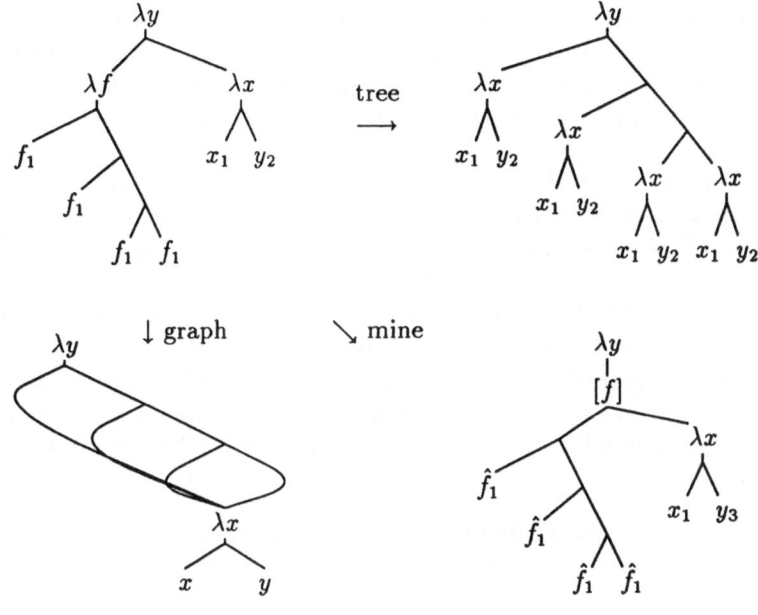

Figure 3: β-reduction in three guises

Using a special syntactic structure to indicate manipulable delayed substitutions is nothing new, being related to the use of environments in many implementations. I got the basic ideas from one of Staples's early papers on graph rewriting [12]; the rules he gives turn out to be related to Révész's rules for breaking substitution into smaller steps [13]. In their recent POPL paper, Abadi et al. present a formidable theory for a λ-calculus with explicit substitutions [14].

β-reduction does not a reducer make. A full reduction step involves:

1. Finding the next redex; for normal-order reduction, this is the leftmost one.

2. Copying (some part of) the redex if it is shared; I am ignoring this messy topic here (but I covered it in my thesis).

3. Doing the β-reduction.

For graph reduction, an underlying primitive operation is pointer-following. Because my basic motto is "Do everything Wadsworth graph-reduction does," I must have something comparable in my tree reducer. I use the hatted $\hat{f}_1$'s in "let $f = stuff$ in ...$\hat{f}$...$\hat{f}$..." as if they are pointers to $stuff$, just as if they were the "real pointers" that graph reduction fiddles with.

Take the matter of looking for the next redex. A graph reducer will glide from node to node, following pointers. My reducer, however, may run into a hatted variable, meaning it is really a "pointer" to a let-bound expression higher up in the tree. Control must be passed in such a way that the search continues up at the let-bound expression. In a conventional graph reducer, this may involve pushing pointers onto a stack. My reducer marks the hatted symbol in the cell it is leaving behind—it "changes its hat"—and then continues working on the pointed-to part of the flattened-tree string. To return from a pointer-following, an FFP Machine implementation can just use the associative-matching power of the processing array to detect the hat that was changed before the transfer of control.

I emphasize that the "pointer-following" in an FFP Machine implementation is messy and not worthy of direct emulation. It is interesting because it can be done, and because it is novel and entertaining. The gruesome details are in my thesis. There, you will also find much effort devoted to tidying expressions, to remove let-expressions that can cause "pointer-following" to become prohibitively expensive, thus breaking the direct comparison with Wadsworth's graph reducer. That effort is analogous to a graph reducer removing indirection nodes.

Despite the general messiness of "pointer-following" in my reducer and the overhead of tidying as a fourth part of every reduction step, some nuggets remain. The basic algorithm to find the leftmost redex in a tidied λ-term on an FFP Machine is just this:

1. Every cell indicates to its right neighbor if it is a left parenthesis (indicating an application) or not—one segmented scan (the lateral connections are not used).

2. All left braces receiving a positive indication contribute to a "vote" as to which is leftmost—one more scan.

3. The parenthesis/brace finding itself voted leftmost is the left delimiter of the next redex.

The whole operation takes $O(\log A)$ time, independent of the size of the λ-term and where the redex actually is within the term. This is a cheap operation!

A quirky result I came across has to do with the difference between full reduction and weak reduction; the latter does not reduce inside lambdas. Conventional implementations of graph reduction vastly prefer some form of weak reduction; it is part of their arsenal to avoid α-conversion. For my FFP Machine implementation, however, brief examination suggested that weak reduction would actually be more difficult than full reduction.

6 Conclusions

Tree reduction of the λ-calculus, suitably souped up and with appropriate underlying hardware, is not a silly idea. It deserves better than the one-thoughtless-sentence write-off that it usually gets. This is *not* to say that tree reduction is practical in the form I have outlined. I assume that the problem calls for a full a set of architecture and compiler tricks to make it effective, just as for other implementation models. A serious implementer would also have some flexibility about evaluation order, stopping at weak head normal form, speculative evaluation—all of which were "out of bounds" for my purposes.

Anyone interested in highly parallel implementations of functional languages must take seriously small-grain machines with thousands or millions of processors.

The Connection Machine is a realistic example, the FFP Machine a more speculative design. This class of machines has the wonderful economics of VLSI technology behind it. Functional programming implementors using such hardware must re-evaluate their assumptions about what is "expensive" and what is "cheap" in the reduction process. My almost-trivial algorithm to find free or bound variables in a λ-term—something usually avoided at all cost—makes this point. If the experience of many people with these types of machines is any guide, scan operations will play an important role in effective implementations.

Acknowledgments. I did this work amidst the invigorating functional programming group at the University of North Carolina at Chapel Hill. Its members, particularly the FFP Machine hackers, deserve at least partial credit for any good ideas herein. My advisor, Gyula Magó, merits a special accolade for his patient remolding of the cantankerous graduate-student material that befell him. I also offer my thanks to Jak Deschner, Kevin Hammond, Simon Peyton Jones, and Paul Roe, all of Glasgow, for their helpful criticism of the earlier draft of this paper.

References

[1] William D. Partain. *Graph Reduction Without Pointers.* PhD thesis, University of North Carolina at Chapel Hill, November 1989.

[2] Christopher P. Wadsworth. *Semantics and Pragmatics of the Lambda-Calculus.* D. Phil. thesis, University of Oxford, September 1 1971.

[3] W. Daniel Hillis. *The Connection Machine.* MIT Press, 1985.

[4] Thomas Johnsson. The G-Machine. An abstract machine for graph reduction. In *Proceedings of the Declarative Programming Workshop*, pages 1–20, University College, London, April 11–13 1983.

[5] N. G. de Bruijn. Lambda calculus notation with nameless dummies, a tool for automatic formula manipulation. *Indagationes Mathematicae*, 34(5):381–392, 1972.

[6] Klaus J. Berkling. A symmetric complement to the lambda calculus. Technical Report ISF-76-7, Gesellschaft für Mathematik und Datenverarbeitung (GMD), Bonn, W. Germany, September 14 1976.

[7] Klaus J. Berkling and Elfriede Fehr. A modification of the λ-calculus as a base for functional programming. In M. Nielsen and E. M. Schmidt, editors, *9th International Colloquium on Automata, Languages and Programming (ICALP)*, volume 140 of *Lecture Notes in Computer Science*, pages 35–47, Aarhus, Denmark, July 12–16 1982. Springer-Verlag.

[8] John T. O'Donnell, Timothy Bridges, and Sidney W. Kitchel. A VLSI implementation of an architecture for applicative programming. *Future Generations Computing Systems*, 4(3):245–254, October 1988.

[9] Guy J. Blelloch. Scans as primitive parallel operations. In Sartaj K. Sahni, editor, *International Conference on Parallel Processing (ICPP)*, pages 355–362, University Park, PA, August 17–21 1987. Penn State University.

[10] John W. Backus. Can programming be liberated from the von-Neumann style? A functional style and its algebra of programs. *Communications of the ACM*, 21(8):613–641, August 1978.

[11] Gyula A. Magó and Donald F. Stanat. The FFP Machine. In Veljko M. Milutinović, editor, *High-Level Language Computer Architectures*, pages 430–468. Computer Science Press, 1989.

[12] John Staples. A graph-like lambda calculus for which leftmost-outermost evaluation is optimal. In Volker Claus, Hartmut Ehrig, and Grzegorz Rozenberg, editors, *Graph-Grammars and their Application to Computer Science and Biology*, volume 73 of *Lecture Notes in Computer Science*, pages 440–454, Bad Honnef, W. Germany, October 30–November 3 1978. Springer-Verlag.

[13] G. E. Révész. *Lambda-Calculus, Combinators, and Functional Programming*, volume 4 of *Cambridge Tracts in Theoretical Computer Science*. Cambridge University Press, 1988.

[14] M. Abadi, L. Cardelli, P.-L. Curien, and J.-J. Lévy. Explicit substitutions. In *17th ACM Symposium on Principles of Programming Languages (POPL)*, pages 31–46, San Francisco, CA, January 17–19 1990.

Calculating lenient programs' performance

Paul Roe[*]

December 10, 1990

Abstract

Lenient languages, such as Id Nouveau, have been proposed for programming parallel computers. These languages represent a compromise between strict and lazy languages. The operation of parallel languages is very complex; therefore a formal method for reasoning about their performance is desirable. This paper presents a non-standard denotational semantics for calculating the performance of lenient programs. The semantics is novel in its use of time and time-stamps.

1 Motivation

Recently interest has grown in parallel programming using functional languages, particularly lenient languages such as Id Nouveau [8]. In order to derive and debug the performance of parallel programs, it is necessary to reason about their performance (execution time). Reasoning about the performance of sequential functional programs has always been an informal affair. However given the inherent *operational* complexity of parallel functional languages, a more formal approach to performance analysis is desirable. A possible exception to this are languages for SIMD machines. To tackle this problem a non-standard semantics has been developed for calculating the performance of lenient functional programs.

2 Background

How should parallel performance be measured ? To measure sequential performance it is sufficient to count the total number of operations (perhaps only certain ones) that are performed during an evaluation. The performance of a parallel program depends on many aspects of the machine on which it is run, including: the machine's number of processors and its scheduling policy. Including these aspects in reasoning

---

[*]Author's address: Department of Computing Science, The University, 17, Lilybank Gardens, Glasgow. G12 8QQ. Email: proe@cs.glasgow.ac.uk

about performance is too complicated. Eager [2] states that the *average parallelism* of a program is a useful performance measure. This may be used to bound the performance of a program running on a P processor machine. Eager proves that the average parallelism is equivalent to the ratio of the single processor execution time, to the execution time with an unbounded number of processors. Thus a good guide to a program's parallel performance may be calculated with its sequential evaluation time and its evaluation time with an unbounded number of processors. Some shortcomings with this method are discussed in section 6.

Lenient languages represent a compromise between strict and lazy languages. Strict languages are simple to reason about because their operational behaviour is compositional. For example the sequential cost (performance) of the (full) application $f\ E_1\ E_2$ is the sum of the costs of E_1, E_2 and the application. The cost of the application if E_1 and E_2 are evaluated in parallel (with an unbounded number of processors) is the maximum of the costs of E_1 and E_2 plus the cost of the application. This kind of technique is called *step counting*, and it forms the basis of the work in [6, 7], which concerns the automatic complexity analysis of a strict FP language. A problem with these languages, and the step counting technique, is that they do not support pipelined parallelism.

Lazy languages are difficult to analyse because their operational behaviour is not compositional. Approaches to the performance analysis of sequential lazy languages, such as [1, 10, 11] are essentially based on strictness analysis. They use strictness analysis to determine the degree to which expressions will be evaluated. This can then be used to determine the costs of evaluating expressions. Unfortunately this approach is not sufficient to analyse parallel lazy languages. This is because it is not sufficient to know to what degree expressions are evaluated; in addition it is necessary to know, *when* expressions are evaluated.

Hudak and Anderson [5] have devised an operational semantics for parallel lazy languages, based on partially ordered multisets. This could be used as the basis for a performance semantics. However the approach is extremely complicated and unwieldy, and there are some technical problems with it.

3 A lenient language

This section informally describes the lenient language which later will be analysed. Lenience means that the language is strict in expressions which are sequentially evaluated and lazy in expressions which are evaluated in parallel. Thus the language supports pipelined parallelism, unlike parallel strict languages. However this language is not as expressive as a lazy one. This lenient language differs from Id Nouveau because it explicitly expresses parallel and sequential evaluation.

3.1 Rationale

The syntax of the lenient language is shown in Figure 1. The language constructs

```
c      ∈ Con
v, h, t  ∈ Var

E  ::=  c
    |   v
    |   E E
    |   \v . E
    |   let v=E in E
    |   plet v=E in E
    |   letrec v=E in E
    |   E:E
    |   case E of []->E  (h:t)->E
    |   (E)
    |   {E}
```

Figure 1: Syntax

should be familiar except for `plet` and {E} (parentheses (E) denote expression grouping).

The `plet` construct is a parallel let; its binding is evaluated in parallel with its main expression. A more general approach is to evaluate all function applications and other constructs in parallel. However, most parallel programs have only a few places where parallel evaluation is necessary. Therefore, for simplicity *all* parallelism will be made explicit via `plet`; there will be no implicit parallelism. The `plet` construct is the only source of parallelism in the language; however other parallel constructs such as those proposed in [3] could easily be added and analysed.

Rather than fixing the costs of operations into the semantics, an explicit annotation is used to label expressions whose evaluation should be 'counted'. The annotation {E} means that the evaluation of {E} should take one step in addition to the cost of evaluating E. For example to analyse the cost of a parallel sorting program, only comparisons might be measured; thus applications of the comparison operator would be annotated with curly braces.

3.2   An informal explanation of the language's evaluation

The evaluation of the lenient language is unusual; therefore before explaining the semantics some example expressions are shown and their evaluation are discussed. Note that providing E1 is completely defined, the two expressions shown below have the same meaning but not necessarily the same performance.

```
let v = E1 in E              plet v = E1 in E
```

Consider the three expressions shown below:

```
let f = \x.[] in    let f = \x.[] in    let f = \x.[] in
    let y = ⊥ in      plet y = ⊥ in      plet y = ⊥ in
       f y                 f y                f (case y of
                                                  []    -> 0
                                                  (h:t) -> 1)
```

The first expression evaluates to bottom, because let is strict and hence
let y = ⊥ in f y does not terminate. The second expression evaluates to [].
The plet evaluates y and f y in parallel. Applications, like f y, evaluate their
arguments. However like strict languages variables need not be evaluated because:

> In the lenient language all variables' evaluation is *started* at binding time
> but their evaluation is *not* necessarily completed then.

Thus all variables are either evaluated or being evaluated. The third expression
evaluates to bottom. This is because the application of f causes its argument to
be evaluated. The evaluation of case *needs* the value of y. Therefore the case
expression fails to terminate, as does the f application.

4 A performance semantics

4.1 Time

Step counting does not work for lenient languages. Consider the evaluation of
plet v = E_1 in E; the evaluation of E_1 and E should proceed in parallel, with no
unnecessary synchronisation. Synchronisation only occurs if E tries to access the
value of v. When this happens two possibilities arise: either v's evaluation will
have completed or it will still be being evaluated. If v's evaluation has completed
it should be accessed exactly the same as if it had been evaluated sequentially by
a let. If the evaluation of v has not completed E should wait for its evaluation to
complete. (In an implementation this arises as one task blocking on another.) To
reason about the length of one task (v) and the time for another task (E) to require
its value, a notion of *time* is required. Thus rather than counting the number of
steps to evaluate an expression, all expressions will be evaluated at some time and
the time at which evaluation completes will be calculated.

To do this expressions must be evaluated relative to some time, just as expressions are evaluated within an environment. Two pieces of temporal information
are required about evaluations. Firstly the time spent *evaluating* an expression is
required. Secondly the time at which values become *available* is needed. These
times may be different, since the result of one task may be several values which do
not simultaneously become evaluated. For example a list whose evaluation starts at
time t may become fully evaluated at time t'. However individual elements of the

list may become evaluated at times before or after t'. In a sequential system this is of no consequence; in a parallel system this can affect performance. Specifically, pipelining relies on this; for example, one task may consume elements of a list while another task produces elements of the list.

Times have also been used in real time functional languages, for example Ruth [4]. However, in these languages times are used for a different purpose; they are used to respond to real-time events and to avoid non-determinism.

4.2   The semantics

Rather than augment a standard semantics with temporal information, a combined semantics has been defined. In this semantics, the standard semantics and temporal information are mutually dependent.

The valuation function $\mathcal{M}$ has the form:

$$\mathcal{M} : E \rightarrow Env \rightarrow Time \rightarrow Ans$$

Expressions are evaluated within an environment and at a specific time to produce answers. The semantic domains are:

$$
\begin{aligned}
Ans &= D \times Time \\
\alpha, \beta \in D &= Basic + Fun + List \\
Basic &= B \times Time \\
Fun &= (Ans \rightarrow Ans) \times Time \\
List &= (nil + (D \times List)) \times Time \\
t \in Time &= Nat_{\perp} \\
\rho \in Env &= Var \rightarrow D \\
B &= \text{constants and primitive functions}
\end{aligned}
$$

All values (D) are time-stamped with the time at which they become available. Each evaluation returns a pair (Ans), comprising a value (D) and a $Time$ representing the time at which the evaluation finished. In general, the time required to evaluate an expression is not the the same as the time at which the expression's value becomes available. For example variables already spawned by `plet` require no evaluation, but they may not yet be available. Also, the elements of a list may become available before the entire list is evaluated; this is necessary for pipelined parallelism.

The meaning of a variable v, in an environment ρ and at time t, is:

$$\mathcal{M}[\![v]\!]\, \rho\, t \;=\; \langle \rho[v], t \rangle$$

The time-stamped value is looked-up in the environment. The variable is either evaluated or being evaluated, thus no time is required to evaluate it. Therefore the input time t is returned as the new time after v's evaluation.

The meaning of let is:

$$\mathcal{M}[\![\texttt{let } v = E_1 \texttt{ in } E_2]\!] \, \rho \, t \;=\; \mathcal{M}[\![E_2]\!] \, \rho[v \mapsto \alpha] \, t'$$
$$\langle \alpha, t' \rangle = \mathcal{M}[\![E_1]\!] \, \rho \, t$$

The let construct evaluates its binding (E_1) and then it evaluates its main expression (E_2). Thus the binding is evaluated at the current time t and the main expression is evaluated at the time when the evaluation of the binding finishes. The valuation function is strict in its time argument: $\mathcal{M}[\![E]\!] \, \rho \perp \;=\; \langle \perp, \perp \rangle$. Therefore if the let binding evaluates to bottom, t' will be bottom and hence the whole construct will evaluate to bottom. In this way times are used to ensure the strictness of sequential evaluation.

This may be contrasted with plet:

$$\mathcal{M}[\![\texttt{plet } v = E_1 \texttt{ in } E_2]\!] \, \rho \, t \;=\; \mathcal{M}[\![E_2]\!] \, \rho[v \mapsto \alpha] \, t$$
$$\langle \alpha, \_ \rangle = \mathcal{M}[\![E_1]\!] \, \rho \, t$$

The difference between plet and let is that for plet, the main expression's evaluation (E_2) begins at the same time as the bindings evaluation (E_1). Unlike the sequential let, the binding may evaluate to bottom and the main expression may still be defined. Synchronisation occurs when E_2 requires v's value.

The meaning of cons is:

$$\mathcal{M}[\![E_1 : E_2]\!] \, \rho \, t \;=\; \langle \langle cons \; \alpha \; \beta, t \rangle, t_2 \rangle$$
$$\langle \alpha, t_1 \rangle \;=\; \mathcal{M}[\![E_1]\!] \, \rho \, t$$
$$\langle \beta, t_2 \rangle \;=\; \mathcal{M}[\![E_2]\!] \, \rho \, t_1$$

Operationally cons produces a cons cell, then the head of the cons is evaluated and then the tail of the cons is evaluated. Many different patterns of evaluation for cons are possible; for example E_1 and E_2 could be evaluated in parallel. This cons, although sequential, can give rise to pipelining. Notice that the cons value is time-stamped with the current time. The head and tail will often have different time-stamps from this cons time-stamp.

The semantics for {E} simply increments the time at which E is evaluated:

$$\mathcal{M}[\![\{E\}]\!] \, \rho \, t \;=\; \mathcal{M}[\![E]\!] \, \rho \, (t+1)$$

The crucial semantics is for case:

$$\mathcal{M}[\![\texttt{case E of} \qquad\qquad = \quad case \; \mathcal{M}[\![E]\!] \, \rho \, t$$
$$\texttt{[]} \qquad \texttt{->}E_1 \qquad\qquad \langle \langle nil, t_1 \rangle, t_2 \rangle \qquad\qquad : \; \mathcal{M}[\![E_1]\!] \, \rho \, (max \; t_1 \; t_2)$$
$$\texttt{(x:xs) ->}E_2]\!] \, \rho \, t \qquad \langle \langle cons \; \alpha \; \beta, t_1 \rangle, t_2 \rangle \quad : \; \mathcal{M}[\![E_2]\!] \, \rho' \, (max \; t_1 \; t_2)$$
$$\rho' = \rho[x \mapsto \alpha, xs \mapsto \beta]$$

The `case` construct evaluates E at time t. Since `case` requires the value of E, if necessary, it must wait for this value to become available (synchronise). It does not wait for the whole list to become evaluated but only the top cons or nil. The value E become available at time t_1. The evaluation of E takes until t_2. Therefore evaluation of E_1 or E_2 starts at the later of the two times t_1 and t_2. All primitive operators, such as addition, must synchronise in this way. That is all primitive operators must wait for their strict operands to become available.

The complete semantics, except for primitive operators and constants, is shown in Figure 2.

5 A simple proof

Using the semantics proofs can be constructed about the performance of parallel programs. As with conventional complexity analysis one does not calculate the performance of arbitrary programs. Rather the performance of core algorithms and library functions are calculated.

Below, two program fragments are proved to have the same performance. A kind of idempotence is proved. This allows some redundant `plets` to be removed from programs; this will improve programs' efficiency. Any expression having the form of the left hand side may be replaced by the more efficient form shown on the right.

$$\begin{array}{ll} \text{plet a = E in} & = \quad \text{plet a = E in} \\ \quad \text{plet b = a in} & \qquad \text{Emain [a/b]} \\ \qquad \text{Emain} \end{array}$$

The left hand side is equal to, at time t and in an environment ρ:

$$\mathcal{M}[\text{Emain}] \; \rho' \, [b \mapsto fst(\mathcal{M}[a] \, \rho' \, t)] \; t$$
$$\rho' \;=\; \rho \, [a \mapsto fst \, (\mathcal{M}[E] \, \rho \, t)]$$

= var semantics

$$\mathcal{M}[\text{Emain}] \; \rho' \, [b \mapsto \rho'[a]] \; t$$

= by substitution

$$\mathcal{M}[\text{Emain [a/b]}] \; \rho' \; t$$
$$\rho' \;=\; \rho \, [a \mapsto fst \, (\mathcal{M}[E] \, \rho \, t)]$$

= meaning of the right hand side $\square$

This proof may seem intuitively obvious; however beware, for example `plet x = E in x` and E have the same meaning, but they do not have the same performance.

$$\mathcal{M}[\![E]\!]\,\rho\,\bot \quad\quad\quad = \quad \langle\bot,\bot\rangle$$

If $t \neq \bot$:

$$\mathcal{M}[\![v]\!]\,\rho\,t \quad\quad\quad = \quad \langle\rho[v],t\rangle$$

$$\mathcal{M}[\![E_1\ E_2]\!]\,\rho\,t \quad\quad = \quad f\ (\mathcal{M}[\![E_2]\!]\,\rho\,t_1)$$
$$\langle\langle f,\_\rangle,t_1\rangle = \mathcal{M}[\![E_1]\!]\,\rho\,t$$

$$\mathcal{M}[\![\backslash v.E]\!]\,\rho\,t \quad\quad = \quad \langle\langle\lambda\langle\alpha,t'\rangle.\ \mathcal{M}[\![E]\!]\,\rho[v\mapsto\alpha]\,t',t\rangle,t\rangle$$

$$\mathcal{M}[\![\text{let } v = E_1 \text{ in } E_2]\!]\,\rho\,t \quad = \quad \mathcal{M}[\![E_2]\!]\,\rho[v\mapsto\alpha]\,t'$$
$$\langle\alpha,t'\rangle = \mathcal{M}[\![E_1]\!]\,\rho\,t$$

$$\mathcal{M}[\![\text{letrec } v = E_1 \text{ in } E_2]\!]\,\rho\,t \quad = \quad \mathcal{M}[\![E_2]\!]\,\rho[v\mapsto\beta]\,t'$$
$$\langle\beta,t'\rangle = \mathit{fix}\ (\lambda\langle\alpha,\_\rangle.\ \mathcal{M}[\![E_1]\!]\,\rho[v\mapsto\alpha]\,t)$$

$$\mathcal{M}[\![\text{plet } v = E_1 \text{ in } E_2]\!]\,\rho\,t \quad = \quad \mathcal{M}[\![E_2]\!]\,\rho[v\mapsto\alpha]\,t$$
$$\langle\alpha,\_\rangle = \mathcal{M}[\![E_1]\!]\,\rho\,t$$

$$\mathcal{M}[\![[]]\!]\,\rho\,t \quad\quad\quad = \quad \langle\langle\mathit{nil},t\rangle,t\rangle$$

$$\mathcal{M}[\![E_1\!:\!E_2]\!]\,\rho\,t \quad\quad = \quad \langle\langle\mathit{cons}\ \alpha\ \beta,t\rangle,t_2\rangle$$
$$\langle\alpha,t_1\rangle = \mathcal{M}[\![E_1]\!]\,\rho\,t$$
$$\langle\beta,t_2\rangle = \mathcal{M}[\![E_2]\!]\,\rho\,t_1$$

$$\mathcal{M}[\![\text{case } E \text{ of} \quad\quad = \quad case\ \mathcal{M}[\![E]\!]\,\rho\,t$$
$$\phantom{\mathcal{M}[\![}[]\quad\quad \text{->}E_1 \quad\quad\quad\quad \langle\langle\mathit{nil},t_1\rangle,t_2\rangle \quad\quad : \mathcal{M}[\![E_1]\!]\,\rho\ (max\ t_1\ t_2)$$
$$\phantom{\mathcal{M}[\![}(x\!:\!xs)\ \text{->}E_2]\!]\,\rho\,t \quad \langle\langle\mathit{cons}\ \alpha\ \beta,t_1\rangle,t_2\rangle : \mathcal{M}[\![E_2]\!]\,\rho'\ (max\ t_1\ t_2)$$
$$\rho' = \rho[x\mapsto\alpha, xs\mapsto\beta]$$

$$\mathcal{M}[\![\{E\}]\!]\,\rho\,t \quad\quad\quad = \quad \mathcal{M}[\![E]\!]\,\rho\ (t+1)$$

Figure 2: The semantics

6 Discussion

The main problem with the semantics is its complexity. In [9] a pipelined version of Quicksort is analysed; this occupies five pages! In many ways this is not surprising; the operational behaviour of parallel programs is very complex.

The semantics may be regarded as a specification for a parallel interpreter or simulator. By treating the semantics as a set of transformation rules, parallel program simulation may be performed by program transformation. The semantics may also be augmented to collect other information, for example: task length statistics and parallelism profiles. This information is hard to reason about using the semantics but it may be useful for simulation purposes.

The semantics can on some occasions be too abstract. For example the semantics does not specify that tasks must terminate. Thus speculative tasks may be generated, which are difficult to implement. A more fundamental problem is that average parallelism is not always an accurate measure of performance. The optimal algorithms for some problems, like sorting, depend not only on the input data but also on the number of processors a parallel machine has. Many problems have different optimal algorithms for sequential and parallel evaluation, for example parallel prefix.

7 Conclusions

A semantics for the time analysis of a lenient language has been presented. The semantics can be used to analyse small programs but the analysis of larger programs is problematic. In general more theorems concerning the performance of general patterns of computation are required. Alternatively a higher level language could be used to simplify the programs which must be reasoned about. For some programs a more detailed analysis involving a finite number of processors is desirable. The lenient language is more expressive than a strict language but not as expressive as a lazy language. It seems difficult to apply this approach to a parallel lazy language.

8 Acknowledgements

I would like to thank my supervisor, Professor Simon Peyton Jones, for his encouragement and for helping me to debug many of my ideas.

References

[1] B Bjerner and S Holmstrom. A compositional approach to time analysis of first order lazy functional programs. In *1989 ACM Conference on Functional Programming Languages and Computer Architecture, London*, pages 157–165, 1989.

[2] D L Eager, J Zahorjan, and E D Lazowska. Speedup versus efficiency in parallel systems. Technical Report 86-08-01, Dept. of Computational Science, University of Sasketchewan, August 1986.

[3] C Hankin, G Burn, and S L Peyton Jones. A safe approach to parallel combinator reduction. *Theoretical Computer Science*, 56:17–36, 1988.

[4] D Harrison. Ruth: A functional language for real-time programming. In *PARLE*, pages 297–314, 1987.

[5] P Hudak and S Anderson. Pomset interpretations of parallel functional programs. In *Proceedings IFIP Conference on Functional Programming Languages and Computer Architecture, Portland*, pages 234–256. Springer Verlag LNCS 274, September 1987.

[6] S B Jones. Investigation of performance achievable with highly concurrent interpretations of functional programs. Final Report, ESPIRIT project 302, October 1987.

[7] D LeMétayer. Mechanical analysis of program complexity. *ACM SIG-PLAN Symposium on Programming Languages and Programming Environments*, 20(7), 1985.

[8] R S Nikhil, K Pingali, and Arvind. Id Nouveau. Technical Report memo 265, Computational Structures Group, Laboratory for Computer Science, MIT, July 1986.

[9] P Roe. *Parallel Programming using Functional Languages*. PhD thesis, Department of Computing Science, University of Glasgow, in preparation.

[10] M Rosendahl. Automatic complexity analysis. In *1989 ACM Conference on Functional Programming Languages and Computer Architecture, London*, pages 144–156, 1989.

[11] D Sands. Complexity analysis for a lazy higher order language. In K Davis and J Hughes, editors, *Functional Programming: Proceedings of the 1989 Glasgow Workshop, 21-23 August 1989, Fraserburgh,, Scotland*, Springer Workshops in Computing. Springer Verlag, July 1990.

Problems & Proposals for Time & Space Profiling of Functional Programs

Colin Runciman and David Wakeling
University of York*

1 Problems

Many functional programs are quick and concise to express but large and slow to run. A few critical parts of the program may account for much of the time and space used: replacing these with something cheaper, or applying them less often, significantly improves overall performance of the program. The repetition of this refinement process, starting from a deliberately artless prototype, is a popular strategy for software development. But its effectiveness depends on the ability to identify the "critical parts", and this is far from easy in a lazy functional language. Commenting on the experiences of a colleague developing a large application with their LML system, Augustsson and Johnsson note that

> After long and painful searching in the program he finally found three places where full laziness was lost, each of which accounted for an *order of magnitude* in time (and it is not guaranteed that all such places were found) ... If a program does not run fast enough it can be quite difficult to find out why [1].

(The italics are ours.) There is now general agreement in the functional programming community that a major weakness of lazy functional languages is the difficulty of reasoning about their space and time behaviour [2].

1.1 Why Conventional Profilers May be Inapplicable

Conventional programming systems have tools for profiling such as *gprof* [3] and *mprof* [4]. These automate the installation and reading of *meters* to record information such as the number of times each procedure is called for each static point of call, the proportion of time spent in each procedure (estimated by regular sampling of the program counter), and the amount of memory dynamically allocated by each procedure. Costs incurred by lower level procedures are also aggregated appropriately so that they can be attributed to calling procedures higher up in the program call graph. The availability of such information greatly eases the task of identifying the critical parts of a program. However, these profiling tools of procedural programming systems may be of limited use to the functional programmer, for reasons such as the following.

*Authors' address: Department of Computer Science, University of York, Heslington, York Y01 5DD, United Kingdom. Electronic mail: colin@uk.ac.york.minster, dw@uk.ac.york.minster

1. *The semantic gap*: Program counter sampling may give good estimates of the proportion of time spent in different parts of the *object* code, but this accuracy is not very useful if these "parts" cannot be identified in the *source* code. Functional programs, unlike procedural ones, do not map very directly into computer instructions; functional language implementations involve radical transformation. Measurements of a run-time profiler may therefore be difficult to associate with structural units of the source code, and programs tuned under one implementation may need significant re-tuning to run well under others.

2. *Hidden routines*: Not only may the structure of compiled code depart radically from the source, the auxiliary routines of a functional run-time system may carry out a significant proportion of the computational work. Storage management in general, and garbage collection in particular, may be expensive. Simply passing responsibility up the call graph, as a conventional profiler would, unreasonably charges the full cost of a garbage collection to the program part whose request for memory allocation happened to trigger it.

3. *Global laziness*: Lazy evaluation makes it difficult to assess the costs of isolated program parts. Laziness is a global policy not a local programming technique. The extent of evaluation and the degree to which computational work is shared or avoided is context dependent in subtle ways. For example, a supposed refinement that avoids the evaluation of a costly expression may only shift the point of evaluation to a different context where the result was previously shared.

4. *Space leaks*: In view of the current multi-megabyte storage requirements of many functional programming systems, space costs are perhaps even more important to address than time costs. The lazy evaluation strategy can cause large memory demands of a distinctive kind. Laziness cuts the number of reductions by evaluating expressions only if needed, and then only once. However, this means expressions may be held unevaluated even though their results would occupy much less space: conversely, large results of evaluating small expressions may be retained for a long time until they are used again (or until it is realised that they are no longer needed).

5. *Recursion & cycles*: Profilers for conventional languages, such as *gprof* [3] and *mprof* [4] actually attach measurements to a *condensed* call graph, collapsing strong components to a single point. Since most functional programs use recursive and mutually recursive functions heavily, such condensation could involve the loss of a great deal of information.

The functional programming world has been aware of some of these difficulties for several years — pertinent observations go back at least as far as [5] — but there have not been many suggestions about how to resolve them. Current implementations of purely functional languages typically provide only very basic computational statistics such as the number of reductions performed (on some abstract machine). the number of memory cells allocated (ditto) and the number of garbage collections.

2 Proposals

2.1 Source-level Evaluation with Parametrised Costs?

It is often assumed that to overcome the *semantic gap* existing implementations must be adapted to preserve more source level information in (or about) compiled code. An alternative approach is to construct an interpretive profiler using a *source level graph reduction model*. The idea is to *approximate* the characteristics of various implementations, estimating the time and space costs by a formula combining raw measurements (*eg.* product of reduction count & number of new graph nodes per contractum for each rule). A particular target implementation is represented by a set of values for parametric weights in these formulae, and the formulae can always be refined by generalising them to take into account additional parameters (*eg.* distinctions between *constructors* and other nodes, or between *binary* and *vector* application nodes).

Advantages? The problem of attaching profiling information to units of the source code is greatly simplified. A *single* development of a comparatively simple system approximates *many* separate modifications of already complex implementations. An interpreter with parametrised profiling might also be a useful tool for comparing the relative importance of implementation strategies for particular applications, and for assessing the potential gains from new implementation ideas.

Disadvantages? An interpretive profiler might only give crude approximations of costs for some kinds of implementation (*eg.* those employing *deforestation* [6]) but even these crude profiles may be better than no profiling information at all. The low speed of an interpreter might limit its application: but even a profiler two orders of magnitude slower than implementations designed for speed can still perform substantial computations while the programmer is eating, sleeping or otherwise occupied. Besides, a single profiling run generates enough information to engage the human programmer for some time in consequent program refinements. Lastly, perhaps some elements of modern functional languages cannot be modelled conveniently using source-level graph reduction: the issue is contentious, but in any case tackling a simplified version of the problem first may be quite sensible. Even for rather limited forms of functional program — say in a first order subset of Haskell [7] with no "extras" such as local definitions or comprehensions — the pragmatics of pattern matching and lazy evaluation pose plenty of difficulties.

2.2 Profiles of Object Program Space?

The main concern of profiling is the changing pattern of resource consumption during a computation, and for most implementation methods space taken up by the program *as distinct from the graph* is fixed throughout. (In interpretive implementations based on fixed combinators, however, the program and the graph may be treated as one; the program is "self-modifying", and indeed "self-optimising" [5]). But recent implementation methods involve a significant expansion of program size, and the degree of expansion varies for different kinds of expression:

> ... functions defined using a fair number of equations, where the patterns in the equations are complex. The pattern matching transformation phase in the compiler *expands such programs considerably* ... [1]

... though the above partial evaluation strategy is safe, it may induce a certain degree of *"code explosion"* ... it may be very efficient with respect to execution time ... but it may be *very inefficient with respect to code size* [7].

(Again, italics are ours.) As Thomas Johnsson has pointed out to us, if a program uses a heap of several megabytes, then it is not unreasonable to expand its size from say 100K to 1M bytes, particularly if this also reduces heap usage. But expanding 1M to 10M bytes would be more problematic! It may therefore be useful to know the size of object code generated for each function definition (say).

2.3   Aggregate Profiles ?

The whole of a functional computation can be regarded as nothing but the production and consumption of pieces of graph. To understand why a graph becomes so large, or why the process of reducing it is so long, one might therefore begin by identifying the high-volume *producers* and *consumers* of nodes.

The graph representing the state of a functional computation may grow and shrink dramatically during its history. It is typically small at the start, representing a "main expression" whose value is to be computed. In mid-computation, it may become a very complex structure occupying several megabytes of memory. In the end it will reduce to nothing as the last reduction permits the output driver to complete whatever remains of its value-printing task. This is illustrated nicely in the paper by Hartel and Veen [8].

Every node in the graph at any point must either have been present in the original graph (representing the "main expression"), or else it must have been created by some previous reduction step. The *producer* of a graph node (let us say) is the reduction rule, whether primitive or a program clause, that caused it to be introduced into the graph — a distinguished producer *main* can be defined for nodes in the original graph.

It is not so easy to define *consumers*. It is difficult even in a simple first order programming system without "apply" nodes — in which, for example, `tail (x:xs)` is represented not by the graph shown in Figure 1(a), but by the the one shown in Figure 1(b).

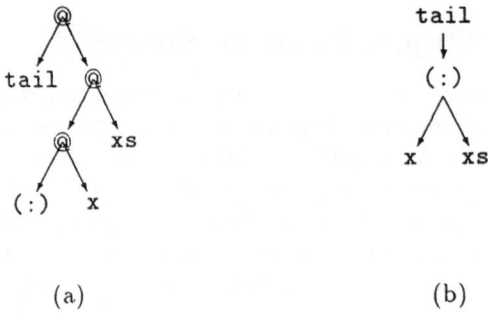

(a)   (b)

Figure 1: Two alternative representations of `tail (x:xs)`

In such a system, reduction by the rule `tail (x:xs) = xs` consumes the graph node for `tail` in the twin sense that it is *used* (it is necessary for the redex to exist) and it is *disposed of* (after the reduction it is no longer part of the graph). But what of the `(:)` node? Though necessary for the reduction it may not disappear from the graph since it may be shared — it may be used but not disposed of. And what of the graph corresponding to `x`? It may be disposed of without being used.

It seems necessary to distinguish between the two forms of consumption. Let's call a primitive or programmed reduction rule r a *user* of a graph node n if some reduction using the rule depends on the occurrence of n in the redex. And let's call it the *disposer* of n if n is finally detached from the graph as an immediate consequence of a reduction using r. If the *output driver* is regarded as a distinguished user and disposer of graph nodes, then each node has zero or more users but exactly one disposer.

Producer-consumer matrices

We envisage a profiling implementation that maintains information about the production and consumption of every graph node. This information can be summarised in a *producer-consumer matrix*, with a column for each producer and a row for each user or disposer. Entries at (i, j) present three figures about nodes *produced* by i: (1) the number of such nodes *disposed of* by j, (2) their *average lifetime* (in reductions), and (3) the number of *uses* of such nodes by j. Rather than have only a single matrix summarising production and consumption of *all* graph nodes, it may be useful to classify nodes in some way and to compute a matrix for *each class*.

To show which classes of graph nodes account for most space used by a program, and which program clauses are most heavily involved in their production, use and disposal, matrices could be ranked (*eg.* by the product of total volume and overall average lifetime of nodes they represent). Similarly, for rows or columns within each matrix. To reduce the amount of information presented to the programmer, matrices/rows/columns representing a low volume of graph nodes could be suppressed.

Notice that both call-frequency and call-graph information is present in producer-consumer matrices since each function call involves the production of an application node tagged with the identity of the "calling" function and its subsequent use and disposal.

It is not obvious how to build a profiler that can produce all this information efficiently. A partial implementation of the idea should be straightforward. Graph nodes can be *tagged* on creation with a production time (*i.e.* reduction number) and the identity of the producer. Lifetimes can be determined approximately by the garbage collector, since the disposal of "fresh" garbage must have occurred at some time since the last collection, and the frequency of collections can always be increased to obtain greater accuracy. Recording node uses is tricky: it could require a lot of space for some nodes, but for applications a single bit may suffice. Determining the identity of disposers could be very expensive: doesn't it require garbage collection in the redex after every reduction, and then in the wake of any processing by the output driver?

Example

Assuming the definitions

$$\text{listmin } (x:y:zs) = \text{listmin } (\text{min } x \ y \ : \ zs) \qquad (1)$$

$$\text{listmin } [x] = x \qquad (2)$$

$$\text{min } x \ y = \text{if } (x < y) \ x \ y \qquad (3)$$

$$\text{if True } x \ y = x \qquad (4)$$

$$\text{if False } x \ y = y \qquad (5)$$

a tagged reduction of `listmin [M,I,N]` where $I < M < N$ is shown in Figure 2, and the producer-consumer matrix for `(:)` nodes during this computation is shown in Table 1. (Note that in this example, users and disposers coincide.)

(:) nodes		Production		
		(0)	(1)	Σ
Use &	(1)	3	2	5
disposal	(2)	0	1	1
	Σ	3	3	6
average lifetime		1.00	1.33	1.20

Table 1: Aggregate production and consumption of `(:)` nodes for `listmin [M,I,N]`

Application to Reducing Graph Space?

A programmer may wish to minimise either the *average* size of the graph, or its *maximum* size. In either case, it should be possible to identify a *target group* of graph nodes. If the aim is to reduce the average then the target group should contain the *longest lasting high volume* nodes, and if the aim is to reduce the *maximum*, the target group should contain the *highest volume nodes in the largest graphs* occurring during the computation.

The first aim is to modify the program to *avoid creating* the nodes in this target group — for example, by fusing together the functions that produce them and the functions that use and discard them. An alternative (or additional) aim is to *shorten the time* for which they are retained in the graph. This may be achieved by forcing earlier evaluation of expressions involving them to yield a small result such as a basic value. Another way to shorten the lifetime of graph nodes is to avoid sharing large results involving them when the uses of these results are a long time apart.

2.4 An Accounting Procedure for Garbage Collection?

The cost of garbage collection in a lazy functional programming system has been estimated at *up to a quarter* of total computing time [9], so it should not be ignored. But what is an appropriate *accounting procedure* for charging collection costs to specific reduction rules of a program?

1. *Charge the disposer?* This is hardly appropriate. Would it be preferable for a rule to retain in the graph as many nodes as possible? Surely not. A disposer should be rewarded, so to speak, for rendering a valuable service!

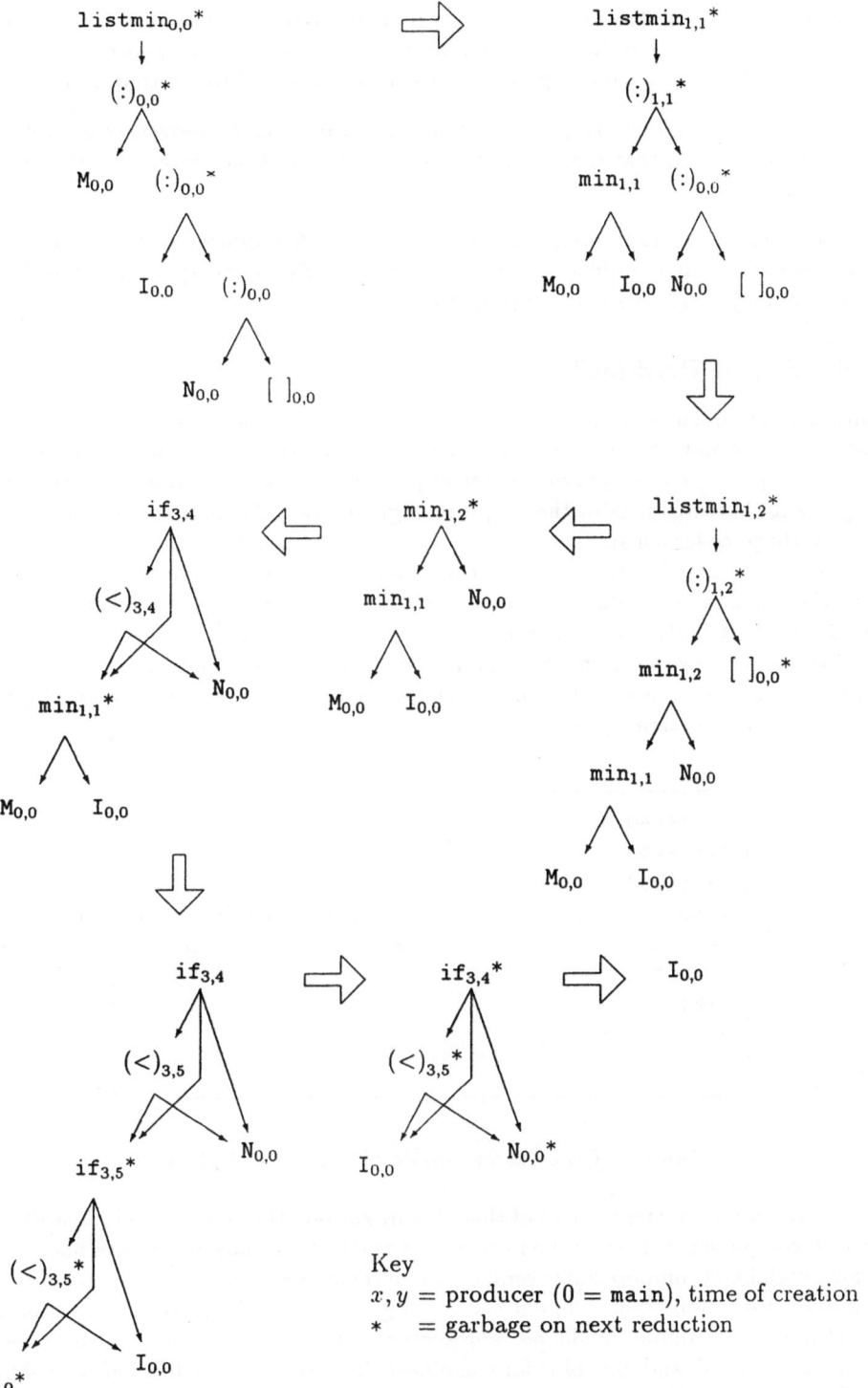

Figure 2: Tagged Reduction of listmin [M,I,N]

244

2. *Charge the producer?* This seems a little more reasonable, until one considers that under lazy evaluation graph production is always in response to the needs of another program component or to the demands of the output driver.

3. *Charge the users?* This seems *far* more reasonable. Moreover, costs could be distributed so that the heaviest users pay the most, not forgetting the output driver.

However, some graph nodes may have *no* users. A producer may generate more graph than is actually needed, in which case it may after all be appropriate to charge it for the recycling of its excess production.

2.5   Serial Profiles?

Summary tables such as producer-consumer matrices provide aggregate information such as *totals* and *averages*, for an entire computation. An alternative or complementary approach is to provide a *serial* profile: that is, a summary of the most important characteristics of the graph at regular intervals (perhaps in conjunction with garbage collections).

Even extremely limited versions of such serial profiles displayed on monochrome ASCII devices can be quite informative. From the crude serial profile of the reduction of `listmin [M,I,N]` shown in Figure 3, one may verify at a glance, for example, that the graph never exceeds its original size. For larger computations, the scale of a profile is easily adjusted by using one character to represent x nodes and sampling after every y reductions.

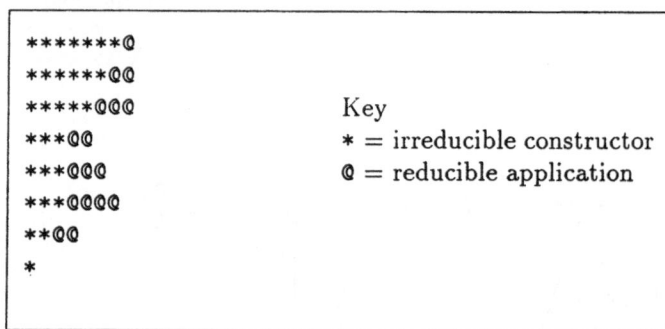

Figure 3: Crude serial profile of `listmin [M,I,N]`

A more satisfying refinement of this idea might be achieved on a colour workstation. A complete profile could be formed as a vertically arranged series of horizontal bands, each band composed of several coloured segments where the colours, arranged in a fixed order, represent different classes of graph nodes. The "cons" nodes of list structures, for example, might be represented in blue — dark blue for those most recently produced, and pale blue for the oldest. The extent of each colour and shade would vary between bands, being be proportional to the volume of the corresponding nodes found in the graph at successive stages in the computation. In this way, high volume node types, including those retained in the graph for a long time, or those predominating in graphs of peak sizes, would stand out at a glance. Ideally such a system would allow its users to specify the colour schemes — for example, depending on the program, colouring by producer may be more informative than colouring by the type of node.

3 Summary & Conclusion

There is no doubt about the outstanding need for profiling tools in lazy functional programming. The subtleties of lazy evaluation and the sophisticated transformations performed by modern functional compilers limit the effectiveness of conventional tools. This paper has put forward only a few tentative proposals: their usefulness must be tested by building and using experimental profiling systems.

4 Acknowledgements

Thanks to Sandra Foubister and the Referees.

References

[1] Augustsson L and Johnsson T. The Chalmers Lazy-ML compiler. *Computer Journal*, 32(2):127–141, April 1989.

[2] Peyton Jones SL. *The Implementation of Functional Programming Languages*. Prentice-Hall, 1987.

[3] Graham SL, Kessler PB, and McKusick MK. An execution profiler for modular programs. *Software — Practice and Experience*, 13:671–686, 1983.

[4] Zorn B and Hilfinger P. A memory allocation profiler for C and LISP programs. *USENIX 88*, pages 223–237, 1988.

[5] Turner DA. A new implementation technique for applicative languages. *SOFTWARE — Practice and Experience*, 9(1):31–50, January 1979.

[6] Wadler P. Deforestation: Transforming programs to eliminate trees. *Theoretical Computer Science*, 73(2):231–248, June 1990.

[7] Hudak P and Wadler P (editors). Report on the programming language Haskell, a non-strict purely functional language (Version 1.0). Technical report, University of Glasgow, Department of Computer Science, April 1990.

[8] Hartel PH and Veen AH. Statistics on graph reduction of SASL programs. *Software — Practice and Experience*, 18:239–253, 1988.

[9] Augustsson L. *Compiling Lazy Functional Languages, Part II*. PhD thesis, Chalmers University of Technology, S-412 96 Göteborg, November 1987.

Solid Modelling in HASKELL

Duncan C. Sinclair*

University Of Glasgow

December 1st, 1990

Abstract

We investigate the suitability of the functional model of programming as applied to the solid modelling field of 3D rendering, with particular reference to expressiveness and efficiency.

We find that functional languages with a good implementation can be more efficient than other languages in certain aspects in the rendering process. Furthermore, recent developments in functional languages allow difficult concepts to be expressed simply within programs, and allow easier expression of the models we wish to render.

1 Introduction

A currently popular area of computing research is functional languages. These are inspired by mathematical notation, and the work of the mathematicians Haskell B. Curry and Alonzo Church. These languages claim to be mathematically pure, which helps program manipulation and proofs.

At the same time, a graphics technique known generally as Constructive Solid Geometry is gaining favour, especially now it has been enlivened with new ray-tracing and texture-mapping methods. Constructive Solid Geometry is a part of the broader field of Solid Modelling, which has a basis within Mathematics and Topology.

It would probably be fair to say that the most prolific users of functional languages are those involved in the design and implementation of functional languages, whether it is the writing of their compilers, or program manipulation systems. Yet there is relatively little use of these languages in the more main-stream branches of computing.

We set out to find whether the functional paradigm is useful for Solid Modelling systems, and what special aspects of functional languages help in this. We use the new functional language HASKELL [1], as the current state of the art, to implement a Constructive Solid Geometry rendering system, and compare it to a similar system in Miranda,[1] which was used for early prototypes.

---

*Author's address: Department of Computing Science, University of Glasgow, Glasgow, G12 8QQ, UK. E-mail: `sinclair@cs.glasgow.ac.uk`

[1]Miranda is a registered trademark of Research Software Ltd.

Our graphical rendering system, christened *Fulsom*,[2] is based on the Constructive
Solid Geometry (CSG) paradigm. CSG in turn, is based on a mathematical model of
solids. The object to be rendered is constructed with mathematical set operations on
simple solids, such as spheres and cubes. The rendering system takes a description
of an object, and produces a grey-scale or colour rendition of the solid that may be
viewed or printed out.

The paper is structured as follows: We start with an overview of HASKELL in
Section 2 with a detailed look at the its overloading features in Section 3. Then we
explain our solid modelling techniques in Section 4 and our particular implementation of it in Section 5. We consider how functional languages can communicate
with graphics devices in Section 6. In Section 7 the process of writing the program
is discussed. Section 8 concludes.

2   HASKELL

We assume a general knowledge of the concepts behind functional languages, and of
the syntax of a typical language like Miranda. A good general introduction for this
is [3].

HASKELL is a general purpose, purely functional programming language. It
incorporates many of the features of the current diverse mix of existing functional
languages that it hopes to take the place of. Regular features include:

- Higher-order functions

- Non-strict semantics

- User-defined algebraic data types

- Pattern matching

- List comprehensions

Also included are some features more often found in conventional languages, to
make the language applicable to real systems. Thus it includes a rich set of numeric
types and operations, arrays and a comprehensive module system.

2.1   New Features in HASKELL

In addition to unifying the features from many other functional languages, HASKELL
includes several new features.

- Abstract data types. These have been split into two components: data abstraction and information hiding.

- The module system. A rigorous module system is provided that separates the
  implementation of a module from its interface. This supplies the mechanism
  used for the creation of abstract types.

---

[2]So called after *Winsom* [2] by Stephen Todd et al.

```
type R3 = (Float,Float,Float)
type R1 = Float

type Row = (Float,Float,Float,Float)
type Mat = (Row,Row,Row)

affine :: Mat -> R3 -> R3
affine (r1,r2,r3) xyz = (x,y,z)
    where
         x = dorow r1 xyz ; y = dorow r2 xyz ; z = dorow r3 xyz

dorow :: Row -> R3 -> R1
dorow (m1,m2,m3,m4) (x,y,z) = (m1 * x) + (m2 * y) + (m3 * z) + m4
```

Figure 1: Geometric Matrix Operation

- A new system interface provides a flexible connection between a program and the operating system it is running upon. This interface is available through both streams and continuations.

- Arrays are supported. Their creation is simplified with the convenient *array comprehension* syntax.

Perhaps the most important addition to the language is an overloading mechanism built into the type system, allowing functions and operators to be defined over different types. This is examined closely in Section 3.

2.2   Example of HASKELL Code

Figure 1 presents a special matrix transformation function written in HASKELL. Conceptually, it multiplies a 4×4 matrix by a homogeneous three dimensional vector, which is 4×1, then normalises the result to ensure that the fourth value in the vector is equal to 1.

This is a common operation in graphics, as this is how all geometric transformations are performed. We have used a common optimisation to reduce the 4×4 matrix to a 3×4 matrix; and to eliminate the normalisation phase [4]. This transformation is sometimes called an *affine transformation*.

The type declarations introduce new *Type Synonyms* [3] which act as abbreviations for other types and are used to make the typings of the functions clearer.

3   Overloading

In Section 2, we stated that HASKELL has a new type system which allows overloading of functions. Overloading in HASKELL is structured by type classes, rather than being a free-for-all as in most of the few languages that support it. These classes are inspired by the classes seen in object-oriented systems, but applied instead to types, rather than objects.

3.1 Classes

A family of operations is grouped into a class. These operations will be overloaded — any instance types of this class are able to define methods for each operation in the class.

3.2 A Numeric Class

Consider the example of simple arithmetic operations. We wish to define addition and multiplication over both integer and floating point types. These operations are grouped into a new class, called Num as all instances of the class will be numeric types.[3]

```
class Num a where
   (+)      ::  a -> a -> a
   (*)      ::  a -> a -> a
```

This declaration states that for a type to belong to the class of Num, it must provide a method for addition (+), and for multiplication (*).

Instances of this class may now be declared.

```
instance Num Integer where
   a + b =  addInteger a b
   a * b =  multInteger a b

instance Num Float where
   a + b =  addFloat a b
   a * b =  multFloat a b
```

The various add and mult functions are assumed to be defined elsewhere. The instance declaration asserts that the type is an instance of the class by virtue of the fact that it provides methods for the class's operations.

These overloaded operators can now be used in the definition of affine, given in Figure 1, to make the matrix function overloaded on *all* types of class Num. In fact to do this, all that needs changed are the type definitions. (See Figure 2.)

Notice that the new type of affine is:

affine :: (Num a) $\Rightarrow$ Mat a $\rightarrow$ R3 a $\rightarrow$ R3 a

This may be read in the style of a polymorphic type definition, where the free type variable a would be universally quantified, but has a constraint placed upon it. The (Num a) $\Rightarrow$ part is called a *context*, it constrains the type a to only those that are instances of type Num. This means that this function is overloaded on all types that are in the class Num. This type would not be valid without this context. The declaration of (R3 a) restricts its own use to places where it is in the scope of the context (Num a).

---

[3]This class Num is a simplified version of actual class Num, part of the large class hierarchy defined in the standard HASKELL *Prelude*.

250

```
type (Num a) => R3 a = (a,a,a)
type (Num a) => R1 a = a

type (Num a) => Row a = (a,a,a,a)
type (Num a) => Mat a = (Row a,Row a,Row a)

affine :: (Num a) => Mat a -> R3 a -> R3 a

dorow :: (Num a) => Row a -> R3 a -> R1 a
```

Figure 2: Types to make Matrix Operation Overloaded.

3.3   Taking Numbers Further - Intervals

The *Fulsom* program uses a non-standard style of numbers called *Intervals*. An interval is a range of values, which *approximates* a unique value within this range. Thus the interval $(3,4)$ represents a single value within the range 3–4; this value could be for example, 3.25, 3, 4 or even π — but only one of them.

Arithmetic operations may be defined over intervals, any resultant interval will represent the range of possible results if the operations were to be performed on the true values.

Addition of intervals is trivial. It is a simple addition of the end points of the intervals:

$$(a,b) + (c,d) = (a+c, b+d)$$

Product is a little more complicated. The product is the maximum range possible, choosing the new end-points from the products of the original end-points. For example, $(-3,2) \times (3,4) = (-12,8)$.[4] Other arithmetic and mathematical operations follow the same techniques.

We shall represent intervals as an algebraic data type. In HASKELL, these are declared with the **data** statement.

```
data Interval = Iv Float Float
```

This allows the interval $(3,4)$ to be represented as **Iv 3.0 4.0**. At the moment we restrict ourselves to intervals over **Float**, but later we show how to remove this restriction using overloading.

In *Fulsom*, we would like to use the standard operators for intervals. To do this the interval type is made an instance of the **Num** class. Using the simplified numeric class from the previous section, the instance declaration might look like this:

```
data Interval = Iv Float Float

instance Num Interval where
  (Iv a b)   +   (Iv c d)   =   Iv (a+b) (c+d)
  a          *   b          =   ivMult a b
```

We assume a definition of multiplication (**ivMult**) elsewhere, but retain the full definition of interval addition for the sake of example.

---

[4] -12 from -3×4 and 8 from 2×4.

3.4   Enhanced Intervals

There are two more things we wish to add to our interval type. Firstly, the data type needs to be enhanced to give better handling for "point intervals", whose range allows only one value (e.g. $(3, 3)$), and also to introduce an infix constructor to build our intervals. Secondly, we require the ability to use intervals over different types of numbers, not just `Float`.

3.4.1   The Data Type

To allow intervals of all types (an interval of characters can make sense) we parameterise the interval type. New constructors are also devised for the point interval and the normal interval.

```
data Interval a = Point a | a :#: a
```

Here the `:#:` is the infix constructor for the interval. Infix constructors must be made up from symbols, and start with a colon.

Our previous `Interval` type is now `Interval Float`, and we can now use other interval types, such as `Interval Char` or `Interval Int`.

3.4.2   Interval Instances

We can now declare our interval types as instances of the class `Num`. This has to be limited to those interval types formed from a type already in class `Num`. We can state this restriction in the form of a type context such as $(Num\ a) \Rightarrow \dots (Interval\ a)$, thus the instance declaration becomes:

```
instance (Num a) => Num (Interval a) where
    a + b = ivAdd a b
    a * b = ivMult a b
```

We have omitted the definition of interval arithmetic on this occasion, as its definition is now more complex with the additional problem of point intervals. The definition of `ivAdd` assumed.

Now that a parameterised interval type exists as an instance of the `Num` class, all functions defined on numbers can be used on intervals, including the `affine` function defined earlier.

4   Solid Modelling

Constructive Solid Geometry is an established technique of Solid Modelling where the object modelled is constructed by manipulations performed on a base set of solids. We shall look at how these models are built, then survey the simple *Boolean* system, and the newer *Potential Field* method.

4.1   The Problem

The basis of Constructive Solid Geometry is that any complex shape of interest can be represented by transforming and combining simple shapes such as cubes and

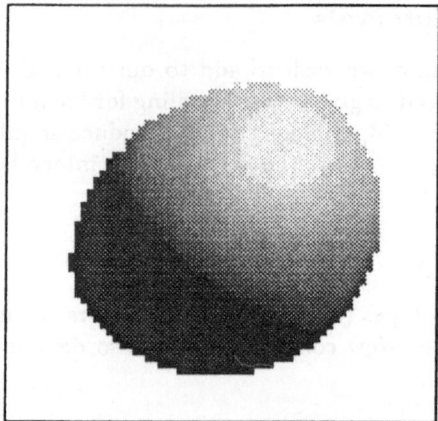

Figure 3: Intersection of a cube and sphere, produces a hemisphere.

cylinders. The transformations are simple geometric operations such as rotations and scaling.

We wish to take a model described as a tree, and produce pictorial views of the shapes described by it — this involves breaking down the model, and reforming it as a raster image for displayed output.

4.2 Intuition

Objects are built using the traditional set operations to combine shapes, to produce new ones. So a sphere intersected with a cube produces a hemisphere, as shown in Figure 3. Other set operations, such as union and difference produce the expected results.

As well as the set operations, shapes may be distorted using the normal graphics transformations, such as scaling, rotation and translation. These operations can be performed on constructed objects as well as primitive ones.

The ability to construct models in this mathematical fashion is responsible for the popularity of CSG in engineering circles [5].

4.3 A Data Type for Primitives

A complex object is represented by a *CSG-tree* with the simple objects at the tips, and geometric and combining operations in the nodes.

This tree can be expressed in HASKELL using an algebraic data type:

```
data CSG = Union CSG CSG           -- Set operations
       | Intersection CSG CSG
       | Minus CSG CSG
       | Scale Point CSG           -- Geometric operations
       | Translate Point CSG
       | Rotate Point CSG
       | Cube Point Float          -- Primitives
       | Sphere Point Float
```

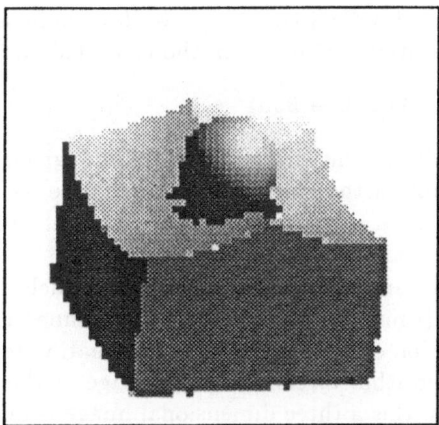

Figure 4: Example of a more complex CSG shape.

```
type Point = (Float,Float,Float)
```

This is only an abstract representation. In the true implementation other information is required.

An example of this structure, used to produce the picture shown in Figure 4, is given below. It describes a cube with two symmetric scoops hollowed out of it by two spheres, unioned with a sphere placed on top.

```
Union   (Sphere (0.0,0.6,0.0) 0.4)
        (Minus (Cube (0.0,0.0,0.0) 1.2)
               (Union (Sphere (0.0,2.8, 1.2) 2.8)
                      (Sphere (0.0,2.8,-1.2) 2.8)))
```

Syntax can also be used to enhance the readability of CSG objects. If we define infix versions of the binary CSG constructors, we can produce a tidier definition of the CSG object.

```
(\_/) = Union
(---) = Minus

cut1 = Sphere ( 0.0, 2.8, 1.2)  2.8
cut2 = Sphere ( 0.0, 2.8,-1.2)  2.8
cube = Cube   ( 0.0, 0.0, 0.0)  1.2
ball = Sphere ( 0.0, 0.6, 0.0)  0.4

shape = ball \_/ (cube --- (cut1 \_/ cut2))
```

4.4 Boolean Model

The Boolean model partitions space into the inside of the object (True), and the outside (False). This allows the set operations to be defined using simple boolean logic operators. Union is implemented by the or operation, intersection by the and operation.

Using our definition of a CSG-tree, once we have built an object, the Boolean model provides the operation isInside on the tree. This would have the type:

```
isInside :: CSG → Point → Bool
```

This operation is actually a front-end for a family of *boundary functions* defined for each possible constructor in the CSG data type. These will often recursively call isInside with new data, in order to determine the final result of whether a point is inside the boundary of the object.

Geometric operations are performed by translating each point using the relevant matrix transformation (using the affine operation defined in Figure 1.)

The isInside function can supply enough information to allow us to perform a scan-line conversion algorithm to construct an image of the object. Each point is tested in turn, and from this a three dimensional image is built up, which can then be mapped down to two dimensions.

In practice, this is too time consuming, requiring a scan of the complete CSG-tree for almost every point in the space, instead the isInside operation is extended to test volumes [6], rather than individual points. This allows a recursive spatial decomposition to be performed. Unfortunately, the use of volumes complicate the boundary functions considerably.

Thus, the process of rasterisation can be simplified, but only by making the boundary functions more complex.

4.5   Potential Field Model

The boolean system only provides simple set operations. These lack the sophistication we would like in order to implement such operations as blends. Blends allow greater flexibility in the operations used to combine objects, in particular they can be used to create fillets between objects joined together.

Quarendon and Todd [2] found a simple enhancement to the boolean method which allows a better implementation, and also an escape from the boolean model's limitations. Rather than having a simple true/false value, instead base the model on *potential fields*, such as those examined in physics labs.

A potential field is basically a mapping from three dimensional points to real values. These are used to model magnetic and electrical (potential) fields in engineering and physics.

When modelled as a function, a potential field might have the type:

```
field :: Point → Float
```

We can apply this model to CSG by assigning each point a value which encodes the information that the boolean model returned, plus extra information which gives greater power.

Points inside an object would be assigned a negative potential, outside an object a positive potential, with zero potential on the surface. The added information is that the value represents a measure of distance from the surface of the object. So, a point 2 "units" from the surface of the object might have a value double that of the value for a point 1 "unit" away from the surface. In practice, such linearity might not be what is required.

Figure 5: Blended union creates smoother curves.

This added information allows us to implement blended unions and intersections. Taking the example of the union operation, the boundary function for union was previously modelled by the **or** binary operation over the result of the boundary functions for its two sub-trees. In the potential field model, it can be modelled with the **min** function — a point is within the shape if at least the lesser value is negative.

A blended union would be a new constructor in the CSG type, and would be have similar operational behaviour to that of the union construct, but with the **min** function replaced by an appropriate blend function, such as:

```
blend        :: Float → Float → Float
blend  a  b  =  −log((exp − a) + (exp − b))
```

The effects of blended union may clearly be seen in Figure 5, where a number of spheres have been blended together, and used to hollow-out the corners of a cube.

Potential Field Functions

By specifying methods for an instance of the numeric class for the CSG type and adding new primitive constructors X, Y & Z, we can express CSG objects using mathematical operations.

The new primitives are potential fields whose value is respective component from the R^3 point. So, the X primitive implements this operation:

$$X\,(x, y, z) = x$$

Likewise for Y and Z.

The CSG data type would now have some new constructors:

```
data CSG = Union CSG CSG
         | Blend CSG CSG
         | ...
         | X | Y | Z
```

Using these facilities, a sphere of radius r can be defined thus:

```
sphere r = sqrt (X^2 + Y^2 + Z^2 - r^2)
```

Compare this definition of a sphere with the true mathematical definition:

$$r = \sqrt{x^2 + y^2 + z^2}$$

This shows another advantage of potential fields. Using potential fields a sphere can be specified directly as input for *Fulsom* without it being required as a primitive — this is not possible in the boolean model.

5 The Implementation

The implementation of the *Fulsom* rendering process is divided into a CSG evaluator which computes potential field values of interval volumes, and a number of conversion phases which transform the CSG-tree into a raster using recursive spatial decomposition on R^3 space.

We first transform the CSG-tree into a oct-tree, where at each level of the tree, we split the space into 8 equal sized voxels.[5] The oct-tree is then mapped from 3 dimensions down to 2, into a quad-tree. This can then be evaluated to generate a raster representation of the objects.

At the top level, *Fulsom* may therefore be viewed as a composition of three translation functions,

```
octcsg :: CSG -> Oct
quadoct :: Oct -> Quad
rastquad :: Quad -> Rast

program :: CSG -> Rast
program = rastquad . quadoct . octcsg
```

The types Oct, Quad and Rast are respectively the types of the oct-tree, the quad-tree, and the output raster form. Each of these phases are discussed later in this section.

5.1 Lazyness

HASKELL has non-strict, or lazy semantics. This means that values are computed only when required. This can give rise to partial values in structured data, where only the required parts of a data structure are computed.

Lazyness allows us to build the translation functions as individual entities. In a strict language the intermediate data structures these routines handle would be too large to be held in memory at one time, thus the phases have to be mixed together, leading to a more complex and hard to understand program. In HASKELL, the intermediate structures have partial values, only as much of the structure as is required is produced, and once used will become garbage for a garbage collector to recover.

Further, the translation functions can be used as they are individually, while in strict systems where the phases must be combined, individual phases are lost, and separate code is required to implement a sub-part of the complete translation.

---

[5]Voxel is from *Volume Elements*, after *pixel*.

5.2 Evaluating the CSG-tree

The core of the system is the CSG `eval` function. This function is passed a csg-tree and a volume, and evaluates the potential field specified by the CSG-tree within that volume. It returns the value given by the field, and a new CSG-tree which can be used in further calls to `eval` within the given volume. The type of this function is:

$$\text{eval} :: \text{CSG} \to \text{R3 (Interval Float)} \to \text{(Interval Float, CSG)}$$

The `eval` function uses intervals, see Section 3.3, the volume passed to `eval` is a triple of real intervals. The resulting value is an interval which represents the range of possible field values within the supplied voxel. This is an approximation: an increasingly better result is guaranteed as the voxel size is reduced.

If the interval value returned is completely below or above zero, then the voxel is inside or outside the object, and recursive decomposition can stop. Volumes outside the object give white space in the result, while volumes inside should not appear in the output — there should at least be a "skin" in front of it.

Pruning of the CSG-tree may take place. Pruning is allowed when one branch of a split in the tree takes no part in producing the value of a voxel, and may be disregarded. This happens most often for the union and intersection constructors. The basic rule for union in the boolean model is that if one branch is completely inside the object, then it can be safely ignored, for intersection this becomes completely outside. The rule extends logically for the potential field model, where the greater information available makes pruning easier. The pruned tree is returned as part of the result of `eval`, so it can be used in sub-volumes.

5.3 Translating a CSG-tree into a Oct-tree

Using the `eval` function, the CSG-tree can be converted into a oct-tree. A spatial decomposition is performed on our image space, evaluating the CSG-tree for each voxel. When the voxel is completely within or outwith of the object — i.e. the interval value returned does not straddle zero — then the recursion stops. Otherwise the recursion is unbounded, and will produce an infinite oct-tree. To stop this the oct-tree is pruned to a fixed depth by an auxiliary function while it is being created.

```
pruneoct :: Oct -> Oct
makeoct  :: CSG -> Oct

octcsg = pruneoct . makeoct
```

At every node and leaf of the oct-tree we need to know the shade or colour to assign to that point when the final image is drawn. We use a simple diffuse shading model [4, page 575]. Using the unit vector of the normal of the surface and the unit vector pointing towards the light source, we take the dot product of this, which gives us an illumination intensity. This can then be used to modify the assigned colour for the object to arrive at a final value. An ambient light component is added for background illumination.

The normal is calculated by a three-dimensional differentiation. Within each voxel we take four point values of the field. One is the basepoint (x, y, z), the others follow the axes $(x + h, y, z)$, $(x, y + h, z)$ and $(x, y, z + h)$. The value for 'h' is proportional to the size of the voxel. The base-point value is subtracted from the axes values to produce a 3D vector, which we then normalise to produce a unit vector.

5.4 Collapsing the Oct-tree down to a Quad-tree

The Oct-tree is a representation of three dimensional space. This needs to be mapped down to two dimensions in order to display it.

The mapping takes the form of a projection of the Oct-tree backwards onto a Quad-tree where parts of the Oct-tree in the "shadow" of other parts do not need to be examined, and so will not be computed.

So the Oct-tree is traversed in a front-to-back order, using the Quad-tree built so far as a mask for areas in the Oct-tree which do not need examined, as they have been obscured.

Loius Doctor [7] covers this algorithm in his report on CSG. He calls the algorithm *Smash*. His version of the algorithm is inefficient, as he constructs the quad-tree from back-to-front, and so needs to re-write parts of the quad-tree that are obscured. In a functional version, this would cause the complete oct-tree to be evaluated needlessly.

5.5 Display of the Quad-tree

During this phase of the rendering process, the quad-tree is evaluated in a depth-first manner to produce a stream of commands sent to an external processor which draws the final output. Burton discusses the use of quad-trees in functional programming in [8], where he rasterises the quad-tree in the functional language. Without the use of efficient array mechanisms I feel this can be better performed outside of the functional language, where dedicated graphics processors can do a faster job. I discuss the interface to the external processor in the next section.

Alternatively, by doing a breadth-first traversal of the quad-tree, it is possible to see the image being formed a low level of resolution, which will gradually increase in detail as we progress down the tree.

6 Graphical I/O in Functional Languages

FPLs have have received a lot of criticism in this area — this is because new techniques are required for input and output in functional languages. The idea that I/O is a side-effect in an otherwise side-effect free functional system is a red herring. The state-changes caused by input and output are as valid as the changes of state in the evaluation graph.

In this section we review the myth relating to functional input/output, we explain what really happens, and then go on to show how it works in practice in our system which communicates with an external graphics processor using input and output streams.

6.1 The Myth

Functional languages cannot handle I/O easily because it is a side effect. Side effects are not possible in functional languages, there is no implicit state upon which the functions can act, and no way in which they could. When an external file system is admitted, side effects must happen within it. Thus when a functional program writes to a file, this is a side-effect. This conflict must be resolved.

The existence of a graphics environment makes the conflict even more acute, when a writable display is made available. How does the functional program read and write to the display without referential transparency being compromised?

This is especially true for graphics systems - how do you capture the changing display without side-effects?

6.2 The Truth

In the streams based model of functional I/O, the output of the program is a stream of messages, containing requests to the operating system. It replies to these requests with responses channeled through the input stream. Thus the program has a general type of:

main :: [Response] $\rightarrow$ [Request]

General output operations such as writing a file or displaying a window will be requests, the response to which will be a just a status value, reporting on the success or otherwise of the requested operation. For input-type operations, we again start by sending a request on the output stream asking for a specific file to be read, or for a pixel to be read on the screen. This is responded to on the input stream, either with an error, or with the requested data.

The problem lies in our concept of what the file-system and graphics display is. It is because we currently think of these as systems that undergo changes in state, rather than taking a functional point of view, where every change made to a system creates a new system. This means that if we read in a file, change it, and then read it again, it is perfectly proper that the second read would be different from the first, as we are reading from a new file system. (In real life we might have to be careful to throw away the data first read from the file after it has been changed so that the changes do not appear in the "previous version" of the file — this depends on the file system, the operating system and the implementation of the run-time interface between the functional program and the operating system.)

6.3 The Practice

Fulsom would be rather academic if we could do little more than get a boring character representation of our scene. As it is, *Fulsom* can produce full colour rasters with good resolution.[6] This is achieved by the output of *Fulsom* being sent to a 'graphics processor'. This is a stream of commands, conveying graphics operations which are performed on the raster as commanded by *Fulsom*. This allows the user to watch the picture develop on-screen as it is being computed. The graphics processor

---

[6]The pictures in this paper do not represent the range of colour and quality of resolution possible from *Fulsom*.

can feed any user input back to *Fulsom*, thus allowing full graphical interaction to take place. Currently *Fulsom* only uses a rectangle-drawing primitive for output. This specifies a rectangle on the raster canvas to be drawn in a particular shade.

7 Program Development

Various stages of development were passes through on the way to completing the implementation. This divides into Implementation Development and Optimisations.

7.1 Implementation Development

There is more to programming than implementing an algorithm. Bugs when they occur in a functional language, tend to be more subtle that in imperative languages. This is because it is not easy to understand how the denotational program produces an operational behaviour.

Here we look at a number of the difficulties faced when writing *Fulsom*.

Shading

The algorithm used to convert from the oct-tree encoding to the quad-tree encoding can be very subtle. Oversights in the coding of this algorithm led to occasional errors in the output of the program. The shape of the output was correct, but the values picked up for the shades were incorrect. This problem was hidden for a long time while the function used to calculate the shade was debugged. It was only after much rewriting of the shading routine that the bug was discovered to be elsewhere.

Overloading Errors

Initially it was hoped to make the CSG `eval` function overloaded on the type of numbers it used, so that we could use normal numbers, rather than intervals while calculating the normal value, which requires four CSG-tree evaluations. This turned out to be unviable. In the complete implementation of the Haskell *Fulsom*, potential field functions may be stored in the CSG-tree for speed. Unfortunately, this was not possible, as the functions being built to be placed in the structure were not over-loaded, as it does not seem possible to create a data structure which contains over-loaded functions. This is what motivated the use of point interval, in an attempt to restore some efficiency.

The Need for a Debugger

The task of fixing bugs is too serious to be left to the programmer unaided. A debugger would allow the programmer to locate a faulty function, and watch it's operation. From this the programmer would be able to locate any problem, and hopefully know how to fix it.

7.2 Optimisations

Initially, the Miranda version of *Fulsom* had space and time complexity problems. A number of unobvious optimisations to the code help solve these problems. Other optimisations were implemented only in the later HASKELL version of the program.

Programming Optimisations

We mean here just general optimisations which can be used to improve the performance of almost any functional program, and not specific to solid modelling.

This included optimisation of list append functions. These can be a source of inefficiency in programs with a lot of output. If the output is strung together with appends, then large portions of the lists are needlessly copied between the append functions. Wadler [9] provided a neat optimisation for removing the list append functions from a program. A similar technique is incorporated into the standard output functions of HASKELL.

There is an obvious difference between depth first and breadth first traversal of a tree. In the breadth first traversal, a list of sub-nodes needs to be maintained. This not only is very large, but because of it's behaviour as a queue, requires new items to be appended to the end. This has quadratic time complexity. It is possible to reduce this back to a linear case by using a non-obvious technique where items are added and removed respectively to and from the front of two lists. When the "from" list becomes empty, the "to" list is reversed and becomes the new "from" list, the "to" list starts empty again.

By pattern-matching at the top-level of a function, memory efficiency can be improved. This is because the constructed data can become garbage sooner. A speed up of an order of magnitude was seen in *Fulsom* when some pattern matching code was moved. This can be seen in any tree traversal algorithm. If a node's sub-trees are held in a fixed size list and we find that map is not appropriate for the task, then we have these two alternatives:

```
walktree1 (Node l) = s
   where
     [l1,l2,l3] = l
     s = ...

walktree2 (Node [l1,l2,l3]) = s
   where
     s = ...
```

In tests, walktree2 runs faster, uses less memory and requires fewer garbage collections. Thus it appears to be better to pattern match the full list on the left-hand side of the function, rather than inside a where clause. The reason we may wish to use walktree1, is that it is less strict than walktree2, which may be advantageous if some sub-trees were not going to be visited. The difference in performance was mainly because memory was freed quicker, which helped prevent the garbage collector from thrashing in memory, copying large areas of memory around which were never going to be used again.

Pruning Strategy

This is a memory optimisation. We attempt to improve (reduce) memory turn-over by trying to prevent the complete re-build of the csg-tree every time we look at it. We do this by using "as" patterns, and by not always pruning the csg-tree, but only when we know the it needs pruned. This reduces memory usage, but can increase time complexity. The run-time increase may be off-set by less time being spent in garbage collection. We achieved this by returning a boolean flag as well as the pruned csg-tree from the csg-tree evaluator. Only if the new pruned tree actually has had any pruning performed on it is it used. Due to lazy evaluation, only those parts of the csg-tree that can be pruned have any pruning attempted on them.

Strictness Bug

Here is an example of how the desire to reduce memory usage and execution time can back-fire, thus increasing both. This bug did not appear as incorrect values in the result, but was only found by examination of the program. In order to reduce the size and complexity of both the quad and oct-trees, we used pruning and optimisation functions upon the trees as they were built. The pruning was insurance against the trees growing too big, while the optimisations folded equal leaf nodes into the one node. It was not until later inspection of the program, looking for bottle-necks that it was realised that these functions were "tail" strict, and thus caused a maximum tree to be built rather than a minimum.

Debugging

These examples again show a need for a debugger. A profiling system incorporated within this would have meant the strictness bug being found sooner.

8   Conclusions

We have implemented a Solid Modelling system in both Miranda and HASKELL. The task of implementing the conceptual potential field algorithms was greatly simplified by the expressive power available in functional languages, and HASKELL in particular.

We feel that the advantages of the lazy system may make functional systems more efficient once better compilers are available. It helps the modularity of the program, and allows the CSG algorithm to be expressed in a natural manner.

The overloading type system which HASKELL provides is a step up from Miranda's normal Milner type system, and far ahead of primitive type systems seen in typical imperative languages. It has allowed us to express the basic concepts of the potential field mathematics directly, by extending the HASKELL numeric classes with an interval system.

We find that the only thing that holds us back is that it is too difficult to reason about the run-time behaviour of a lazy functional program. I suggest that good debuggers, which will allow the run-time behaviour of a program to be monitored can help solve this problem.

The Haskell Advantage

The overloading class system is the best thing about HASKELL: this allowed a more natural implementation of the interval system, and the functions which used it. We feel that the module system could have helped make our program more modular, but failed to use this feature strongly.

HASKELL has the flavour of a cleaned-up version of Lazy ML, made up to look a bit more like Miranda, which can be deceptive to the unwary.

Acknowledgements

This work was supported by a SERC post-graduate research award. Many thanks to my supervisors Simon Peyton Jones, John O'Donnell and, in an unofficial capacity, Stephen Todd, and to those who read and provided comments on early drafts of this paper.

References

[1] P. Hudak, P. L. Wadler, et al, "Report on the functional programming language Haskell," Dept of Computer Science, Glasgow University, April 1990.

[2] Peter Quarendon & Stephen Todd, "Modelling using potential fields," IBM Scientific Centre, Winchester, Sept 1988.

[3] Richard A. Bird & Philip L. Wadler, *Introduction to Functional Programming*, Prentice Hall International, 1988.

[4] J. D. Foley & A. Van Dam, *Fundamentals of Interactive Computer Graphics*, Addison-Wesley, 1982.

[5] A. A. G. Requicha & H. B. Voelcker, "Constructive Solid Geometry," University of Rochester, TM-25 Production Automation Project, New York, November 1977.

[6] Yong Tsui Lee & Aristides A. G. Requicha, "Algorithms for Computing the Volume and Other Integral Properties of Solids. II. A Family of Algorithms Based on Representation Conversion and Cellular Approximation," *Communications of the ACM* **25** (September 1982), 642–650.

[7] Louis Doctor, "Solid Modelling Algorithms Utilizing Octree Encoding," December 1980.

[8] F. W. Burton & John G. Kollias, "Functional programming and quadtrees," Dept of Computer Science, Univ of Utah, Sept 1987.

[9] Philip Wadler, "The concatenate vanishes," Dept of Computer Science, Glasgow University, Dec 1987.

Differentiating Strictness

Satnam Singh *

Abstract

Strictness analysis is viewed as a differencing operation over functions. This results in differencing equations that have a similar form to those found in the calculus of real valued functions.

1   Introduction

In the calculus of real valued functions, the *derivative* is used to measure the rate of change of some function $f : \Re \to \Re$ at a given value x. The derivative of $f(x)$ is written:

$$\frac{df}{dx}$$

A useful collection of laws exists for derivatives e.g. the product rule and the chain rule.

Derivatives can also be defined for boolean functions. The derivative gives the conditions under which a change in a given parameter value will result in a change in the output of the function. The laws for the derivatives of boolean functions are similar to those that hold for real valued functions.

This paper explores the possibility of performing strictness analysis by performing an approximate differentiation of program expressions. Differencing rules are formulated to describe exactly when the output of a function depends on a given parameter. This is then used to assess the strictness in this parameter.

First, boolean differences [1] are briefly presented. Then rules are drawn up for strictness analysis of a first-order language. A simple example is presented and then the chain rule is demonstrated to hold for the given strictness rules. A method for coping with recursive functions is presented.

2   The Boolean Difference

Differences are the discrete analogs of derivatives. The boolean difference of a function f of parameters $x_1, x_2, ..., x_n$ is defined with respect to a parameter x_i where $1 \leq i \leq n$ by:

$$\frac{df}{dx_i} = f(x_1, x_2, ..., x_i, ..., x_n) \oplus f(x_1, x_2, ..., \bar{x}_i, ..., x_n) \tag{1}$$

---

*The University of Glasgow, G12 8QQ.

A function f is said to *depend* on a parameter x_i if a change in x_i results in a change in the value of f. If $df/dx_i = 1$ then f always depends on the value of x_i irrespective of $x_1, ..., x_{i-1}, x_{i+1}, ...x_n$. If $df/dx_i = 0$ then f does not depend on the value of x_i. If df/dx_i is an expression in terms of $x_1, ..., x_{i-1}, x_{i+1}, ...x_n$ then this expression gives the conditions under which f depends on x_i. Boolean differences have familair looking laws that correspond to laws of derivatives real-valued functions.

3 Differencing for Strictness Analysis

The boolean difference gives the conditions under which a given parameter is needed. This idea is extended to perform strictness analysis of a first order functional language.

Let functions be of one parameter only. This parameter may be a tuple, whose elements can be selected by the projection functions π_1, π_2, etc. Thus, for a parameter X, $x_1 = \pi_1, x_2 = \pi_2$, etc.

The difference of a variable x_j with respect to x_i where $i \neq j$ is defined to be:

$$\frac{dx_j}{dx_i} = 0 \text{ where } i \neq j \qquad (2)$$

This reflects the observation that in general a change in x_i does not result in a change in x_j. The difference of a constant is also 0 for the same reason:

$$\frac{dc}{dx_i} = 0 \text{ where } c \text{ is a constant} \qquad (3)$$

A change in x_i certainly changes any expression containing x_i including x_i itself:

$$\frac{dx_i}{dx_i} = 1 \qquad (4)$$

The binary arithmetic operators are assumed to be strict in both arguments. The differencing rule for multiplication is:

$$\frac{d}{dx_i}(a \times b) = \frac{da}{dx_i} + \frac{db}{dx_i} \qquad (5)$$

where a and b are arbitrary expressions, and a plus denotes logical disjunction. Then rules for the other strict binary operators are similar.

The differences rules for application of some function g which takes Y as its parameter is defined as follows:

$$\frac{d}{dx_i}g\langle f_1(X), f_2(X), ..., f_m(X)\rangle = \sum_{j=1}^{m}\left(\frac{dg}{dy_j}.\frac{df_j}{dx_i}\right) \qquad (6)$$

The dot denotes logical conjunction. A variable x_i is considered to be not needed if it is evaluated in any of the arguments $f_1(X), f_2(X), ..., f_m$ which are strict parameters to g.

The difference of the condition expression:

$$f(X) = \textbf{\textit{if }} p(X) \textbf{\textit{ then }} q(X) \textbf{\textit{ else }} r(X)$$

with respect to x_i can be defined by:

$$\frac{df}{dx_i} = \frac{du}{dx_i} + u.\frac{dv}{dx_i} + \bar{u}.\frac{dw}{dx_i} \tag{7}$$

where $u = p(X)$, $v = q(X)$ and $w = r(X)$. A variable x_i is considered to be needed if it is needed in the test for the conditional $p(X)$ or if it is needed in $q(X)$ when the test is true or if it is needed in $r(X)$ when the test is false. The derivative df/dx_i here gives the *conditions* under which x_i is needed.

4 An Example

The rules introduced in the previous section are now used to obtain strictness information for the following function f:

$$f\langle x_1, x_2, x_3, x_4 \rangle =_{def} \textbf{\textit{if }} x_1 = 2 \textbf{\textit{ then }} x_2 \times x_3 \textbf{\textit{ else }} x_2 \times x_4$$

By inspection, we can see that x_1 and x_2 are always needed. The variable x_3 is only needed when $x_1 = 2$ and x_4 is only needed when $x_1 \neq 2$.

The strictness of x_1 is given by:

$$\begin{aligned}
\frac{df}{dx_1} &= \frac{d}{dx_1}(x_1 = 2) \quad + (x_1 = 2).\frac{d}{dx_1}(x_2 \times x_3) \quad + (x_1 \neq 2).\frac{d}{dx_1}(x_2 \times x_4) \\
&= \frac{dx_1}{dx_1} + \frac{d}{dx_1}2 \quad + 0 \qquad\qquad\qquad\qquad + 0 \\
&= 1 + 0 \qquad\quad + 0 \\
&= 1
\end{aligned}$$

This indicates that the parameter x_1 is always needed, irrespective of the values of x_2, x_3 and x_4.

Differencing f with respect to x_2 gives 1. The variable x_3 is only needed when $x_1 = 2$, since $df/dx_3 = x_1 = 2$. Since the strictness of x_3 depends on the value of x_1, f is not strict in this parameter. When the value of x_1 is known, x_3 could be evaluated before calling f if $x_1 = 2$.

Similarly, x_4 is only needed when $x_1 \neq 2$:

5 The Chain Rule

Let the functions g and f be defined as:

$$g(X) = \textbf{\textit{if }} \pi_1(X) > 42 \textbf{\textit{ then }} \langle \pi_2(X) + 7, 14 \rangle \textbf{\textit{ else }} \langle 18 - \pi_1(X), \pi_3(X) \rangle$$
$$f(Y) = \textbf{\textit{if }} \pi_1(Y) = 2 \textbf{\textit{ then }} \pi_2(Y) + 2 \textbf{\textit{ else }} \pi_1(Y) + 3$$

The differences of g w.r.t. x_1, x_2 and x_3 are:

$$\frac{dg}{dx_1} = 1, \quad \frac{dg}{dx_2} = \pi_1(X) > 42, \quad \frac{dg}{dx_3} = \pi_1(X) \leq 42$$

The composition of f and g is:

$$\begin{aligned}
(f \circ g)(X) &= f(g(X)) \\
&= \textbf{\textit{if }} \pi_1(g(X)) = 2 \textbf{\textit{ then }} \pi_2(g(X)) + 2 \textbf{\textit{ else }} \pi_1(g(X)) + 3 \\
&= \textbf{\textit{if }} (\textbf{\textit{if }} \pi_1(X) > 42 \textbf{\textit{ then }} \pi_2(X) + 7 \textbf{\textit{ else }} 18 - \pi_1(X)) = 2 \\
&\quad \textbf{\textit{then }} ((\textbf{\textit{if }} \pi_1(X) > 42 \textbf{\textit{ then }} 14 \textbf{\textit{ else }} \pi_3(X)) + 2 \\
&\quad \textbf{\textit{else }} (\textbf{\textit{if }} \pi_1(X) > 42 \textbf{\textit{ then }} \pi_2(X) + 7 \textbf{\textit{ else }} 18 - \pi_1(X)) + 3
\end{aligned}$$

The differences with respect to x_1, x_2 and x_3 is:.

$$\frac{d}{dx_1}(f \circ g) = 1, \ \frac{d}{dx_2}(f \circ g) = (\pi_1(X) > 42), \ \frac{d}{dx_3}(f \circ g) = (\pi_1(X) \leq 42).(\pi_1(X) \neq 16)$$

Instead of expanding the function applications, the *chain rule* for differentiating the composition of two functions can be used:

$$\frac{d}{dx_i}(f \circ g) = \frac{df}{du}.\frac{du}{dx_i} \text{ where } u = g(X) \tag{8}$$

6 Remarks

The derivative of a real valued function is a real valued expression, This is necessary for higher order derivatives to make sense. Here, derivatives of program expressions are always boolean expressions. Higher order derivatives seem to make no sense for the strictness analysis definitions given here.

It is also difficult to imagine what would be the analogue of the product rule and the quotient rule. The product rule is given below:

$$\frac{d}{dx}\{f(x).g(x)\} = \frac{df}{dx}.g(x) + f(x).\frac{dg}{dx} \tag{9}$$

Again, because the result of the derivative is a boolean expression, there seems to be no straightforward interpretation of these laws.

A real valued function of more than one parameter can be differentiated with respect to one parameter while holding the others constant by forming the partial derivative: $\frac{\partial f}{\partial x_i}$. However, partial derivatives are given a more fundamental definition for boolean differences. The df/dx notation has been employed in the boolean difference literature even if f is a multiple parameter function.

7 Conclusions

Strictness has been viewed as a differencing operation. Instead of measuring the degree of difference, rules have been developed to detect if a difference occurs. These rules are approximations which give the exact circumstances under which a parameter is used. By weakening these rules, we arrive at the usual rules used for strictness analysis.

The chain rule which is useful for differentiating composite functions in calculus has been found to hold for the definitions given here for strictness analysis. The sequence of approximations given by the ascending Kleene chain can be used to find an approximate result for recursive functions [2].

References

[1] F. F. Sellers, Jr., M. Y. Hsiao, and L. W. Bearnson. "Analyzing errors with the Boolean Difference". *IEEE Transactions on Computing*. Vol. EC-17, July 1968, pp. 676-683.

[2] Peyton-Jones S. L. *The Implementation of Functional Programming Languages*. Prentice-Hall, 1987, pp. 387-390.

GENERALISING DIVERGING SEQUENCES OF REWRITE RULES BY

SYNTHESISING NEW SORTS

Muffy Thomas and Phil Watson
Dept. of Computing Science
University of Glasgow

Extended Abstract

1. Introduction

Confluence, termination and typing are crucial issues in term rewriting. When a set of rules is terminating and confluent, then each term has a unique normal form. The Knuth-Bendix completion algorithm [KB70], given a termination ordering, tests for the confluence property by generating a confluent set of rules from a given set of equations. The algorithm is not guaranteed to terminate, even when the word problem defined by the given system of equations is decidable. When the completion (semi) algorithm diverges and results in an infinite sequence of confluent rewrite rules, then we only have a semi-decision procedure for the word problem.

We aim to replace such an infinite sequence of rules with a finite sequence, or set, which is equivalent in the following sense. First, the finite set should preserve the equational theory defined by the given equations, i.e. the finite set should at least be a conservative extension [TJ89] of the infinite sequence. Note, however, that the finite set may be based on a larger signature than the infinite sequence; the rules in the former may use some sorts which do not occur in the latter. Second, the finite set should be canonical, i.e. confluent and terminating. Our approach is based on finding exact generalisations [TJ89] of the varying parts of the infinite sequence of rules. Often, exact generalisations cannot be found with respect to the given signature, but they may exist if we enrich the signature. In [La89], the signature is enriched with new operators; here we enrich the signature with new sorts, sort relations and operator arities: the result is an order-sorted signature. The new sorts allow us to capture exactly the varying parts of the rules, in some cases.

In this extended abstract we present an algorithm for synthesising the required new sorts; a more complete approach to finding generalisations of infinite sequences of rules is contained in [TW90]. We work within order-sorted rewriting and therefore aim to produce regular and monotonic signatures.

In §2 we present an example of the kind of problem to be solved. §3 contains some background material and definitions concerning languages and grammars. §4 contains our algorithm which takes as input a signature and a context-free grammar G (with start symbol S) describing the language of the varying parts of the infinite sequence of canonical rewrite rules. It produces an order-sorted signature with a distinguished sort S such that terms with sort S are exactly those words in the language of G. In §5 we apply the algorithm to the example presented in §2 .

We assume the usual definitions of order-sorted matching and term rewriting as contained in [SNGM87], for example. We briefly review the concepts of monotonicity and regularity from [SNGM87] below.

An order sorted signature Σ is *monotonic* iff for every pair of operator functionalities f:s_1 x ...x s_n → s, f:t_1 x ...x t_n → t, if for all i=1,...,n , $s_i \leq t_i$, then s ≤ t.

An order sorted signature Σ is *regular* iff every term has a least sort. We use the notation LS(t) to denote the least sort of a term t, when it exists.

2. Motivation

Consider the set of rules generated by application of the Knuth-Bendix completion algorithm to the rule:

R)   f(g(f(x))) → g(f(x))

where we assume a single-sorted signature with no operators apart from g: T → T, f: T → T and a constant symbol c: T.

Then the complete set of rules generated is the infinite sequence:

R1)	f(g(f(x)))	→	g(f(x))
R2)	f(g(g(f(x))))	→	g(g(f(x)))
R3)	f(g(g(g(f(x)))))	→	g(g(g(f(x))))
etc.			

We use R^∞ to denote this infinite sequence.

It can easily be seen that the rules in R^∞ fall into a clear pattern:
$$f(g^n(f(x))) \to g^n(f(x)) \qquad \text{for any } n > 0.$$

In fact, we might observe that all terms of the form
$$t = g^n(f(x)) \qquad \text{for any } n > 0.$$
are qualitatively different from all others; these are exactly the terms
for which
$$f(t) \to t.$$

Note that we cannot generalise R^∞ by the rule
$$f(y) \to y$$
where y is a variable of sort T. Such a rule is too powerful - it equates terms which have different normal forms under R^∞. If we add such a rule, then the new rule set is not a conservative extension of the original.

If we were able to define a variable y which could *only* be instantiated by terms of the form $g^n(f(x))$, n > 0, then we would be able to replace the infinite sequence by the single rule f(y) → y. The aim of our algorithm is to define a new sort which contains exactly those terms of the form $g^n(f(x))$, n > 0, and to modify the arities of the operators appropriately.

3. Languages and Grammars

In §1 we informally introduced the idea of regarding an infinite set of rewrite rules as a language; we give the relevant language concepts below.

Definition [HU79]
A *context-free language* is a set of words (finite strings of symbols from our alphabet) each of which is derived from a *context-free grammar* G = (V,C,S,P) where:

> V is a finite set of variables or non-terminals
> C is a finite set of constants or terminals (our alphabet)
> S is a special non-terminal called the start symbol
> P is a set of productions each of which is of the form:
> > A → s

where s is a string of symbols from $(V \cup C)^*$ and A is in V.

Since we are concerned with sets of *terms*, we assume that the symbols "(" and ")" are terminals in every grammar. Moreover, since terminals will be either operator symbols from Σ, brackets, or variables in Σ, we refer to the constant operator symbols as constant-terminals and the variables as variable-terminals. We are interested in a special case of context-free grammar as follows.

Definition
A grammar G is *weakly simple* iff every production rule in G has one of the forms:
> > $N \to f(x_1,...,x_n)$
> or > $N \to f$
> or > $N \to N'$

where each x_i is a terminal or non-terminal, f is a terminal, N and N' are non-terminals.

Lemma
Any *context-free* grammar can be transformed into an equivalent *weakly simple* grammar.

4. The Algorithm

We will now define our algorithm as follows.

From a given rewriting system R over signature Σ, let R^∞ be the infinite sequence of rules generated by the Knuth-Bendix completion algorithm. We partition R^∞ into Q and Q^∞, where Q^∞ is the infinite sequence we wish to generalise; i.e. we aim to replace Q^∞ by a finite set of rules. Note, in general, R^∞ may contain more than one sequence to be generalised, in which case the algorithm may be applied in turn to each sequence.

Provided the language of the varying parts of Q^∞ can be described by a context-free grammar, then we apply the following algorithm which enriches the signature in the appropriate way, so that Q^∞ can be generalised. We do not concern ourselves here with the generation of the grammar from the finite subset of the infinite sequence Q^∞ which we can see up to any one time, but we proceed by inspection.

Algorithm

Let G be a weakly simple context-free grammar with terminals C, non-terminals V and start symbol S such that

> • G generates the language of the varying parts of Q^∞,
> • there is a sort X in Σ such that every term in L(G) has sort X and X is minimal among such sorts.

Let Z = ({X,𝒮}, {(𝒮,X)},{}) be a triple consisting of sorts, a relation < on sorts and operator arities. By an abuse of notation, we identify < with its transitive closure. Note, Z may only be a fragment of a signature. We now proceed to enrich Z and combine it with Σ as follows:

Step 1 (add sorts)

For every non-terminal N in V, add the sort $\mathcal{N}$ to Z (non-terminals are sorts).

For every constant-terminal t in T, if t occurs as an operand in the right hand side of a rule then define a new sort, t, say. Add sort t and operator t: t to Z. If t is a term of sort U in Σ, then add the pair (t,U) to < in Z, i.e. order t < U.

Define the partial function sort: $V \cup T \to$ Sorts of $Z \cup$ VarSorts, where VarSorts is the set of sorts of the variable terminals in G, by:

$$\text{sort}(t) = T \qquad \text{if t is a variable-terminal of sort T,}$$
$$\text{sort}(t) = t \qquad \text{if } t \text{ was defined in Step 1,}$$
$$\text{sort}(N) = \mathcal{N} \qquad \text{if N is a nonterminal.}$$

Step 2 (add operator arities and sort orderings)

For every production of the form $N \to f$, where f is a constant-terminal, add the operator
$$f: \mathcal{N}$$
to Z.

For every production of the form $N \to f(x_1,...x_n)$, $n > 0$, add the operator
$$f: \text{sort}(x_1) \times ... \times \text{sort}(x_n) \to \mathcal{N}$$
to Z.

For every production of the form $N \to N'$ where N' is a nonterminal, add the pair
$$(\mathcal{N}',\mathcal{N})$$
to the relation < in Z, i.e. order $\mathcal{N}' < \mathcal{N}$.

Step 3 (combine Z and Σ)

Let Σ' be the union of Z and Σ.

Step 4 (ensure regularity)

For each n-ary operator f, $n \geq 0$, in Σ', for each pair of arities
$$f: s_1 \times ... \times s_n \to t$$
$$f: s'_1 \times ... \times s'_n \to t'$$
with $\sim(t' \leq t \vee t \leq t')$

for each sequence of sorts $<u_1,...,u_n>$ such that
for all i=1,...,n, $u_i \leq s_i$, and $u_i \leq s'_i$, and u_i is maximal among such sorts,
do:
add the new sort GLB(t,t') to Σ',
add the pairs (GLB(t,t'), t) and (GLB(t,t'), t') to the relation < in Σ',
if for some r we have r < t and r < t',

$\qquad$ then add (r,GLB (t,t')) to the relation < in Σ',
$\qquad$ add a new arity f: $u_1 \times ... \times u_n \to$ GLB(t,t') to Σ'.

(Note: any of these substeps must be omitted if done already. The new sorts are intended to be greatest lower bounds, thus the sorts GLB(x,y) = GLB(y,x), GLB(x,GLB(y,z)) = GLB(x,y,z), etc.)

Step 5 (ensure monotonicity)

For each n-ary operator f, $n \geq 0$, in Σ', for each ordered pair of arities
$\qquad$ f: $s_1 \times ... \times s_n \to t$
$\qquad$ f: $s'_1 \times ... \times s'_n \to t'$
if for all i=1,...,n $s_i \geq s'_i$, then:
$\qquad$ if t'>t then delete the arity f: $s'_1 \times ... \times s'_n \to t'$ from Σ'.

Step 6 (remove redundant sorts)

For every sort s in Σ', excepting S, if s does not occur in an operator arity, then delete s from Σ'.

5. An Example

Consider the language of the varying parts from the example presented in §2: the set of terms {g(f(x)), g(g(f(x))),...}. A grammar for this language is

$S \to$ g(S) | g(F)
$F \to$ f(x)

The result of the algorithm is:

	<	Sorts	F
Step 1			
	$S<T$	T, S, F	
Step 2			
			g: $S \to S$
			g: $F \to S$
			f: $T \to F$
Step 3			
			g: $T \to T$
			f: $T \to T$ $*$
			c: T
Step 4			
GLB(T,F) <T		GLB(T,F)	f: $T \to$ GLB(T,F)
GLB(T,F) < F			
Step 5		(delete $*$)	

Result:

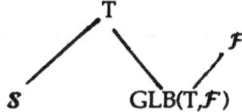

$$(T_{\Sigma'})_S \quad = \quad \{g(f(x)),\ g(g(f(x))),...\}$$

$$= \text{language of start symbol S}$$

Now the single rule
$$f(y) \rightarrow y$$
with variable y of sort S is

i)   a complete, confluent rewrite set;
ii)   a conservative extension of R^{∞}.

Moreover, the order-sorted signature is monotonic and regular.

7. Conclusions

The algorithm which we have given is only a part of the full process of transforming an infinite set of rewrite rules R (or more accurately a divergent case of Knuth-Bendix completion) into a finite complete set of rules. We have shown that if we enrich the original signature Σ in an appropriate way then at least in some cases we arrive at a signature in which at least there exists a complete set of rules which forms a conservative extension of the original set, which may not be true in Σ.

9. References

[HU79] J. Hopcroft, D. Ullman, Introduction to automata theory, languages, and computation, Addison-Wesley, 1979.

[La89]   St. Lange, Towards a Set of Inference Rules for Solving Divergence in Knuth-Bendix Completion, Proc. Analogical and Inductive Inference '89, GDR, Lecture Notes in Computer Science 367, Springer-Verlag, 1989.

[SNGM87] G. Smolka, W. Nutt, J.A. Goguen, J. Meseguer, Order-Sorted Equational Computation, SEKI Report SR-87-14, Universität Kaiserslautern, FRG, 1987.

[TJ89]   M. Thomas, K.P. Jantke, Inductive Inference for Solving Divergence in Knuth-Bendix Completion, Proc. Analogical and Inductive Inference '89, GDR, Lecture Notes in Computer Science 367, Springer-Verlag,1989.

[TW90] M. Thomas, P.Watson, Solving Divergence in Knuth-Bendix Completion by Enriching Signatures, submitted for publication.

Concurrent Data Manipulation in a Pure Functional Language

Phil Trinder

Glasgow University *

Abstract

This paper investigates the feasibility of using a pure functional language to implement data storage and manipulation on parallel declarative machines. A pure functional language is used to construct a data manager that allows efficient and concurrent access to shared data. The interaction between concurrent data manipulation operations is investigated. It is shown that, within certain limits, the rate of processing data manipulating operations is independent of the size of the data structure.

1   Introduction

One means of processing data quickly is to use a multiprocessor machine. Pure functional languages are easily made concurrent and hence are suitable for programming multiprocessors [9, 13]. Indeed, there are now several declarative multiprocessors, i.e. machines specifically designed to evaluate functional languages in parallel [1, 3, 4, 8]. Declarative multiprocessors typically have large memories, which increases their potential data-processing speed. However, when a data structure is changed in a pure functional language, a new version of the structure must be constructed, this is termed *non-destructive update*. Initially it appears to be prohibitively expensive to create a new version of a database every time it is modified.

By storing data in trees it is possible to provide non-destructive data manipulation operations that are efficient in both space and time. These operations, such as a function that updates an entity to have a new value, are termed bulk-data operations. The interaction between concurrent bulk-data operations is investigated. It is shown that, given certain conditions, the rate that a declarative multiprocessor can process bulk-data operations is independent of the size of the database. The conditions required are that all of the database must reside in shared primary memory and there must be sufficient processors to service a pipeline.

A transaction may perform several bulk-data operations atomically, i.e. without risk of interference from competing transactions. The implementation of a transaction manager that processes transactions constructed from the bulk-data operations described here is outlined in [12]. Two problems that restrict concurrency in the

---

*Email: trinder@uk.ac.glasgow.cs. This work supported by both the SERC Bulk Data Types project and the ESPRIT FIDE project

transaction processor were identified in [2]. Three primitives were proposed to resolve these problems, and one of these, optimistic if, has been implemented. For brevity transaction processing in the functional database is not described here.

In some related work the Flagship team have built a small declarative multiprocessor using 15 Motorola 68020 processors. Transactions are provided as primitives in the Flagship operating system, or PRM. Because of the cost of non-destructive update, PRM transactions are impure, i.e. a PRM transaction may have the side-effect of updating many entities atomically. The Flagship machine achieves some impressive results for the Debit/Credit transaction-processing benchmark [10].

Machine	Transactions Per Second
Flagship	45
Sun	5
IBM 4381-P22	22
DEC VAX 8830	27

The Flagship machine demonstrates the transaction-processing potential of declarative multiprocessors. However, the introduction of side-effects destroys the referential transparency of parts of the PRM making the semantics of the transactions complex, reasoning about programs difficult and evaluation order significant. In an attempt to avoid these problems the database described here has been implemented in an entirely pure, or referentially transparent, language. The consequences of using a pure functional language to implement a database are described in some detail in [11].

The remainder of this paper is structured as follows. Section 2 describes the database design. Section 3 describes the hypothetical machine that the bulk data manager is implemented on. Section 4 presents the results obtained when sequences of bulk-data operations are processed. Section 5 concludes.

2   Database Architecture

2.1   Introduction

A *class* is a homogeneous set of data; it may represent a semantic object such as a relation or an entity set. For example a class might represent a collection of bank accounts. For simplicity the bulk data manager described in this paper supports operations on a single class of data. The same principles apply for operations on a database containing multiple classes of data. The design of a more realistic functional database that supports multiple classes, views, security, alternative data structures and two data models is given in [12].

In most existing languages only certain types of data may be permanently stored. Much of the effort in writing programs that manipulate permanent data is expended in unpacking the data into a form suitable for the computation and then repacking it for storage afterwards. The idea behind *persistent* programming languages is to allow entities of any type to be permanently stored.

In a persistent environment a class can be represented as a data structure that persists for some time. Operations that do not modify a such a bulk data structure, for example looking up a value, can be implemented efficiently in a functional

276

language. However, data structures must be modified non-destructively in a pure
functional language, i.e. a new version of the structure must be constructed. At first
glance it appears to be prohibitively expensive to create a new version of a bulk
data structure every time it is modified.

2.2 Trees

A new version of a tree can be cheaply constructed. For simplicity the prototype
data manager uses a binary tree. In a more realistic database a B-tree would be used.
The distinction between binary and B-trees does not affect the efficiency described
in the next Section. A class can be viewed as a collection of entities and there may
be a key function that, given an entity, will return its key value. If et and kt are the
entity and key types then an abstract datatype bdt, for a tree can be written

$$bdt = Node\ bdt\ kt\ bdt \mid Entity\ et$$

Using this definition a function to update an entity can be written as follows.
The update tags its result to indicate success or failure and returns a new version
of the database-tree reflecting the update. A lookup function is similar, except that
it leaves the tree unchanged.

$$update\ e'\ (Entity\ e) = (Ok\ e,\ Entity\ e'),\ \textbf{if}\ key\ e = key\ e'$$
$$= (Error,\ Entity\ e),\ \textbf{otherwise}$$

$$update\ e'\ (Node\ lt\ k\ rt) = (m, Node\ lt'\ k\ rt),\ \textbf{if}\ key\ e' \leq k$$
$$= (m, Node\ lt\ k\ rt'),\ \textbf{otherwise}$$
$$\textbf{where}$$
$$(m, lt') = update\ e'\ lt$$
$$(m, rt') = update\ e'\ rt$$

The database-tree used to produce the results reported in the following Sections
is a binary tree of 512 bank account entities. Each account entity has an account
number, a balance, a class and a credit limit. The database resides entirely in
primary memory. Whilst this data structure is small it is sufficient to demonstrate
the behaviour of the data manager.

2.3 Efficiency

Let us assume that the tree contains n entities and is balanced. In this case its depth
is $\log n$ and hence the update function only requires to construct $\log n$ new nodes
to create a new version of such a tree. This is because any unchanged nodes are
shared between the old and the new versions and thus a new *path* through the tree
is all that need be constructed. This is best illustrated by Figure 2.1 that depicts a
tree that has been updated to associate a value of 3 with x.

Figure 2.1: Original and New Trees

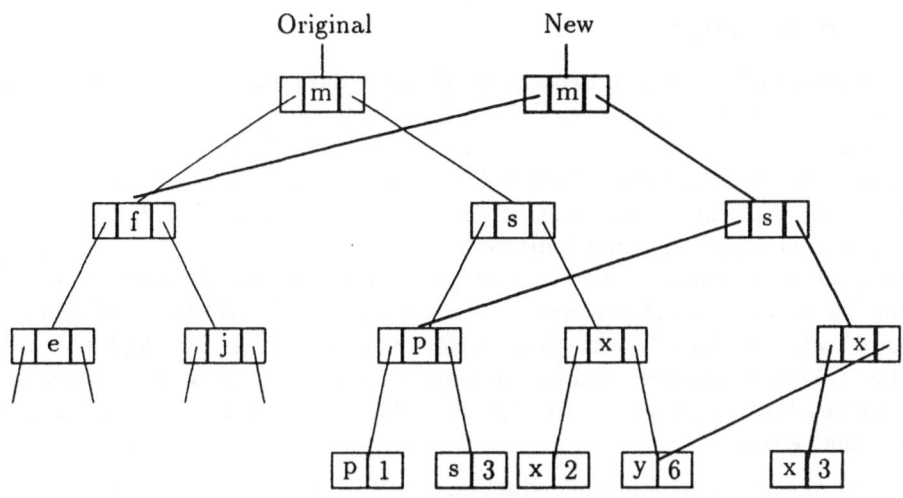

A time complexity of $\log n$ is the same as an imperative tree update. The non-destructive update has a larger constant factor, however, as the new nodes must be created and some unchanged information copied into them. The functional update can be made more efficient using a reference count optimisation [12]. However, when non-destructive update is used, a copy of the tree can be kept cheaply because the nodes common to the old and new versions are shared. These cheap multiple versions facilitate concurrency, make aborting transactions easy and can be used to protect the database from becoming corrupted [2, 12]. The significant points are that when a version is required it is preserved automatically and cheaply. Further, if a version is not required the update can be automatically performed efficiently.

2.4   Data Manager

Bulk data operations are functions that take the database as an argument and produce some output and a, possibly modified, database as a result. That is, they have type $bdt \rightarrow (output \times bdt)$. Let us call this type $bdop$.

The database-tree is controlled by a manager function that processes a stream of bulk-data operations to produce a stream of responses. That is, the manager has type $bdt \rightarrow [bdop] \rightarrow [output]$. A simple version can be written as follows.

$$manager\ d\ (f:fs) = out : manager\ d'\ fs$$
$$\textbf{where}$$
$$(out, d') = f\ d$$

The first bulk-data operation f in the input stream is applied to the database and a pair is returned as the result. The output component of the pair is placed in the output stream. The updated database, d', is given as the first argument to the recursive call to the manager. The manager can be made available to many users simultaneously using techniques developed for functional operating systems [6].

3 Hypothetical Machine

3.1 Architecture

For the purposes of the current experiment the bulk data manager is evaluated on a pseudo-parallel interpreter that emulates a hypothetical machine. The architecture of this machine determines the nature of the parallelism. Fuller details of the architecture and instrumentation can be found in [12]. It is assumed that the secondary storage underlying the persistent environment is based on disks. The machine is assumed to have a shared primary memory.

The machine is assumed to be a multiple-instruction multiple-data, or MIMD, machine. Hence each of the processing agents is capable of performing different operations on different data. The machine performs super-combinator graph reduction [7]. The evaluation strategy used in the machine is lazy except where eagerness is introduced by the primitives described in the following Section. In a machine cycle an agent may either

- Perform a super-combinator reduction, or

- Perform a delta-reduction, i.e. evaluate a primitive such as 'plus', or

- Perform a house-keeping activity such as sparking a new task.

The work to be performed by the program is broken into tasks. Each task reduces a subgraph of the program graph. Initially only one task exists. New tasks are sparked by the eager primitives described later. Task synchronisation occurs as follows. A task marks the nodes it is processing as busy. A task encountering a busy node is marked as *blocked*. As soon as the required node is no longer busy the blocked task resumes. A task that is not blocked is termed *active*. The scheduling strategy used in the hypothetical machine is both simple and fair: every active task is assigned to a processing agent and in a machine cycle the next redex in each active task is reduced.

The hypothetical machine is simple, but consistent with existing models of parallelism [5, 9]. The machine is simplistic in not supporting throttling or granularity control, in having a uniform machine cycle and in reducing newly sparked tasks immediately.

3.2 Instrumentation

The hypothetical machine is instrumented to record the following statistics during the evaluation of a program: the number of super-combinator and delta- reductions, the number of graph nodes allocated, the number of machine cycles and the average number of active processes. The number of super-combinator and delta- reductions is a measure of the time-complexity of the program. The number of graph nodes allocated is a measure of a program's memory usage. Under the assumption that machine cycles take constant time, the number of machine cycles is a measure of the elapsed-time taken to evaluate a program. The average number of active tasks gives the average concurrency available during a program's evaluation. In addition to the above figures, every 10 machine cycles the average number of active tasks during those cycles is recorded. This information is used to plot a graph of the average number of active tasks against time, measured in machine cycles.

4   Concurrent Operations

4.1   Potential

A purely lazy, or demand-driven, evaluation of bulk-data operations does not lead to any concurrency. It is reasonable to assume that the result of all of the operations will be demanded. Thus a task can be sparked to evaluate a subsequent operation before the current operation has completed. This effect can be achieved using an eager constructor. An eager list constructor sparks tasks to evaluate both the head and the tail of the list concurrently. Consider the manager from Section 2:

$$manager\ d\ (f:fs)\ =\ out:manager\ d'\ fs$$
$$\textbf{where}$$
$$(out,d') = f\ d$$

To introduce concurrency an eager list constructor is used to create the output list. As a result a task is sparked to evaluate the output of the current operation and another is sparked to evaluate the manager applied to the subsequent operations.

4.2   Lookups

Consider the manager processing a sequence of lookups. The eager output-list constructor in the manager sparks tasks to perform the first lookup and to apply the manager to the remaining lookups. Because the first lookup does not change the database it is immediately available for processing the second lookup. On encountering each of the remaining lookups the manager will spark a task to perform the lookup and another to evaluate the manager against the remaining input stream.

There is no limit to the number of tasks that can be sparked in this way. Hence a fair scheduler is required to ensure that, not only are new lookups sparked, but those already in the database make progress. The scheduling strategy employed in the hypothetical machine is fair because it attempts to perform a reduction in every active task in each machine cycle. As a consequence the first lookup will complete at

some point. From this point onwards earlier lookup-tasks will complete at the same rate as the manager sparks new ones. The manager has reached a state of dynamic equilibrium. If the input stream is finite, then, once the last lookup has been sparked, the number of active processes will decline as the earlier lookup-tasks complete.

This behaviour is exhibited by the manager processing a sequence of 30 lookups directed to different entities. The lookup program is simply an invocation of the manager applied to the database and a list of 30 lookup functions directed to different entities, $manager\ d\ [lookup\ 8230;\ lookup\ 1540;\ ...\ ]$. The active task graph for the eager evaluation of this program is shown in Figure 4.1.

280

Figure 4.1 30 Lookups

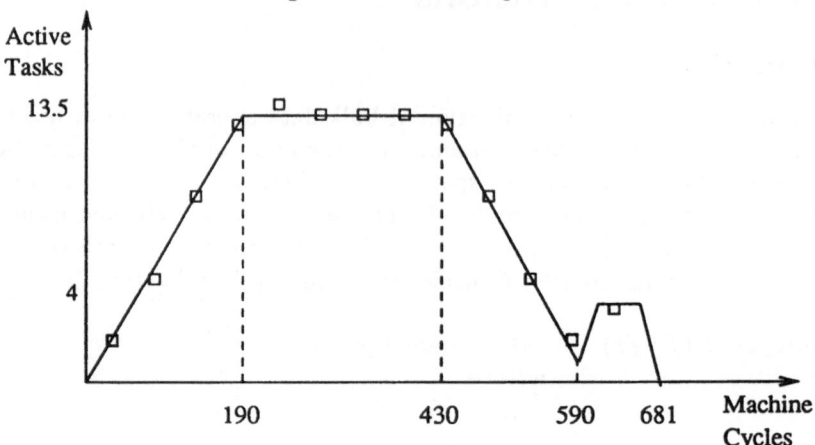

The first lookup completes after approximately 190 cycles and the maximum concurrency is reached at this point. The average of 13.5 active tasks represent the manager and 12.5 lookup-tasks. After the last lookup-task is sparked at approximately 430 cycles the concurrency declines steadily until the output phase is entered at cycle 590. The manager function requires 430 machine cycles to spark all 30 tasks, indicating that it requires approximately 14 cycles to spark a new task. Note that the number of active tasks depends on this delay and the number of machine cycles each task takes to complete. The small peak between cycles 590 and 681 represents an output phase.

30 LOOKUPS

Metric	Lazy	Eager
Number of super-combinator reductions	1923	1923
Number of delta-reductions	1573	1573
Number of graph nodes allocated	32366	32366
Number of machine cycles	5734	681
Average number of active tasks	1.04	8.82

Note that the average concurrency during the lazy evaluation of the program is not 1.00. This is because a strict primitive in the lazy program will spark a sub-task and for a brief period both parent and child tasks are active before the parent task discovers that it is blocked. To compensate for this calibration error the average concurrency in the eager evaluation can be divided by the lazy average concurrency to give an *adjusted average concurrency* of 8.48 active tasks. Note that the elapsed-time to evaluate the eager program has been reduced by a factor of 8.42. The *elapsed time reduction factor* is reassuringly close to the adjusted average concurrency, indicating that the additional tasks are reducing the elapsed time by performing useful work.

4.3   Updates

Not all of the parallelism is unbounded. Consider a stream of updates directed at the same entity. Each update must wait until the path in the tree being created by the preceding update exists. As a result the parallelism is bounded by the depth of the tree. This is illustrated by the following diagrams. Initially the first update-task has control of the original root and is constructing a new one.

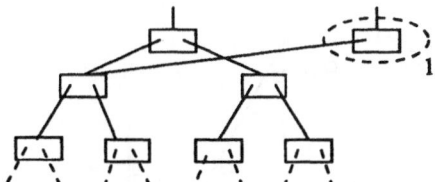

Once the first update has constructed a new root the second update is activated.

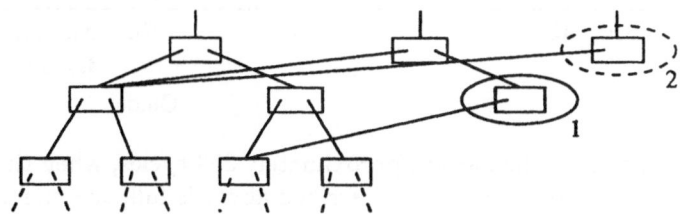

Similarly, once the second update has constructed a new root, the third update is reactivated.

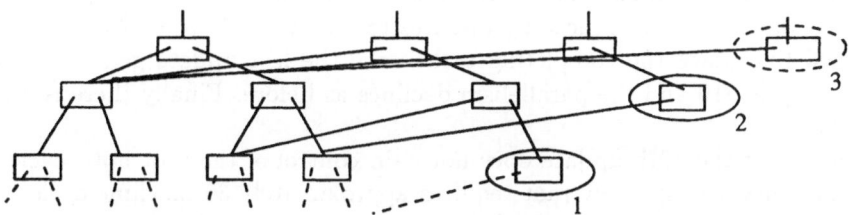

Note how a tree-node just created by an update is immediately consumed by the following update. This is pipelined behaviour. In fact the pipeline is slightly more complex than the preceding figures indicate because the tree constructor releases a node once it is in weak head normal form, i.e. before the sub-trees are complete. As a consequence two tasks can perform useful work at each level in the tree :- one selecting a subtree to update and the other constructing a new sub-tree. Because these two activities take different times, there will not always be two active tasks at each level in the tree. For example, as the account tree has 10 levels, there can be at most 20 active tasks in it. The manager will also be active, giving a maximum of 21 active tasks. In the following example the maximum number of active tasks recorded is 19. The program to direct 30 updates to the same entity is very simple:

282

manager d [*update* (*Entity* 1400 745 'A' 40); *update* (*Entity* 1400 345 'A' 40); ...].
The active task graph for this program is shown in Figure 4.2.

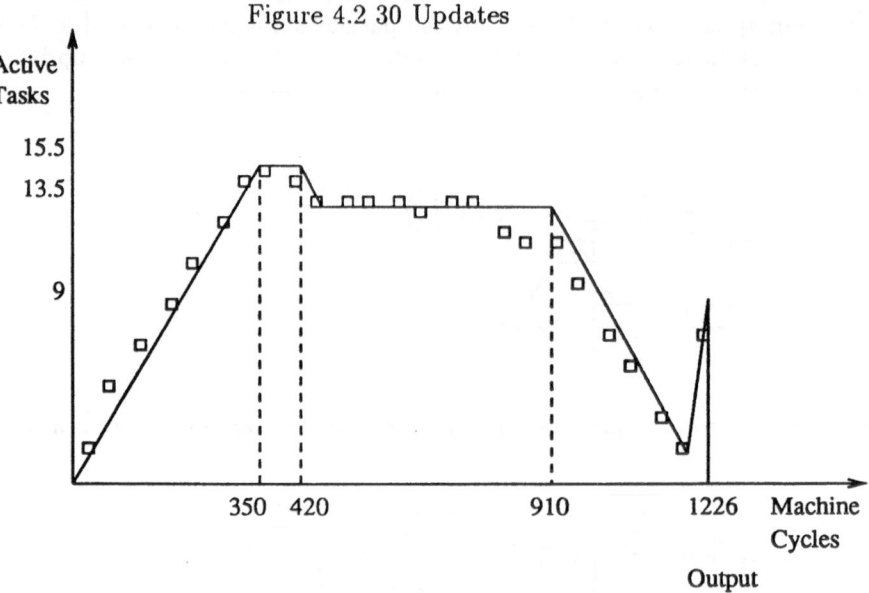

Figure 4.2 30 Updates

Maximum concurrency is reached after approximately 350 cycles, when the first update completes. At this point the pipeline described above is full, the manager is active and there may be an update that has been sparked but has not yet demanded the root of the tree, i.e. entered the pipeline. Recall that the manager requires approximately 14 cycles to spark a new operation. By cycle 420 the manager has sparked all 30 of the updates and the number of active processes drops at this point. The pipeline remains full until cycle 910. The later update-tasks, although sparked, are blocked waiting for the preceding updates to create a new root. No more tasks are sparked to replace the completing tasks once the last update gains control of the root at cycle 910 and the parallelism declines as before. Finally there is a brief output phase.

The fact that the 30th update does not gain control of the root until cycle 910 shows that constructing a new root requires approximately 30 machine cycles. For updates the construction time is the bottleneck, rather than the time the manager requires to spark a new task. The effect of this bottleneck on a more realistic mix of operations is investigated in [12].

30 UPDATES

Metric	Lazy	Eager
Number of super-combinator reductions	2973	2973
Number of delta-reductions	2783	2792
Number of graph nodes allocated	46515	46524
Number of machine cycles	10373	1226
Average number of active tasks	1.15	10.34

Giving an elapsed-time reduction factor of 8.46, and an adjusted average concurrency of 8.99 tasks. The updates require more work in total than the lookups because each one is constructing a new version of the database. The eager manager constructs entities that are not demanded and hence does slightly more work and uses slightly more memory than the lazy manager. Under the assumption that all of the database will ultimately be realised this work is not wasted. Again the adjusted average concurrency and elapsed-time reduction factors are reassuringly close. The discrepancy between these two statistics is consistent for all programs: the elapsed-time reduction factor is always less than the adjusted average concurrency.

4.4 Effect of Database Size

Primary Memory

If all of the database resides in primary memory the time to complete an operation is proportional to the log of the database size. Hence an operation on a larger database takes longer to complete. As a result more operations are able to pass the bottleneck at the root before the first operation completes and greater concurrency is possible. As in a smaller database, once the first operation completes, earlier operations will complete at the same rate as they pass the bottleneck. In consequence the manager delivers the results of operations on the larger database at the same rate as on a smaller database. Recall that the hypothetical machine guarantees that there are always enough agents to evaluate the extra tasks required by the larger database.

For example, consider a database only an eighth of the size of the account database. Such a database-tree has only 7 levels and contains only 64 entities. Figure 4.3 plots the active processes when the stream of 30 lookups from Section 4.2 is consumed by two instances of the manager. One instance processes the lookups against the large database and the other against the small database.

Note that the first lookup in the larger database takes longer to complete and hence the time to reach maximum concurrency is greater. This larger set-up time results in a small 13% increase in elapsed time. Also note that the last lookup starts at the same cycle in both instances. This fact and the small increase in elapsed-time confirm the expectation that operations on a large database occur at the same rate as in a small database.

Secondary Storage

If the lower levels of the database-tree are in secondary storage then the time to perform an operation is greatly increased because of the disk access delay. The time to perform a disk access is typically three orders of magnitude greater than the time required to perform a machine instruction. As a result many more operations can pass the bottleneck at the root in the time taken for the first operation to complete.

If the operations depend on each other it is reasonable to assume that the path to any shared entity is preserved in cache. In this case the first operation retrieves the path into cache and subsequent operations occur in relatively high-speed primary memory. If the operations are independent then multiple disk-accesses can occur concurrently.

284

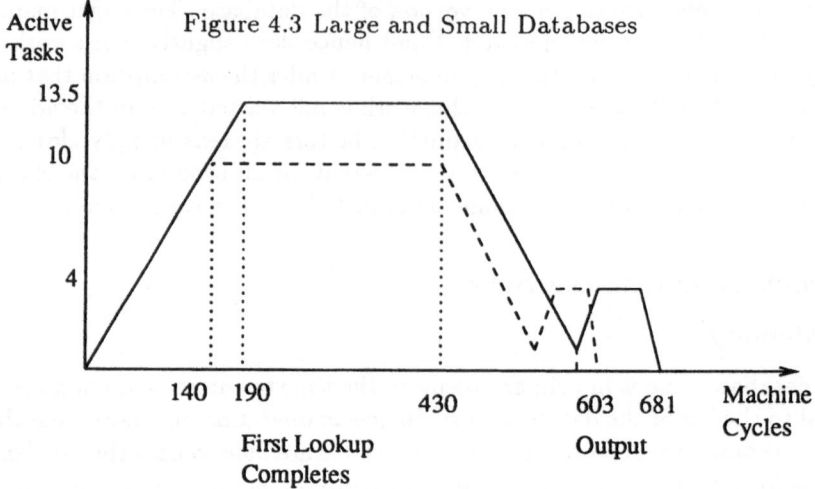

Figure 4.3 Large and Small Databases

Key

Large Tree

Small Tree

The effect of disk accesses is difficult to demonstrate in the prototype data manager because all of the database-tree resides in memory. To simulate the effect of a disk access to retrieve the leaves of the tree a delay function has been added to the lookup and update operations so that they wait for approximately 750 cycles on demanding a leaf. The update operations are made slightly more eager to force them to perform the delay-function even when the value of the updated entity is not demanded. The additional concurrency this introduces is apparent in the average concurrency for the 'lazy' version of the program. When only 15 updates with a disk-delay are directed to different entities in the database the following information is recorded.

15 UPDATES WITH DISK DELAY

Metric	Lazy	Eager
Number of super-combinator reductions	6123	6123
Number of delta-reductions	5917	6167
Number of graph nodes allocated	70294	70453
Number of machine cycles	15942	1449
Average number of active tasks	1.40	15.89

Giving an elapsed-time reduction factor of 11.00, and an adjusted average concurrency of 11.35. The 22 active tasks represent 15 'disk accesses', the output of each update being eagerly constructed and some calibration error.

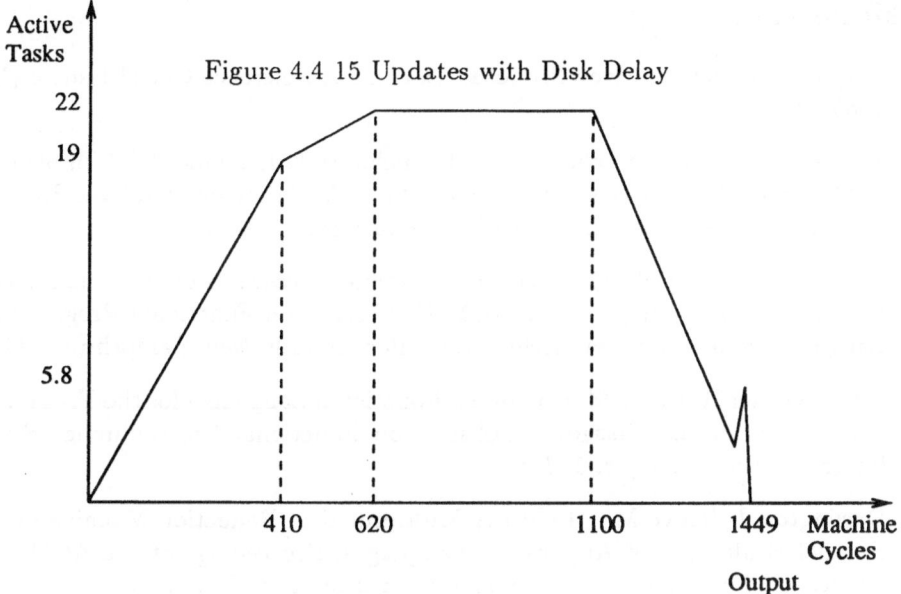

Figure 4.4 15 Updates with Disk Delay

5 Conclusion

A bulk data manager has been constructed in a pure functional language and evaluated on a simulated declarative machine. The manager allows efficient and concurrent manipulation of shared data. It has been shown that, given certain conditions, the rate that a declarative multiprocessor can process bulk-data operations is independent of the database size.

The Flagship results show that a fast transaction manager can be built in a functional language with impure constructs. The results presented above show that a fast bulk-data manager can be built in a pure functional language. However, transaction processing is more difficult than bulk-data processing as a transaction performs several bulk-data operations atomically. As yet, the transaction processing examples are too small to be good evidence that sufficient concurrency is provided for transaction processing [12].

Further work entails constructing a more realistic implementation, possibly on a genuine multiprocessor. Larger transaction-processing examples might then be constructed. The suitability of more complex data structures, such as trees with secondary indices, might also be demonstrated.

Acknowledgements

The design of the database was joint work with Guy Argo, Jon Fairbairn, John Hughes and John Launchbury. Murray Cole, John Hughes, Simon Peyton-Jones and Phil Wadler all made useful comments on the parallelism results.

286

References

[1] Flagship Project — Alvey Proposal. Document Reference G0003 Issue 4 (May 1985).

[2] Argo G. Fairbairn J. Hughes R.J.M. Launchbury E.J. Trinder P.W. Implementing Functional Databases. Proceedings of the Workshop on Database Programming Languages, Roscoff, France (September 1987), 87-103.

[3] Burton F.W. Sleep M.R. Executing Functional Programs on a Virtual Tree of Processors. Proceedings of the ACM Conference on Functional Programming Languages and Computer Architecture, Portsmouth, New Hampshire (1981).

[4] Cox S. Glaser H. Reeve M. Compiling Functional Languages for the Transputer. Proceedings of the Glasgow Workshop on Functional Programming, Fraserburgh, Scotland (August 1989).

[5] Darlington J. Reeve M. ALICE: A Multiprocessor Reduction Machine for the Parallel Evaluation of Applicative Languages. Proceedings of the ACM Conference on Functional Programming Languages and Computer Architecture, Portsmouth, New Hampshire (1981).

[6] Henderson P. Purely Functional Operating Systems in *Functional Programming and its Application*. Darlington J. Henderson P. Turner D.A. (Eds) Cambridge University Press (1982).

[7] Hughes R.J.M. The Design and Implementation of Programming Languages. D.Phil. Thesis, Oxford University Programming Research Group Technical Monograph PRG-40 (July 1983).

[8] Peyton Jones S.L. Clack C. Salkild J. Hardie M. GRIP - a High-performance Architecture for Parallel Graph Reduction. Proceedings of the IFIP Conference on Functional Programming Languages and Computer Architecture, Portland, USA (September 1987), 98-112.

[9] Peyton Jones S.L. *The Implementation of Functional Programming Languages.* Prentice Hall (1987).

[10] Robertson I.B. Hope[+] on Flagship. Proceedings of the 1989 Glasgow Workshop on Functional Programming, Fraserburgh, Scotland (August 1989).
Hardware. Cambridge University Ph.D. Thesis (December 1985).

[11] Trinder P.W. Referentially Transparent Database Languages. Proceedings of the 1989 Glasgow Workshop on Functional Programming, Fraserburgh, Scotland (August 1989).

[12] Trinder P.W. A Functional Database. Oxford University D.Phil. Thesis, (December 1989).

[13] Turner D.A. Recursion Equations as a Programming Language in *Functional Programming and its Application*. Darlington J. Henderson P. Turner D.A. (Eds) Cambridge University Press (1982).

Author Index

Argo, G. 1
Bondorf, A. 9
Davis, K. 23
Hall, C. 44
Hamilton, G. W. 66
Hammond, K. 44
Hankin, C. 54
Holst, C. K. 71, 83
Hughes, J. 83, 101
Hunt, S. 114
Hutton, G. 126
Jensen, T. 141
Johnsson, T. 146
Jones, S. B. 66, 172
Jørgensen, J. 177
Kirkwood, C. 196
Launchbury, J. 101
Murphy, D. 201
O'Donnell, J. 44
Partain, W. D. 218
Roe, P. 227
Runciman, C. 237
Sinclair, D. C. 246
Singh, S. 264
Thomas, M. 268
Trinder, P. 274
Wadler, P. 23
Wakeling, D. 237
Watson, P. 268
White, M. 172